RY ROE CLOUD SERIES ON AMERICAN INDIANS AND MODERNITY

ditors
ckhawk, Yale University
. Reid, University of Washington
Shanley, University of Montana
Bear, University of Alberta

ission Statement
in honor of the pioneering Winnebago educational reformer
known American Indian graduate of Yale College, Henry Roe
Class of 1910), this series showcases emergent and leading
hip in the field of American Indian Studies. The series draws
altiple disciplinary perspectives and organizes them around the
Native Americans within the development of American and
n modernity, emphasizing the shared, relational ties between
us and Euro-American societies. It seeks to broaden current
literary, and cultural approaches to American Studies by fore-
ng the fraught but generative sites of inquiry provided by the
Indigenous communities.

THE MAKINGS A
OF AMERICANS

THE HEI

Series E
Ned Bla
Joshua
Kate W.
Kim Ta

Series N
Named
and firs
Cloud
scholar
upon n
place c
Europe
Indigen
historic
ground
study c

THE MAKINGS AND UNMAKINGS OF AMERICANS

INDIANS AND IMMIGRANTS IN AMERICAN

LITERATURE AND CULTURE, 1879–1924

CRISTINA STANCIU

Yale UNIVERSITY PRESS

New Haven and London

Published with assistance from the foundation established in memory of
Amasa Stone Mather of the Class of 1907, Yale College.

Yale University Press books may be purchased in quantity for educational, business,
or promotional use. For information, please e-mail sales.press@yale.edu (U.S. office) or
sales@yaleup.co.uk (U.K. office).

Set in Sabon and Berthold City Bold types by Newgen North America.
Printed in the United States of America.

Library of Congress Control Number: 2022935754
ISBN 978-0-300-22435-1 (hardcover: alk. paper)

A catalogue record for this book is available from the British Library.

This paper meets the requirements of ANSI/NISO Z39.48-1992 (Permanence of Paper).

10 9 8 7 6 5 4 3 2 1

This book is lovingly dedicated to Bogdan Stanciu, our children, and our parents

Contents

Illustrations

Introduction

Indians and Immigrants: Toward a Cultural History of Exclusion

It turns out that the most American thing ever is in fact American Indians.

—Paul Chaat Smith, 2017

In order to become an American patriot, one must be an Indian. . . . Is it possible to be a patriot of two countries simultaneously, for instance, of America and Ireland, of America and Germany, of America and Poland?

—"The Press Criticizes the United States Government for Mistreatment of the American Indians." *Dziennik Chicagoski*, January 6, 1891

THE *INDIAN* AND IMMIGRANT "PROBLEMS"

IN DECEMBER 1923, on the eve of the country's first comprehensive immigration legislation, the *New York Times* published an article positioning "Americans" between two groups rarely considered in the same context. The article, titled "Aborigine and Immigrant," went on to alert the readers: "With the problem on the one hand of the admission of the immigrant who has come *after us* and that of just dealing on the other with the aborigine who was here *before us*, the people who occupy as citizens a minor part of the American Hemisphere, but call themselves 'Americans' have a delicate and difficult time of it" (my emphasis). "Aborigine and Immigrant" signaled two seemingly pressing problems the settlers in the United States faced: "If the former is to be encouraged in his *primitive* and distinctive crafts, what shall be said of those who come from other lands with ancient crafts in their hands and folksongs in their memories?"[1] Spelling out immigration and Indigeneity as "problems," the article placed the dilemma on the

1

American citizen settlers, "the people who occupy as citizens a minor part of the American hemisphere." It also framed a pervasive impasse in white America's exceptionalist imaginary: it relegated Native life to primitivism and "crafts," and reaffirmed settler centrality and responsibility, the imperative to redress the groups and to remake them into "good Americans."

Dealing with new immigrants and Indigenous people was a settler "problem" to be solved by Progressive Era Americans. The *Times* article framed the dilemma of those who measured progress in terms of "before us" and "after us" as one of moral and civic responsibility. Americans sought to understand themselves as part of a changing landscape, reshaped by recent immigration and its supposed threats to whiteness and Anglo-Saxonism. By 1923, the U.S. had already launched a campaign to assimilate Native Americans through federal policy, neglect, separation from Indigenous communities, a drastically diminished land base, and the removal of children to off-reservation boarding schools. Other attempts at naturalizing Indigenous people in the United States preceded the Indian Citizenship Act of 1924, passed shortly after the Immigration Act of 1924. These two pieces of legislation constituted temporary responses to the so-called Native and immigrant problems in the U.S. Larger structural mechanisms of cultural and legal exclusion solidified the popular understanding of Native and immigrant presence in the U.S. as a menace.

Anglo-American references to *Indians* and immigrants as problems abound in what Anashinaabe writer and literary critic Gerald Vizenor calls "the literature of dominance," yet, such misrepresentations continue to inform popular understandings of Indigenous people in North America.[2] During the Progressive Era, cultural venues and practices, such as the Wild West shows, silent films, popular literature, and advertising, helped spread and institutionalize racist representations of ethnic groups. When novelist Henry James returned to "the American scene" in 1904, he panicked at the sight of what he described as the "ubiquitous alien" in New York City—especially the Jewish immigrants— whom he saw as a threat to the so-called old-stock Americans. In both cases, the literary market was less invested in Native or immigrant self-representations and more in the perpetuation of white representations of immigrants and *Indians*, which is not the focus of this book. Instead, this book focuses on Native and new immigrant self-representations to show how, despite U.S. exclusionary efforts, new immigrants and Native Americans co-constitute what it means to be (and not to be) an American.

This book sets out to rethink arguments about national belonging, citizenship, and literary and cultural production within and across these two groups and in relation to Americanization. As a cultural, political, and ideological project, Americanization has so far offered a narrow paradigm for understanding American national formation. Within this grand narrative, Americans can be *made*, transformed into loyal citizens who renounce foreign loyalties. The shared spaces, gaps, and erasures occupied by both Native Americans and new European immigrants in the American imaginary at the turn into the twentieth century are at the heart of this book, along with the following historical and theoretical concerns. How did the legal and cultural dynamics of Americanization affect these two groups that are rarely read together? How did these largely different groups engage in those dynamics through print and film? What does this reading of parallel and intersecting visions of national belonging reveal about Indigeneity and immigration as conditions central to American identity? As such, this book offers a critical lens to understand how the nation-state reproduced itself in two disparate yet intimately connected arenas in the "domestication" and Americanization of both colonized and "foreign" people. As Amy Kaplan reminds us, "domestic" and "foreign" are not neutral legal and spatial descriptions but "heavily weighted metaphors imbued with racialized and gendered associations of home and family, outsiders and insiders, subjects and citizens."[3] In its promise of homogenization, Americanization attempted to amplify Anglo-Saxon fears and anxieties about foreign people.

Although some immigrant groups enjoyed the privilege of whiteness, racial difference also drove the white invention of the so-called immigrant and *Indian* problems during the Progressive Era. In "The Possessive Investment in Whiteness," George Lipsitz recalls expatriate Richard Wright's response to a French reporter who asked him about the "Negro problem" in the U.S. Wright replied, "There isn't any Negro problem; there is only a white problem." Wright's response shifted the attention on racial polarization away from African Americans; rather than framing Black people as a "problem" for whites, Wright diagnosed the problem in whiteness itself. To Wright and other writers of color, "American" signified whiteness. Similarly, Native doctor, writer, and public intellectual Carlos Montezuma wrote in 1916: "The Indian problem is a problem because the country has taken it and nursed it as a problem; otherwise it is not a problem at all."[4] Although racial discrimination and prejudice against new immigrants in the U.S. was widespread at the end of the nineteenth century, the continued dispossession of and discrimination against African Americans and Native Americans made the challenges faced by European immigrants less entrenched in racial prejudice. Like Native Americans, African Americans were part of the repertoire of "undesirable" American subjects, whose presumed racial inferiority informed eugenicist attempts to create a homogenous (white) nation. In this logic, African Americans were also unassimilable and "outside of Americanization," as Desmond King has shown.[5] Although groups like Italian immigrants, often read as "white on arrival," had their whiteness questioned, new European immigrants largely benefited from the privileges that whiteness afforded them.[6] The investment in whiteness as a fictive identity had deep roots in the history of the country's colonization, Indian policy, slavery, and immigration restriction policy. As threats and sources of pride, identification, and kinship, the *Indian* and immigrant "problems" spoke less about the communities they purported to represent and more about Anglo-American fears and their investment in perpetuating white supremacy. Just as the *Times* article lamented the challenges that new immigrant arrivals and Indigenous people posed to *old Americans*, white Americans expressed mixed emotions about what they considered the *Indian* and immigrant problems.

Yet, how did Native Americans fit into the story of Americanization? How did the new immigrants envision their imposed transformation? This book contributes to recent scholarship that challenges the assumptions about Americanization as a top-down phenomenon and, instead, shows how Native communities negotiated, and sometimes *authored*, the terms of Americanization. In *Shades of Hiawatha*, Alan Trachtenberg opened a necessary conversation in American Studies about the circulation of images of Native Americans and immigrants in this period. Relevant to his argument is not the idea of how they viewed each other, but how the dominant culture viewed each. Although very much indebted to Trachtenberg's work, this book differs from it in making new immigrant and Native voices central to national debates over

Americanization, and it opens the archive to lesser-known writers and activists, as well as nontextual expression through performance and silent film. As they navigated troubling nationalist narratives, Indigenous activists and intellectuals of the Progressive Era often borrowed from the discourse and practice of their new immigrant peers—implicated in larger numbers in the work of the Americanization project from factories to community schools—just as the federal government sought to homogenize Americanization practices for both groups.

During the Progressive Era, Americanization signified assumed compliance to norms of homogenization, patriotism, and allegiance to forms of nationalism, embraced by many immigrant communities yet antithetical to many Native communities' conception of sovereignty. A key distinction between Indigenous people and (im)migrants is that Indigenous people are members of sovereign nations. Yet the continued erasure of Native Americans from the story of America over the last few centuries has legitimized the larger settler colonial project of elimination and territorial expansion. Settler colonial studies scholar Patrick Wolfe has argued that the impetus of settler colonialism has not been race or ethnicity but access to territory: "Territoriality is settler colonialism's specific, irreducible element."[7] The accumulation of land through violent acts of dispossession has characterized the North American settler colonial project, which justified the ongoing violence against Indigenous communities. Similarly, the central and eastern European project of the Austro-Hungarian empire left many communities landless and destitute, forcing immigration to the U.S.[8] At the heart of this erasure caused by the American settler colonial project and the central European imperial project is capitalist accumulation and territorial expansion.

In this book I rethink popular understandings of Americanization and argue that, in their interactions with Americanizers, new immigrants and Native Americans not only challenged the intellectual and cultural debates over inclusion and exclusion but also expanded the narrow definitions of American identity. Throughout the Progressive Era, analogies between the so-called immigrant problem and the Indian problem translated mainstream derogatory associations of Native people with markers of savagery into strategies of identification, alliance building, and resistance to dominant ideologies of race and racial discourse—what I call in a later chapter "convenient affiliation." They also framed the putative problem of the "aborigine and immigrant" in terms of what Ali Behdad calls "national hospitality," and which I read more as an instance of national hostility. The myth of immigrant America as a narrative of hospitality—where (white) Lady Liberty welcomes immigrants with open arms—depends on recuperating and challenging the national historical amnesia and hostility toward immigrants.[9] At the same time, immigration history has yet to examine "hospitality" from an Indigenous perspective. By recasting the story of American Indians and new immigrants as one of exclusion and a careful recalibration of identity to facilitate membership (if not inclusion) in American society, we can begin to illuminate the common project of the two (admittedly diverse) groups: rejecting exclusion.

AMERICANIZATION REDUX

Throughout this book I read Americanization as intrinsic to the American imperial and capitalist project, a continuation of late nineteenth-century imperial consolidation tactics through westward expansion, race-based immigration policy (including the first major legislation to exclude immigrants, the Chinese Exclusion Act of 1882), the genocide of Indigenous people (including Indian wars and later, boarding schools aimed at Americanizing Indigenous children, and continued settler intrusion on Indigenous lands and kinship structures), and the consolidation of imperial economic power through importing (cheap) new immigrant labor from southern and eastern Europe. Americanization also signified exclusion and rejection of perceived un-American practices. Although historians have studied the social phenomenon that Americanization represented during the 1910s, I expand this timeframe to show the longer and more deeply engrained roots of this phenomenon in the American imaginary.[10] I take the founding of Carlisle Indian Industrial School in 1879 and the opening of the immigration door to *new* immigrants (southern and eastern European) in 1883 as starting points. I end in 1924, a year with significant legal and historical resonances for both groups, with the passing of the Immigration Act and the Indian Citizenship Act.

At the end of the nineteenth century, the distinctions between the "old" and "new" immigrants grew more trenchant in the American popular and legal imaginary. A growing preoccupation with national identity emerged as a new "Babel of tongues," from non-Protestant religions (Catholic, Jewish, and Eastern Orthodox), refused to be tamed into a uniform mass of Americanism.[11] The concept of "American" itself attracted more and more scrutiny, and some of the optimists of immigrant assimilation in the early 1880s became the skeptics and immigration restrictionists of the 1900s and beyond. American imperialism also heightened the sense of Anglo-Saxonism, nationalism, and nativism. What Hector St. Jean de Crèvecoeur had optimistically envisioned as an amiable melting of "individuals of all nations" into "a new race of men" during the revolutionary era turned into a distrust of difference as intolerance fueled a national campaign to Americanize new immigrants. Because the composition of the American population had changed so drastically—with more than twenty million immigrants entering the U.S. between 1890 and 1924—the new immigrants became a suspect category.[12] The term "new immigrants" placed southern and eastern European immigrants in opposition to the "old immigrants" of Nordic and Anglo-Saxon stock, accentuating their foreignness. New immigrants were (perceived as) deficient in terms of race, social class, and relationship to Anglo-Saxonism. An evolutionary model of social development informed Progressive Era thinking, with ramifications for federal Indian policy, immigration policy and programs, and the United States' colonial policy in the Pacific. Because the Native population was lower than 300,000 in 1910, many white Americans saw the "immigrant problem" as a more pressing national concern than the "Indian problem."[13]

If, for many immigrant groups, Americanization signified possibility, for Indigenous communities Americanization signified an end to tribal sovereignty, a stamping out of tribal identity, the dispossession of land, the erasure of Native languages, and the imposition of English. Given that tribal sovereignty is tied to land, Americanization also signified loss of territory. Although the rhetoric of Americanization implied that Indigenous people would be allowed to join American society as Americans, Americanization campaigns asked Native people to reject the ways of their ancestors without offering them the benefit of full participation in American life. In the late 1860s, many reservations had no schools—except for mission schools and the schools organized by Cherokees, Choctaws, Chickasaws, and Creeks for their own communities. Ulysses S. Grant's Peace Commission, which Congress had established in 1867 and tasked to assess the source of friction between Indians and whites in the West, recommended that compulsory schools be established, where Native languages would be replaced with English. Because the commission considered Native people as "barbarous" and "savage," it refused to recognize that Native languages could communicate the same emotional and intellectual needs as English. This assumption about the colonial linguistic superiority of English explains, in part, the perpetuation of structures of domination through linguistic control.[14] The imposition of English also fulfilled a more immediate and utilitarian need, ensuring Native entrance into the capitalist and individualist economies beyond reservations.

In several chapters, I use the concept "affective Americanization" to show the insidious ways that Americanization as ideology and practice inserted itself into the most vulnerable populations, from Native children attending the Indian boarding schools and immigrant mothers "educated" by their American children, to Native communities captured on film reacting to artificial patriotic rituals, and immigrant spectators exposed to Americanization on screen via industrial and educational films. Sara Ahmed and other theorists regard emotions not only as psychological states but also as social and cultural practices. Raymond Williams places the "structure of feeling" at the intersection of the official discourse, popular responses to the official discourse, and its use in literary and cultural texts.[15] I read affective Americanization as a structure emerging at the intersection of official discourse (federal and state governments spelling out the parameters of Americanization and acculturation), popular responses to the official discourses (in visual culture, particularly cartoons and silent film), and literary representations. Print, film, and cultural texts carry and reveal feelings and emotions. In the period I'm studying, such emotions were often stifled by institutional control, especially during the more militant phase of Americanization in the 1910s. Instances of affective Americanization formed specific sites of encounter between institutions and Native and new immigrant subjects. In these affective economies, how Native and immigrant subjects decoded and negotiated forms of belonging affected both the person and the community. We know about the (dominant) nationalist narrative of this era and the many impositions regulating the Native and immigrant sense of belonging and citizenship. But what "structure of feeling" do the stories told by Native and immigrant writers and activists reveal? As a structure, affective Americanization—emerging from Native and immigrant documents and performances—circumvents, troubles, and negotiates the strictures of the Progressive Era "search for order."[16]

Americanization had larger ramifications for immigrant and Native American communities than scholars have supposed. This period in American history allowed Native and new immigrant activists to write Americanization on their terms. Print and public performances offered the venues for these new voices. Scholars of American Studies have tended to agree that *Indians* and immigrants shared a key place in the U.S. imaginary as *others*, as a repertoire of images that Anglo-Americans used as oppositional figures to define their Americanness. As rhetorical figures, the *Indian* and the immigrant continue to have a larger appeal in the American settler imaginary than the real, living communities. Building on this scholarship, I argue that new immigrants and Native Americans shared similar roles in what I read as the drama of Americanization and assimilation at the turn of the twentieth century. Progressive Era reforms to "civilize" and domesticate the *Indian* and the immigrant participated in larger national contests over the meaning of citizenship, whose unwritten cultural norms were western Europe (as the parent culture), English (as the official language), and whiteness (as the color of "true citizenship").

Americanization depended on both visual and print culture to fulfill its mission of "making" Americans in both Indian boarding schools and Americanization classrooms. The project of Americanization, relying on education programs as well as literary, epistolary, and filmic texts, depended on the confluence of two events rooted in industrial modernity: on one hand, (new) immigration from southern and eastern Europe called for different forms of "education" and acculturation than (old) immigration from western Europe; on the other, new media technologies—the growth of commercial periodical press, the accessibility of mass market books, and the emergence of visual technology like the silent film—facilitated the work of Americanization. The growing visual instruction movement in the early twentieth century, aided by the new technology, made "visualizing citizenship" into a visual pedagogy project. Technology appealed to industrial conglomerates (such as Ford Motor Company or U.S. Steel, discussed in chapter 7); it promised to transform workers into compliant industrial citizens. Similarly, the settler colonial visual narrative this new technology helped create allowed for Native presence on and off screen, either as documentary footage or as instances of what Michelle Raheja calls "visual sovereignty."[17]

Besides visual culture, print culture, in its various forms, is central to this book's archive: papers as legal documents, as records and archival documents, as letters and fragments, as monolingual and bilingual newspapers and leaflets produced by Native and new immigrant communities, as "citizen papers" that immigrants received after civics training and that Native people did not, as traces of print culture left by Native and immigrant communities in both English and Native languages, as lectures at Native conferences or immigrant gatherings, as readings in book clubs, as debates in debate clubs, and as literature and cultural documents. Papers as records of knowledge and papers as legal documents (treaties, congressional acts, etc.) include and exclude; they codify who can (and cannot) be American. Papers also textualize and authorize knowledge and exclude stories circulating orally. Historically, the use of legal documents, inherited from European colonial governments, has provided a legal façade aimed at denying Native rights. On one hand, historically, "papers" determined and invented the racial composition of the country by keeping the inconvenient immigrants out through a series of draconic immigration restriction acts at the beginning of the twentieth; on the other, they dispossessed Native people of millions of acres of land through war, genocide, and seemingly benevolent provisions of legislation supported by Progressive Era Friends of the Indian.[18]

NOT "A NATION OF IMMIGRANTS"[19]

One pervasive narrative—the United States as a nation of immigrants—continues to solidify the American myth of national hospitality and to erase Native presence in the American story of origin. In the twenty-first century, Indigenous people continue to be largely absent from the story of America.[20] But what happens when we make Native narratives central to understanding American history and cultural production? This book reexamines the centrality of Native cultural production in the context of Americanization and ongoing colonization through what I call "Native Acts"—rhetorical and performative, militant and imaginary, legal and fictional—alongside the better-known "immigrants acts," which I read in their legal and cultural contexts. This focus reveals key ways that these two very large and different groups—new immigrant and Indigenous communities—adapted to and reframed the script of Americanization, or what I call "the makings and unmakings of Americans." Although the title of this book may bring to mind Gertrude Stein's *The Making of Americans* (1925) and the privileged Americanism Stein enjoyed, and which I discuss briefly in chapter 2, the title of this book is not an homage to the highly unreadable modernist novel; it is, rather, an attempt to render the multiplicity and contradictions of the Americanization campaigns and media engaging Native and new immigrant subjects. This multiplicity also allows for occasional agential autonomy, whereby Native and new immigrant subjects may (choose to) become American on their terms.

Recent scholarship in postcolonial and settler colonial studies has helped redefine our understanding of an Indigenous past beyond the framework of "assimilation" into the nation-state. By deemphasizing the idea of Native progress from "savagery" to "civilization," the field of settler colonial studies insists on understanding Indigenous encounters with modernity as ongoing struggles with the settler colonial rule both during this book's focal period and beyond. I read the work of Indigenous students, writers, and activists as part of a continued struggle with colonialism and acknowledge Native agency and sovereignty despite the homogenizing imprint of the Americanization campaigns. Lorenzo Veracini reads "colonial systems of relationships" as premised on the subjugation of exploitable Others. Similarly, Patrick Wolfe acknowledges settler colonialism's "logic of elimination" against exploitable Others as well as those who hindered the settlers' access to land and resources. For Wolfe, settler colonialism, through its invasion—as "a structure, not an event"—creates its own reasons for staying, for taking hold of people and resources. Native dispossession becomes, in this model, complicit with settler colonial agendas, including assimilation through boarding school education and other means of "whitening" non-white subjects. Assimilation reverses the American republican phenomenon: people no longer constitute the government, but the government constitutes the people.[21]

Although settlers and immigrants are often read together, both historians of Indigenous Studies and those who specialize in Immigration

Studies make sharper distinctions between old and new immigrants and read old immigrants as complicit with the U.S. colonial project. According to Daniel Heath Justice, "not all newcomers are colonial agents."[22] In the words of Mahmood Mamdani, "Immigrants join existing polities, whereas settlers create new ones." Mamdani also distinguishes between the political project of the settler, which is "to create and fortify the colonial nation-state," and the nonpolitical project of the immigrant, who merely seeks to take advantage of what the state allows every citizen."[23] Lorenzo Veracini also distinguishes between settlers and migrants, rethinking the category of immigrant/migrant in relation to Native communities: "Settlers are not migrants." According to Veracini, although both settlers and immigrants move across space, what distinguishes the settlers from the immigrants is conquest: "They are defined by conquest. Settlers are *founders* of political orders and carry their sovereignty with them." Both Indigenous people in settler societies and the immigrants moving to settler societies share a lack of sovereignty.[24] Eve Tuck and K. Wayne Yang make a similar argument, distinguishing further between settler and immigrant nations: "Settlers are not immigrants. Immigrants are beholden to the Indigenous laws and epistemologies of the lands they migrate to. Settlers become the law, supplanting Indigenous laws and epistemologies. Therefore, settler nations are not immigrant nations."[25] Separate patterns of exclusion governed Native and new immigrant access to American citizenship, whether they desired that citizenship or not. For instance, Native people occupied an anomalous position in the naturalization process, finalized with the passing of the Indian Citizenship Act (1924), when racist restriction quotas drastically limited the access of new immigrants to the U.S. (see chapter 1). Before this act, Native people were naturalized as citizens just like immigrants, but this blanket Indian Citizenship Act granted birthright citizenship to all Native people in the U.S. This moment of redefining American citizenship along exclusionist lines, I argue, is symptomatic of crucial changes in racial, ethnic, and nationalist discourses during the Progressive Era.

As a cultural history, *The Makings and Unmakings of Americans* investigates how Indigenous and immigrant writers wrote about— sometimes against, sometimes alongside—dominant articulations of Americanization. It also points to rare instances of occasional recognition—when members of these distinct groups wrote about each other.

The legibility of one group for the other remains elusive during the Progressive Era, when instances of misreading, misrecognition, and ignorance abounded in scholarly and popular representations, particularly of Native people by immigrants, and also of both groups by the dominant culture. Besides resorting to *Indians* and immigrants as rhetorical figures, Progressive Era Euro-Americans sometimes misrepresented Native Americans *as* immigrants, as Alan Trachtenberg and Joel Pfister have shown. Pfister has made a persuasive case about the role of "individualizing" in the Americanization efforts, a concept antithetical to Native and immigrant emphasis on group and community affiliation.[26] Few immigrants were exposed to Indigenous history before they came to the U.S. The public schools and the Americanization classes offered by the states painted Native communities in the light of extinction, with few references to contemporary issues. As Indigenous historians have noted, American readers often bought into the national narrative of the "vanishing Indian," which legitimized settler land ownership and authorized the erasure of Indigenous histories from cultural memory.[27] Native print culture, one of the main archives used in the writing of this book, mitigated this erasure and continued to educate American readers—white, middle class, politically influential, such as the Friends of the Indian, who lobbied for Native assimilation and belonging as Americans—from a modern Indigenous point of view.[28]

Native and new immigrant writers and intellectuals *adopted* and *adapted* the settler colonial script; they negotiated Americanization on their own terms and had a lot to say in the debates over assimilation, citizenship, and Americanization. Some immigrant writers went the extra mile to emulate settler exceptionalist discourse. In the short story "American and I," published in *Children of Loneliness: Stories of Immigrant Life in America* (1923), Anzia Yiezierska, a Jewish immigrant from Poland, described her coming of age as a writer in settler terms: "I felt like Columbus, finding new worlds through every new word." In another story published in the same volume, Yiezierska burst with settler pride: "When I saw my first story in print I felt bigger than Columbus when he discovered the New World."[29] Although immigrant writers like Marcus E. Ravage, discussed in chapter 6, were critical of this rhetorical performance of Americanization, many others embraced it. In the early twentieth century Native and immigrant writers borrowed rhetorical strategies from each other and from the larger American settler narrative to withstand and negotiate the larger perils of forced assimilation and transformation into imagined "Americans." This book also reveals the unwritten parallel alliances which shared similar purposes: maintaining cultural specificity in the face of mounting pressures to Americanize. Both legal and performative "acts" are at the heart of this study, which offers archivally derived readings framed by the legal discourse around individuals and groups "making" themselves as Americans. Working through parallel legal histories of exclusion and building on the work of historians of immigration and historians of Native America, I tease out the implications of terms such as "Native acts" and "immigrant acts" as legal and cultural constructs. What possibilities do these "acts" reveal for reading Native and immigrant agency and for their intervention in their own making as Americans? The archival and published texts by members of these groups press against the legal language, creating moments of undecidability in the cultural text—Derridean aporias—contradictions, misunderstandings, and gaps in the myth of national identity, which invite further inquiries.

Recentering the story of U.S. exceptionalism helps illuminate the continued erasure of Native sovereignty. What happens when we conceive of American Indians and new immigrants not only as the laborers trained in the country's Americanization programs—from the Indian boarding school to the factory—but also as the writers, thinkers, activists, and artists, who reconciled the rigid confines of American exceptionalism with their daily acts of resistance and a continued investment in their own communities? As such, they challenged the premises of Americanization by rewriting themselves into American literary history, by negotiating and inventing their "America."

Whereas immigrant writers in the U.S. throughout the Progressive Era sometimes *adopted* a settler colonial stance to legitimize their claim to Americanness, Native writers *adapted* the settler colonial paradigm to fit their political and cultural needs. I call this phenomenon "Americanization on Native terms." The following chapters bring together well-known and lesser-known archives of Native and settler colonial writing, focusing on the work of the so-called Red Progressives—Native writers and activists who came of age as the boarding school experiment of Americanization took shape. These writers were not only more critical of Americanization than previously known, but, by reframing and constantly negotiating discourses on "racial difference," they also *authored* Americanization on Native terms. The body of work of the Society of American Indians, for instance—in print and performance— is a case in point. As they debated pressing issues for Native communities, the Red Progressives grew more critical of Americanization than scholars have credited them, and they also became more attuned to mainstream discourses on "racial difference." This book attempts to fill a gap by showing how competing nationalisms—in this case, American and Indian, often overlapping—were central to print and public Native debates over American citizenship. One especially fascinating archive, which deserves more attention from literary scholars, is the print work of Dr. Carlos Montezuma (see chapter 5). His political newspaper *Wassaja* is as an example of Indigenous "editorial sovereignty," an instance of Native control of meaning and knowledge production in print. As a writer, editor, fundraiser, and publicist, Montezuma used print culture to record and shape a vision for Native people facing the new economic and political challenges of his time.

Historically, most immigrants were not exposed to Native American history—or Native people—before and often after they arrived in the U.S. Public schools and the Americanization classes they attended painted Native communities in the light of extinction, of vanishing, with few references to contemporary issues. Beth Piatote has pointed out that Indigenous experience resonates with immigrant experience "in relationship to larger forces of national domestication." Yet, she cautioned, "as Native American experience becomes more central to American studies scholarship, this difference must maintain its visibility and significance in order for fruitful comparisons to emerge."[30] Similarly, Jodi Byrd acknowledged that it is "all too easy, in critiques of ongoing U.S. settler colonialism, to accuse diasporic migrants, queers, and people of color for participating in and benefiting from Indigenous loss of lands, cultures, and lives, and subsequently to position Indigenous otherness as abject and all other Others as part of the problem, as if they could always consent to or refuse such positions or consequences of history."[31] Piatote and Byrd articulate the centrality of Native experience to American Studies and offer useful critiques to rethink the nation of immigrants matrix. It is time to decolonize our reading of immigrant writing by inviting critics to expand our understanding of American literature beyond American exceptionalism and the supposition of inevitable assimilation. Such a decolonized reading entails a paradigmatic shift, with, on one hand, the recovery of immigrant writing as immigrant writing—not as "ethnic" or "multicultural" or as a supplement to the Anglo-American exceptionalist narrative—and, on the other hand, a renewed focus on immigrant writing as central to American literature. Understanding both the potential and the limits of immigrant literature as American literature could open productive interdisciplinary conversations.

Like American history, American literary history has yet to fully engage the role of Indigenous communities—real and imagined—in the making of America. Historians agree that we cannot teach American history without American Indians because Indigenous nations shaped the formation of the U.S., forged through what Ned Blackhawk has called "violence over the land." Teaching American history as settler colonial history tells a different story from teaching it as an American exceptionalist triumph of manifest destiny and a nation of immigrants. Just as we can no longer teach American history without American Indians, we can no longer teach American literature without American Indians.[32] Working within the nation of immigrants framework obscures other aspects of national formation and the opportunity to wrestle with a traumatic history rooted in the genocide of Indigenous people, African American enslavement, and the exploitation of immigrant labor. The disavowal of these origin narratives prevents the recuperation, rethinking, and rewriting of a story of America where Indigenous people do not disappear into a sepia landscape and where settlers do not prevail.[33]

Two recent examples in immigrant literary criticism make this theoretical and methodological intervention timely. First, Thomas Ferraro calls the self-transformation that an immigrant (or immigrant offspring) undergoes to become a writer an "ethnic passage." This transformation, this ethnic passage, Ferraro contends, "unites immigrant writers of all backgrounds." As interesting as this concept is, the definition of immigrant writers' self-transformation as ethnic passage (presumably from ethnicity to "American") is inherently problematic in its adherence to an exceptionalist framework Ferraro purportedly critiques. More specifically, ethnic passage suggests a necessary transformation to access "the larger world of letters," the rarefied world of Stein, James, and Faulkner. Ethnic passage indirectly implies conformity to dominant cultural norms and, in a sense, Americanization. When he dismisses them as "so-called immigrant writers," Ferraro subscribes to an exceptionalist paradigm of who does and does not have access to the higher realms of American literature.[34]

Second, in an otherwise astute study of contemporary immigrant fiction, David Cowart finds many commonalities between first generation immigrant writers and later writers, as he also theorizes a semiotics of immigrant fiction from narrative fragmentation to a reversal of generational roles. He reads immigrant fiction as a shared site of symbolic initiation, along the lines proposed by Werner Sollors in *Beyond Ethnicity;* in this reading, new immigrant characters come to terms with the inevitability of becoming American, an inevitability reminiscent of old immigrant characters' struggles with Americanization. While Cowart's study does a good amount of work incorporating a variety of writers from different countries of origin, he offers a dangerous conclusion: *"The American subject was always already an immigrant."*[35] Cowart's assertion reinforces a long-standing oversight of Indigenous contributions to American history and subject formation. The American subject could not have "always already been an immigrant" because the first petitioner for a "subject position as an American"—and a forced petitioner at that—was Indigenous. The continued erasure of Indigenous history perpetuates a framework of U.S. formation as a putative nation of immigrants, disregarding and erasing its formation as a settler nation, not an immigrant nation, but one built on the displacement and genocide of Indigenous people and uninhibited westward movement. Erasing this history from scholarship on immigrant literatures and cultures dangerously perpetuates settler subjectivity, even when it textualizes it as either new or old immigrant fiction.

Recent studies have provided a critical paradigm for the conceptual undoing of American exceptionalism in Indigenous Studies and Immigration Studies, and in this book I shift these conversations in American Studies in several ways. First, my work is grounded in archival research, recovering Indigenous and new immigrant voices in literary and public spheres, from Native writers and activists to Carlisle Indian School students, to immigrant writers of eastern European origin, to writers for the Chicago Foreign Language Press Survey, to "undistinguished Americans" in Americanization classes, and to the Yiddish modernist poets in New York. Second, it is informed by literary and critical race theory, immigration history, sociology, and political theory. I show how, while many new immigrants enjoyed the privileges of being (read as) "white on arrival," Native exclusion from U.S. citizenship and its privileges has been determined not only on racial grounds but also on the settler colonial logic of elimination—of denied access to land through various forms of Native dispossession and elimination. In a Native context, the acquisition or the *gift* of U.S. citizenship was also a way of dispossessing Native communities, since retaining treaty rights was incompatible with U.S. citizenship. While different from their settler predecessors, new immigrants were complicit with the American empire although they questioned and resisted total institutions, such as the Americanization classes, just as many Native people began to negotiate the effects of the federally sponsored boarding schools and other forms of Americanization. I approach immigrant and Native assertion and contestation of citizenship as a negotiation of Indigenous sovereignty and immigrant agency.

Third, I build on the work of immigration and citizenship historians to foreground the suspect ways that the U.S. reproduced its citizenry through competing naturalization practices. The Native and immigrant performances of citizenship—which I dicuss in later chapters—reveal moments of contradiction and gaps in the myth of national identity (see chapter 1). Fourth, I join the recent work of literary and film historians and their interventions in reconceiving Native and immigrant writing and performance as crucial to redefinitions of nation and modernity. Whereas they read *Indians* and immigrants separately, I bring these seemingly dissonant voices of modernity into dialogue with the larger ramifications of the Americanization project and intervene in several overlapping fields of interdisciplinary scholarship in American Studies: Native American and Indigenous Studies, as well as literary studies, silent film studies, and immigration studies. I use materials from multiple archives that are usually not in conversation with each other, such as letters, cartoons, print journalism, legal cases, Americanization manuals and government documents, writing specimens, fiction, memoir, poetry, performance, and silent film. What emerges is an analytic lens for understanding ethnicity, race, Indigeneity, and cultural production during the Progressive Era in the context of Americanization. This book does something unconventional, in the line proposed by Lisa Brooks: it makes Native voices central to the story of America; it reads immigrant cultural work and literature through the lens of Americanization first tested on Native communities, later refined in immigrant contexts.[36] It also reads Native absence and presence in the new popular medium of silent film, revealing its potential for Native representation of dissent and pluralism (see chapter 8).

BOOK STRUCTURE

Before describing the arc of the book, I wish to note my own positioning in navigating these often uncomfortable yet necessary conversations. I write as an eastern European immigrant and naturalized American citizen who is privileged to work in the academy, who teaches and writes in several fields—including Indigenous Studies, critical race theory, and multiethnic literatures of the United States—and who is an ally to anti-racist struggles for Indigenous recognition. I share Melanie Benson Taylor's concern about the danger of multiculturalism rendering Native Americans less visible when lumping them together with other racial and ethnic groups: "No other 'minority' group in America has had the distinctive experience of being unsettled, removed, forcibly assimilated, slaughtered, and undone in the land of their own origins. To insist on comparative and multicultural methodologies is to diminish those histories and obscure the particularities of Native cultures."[37] Yet, that is not my approach in this book. Rather, I focus on Native and new immigrant representations and use examples of immigrant writing to amplify the claims about Native presence, agency, and representation.

The first chapter, "Native Acts, Immigrant Acts: Citizenship, Naturalization, and the Performance of Civic Identity," turns to legal texts to draw attention to the complicity of immigration restriction laws and federal Indian policy with organized Americanization in legislating the desirable "new American." For Native people, Americanization and the imposition of citizenship were extensions of settler colonialism. For new immigrants, Americanization meant a renunciation of political allegiance to other sovereigns, the acquisition of English, and civic education for citizenship. Both groups were targeted by legislative acts in 1924: the Johnson-Reed Immigration Act and the Indian Citizenship Act. In this chapter I challenge the myth of the U.S. as a nation of immigrants and the settler colonial nation-state's ongoing infatuation with its colonial project. I find that the consensual model of American citizenship for these groups was inadequate—with Native people resisting the slow coercion into citizenship and new immigrants becoming gradually barred from it.

Chapter 2, "'You Can't Come In!—the Quota for 1620 Is Full': Americanization, Exclusion, and Literary History," defines and historicizes Americanization as an ideology and as a state- and federally sponsored program, situating the debates over national identity and citizenship in a broader racial and ethnic context. The chapter starts with the uneasy places *Indians* and immigrants occupy in the American settler imaginary, in narratives of deficiency that the work of Americanization sought to reinforce. Although many non-Anglo-Saxon peoples were intimately implicated in or co-opted by Americanization, my focus is on Native and new immigrants, two groups rarely read together. Drawing on Indigenous and immigrant literary history, I reveal connections between old Anglo-Saxon anxieties over *Indians* and new(er) anxieties over new immigrants. The chapter begins and ends with analyses of political cartoons, which speak to larger concerns about Americanization, exclusion, and representation.

Chapter 3, "'That Is Why I Sent You to Carlisle': Native Education, Print Culture, and Americanization at Carlisle Indian Industrial School, 1879–1918," engages a key archive of this book: the records of Carlisle Indian Industrial School, the first federally funded off-reservation boarding school. Examining surviving student letters and publications from Carlisle and other federal boarding schools offers a glimpse into a tumultuous period of Americanization. Writing and reading practices mitigated some of the damage that industrial training did to Native education; print culture offered a platform for creative expression and shaped this period in the American Indian intellectual tradition. Why was Native student writing complicit with the institution's ideology, popularized by the school's founder, R. H. Pratt, yet sometimes critical of the demands the institution made of its students? In this chapter I show that education for Americanization aimed at erasing tribal identity and instilling patriotism into students, but how Native students integrated Indigeneity into their writing and expressive culture tells a more nuanced story. The rhetorically bold writings and performances at Carlisle set the stage for the cultural work of the Society of American Indians (SAI).

Chapter 4, "'Sing, Strangers!': Education, Print Culture, and the Americanization of New Immigrants," explores Americanization—this time in a new immigrant context. The Americanization of new immigrants through education consolidated the U.S. empire by producing imagined compliant new citizens, ready to supply the expanding demands of the country's labor market after the Chinese Exclusion Act of 1882. Like their emerging Native intellectual peers, new immigrant writers and activists revised the script of Americanization as they shaped a new immigrant literature. In this chapter, focusing on the work of public schools and foreign language newspapers in New York City and Chicago, I trace ways that immigrant education and print culture supported the work of Americanization and illustrate what I call "affective Americanization," an insidious form of co-optation through the affective bonds across time and space. In this chapter I also seek to fill a gap in the current scholarship on the immigrant press and its role in the Americanization project, as well as the immigrant treatment of *Indian* tropes in foreign language publications.

Chapter 5, "Americanization on Native Terms: The Society of American Indians, Citizenship Debates, and Tropes of 'Racial Difference' in Native Print Culture," builds on the argument of chapter 3—that Carlisle students' writing and performance set the stage for the more militant cultural work of the Society of American Indians. The Native intellectuals of the Progressive Era used the analogy to the European immigrant to argue for Indian citizenship. If the immigrant could easily become a citizen, why not the Indian? Through their criticism of Americanization, I show that Native intellectuals rewrote the mainstream discourses on "racial difference" and authored Americanization on Native terms. Two competing nationalisms, American and Native—often overlapping—drove these spirited debates over American citizenship, as the SAI journal and Carlos Montezuma's political newspaper, *Wassaja*, reveal.

Chapter 6, "'This Was America!': Americanization and Immigrant Literature at the Beginning of the Twentieth Century," turns to Americanization in new immigrant literature, using Jewish American writers and their contributions to the literature of Americanization to complement other ethnic groups, and to chart some strategies new immigrant writers used to negotiate Americanization. Like their Native American intellectual peers, new immigrant writers revised the script of Americanization as they shaped the beginnings of new immigrant literature. Foregrounding the work of first-generation immigrant writers, I show how these counternarratives to Americanization are part of an incipient counterdiscourse, which I call the "unmaking of Americans."

How does the settler nation include or exclude its aspiring citizens, especially when nationalism and nativism preclude the nation from *seeing* the difference of its subjects? In the last two chapters I explore the complicity of the silent film industry with the Americanization campaigns in exploiting the potential of this new medium to reach wider and wider audiences in the U.S. Early motion pictures perpetuated ideologies of national and racial difference. Like print and other cultural texts, silent film carried and revealed feelings through what I call "spectacular nationalism." Early silent films not only socialized and instructed viewers, but they also introduced immigrant, Indigenous, and American-born audiences to xenophobia and racism.

Chapter 7, "Spectacular Nationalism: Immigrants on the Silver Screen, Americanization, and the Picture Show," asks: what cultural work did silent film do for Americanization, the active and sometimes coercive campaign to *make* new immigrants into *good* Americans? I argue that early American cinema was both complicit with and critical of Americanization. The rise of the moving image expanded the institutionalization of Americanization, with federal and state governments and capitalist concerns, like Ford Motor Company, using film strategically in their efforts to Americanize the new immigrants. Yet, early American cinema was also critical of Americanization, as it negotiated new immigrant concerns about labor, literacy, gender, and representation. In many ways, silent film was a welcoming forum where racial, ethnic, and linguistic differences were temporarily suspended. This seemingly democratic and democratizing new public sphere brought audiences together while it also alienated them from each other.

Chapter 8, "From 'Vanishing Indians' to 'Redskins:' American Indians on the Silver Screen," examines some of the possibilities and limitations of the cultural work that silent film did in the Americanization project. The silent film industry played no small part in negotiating modernity on Native terms, even when those terms were uneven. In 1910, Westerns represented Indigenous people as quintessentially American subjects. Films about "the good Indians" appealed to working-class immigrant audiences and informed their ideas about Americanization. But what happens when the *Indian* becomes not only the object but also the subject of representation? Film enabled white directors and producers to bring representations of Native people to wide audiences, and to reinforce white supremacist ideology. Occasionally, large studios employed Native actors and directors, and some films had an all-Native cast. Mediating between the demands of the genre and the commitment to tribal specificity, these films challenged misconceptions about Native representation. In silent feature, documentary, and ethnographic film, the *Indians*' hypervisibility was a reminder of the absence of Indigenous people from the American settler colonial imaginary and a document of their continued presence despite the violence against both the Native body and image.

A note on the book's organization, structure, and terminology: the story moves from two introductory chapters, which lay out my core arguments, to two chapters that trace the interconnected work of Americanization, education, and print culture in Native and new immigrant contexts. It continues with the examination of Native and immigrant print culture, also turning to literary archives to tease out representation of Americanization in traditional genres and venues. Although a strong literary Native tradition emerged in the first decades of the twentieth century, my material choices and argument led me to focus on the lesser-known (print) work of the SAI and Carlos Montezuma's political newspaper. Chapters 7 and 8 expand my argument through analyses of silent film. In a sense, the archival evidence I was able to collect also contributed to this structure.

I use the term "new immigrant" throughout the book, yet I also refer to specific ethnic groups—Polish, Russian, Romanian, Lithuanian, Slovakian, and others. I use terms such as "Indigenous," "American Indian," and "Native" interchangeably; wherever possible, I refer to specific Native nations and languages. I use the term *Indian* to signal Anglo-American representations, appropriations, and distortions.

1 Native Acts, Immigrant Acts

Citizenship, Naturalization, and the Performance of Civic Identity

The Indian Citizenship Act did pass in 1924 despite our strong opposition. . . . This was a violation of our sovereignty. *Our citizenship was in our own nations.* We had a great attachment to our style of government. We wished to remain treaty Indians and preserve our ancient rights.

—Chief Clinton Rickard, Tuscarora, 1973 [my emphasis]

Those who have lived in bondage can seek freedom here. Here they breathe freely, and rest in peace, and here, with pride, they become citizens of a free country, which is not ruled either by a czar or knout.

—*Dziennik Chicagoski,* 1891

IN HIS PULITZER-PRIZE-WINNING book *The Uprooted,* a highly influential study in immigration history, historian Oscar Handlin confessed that he wanted to write a history of immigrants in the U.S. and, in the process, found that "immigrants *were* American history."[1] Positioning U.S. history as immigration history, Handlin did not acknowledge that this history is also one of colonization, relocation, usurpation, genocide of Native people and exploitation of African enslaved people. Recent studies also continue to refer to the U.S. as "a nation of immigrants," although historians like Roxanne Dunbar-Ortiz have started to challenge this paradigm.[2] Perpetuating the myth of immigrant America, Handlin's vision of (old) American history reinforced American exceptionalism through a disavowal of the violence inflicted on Indigenous people.[3]

Although scholarship in Immigration Studies has dominated critical debates over citizenship and national belonging, scholars in Native American and Indigenous Studies have started indigenizing other fields by bringing Indigeneity to the center of conversations about the U.S. empire. Immigration Studies has yet to rethink the settler colonial paradigm of the U.S. as a nation of immigrants and to revise its origin narrative with Indigenous people at the center of that story. What if we revised Handlin's sweeping statement to read, "American Indians *were* [are] American history"? More than five hundred federally recognized nations in the U.S. today are descendants of the fifteen million original inhabitants, and international Indigenous movements continue to advocate for territorial rights and Native self-determination.[4] In a context where "the settler colonial present is also an Indigenous one," as Lorenzo Veracini has argued, and where categories such as "settler" and "migrant" share more differences than similarities, how does this paradigm shift affect our conceptualizations of American citizenship and national belonging?[5]

The myth of the U.S. as a nation of immigrants has been solidified rhetorically by writers, educators, and public figures,[6] yet the United States has never been a nation of immigrants; it was and has continued to be an occupied country, whose capitalist and political investments have justified the continued extraction of resources and perpetuated the myth of the welcoming nation, the mother of refuge for what poet Emma Lazarus called the world's "poor, tired masses." The Marshall Court's wording of *Johnson v. McIntosh* (1823) supports the idea of the inevitability of settler acquisition and later governance of a country inhabited by what the court called "fierce savages": "However extravagant the pretension of converting the discovery of inhabited country into conquest may appear; . . . if the property of the great mass of the community originates in it, it becomes the law of the land, and cannot be questioned."[7] The various immigration acts served the United States' growing anxiety about the new immigrants' putative inability to assimilate, supported by pseudo-scientific evidence about the superiority of Anglo-Saxonism.[8] To understand the stakes of civic participation through citizenship—the imagined *reward* to the naturalized immigrant subject and *gift* to the Native subject—I look at the contested meanings of citizenship in these two contexts. Citizenship law defines membership in a national community and also defines the boundaries of that community. Yet, Indigenous people are tribal citizens of their respective nations, a unique political status that distinguishes them from other marginalized communities or immigrant groups in the U.S. The treaties signed between the federal government and Native nations are binding documents between political entities (and not between a political entity and a racial group).[9]

Whereas immigrants and migrants figure in the U.S. national imaginary as subjects who desire the U.S., that was not the case with Native Americans. They did not seek membership in the U.S., and although their land was desired, they were not. Under the pretext of Americanization, restrictive immigration laws and federal Indian policy combined to legislate a desirable "new American," at a time when resurgent nativism threatened to limit undesirable immigration and to Americanize Indigenous people. Following the 1882 Chinese Exclusion Act, large numbers of European immigrants started coming to the U.S. For the new immigrants, forced by economic and political constraints to migrate, Americanization meant a renunciation of political allegiance to other sovereigns, the acquisition of the English language, and civic education for citizenship. The position of the Native people was more complex when it came to Americanization. For them, the imposition of American citizenship was an extension of settler colonialism, adding one civic status over another—domestic dependent, ward, or U.S. citizen. In this chapter I challenge the myth of the United States as a "nation of immigrants" and the settler colonial nation-state's ongoing infatuation with its colonial project, and I argue that Native acts and immigration acts as public manifestations of consent and dissent speak back to the rigidity of the legal acts.

Native acts and *immigrant acts* serve as this chapter's operating frameworks.[10] First, as legal acts, Native acts and immigrant acts name the context and history of the legal discourse regulating Native and new immigrant subjectivity and citizenship. Second, through performance, they produce Native and Immigrant subjects, revealing their negotiation of the legal text; such performances showcase moments of contradiction and gaps in the myth of national identity. Native acts and immigrant acts are legal and cultural acts; performance allows the Native and Immigrant actors to control and create a space that simultaneously contests the strictures of legal discourse and affirms political subjectivity. Cultural citizenship—such as embodied citizenship through public performance, or what Carroll Smith-Rosenberg calls "citizenship as process"—calls into question the rigidity of the legal text.[11] I expand on this idea by pointing to the inconsistencies of naturalization practices and by showing how Native acts and immigrant acts resist the rigidity of the legal text, how the *desired* new American citizen simultaneously inhabits and contests the strictures of legal citizenship.

NATIVE ACTS, IMMIGRANT ACTS

In two political cartoons of 1924, Dutch American historian, writer, and illustrator Hendrick Willem Van Loon dramatized contemporary immigration policy.[12] In the first he reimagined the scene of immigrant arrival and Native hospitality through a dialogue between a Native man and two pilgrims, who are told that they are not welcome: "The quota for 1620 is full." Granting Native Americans control over settler arrivals—"You can't come in!"—Van Loon draws the reader's gaze to a ship in the distance, waiting to take the settler colonists back to their countries (figure 1). The cartoon appeared in the March issue of *The Survey*, in the context of impending immigration restriction. "You Can't Come In" preceded the article "Taking the Queue Out of Quota," which included an interview with W. W. Husband, commissioner general of immigration, who expressed concerns about the expiration date of the quota law (June 30, 1924). A statistical tool for the federal government, the word "quota" soon signified nightmares for immigrants detained at Ellis Island.[13] The second cartoon spelled out immigration restriction in terms of privileged European geography: a pious-looking man walks on the shore in front of a sign that reads "Only Nordics Need Apply" (figure 2). One reading of this cartoon could be that, taking the absurdity of the quota law to the extreme, it responds to the imminent quota act's favoring of "Nordics." This man—an almost sanctified, robe- and halo-wearing Christian—can come in. Another reading might suggest the discrepancy between what the Christian nation had promised previously persecuted groups (suggested by the Jesus-like figure on the shore) and the reality of the new immigration policy, which kept undesirable immigrants at bay (suggested by the ship in the distance).

Articles in the foreign language press of the time, translated by the Foreign Language Information Service, protested the growing

Drawn by Hendrik Willem Van Loon

You can't come in. The
quota for 1620 is full.

Hendrik Willem Van Loon

Fig. 1. Hendrik Willem Van Loon,
"You Can't Come in. The Quota for
1620 Is Full," *The Survey*, 1924.

Fig. 2. Hendrik Willem Van Loon,
"Only Nordics Need Apply," *The
Survey*, 1924.

mechanisms of exclusion. The *Jewish Daily Forward* opined: "The new
project makes an attempt to divide the coming immigrants into two
different classes: the desirable and the undesirable immigrants. Those
who come from England, Norway, Sweden, Finland, and Germany,
are welcomed guests; those, however, who were born in the eastern
and southern part of Europe, should better remain at home." Russky
Golos, a Russian from New York, criticized the work of immigration
restrictionists and nativists, whose proposed restriction of immigration
was nothing more than "a bone that the republican administration is
throwing to the Ku Klux Klan and to the American Legion." An editorial in *The Day*, a Jewish publication in New York City, protested the
bill on behalf of "the insulted nationalities . . . the Slav, the Latin, and
the Jew." Svijet, a Croatian from New York, decried the abandonment
of non-Anglo-Saxon groups, "good enough once"—when their labor
was needed—and deemed "undesirable" by the new quota act. Despite

vociferous protests and satirical attempts in cartoons, the quota act was there to stay.[14]

On May 26, 1924, President Calvin Coolidge signed into law the Immigration Act (the Johnson-Reed Act), which reduced drastically the number of new immigrants from southern and eastern Europe; their difference from the old, northern and western European immigrants—the original settlers—made them less desirable to their adoptive country.[15] The Immigration Act introduced a quota system based on national origins, spelling out the contours of American citizenship for decades. Relying on quotas based on the 1890 census, not the 1910 census—which would have allowed for a larger pool of southern and eastern European immigrants—the 1924 act closed the door on several decades of immigration from southern and eastern Europe. Before this drastic shift in policy, immigrants performed agricultural and industrial labor, settling on conquered territories repossessed from Native nations. The new immigrants—the industrial empire's new laborers—were different from the original settlers, the descendants of English pilgrims, Scots, Scots-Irish, and French Huguenots who settled a putatively "savage" or "virgin land" and displaced an entire network of Native nations.[16] The settlers' belief in the sacred, God-given covenant—the origin myth at the basis of American exceptionalism—justified their claims to land through the infamous "doctrine of discovery," which granted the discovering European nation legal title to lands in what would become the United States. As David E. Wilkins and K. Tsianina Lomawaima have shown, this doctrine gave "exclusive, preemptive rights" to European nations.[17] In this way, "European and Euro-American 'discoverers' had gained real-property rights in the lands of Indigenous peoples by merely planting a flag."[18] Planting a flag on stolen lands defined patriotism for the *nation of immigrants*. To be accepted into this exclusive settler club, the new immigrants had to prove their loyalty to the covenant, as well as their patriotism. As Mae Ngai has documented, by limiting the number of new immigrants from undesirable nations—the "backward" European countries—the Immigration Act legislated the racial and ethnic contours of the country and instituted new hierarchies of difference and (racial) desirability. Mexico and other countries in the Western Hemisphere did not fall under the purview of this act; for naturalization purposes, Mexicans were considered white under the law. But the law excluded all immigrants from East and South Asia, who were ineligible for citizenship.[19]

On June 2, 1924, President Coolidge signed into law the Snyder Act, or the Indian Citizenship Act (ICA). At the time, there were close to 300,000 Native people in the United States, two-thirds of whom had already become citizens through various congressional acts. Before the ICA, the General Allotment Act of 1887 (also known as the Dawes Act) was the most common way of naturalizing Native allottees. If they left the tribe, received an allotment of land, and "adopted the habits of civilized life," Native people were rewarded with "national citizenship."[20] The ICA held that "all noncitizen Indians born within the territorial limits of the United States be, and they are hereby, declared to be citizens of the United States: *Provided*, That the granting of such citizenship shall not in any manner impair or otherwise affect the right of any Indian to tribal or other property." Unlike previous statutes or treaties, the ICA did not mandate that Native people relinquish their allegiance to their tribe in order to become American citizens.[21] Although race and ethnicity have informed and justified immigration restriction policy historically, the dispossession of Indigenous people of their territories and their near elimination brings other categories of analysis to the forefront of understanding national belonging and citizenship. Concepts such as colonization, genocide, and dispossession (rather than race) are especially relevant to understanding Indigenous definitions of belonging and citizenship beyond those codified in the Indian Citizenship Act.

The renewed interest in the "citizen Indian" in the 1920s, at a time when the vanishing Indian trope dominated popular and scientific venues, was symptomatic of (white) anxieties about national identity. Whereas the acquisition of American citizenship ended immigrant second-class citizenship status, for American Indians citizenship in 1924 did not end their status as wards of the federal government. As domestic subjects by law, Native Americans were legal wards of the federal government, living within the borders of the nation-state but lacking full rights as individuals. The aim of the Johnson-Reed Immigration Act and the Indian Citizenship Act was to make new immigrants and American Indians into "good Americans" and law-abiding citizens. American citizenship was the ultimate goal of the Progressive Era Americanization campaigns, which were supported by federal, state, and private organizations. Whereas the blanket naturalization offered by the ICA may be read as a corrective to earlier exclusionary legal history, immigrant naturalization is part of the pseudo-inclusionary legal history, blending the immigrant into the homogenous mass of Americanism.[22]

UNNATURAL NATURALIZATIONS: IMMIGRATION RESTRICTION

Although Article I of the U.S. Constitution granted Congress the power to establish "a uniform Rule of Naturalization," no clear naturalization policy was in place before 1906.[23] The Naturalization Act of 1790 established a contractual relation between the immigrant and the state, holding that "any alien, being a free white person, who shall have resided within the limits of and under the jurisdiction of the U.S. for the term of two years, may be admitted to become citizen thereof."[24] It was the first federal law to refer to race explicitly, making whiteness a prerequisite to citizenship (until 1952).[25] Restricting naturalization to "free white persons," the Naturalization Act established that African Americans, Asian Americans, and American Indians were not naturalizable. Several terms of future immigration restriction were defined before the Civil War, especially the issue of state versus federal jurisdiction over immigration. In the 1790s, three pieces of anti-alien legislation set the tone for direct anti-alien sentiment and vigilance in the next century—the Naturalization Act (June 1798), the Aliens Act (June 1798), and the Alien Enemy Act (July 1798).[26] Subsequent exclusionary logic based on race continued to inform nineteenth-century immigration legislation.[27]

The naturalization of Native Americans was enacted by various congressional acts responding to specific socioeconomic and political circumstances. Native tribes were held under the jurisdiction of the War Department, the Department of the Interior, and later the Bureau of Indian Affairs. To begin the naturalization process, a Native person first applied to the local superintendent by filling out a questionnaire that demonstrated "competency" and then completing applications for fee patents. (Fee patents refer to Native land held in fee by the owner; this type of land ownership is different from Native land held in trust by the federal government.) In some cases, "recalcitrant Indians" refused to sign applications, expressing direct dissent to naturalization; in others, federal commissioners forced patents in fee simple on unqualified Native people.[28] Whereas new immigrants could live in the U.S. and own land without being required to naturalize, Native people could receive a land allotment and acquire citizenship only if they proved their competence and industriousness.[29] Native Americans were also made citizens against their will, at the recommendation of a Competency Commission, and in some cases made into citizens although they neither applied nor consented.[30]

Naturalization procedures for immigrants became more centralized between 1883 and 1913. Under the Immigration Act of 1891, immigration was placed under federal authority, and Ellis Island became the legitimate port of entry, opening its doors in January 1892.[31] Unlike federal Indian policy, which overlooked Native people's desire or willingness to naturalize (consent being a key element of naturalization), immigration policy was organized around the concept of desirable versus undesirable aliens. A desirable alien could not be an idiot, an epileptic, or a lunatic; for a country imagining its own homogeneity of identity despite a growing racial and ethnic diversity, the new American must be a white Anglo-Saxon Protestant (WASP). In addition to racial determination of whiteness, the Immigration Restriction League (IRL) contributed to a growing repertoire of "excludable" categories.[32] The reports of the Dillingham Commission (produced between 1907 and 1911)—which ultimately recommended that Congress enact restrictions on immigration based on what it found to be the "unassimilable character of recent immigrants"—also offered analogies between the perceived intellectual differences between new immigrants and the old: "The new immigration as a class is far *less intelligent* than the old."[33] Through a similar racist logic, the commissioner of Indian Affairs had commented on Native Americans' intelligence just a few decades earlier: "We have within our midst two hundred and seventy-five thousand [Native American] people, *the least intelligent* portion of our population, for whom we provide no law, either for protection or for the punishment of crime committed among themselves."[34]

When the Naturalization Act passed in 1906, it brought the concerns of Americanizers to bear on those shaping naturalization, posing more procedural obstacles to undesirable immigrants who wanted to naturalize. The immigrants interested in becoming naturalized had to file a "declaration of intention" two to seven years before applying for citizenship. To receive their first papers, they were required to present a "certificate of arrival" issued by the Bureau of Immigration. Under the new law, naturalization was under the purview of the federal government, no longer overseen by state and local institutions. Gradually, the overarching control of the federal government made immigrant agency in the naturalization process minimal and tightened federal control over naturalization.[35] Although the new naturalization law did not define the minimum standards of linguistic or constitutional knowledge, immigration restrictionists read the 1906 act and its provisions as a way to make formal Americanization part and parcel of preparations for U.S. citizenship. In 1906, the Department of Commerce and Labor established the U.S. Bureau of Naturalization, and naturalization and immigration were placed under the jurisdiction of federal courts. Competency in English and knowledge of the U.S. Constitution were added as requirements for naturalization.[36]

In 1907, Congress created a commission, named for its chairman, Senator William P. Dillingham of Vermont, to investigate the sources of European immigration. Members of the Dillingham Commission traveled to southern and eastern Europe to gather information to help determine whether the so-called immigration problem was imported or was caused by conditions at home.[37] After studying data it had collected from approximately 3.2 million people, the commission concluded that, if there was indeed an immigration "problem," it did not originate in Europe but in the U.S.[38] Fueled by nativist concerns caused by the changing demographics in the U.S., the commission made few derogatory references to immigrants. Between 1907 and 1911, the commission produced a forty-one-volume study about the history of immigration to the United States. Despite promising conclusions about the vital role of immigrants in American economic and industrial growth, the Dillingham Commission ultimately recommended that Congress enact restrictions on immigration based on what it found to be the "unassimilable character of recent immigrants." Among the drastic measures it proposed were a literacy test; fixed quotas by race; exclusion of unskilled workers unaccompanied by dependents; annual limits on the number of immigrants admitted; requirements for a fixed amount of money allowed on arrival; and an increase in the head tax, more lenient toward men with families.[39]

Americanization became the arc framing the imagined national identities of Native Americans and new immigrants in the first decades of the twentieth century. As the U.S. entered World War I in 1917, a new brand of patriotic Americanism shaped new formulations of national identity and brought the reward of citizenship to Native and immigrant soldiers who fought in World War I. Yet, as with the Indian Citizenship Act that was enacted *after* the Immigration Act in 1924, the Native soldiers were naturalized months *after* their immigrant peers, almost as an afterthought.[40] Granting American citizenship to Native Americans was yet another colonial gesture, framed as a *gift* from the federal government to the Native wards of the state: an inclusion into the national body yet signifying dispossession and further exclusion under the façade of American citizenship.[41]

Nativism, which was at the heart of immigration restriction legislation, informed definitions of citizenship and national identity as normative and exclusionary. With the Immigration Act, the shift to "national origins" was rooted in questions of race and difference. As new immigrants were increasingly different from the previous generations of immigrants, the concerns over the assimilability of old immigrants turned into scientifically justified claims of new immigrants' racial inferiority. The perceived threats to American institutions and the failure of the Americanization campaigns to "meld" the new immigrants into good Americans also motivated the move toward restriction. President Coolidge summed up his defense of immigration restriction: "Restrictive immigration is not an offensive but a purely defensive action. . . . We must remember that every object of our institutions of society and Government will fail unless America be kept American."[42] Determined to keep America American, President Coolidge signed both the Johnson-Reed Immigration Act of 1924 and the Indian Citizenship Act of 1924, within days of each other. One act restricted immigrants' access to the U.S. and their eventual chance to naturalize while the other extended citizenship to Native people.

OUT BY LAW: THE AMERICAN INDIAN, FOREIGNER AT HOME

One of the goals of Progressive Era reformers was to make Native people feel more at home in America—a paradoxical goal that came at the cost of eroding Native sovereignty and dispossessing Native nations.[43] While this gesture signals *inclusion*, it also implies Indigenous *exclusion* from the American polity and American land. Throughout the nineteenth century, many Native nations had been removed from their ancestral homes and land bases, so the Progressive Era idea of "home" was an abstract construct at best, often contradicting material realities. For white America, Indian removal was not just a forced relocation from one geographic space to another, but a removal from white America's mind. White America has historically perceived Native people as "essentially foreign," as Kenneth Johnson has argued.[44] During the colonial period, the Native nations' title of self-government was recognized under the law of nations and treaties signed between Great Britain and the colonies. Native nations established a relation of imperium in imperio, or a sovereign within a sovereign nation. The doctrine of discovery perpetuated "a second-class national status for tribal nations and relegate[ed] individual Indians to second-class citizenship," stripping "tribes and individuals of their complete property rights." The formal relations between the U.S. and Native nations were subsequently carried out through treaties. Many of these treaties transferred land titles from Native nations to the United States, and the federal government recognized tribal ownership of Native land in the trade and intercourse acts.[45]

As early as the 1787 Constitutional Convention the policy of Indigenous exclusion is apparent. In its wording the Constitution makes clear that Native tribes and their members were nonparticipating inhabitants of the U.S.[46] The only provision to mention Native tribes was the Commerce Clause, which treated them as entities distinct from the states. Congress was authorized to "regulate Commerce with foreign Nations, and among the several States, and with the Indian tribes."[47] The Treaty Clause granted exclusive authority to the federal government to enter into treaties with Indigenous nations.[48] "Indians not taxed" were excluded by Article I and the Fourteenth Amendment from representation and taxation, had no participatory rights, but were considered "free persons"—as distinct from enslaved people, who were subject to the internal laws of the United States without their consent or participation.[49] Although politically and legally "foreign" to the U.S., tribes became a matter of domestic concern when Congress discontinued the practice of treaty making in 1871 and prohibited the recognition of

Native tribes as sovereign political entities. Indigenous people inhabited an in-between political status characterized by domestic dependence on the U.S. in a foreign sense.[50] Whereas the designation of Native nations as foreign nations acknowledged their political sovereignty, Native sovereignty remained, at best, nominal.

Two landmark U.S. Supreme Court cases following the 1830 Indian Removal Act—*Cherokee Nation v. Georgia* (1831) and *Worcester v. Georgia* (1832)—provide legal evidence of the Supreme Court's reinterpretation of the status of Native nations as foreign states, and for understanding "wardship," the opposite status of full citizenship. The Removal Act authorized the president to exchange land west of the Mississippi River for land tribes held in any state or territory.[51] After Georgia extended its state laws over Cherokee lands, in 1831 the Cherokee Nation sued the state of Georgia in the Supreme Court, using its prerogative as a "foreign state" to challenge the enforcement of Georgia's jurisdiction within the Cherokee Nation. Chief Justice John Marshall, who delivered the opinion of the court in *Cherokee Nation v. Georgia*, declined the Cherokee Nation's wish to sue, as a foreign nation, under the court's doctrine of original jurisdiction. Asking "Is the Cherokee nation a foreign nation in the sense in which that term is used in the constitution?" Marshall declared that it was not a foreign nation, but a *domestic dependent nation* and could not challenge state laws. Marshall granted the Cherokees, and by extension, all Native nations, a new designation—domestic dependent nations. Marshall analogized their relation to the U.S. as "like that of a ward to his guardian," emphasizing the idea of dependence: "They look to our government for protection; rely upon its kindness and its power; appeal to it for relief to their wants; and address the president as their great father." The Marshall court imposed the term "domestic dependent nations," erasing Native sovereignty with a stroke of the pen, claiming that foreign nations and the U.S. considered Indigenous tribes "under the sovereignty and dominion of the United States."[52]

Whereas provisions for the naturalization of immigrants were established as early as 1790 (by the Naturalization Act), the only Native people considered citizens by birth under the Constitution before the Allotment Act of 1887 were "those not born into membership in a tribe or whose tribe no longer existed as a distinct entity." In the infamous case *Dred Scott v. Sanford* (1857), the Supreme Court declared that neither free Blacks nor slaves were citizens of the U.S., a decision overruled in 1868. This court case brought debates over citizenship to the forefront of national debates over slavery. In its discussion of citizenship, the court said that Native people were not originally citizens in the constitutional sense but that, unlike Blacks, Congress had the power to naturalize them because they were aliens for that purpose.[53] In 1883, another case brought before the Supreme Court reinforced the idea that federal courts had no jurisdiction on reservation land. Crow Dog (Brulé Sioux) was sentenced to death by a Dakota district court for the murder of Spotted Tail, of the tribe. From prison, Crow Dog brought his case to the Supreme Court and asked to be released, claiming that federal courts had no jurisdiction over crimes committed on reservations by one Native person against another, declaring that "the conviction and sentence are void, and that his imprisonment is illegal."[54] Crow Dog was subsequently freed, and the landmark case *Ex parte Crow Dog* (1883) reinforced the idea that federal courts did not have jurisdiction on reservation land and tribal citizens. Passed in direct response to *Ex parte Crow Dog*, the Major Crimes Act (1885) declared that seven crimes committed by Native people on reservations—including the murder of one Native person by another—would fall under the jurisdiction of U.S. courts, not of tribal courts. In 1976, the Indian Crimes Act extended the number of crimes listed in the 1885 act to fourteen; both acts constituted violations of tribal sovereignty.[55]

In another landmark case, *Elk v. Wilkins* (1884), the Supreme Court declared that Section 1 of the Fourteenth Amendment did not include Native men born under tribal authority.[56] After he was denied the right to vote in Omaha, Nebraska, John Elk, of the Winnebago/Ho-Chunk Nation, and a self-declared "civilized Indian," brought his case to the Supreme Court, and asked for recognition of his American citizenship. Elk, born in an Oklahoma tribe, had moved to Omaha, purchased a home, became a member of the state militia, and paid taxes. His deliberate removal from his tribal lands and his willingness to vote in state elections were encouraged by Nebraska laws.[57] In his dissent to *Elk v. Wilkins*, Justice John Marshall Harlan pointed out the absurdity of Native continued exclusion from citizenship: "There is still in this country a despised and rejected class of persons with no nationality whatever, who, born in our territory, owing no allegiance to any foreign power, and subject, as residents of the states, to all the burdens of government, are yet not members of any political community, nor entitled to any of the rights, privileges, or immunities of citizens of the United States."[58] The court ultimately declined Elk's application for citizenship, holding that, because Native people owed allegiance to their tribe, they did not acquire citizenship at birth.[59]

As a counterpoint to *Elk v. Wilkins,* which decided that a Native man born in the U.S. was not a citizen according to the Fourteenth Amendment, in *United States v. Wong Kim Ark* (1898) the Supreme Court decided that a Chinese man born in the U.S. (whose parents were born in China) was a U.S. citizen according to the Fourteenth Amendment. This case offers a particular exception to naturalization practices after 1882, in the context of the contentious debates over fitness for citizenship, race, and increased federal control. Although the Chinese Exclusion Act of 1882 made it explicit that the Chinese were ineligible for naturalization, the search for citizenship in a Chinese American context at the end of the nineteenth century continued. Unlike John Elk, Wong Kim Ark sought (and ultimately obtained) American citizenship so that he could maintain a transnational relationship with his family in China, at a time when exclusionary laws against Asian Americans threatened to further isolate him. Wong Kim Ark was eventually naturalized in 1898; his citizenship made it possible for his sons to become American citizens as well. After an undistinguished career as a cook, Wong retired to China in the 1930s and never returned to the U.S. After *Elk v. Wilkins,* the United States *gave* citizenship to Native allottees and *took* their land, children, and sense of sovereignty. After *Wong Kim Ark,* the U.S. *extended exclusion* beyond the Chinese immigrants to include other less desirable immigrants—this time from southern and eastern Europe—based on race and national origin.

In the aftermath of these legal decisions, Native Americans and new immigrants continued to contest the limitations these acts placed on their respective communities. Through racially exclusionary immigration acts such as these, the U.S. perpetuated a putatively racial superiority in its naturalization practices.[60] *Elk v. Wilkins,* however, precipitated the inclusion of a citizenship clause in what became the Dawes Act of 1887. By this time, the overarching goal of Indian policy reform was the complete assimilation and Americanization of Native people.[61] The promise of citizenship permeated the rhetoric of the "total assimilation" policy in the late nineteenth century. Reformers were united by three key concerns: breaking up tribal relations and the reservation land base; individualizing Native people and transforming them into U.S. citizens; and providing a universal government school.

The Dawes Act called for allotting all Native reservations (except the so-called Five Civilized Tribes) in severalty to individual Native people, with the goal of breaking up tribal land and relations. It included a citizenship proviso for Native allottees and a grant of land, to be held in trust for twenty-five years by the federal government.[62] Assimilation was to be performed gradually. If, like John Elk, Native allottees left their reservation homes and "adopted the habits of civilized life," they would become citizens of the U.S. and of the state where they resided, and they would receive title to their allotments in twenty-five years.[63] In 1906 the Burke Act amended the Dawes Act and deferred citizenship for twenty-five more years, a time during which the federal government would hold their land in trust.[64] The Burke Act had harmful consequences for Native people, as the government removed them from its care before they were able to support themselves and take care of their land allotments. Many Native people lost their lands and livelihoods.[65]

Before the Indian Citizenship Act, Native people could become citizens in several ways: through treaty provisions and special statutes; through receipt of patents in fee simple (starting in 1906); by "adopting the habits of civilized life"; through marriage (starting in 1888, Native women who married U.S. citizens became American citizens); through parentage (minor children whose Native parents became citizens also became citizens); by birth (a Native child born in the U.S. of citizen Native parents or legitimate children of a Native woman and a white father were citizens); and by special acts of Congress. In 1901, citizenship was granted to all members of the Five Civilized Tribes in Indian Territory (the Cherokee, Chickasaw, Choctaw, Creek, and Seminole).[66] Congress made World War I Native veterans into American citizens in November 1918.[67]

With little congressional debate and dismal public attention, President Coolidge signed the Indian Citizenship Act on June 2, 1924. It extended citizenship to all Native people, allowing for the retention of Native tribal citizenship and rights, including property rights. Under the final bill, unlike earlier drafts, tribal rights were not affected; citizenship did not depend on place of residence or land tenure.[68] Citizenship offered the façade of a uniform membership, although it contradicted many tribal values and allegiances. But the ICA did not put an end to wardship; at best, it extended federal dependence under the umbrella term "universal citizenship." The right to vote in state and federal elections remained, for a long time, the only direct benefit of citizenship yet many states denied Native people this right until the 1950s.[69] Before 1924, noncitizen Native people had a rather unusual status under federal law: they could not naturalize under the naturalization processes offered to immigrants.[70] Yet, citizenship, when it came to Native people was, ultimately, disastrous. As legal historian Bethany R. Berger put it, "In the name of citizenship, Indians had lost their land, their children, and their legal independence and got almost nothing in return."[71] Despite the imposition of American citizenship, many Indigenous people maintained tribal citizenship and remained members of Native communities, a double affiliation often at odds with the white, capitalist citizenship envisioned for them through federal acts.

Although the Indian Citizenship Act was the official naturalization law, not all Native people consented to it. Whereas politicians, legislators, and reform organizations like the Friends of the Indian conceived of legal citizenship as the only way for Native people to enter modernity, this supposed gift of citizenship was not unanimously accepted; Native communities had their reservations (pun intended). Through their actions, Native people on reservations challenged the meaning of American citizenship in several ways: by writing letters, forming delegations, signing petitions, joining religious movements, and partaking in traditional dance and musical performances. Writing in June 1918, from the Warren Springs Reservation, Oregon, to Yavapai Dr. Carlos Montezuma, Jake Culps asserted his position as a citizen of his tribe. He was uninterested in American citizenship, which would bring with it the potential of being drafted to fight in World War I: "I never asked no time for citizenship. There for [sic] I do not know myself as a citizen."[72] Benjamin Caswell, president of the Chippewa Indians, Inc., saw citizenship as a threat to tribal property rights, which could lead to the disintegration of Indigenous communities. In his memoirs, Carlisle graduate Luther Standing Bear, Sioux, called the act "the greatest hoax perpetuated on Indians."[73] One of the loudest voices of dissent was Jane Zane Gordon, Wyandotte, who expressed her views in the pages of the *Los Angeles Examiner,* arguing that the ICA violated the basic political principle of consent.[74]

A better-known example of Indigenous rejection of U.S. citizenship is that of the Haudenosaunee, or Six Nations Iroquois Confederacy, whose grand council sent letters to the president and Congress declining U.S. citizenship and rejecting dual citizenship. Tuscarora chief Clinton Rickard described the Iroquois resistance to the ICA, which he called a "violation" of Native sovereignty: "The Indian Citizenship Act did pass in 1924 despite our strong opposition. . . . This was a violation of our sovereignty. *Our citizenship was in our own nations.* We had a great attachment to our style of government. We wished to remain treaty Indians and preserve our ancient rights."[75] The Six Nations, which included Chief Rickard's nation, the Tuscarora, protested the federal pressure to make Native people into U.S. citizens."[76] They protested the passage of the ICA, arguing that the ICA was passed without their knowledge and consent.[77] An overlooked effect of the Johnson-Reed Immigration Act was that it regulated crossings of the U.S.-Canadian border for Native Americans traveling to religious ceremonies. Because the Six Nations of the Iroquois Confederacy lived on both sides of the border, the act threatened their cultural and political relations. Chief Rickard lobbied Congress to amend the Johnson-Reed Act, and in 1928, President Coolidge signed an amendment "guaranteeing that its border regulations did not apply to Indigenous people,"[78] thus acknowledging their sovereignty to travel freely across the border.

The ICA was the culmination of decades of work by Progressive Era organizations, government officials, and federal employees, but what did U.S. citizenship ultimately mean for Native people? The law acknowledged Native triple citizenship—federal, state, and tribal—that is still recognized today. Unlike previous naturalization statutes, the ICA did not require the consent of Native people, nor were there other preconditions for naturalization. Although there was significant Native support for citizenship and tribal claims, including from Native organizations such as the Society of American Indians (SAI), the push toward Americanization during the 1910s and 1920s obscured the complex status of Native citizenship (tribal, state, federal); Native Americans were first citizens of their sovereign nations, then American citizens.

RIGHTS AND RITES: CITIZENSHIP AND PERFORMANCE

In addition to dissenting to the *gift* of American citizenship, some Native communities used the privileges offered by American citizenship strategically to assert their Indigeneity. In the early 1920s, the Lakotas established what historian John Troutman calls "a citizenship of dance" to assert their right to dance as part of their newly granted U.S. citizenship.[79] Despite the federal government's attempt to suppress Indigenous dance, it remained a powerful act of community expression. After the 1870s, the Office of Indian Affairs considered Native ceremonial dances pagan, uncivilized rituals and attempted to eradicate them, targeting "the old Indian dances." Despite federal attempts to control their expressive culture and impose a uniform (American) political identity, Native Americans remained citizens of their nations and continued to perform their traditional dances on their land allotments.[80] Native people used American holidays to justify tribal ceremonies, swaying Indian agents, often under the aegis of the American flag. In the process, "citizen Indians" found they could remain Native only by becoming American. Preserving a sense of Indigeneity often came at the cost of public declarations of American patriotism even though such declarations were often pro forma.

Native people used American citizenship for their own cultural agendas, especially when their celebrations coincided with Fourth of July ceremonies. A missionary at the Cheyenne River Reservation reported to the Office of Indian Affairs in 1922: "The 4th of July celebration in Indian country and the 4th of July celebration by the whites are two different things. . . . The Indians celebrate the 4th of July with a regular Powwow with all its frills and fixings that go with it."[81] Although reformers and federal agents worked to prevent the spectacle of what reformers called "prurient rituals"—a disavowal of tribal traditions and performances—they failed to eradicate Indigenous dance and performance during the reservation era. Indian agents threatened many Native communities, but dance prevailed. Clyde Ellis recounts the story of an elderly Kiowa man who resisted the threats of an Indian agent to continue withholding government rations: "We don't want your rations. We want this dance."[82]

Dancing on the Fourth of July was a safer form of Native expression because it assumed a celebration of things "American." Native dances on such occasions were celebrations of entire communities, appeasing federal anxieties about the dangers of such "prurient rituals." As Rayna Green and John Troutman have shown, "having learned in the schools that publicly displaying Indianness while promoting citizenship was acceptable to the ever-anxious white man, reservation Indians began to schedule feast days and ceremonials during 'American' and 'patriotic' holidays and celebrations." Draping themselves in the American flag, figuratively and sometimes literally, Native communities used patriotic holidays like the Fourth of July, Memorial Day, and Arbor Day to convince federal agents that they had a reason to dance.[83] If in the early 1880s Native dances were a threat to Americanization, by the 1910s tribes regained control of traditional dances, sometimes modifying the role and use of dancing, despite the continued attempts of the Office of Indian Affairs to suppress their performances.[84]

Patriotic Native ceremonies organized and funded by Indian enthusiasts flourished throughout the American West in the 1910s. Two examples are the Rodman Wanamaker Expedition of Citizenship to the North American Indian in 1913 and the citizenship ceremonies organized by the federal Competency Commissions in 1916. The Wanamaker 1913 expedition was an elaborate didactic exercise in American patriotism, a long parade organized by self-proclaimed Indian enthusiast Joseph K. Dixon, sponsored by wealthy Philadelphia entrepreneur Rodman Wanamaker. The third expedition to the American West for Dixon, it carried President Woodrow Wilson's message of patriotism, recorded on gramophone, to Native reservations: "All the tribes must feel the same thrill of patriotism—the stars and the stripes must be lifted by Indian hands upon every reservation" (figure 3).[85]

The gramophone, a new technology co-opted by Americanization fervor, made Wilson's voice resonate on reservations. The expedition also included a parading of the American flag on Native lands—sometimes to the sound of Native drums—and a signing ceremony of a "Declaration of Allegiance of the North American Indian to the United States" by Native people. Each ceremony followed a similar pattern: first, Dixon explained the symbolism of the flag, followed by dedications to the flag, the raising of the flag, and lastly, the signing or X-marking of a declaration of allegiance. The audiences of the 1913 Wanamaker expedition reached an estimated nine hundred tribal leaders. A Native

Fig. 3. Native Americans assembled to listen to President Wilson's speech on the phonograph as part of the patriotic ceremony during Joseph K. Dixon's third Wanamaker Expedition of Citizenship to the American Indian. Indiana University Museum of Archaeology and Anthropology, Mathers Ethnographic Collections. Accession Number: 1962–08–3476.

interpreter was typically present to translate the message of patriotism to the Native people in the audience (figure 4).[86]

The preserved film footage of the Wanamaker expedition expands the repertoire of Native resistance to Americanization beyond instances recorded in the newspapers. In the segment filmed at Fort Belknap, Montana, a Native man in traditional regalia spits near the American flag; he is never seen signing the declaration of allegiance. It is a fleeting moment, barely noticeable in the footage, yet it speaks volumes about nonverbal Native dissent seldom preserved on camera or in national newspapers. Although major newspapers reported on the success of the

Wanamaker expedition, there was also opposition to it. The strongest resistance was recorded among the Pueblos, Hopis, and Navajos, who refused to acknowledge the flag until the rights to their lands were recognized. Pablo Abeita, governor of the Isleta Pueblo in New Mexico, refused to sign the declaration of allegiance because his people had not been treated fairly. Native intellectuals of the era also called the expedition "a theatrical affair." Arthur C. Parker opined that "the very name [of the expedition] smacks of Jingoism and impresses one with the expressions of a circus manager."[87] The expedition of citizenship was marked by sensationalism, as Americanizer Dixon seized the opportunity to advance his own fame rather than the rights of Native people.

The American fascination with outdoor, highly publicized ceremonies continued throughout the 1910s. The citizenship ceremonies orchestrated by the Competency Commission were another bizarre,

Fig. 4. Dr. Dixon presents the American flag to Native leaders during Joseph K. Dixon's third Wanamaker Expedition of Citizenship to the American Indian. Indiana University Museum of Archaeology and Anthropology, Mathers Ethnographic Collections. Accession Number: 1962–08–4828.

imposed patriotic performance. Following up on the provision of the 1906 Burke Act that allowed the secretary of the Interior to grant "certificates of citizenship" to individual allottees found "competent," in April 1915 secretary of the Interior Franklin Lane sent the first Competency Commission to reservations to determine the "competency" of Native people. Were they industrious, thrifty, and worthy of American citizenship? Many were declared so, based on the commissioners' subjective assessments of their self-sufficiency and knowledge of English. When they were found competent, Native men received patents in fee simple for their land.

In 1916, the Competency Commission spiced things up by adding an outdoor, public ceremony to dramatize the changes in the life of the potential Native citizen.[88] Under Secretary Lane, this ceremony, ornate with all the capitalist accoutrements and performed on reservations, dramatized the transition to an agrarian economy.[89] Lane called on each Native applicant by his white name, asked him for his Native name, handed him a bow, and instructed him to shoot his last arrow. Citizenship, in this public performance, was a site of abandoning traditional rituals. The Native citizen-to-be was then asked to put his hand on a plow handle, the metonym of the new Native farmer. At the end of this humiliating ritual, each soon-to-be-citizen was given a leather purse (to save money), a small flag (to cultivate patriotism), and a gold-colored badge with the inscription "A Citizen of the United States."[90] Let us examine closely a transcript of this ceremony:

Representative of [Government] speaking:

> For men: (*Read white name*), what is your Indian name? (*Gives Indian name*)
>
> (*Indian Name*), I hand you a bow and arrow. Take this bow and arrow and shoot the arrow. (*Shoots arrow.*) (*Indian Name*), you have shot your last arrow. That means that you are no longer to live the life of an Indian. You are from this day forward to live the life of a white man. But you may keep that arrow, it will be to you a symbol of your noble race and of the pride you feel that you come from the first of all Americans.
>
> (*White name*), take in your hand this plow. (*Takes plow.*) This act means that you have chosen to live the life of the white man—and the white man lives by work. From the earth we all must get our living, and the earth will not yield unless man pours upon it the sweat of his brow. Only by work do we gain a right to the land or the enjoyment of life.

(*White name*), I give you a purse. This purse will always say to you that the money you gain from your labor must be wisely kept. The wise man saves his money, so that when the sun does not smile and the grass does not grow, he will not starve.

I give into your hands the flag of your country. This is the only flag you have ever had or ever will have. It is the flag of freedom, the flag of free men, the flag of a hundred million free men and women of whom you are now one. That flag has a request of you (*White name*); that you take it into your hands and repeat these words:

"For as much as the President has said that I am worthy to be a citizen of the United States, I now promise to this flag that I will give my hands, my head, and my heart to the doing of all that will make me a true American citizen."

And now beneath this flag I place upon your breast the emblem of your citizenship. Wear this badge of honor always; and may the eagle that is on it never see you do aught of which the flag will not be proud.[91]

The ceremony for women was almost identical, but instead of a plough, women received work bags. After the Native person declared allegiance to the flag, Secretary Lane pinned a badge decorated with the American eagle and national colors onto their clothes, concluding the ceremony on a high patriotic note.[92]

A closer look reveals the absurdity of this citizenship ritual, different from the immigrant naturalization ceremonies. It marked a *potentiality* rather than a celebratory moment. The mechanical repetition of a degrading script, pledging one's mind, body, and soul to the U.S.—"I will give my hands, my head, and my heart"—speaks to the larger settler colonial context that underlay public performances of American patriotism. Repeating the scripted pledge placed the Native person in a subservient position. There was a stark distance between the image evoked by the ceremony and the reality of reservation life, from the Office of Indian Affairs (official) and reservation (Indigenous) conceptions of citizenship. The reluctance to American citizenship officials encountered on reservations was in sharp contrast to the ceremony they presented. In some instances, the Native patentees had already arranged to sell their land, which made the ceremony even more unnecessary.

For one citizenship ceremony, a crowd of more than 2,000 people gathered on the Yankton Reservation in South Dakota in May 1916. Government officials, reporters, and motion picture crews were also present, along with local officials. So pleased was Secretary Lane with the public naturalization of more than 150 "competent Indians" that day that he suggested that a similar ceremony be used in granting citizenship to new immigrants: "'Surely,' he remarked, 'it tends to instill patriotism and presents the duties of citizenship in a manner that leaves a lasting impression.'"[93] Although Native women were also part of this ceremony, the men were central to newspaper accounts of the event; one reporter was especially taken with the closing moments, when Native men "gathered about a big American flag, each laying his hands on it and pledging allegiance to the country that had given him citizenship."[94]

The *Immigrants in America Review,* a short-lived yet ambitious magazine, featured a short editorial, "Citizenship for Indians," about the ceremony on the Yankton reservation. Its author, Americanizer Frances Kellor, admired the ceremony for making Native people into thrifty and patriotic new citizens; she found it "impressive and thrilling." Like Lane, Kellor called for a similar "ritual" for new immigrants: "Why would not a corresponding ritual adapted to the immigrant's situation and to his needs be a good thing to mark the entry of immigrants into the body of American citizens? . . . Why should not the naturalization of aliens be made a solemn and significant rite?"[95] Although more than 200,000 civilians were naturalized in 1919, most immigrants were sworn in by judges in small ceremonies (figure 5).[96]

Other Americanizers shared in this view. Secretary Lane agreed to lead one of the first public naturalization ceremonies for immigrants. On July 4, 1919, in Washington, D.C., Lane gave the oath of citizenship to fifty-one women and fifty-one men, representing the states and territories of the U.S. It was one of the first group citizenship ceremonies on the Fourth of July.[97] After the public naturalization ceremonies of foreign soldiers in 1918, naturalization ceremonies received increased national attention.

The naturalization ceremony on the 4th of July 1919 was part of a larger Peace Pageant organized in Washington, D.C. Homeowners were urged to display American flags; many nations with diplomatic representatives in the country's capital paraded in this naturalization ceremony. Secretary Lane had a scripted ritual for these soon-to-be citizens as well. Less elaborate than the ritual prepared for Native reservations, it included the following oath:

> I enter into American citizenship with this pledge made before my fellow citizens, that the rights and powers given me by this country shall

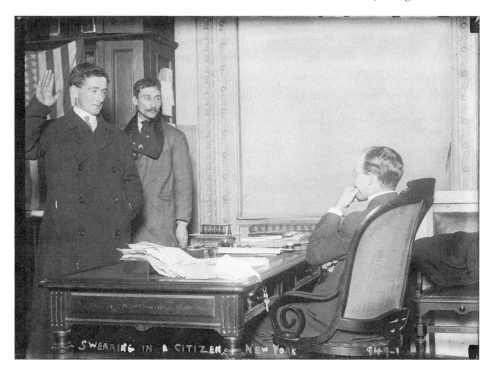

Fig. 5. A judge in his chambers swearing in a new citizen, New York, ca. 1910. Library of Congress Prints and Photographs Division. LC-DIG-ggbain-04470.

be so used that the people of America shall the more perfectly enjoy the benefits of free institutions and increasingly present to the world the strength and security which come from a high regard for the rights of others.[98]

Let us now consider the oath of the Native American citizen-to-be:

For as much as the President has said that I am worthy to be a citizen of the United States, I now promise to this flag that I will give my hands, my head, and my heart to the doing of all that will make me a true American citizen.

For Secretary Lane, whose office orchestrated this performance, the transformation of Native people was total; the citizen-to-be pledged his "hands," "head," and "heart" in the final chapter of Americanization: citizenship. The immigrant citizen-to-be entered a community of fellow citizens, and his oath emphasized concepts unimaginable by his Native counterpart, such as "power" and "rights." Although the naturalization oath new citizens take in the twenty-first century is similar, the "oaths" in these two contexts in the 1910s were highly improvised, the rhetorical products of their ideological moment. And, although the newspapers advertised the events as bringing all nations together—the pageant following the naturalization ceremony, "A Parade of All Nations," included representatives of over three dozen nations, and smaller nations like Romania and Lithuania—no Native nation was represented in the parade, which ended with the float of Uncle Sam and "$6,000 worth of fireworks."[99] The conspicuous absence of Native nations from these 1919 ceremonies amplified the further erasure of Indigenous people from both the national scene and the American imaginary.

Other national holidays became occasions for immigrant naturalization. On George Washington's birthday in 1922, the city of Rochester, New York, held a naturalization ceremony. The ceremony began with a dinner, with patriotic songs as entertainment, followed by a gathering at the Chamber of Commerce, with thousands in attendance. School children sang patriotic songs, and the Boy Scouts marched on the platform carrying American flags. One by one, the mayor called the applicants to the platform, where they passed under the American flags, shook hands with the mayor, and received a flag, a copy of the Constitution from a girl dressed as Miss Columbia, and a certificate of citizenship from a clerk. The presiding judge, Frederick E. Crane, recommended that New York City follow suit by publicly welcoming its new citizens.[100] After 1924, naturalization ceremonies became larger and more elaborate, as fewer and fewer undesirable Americans were admitted into the U.S. after the Immigration Act of 1924.

At Ford Motor Company, a public pageant was incorporated into its Americanization Program, to mark the symbolic transformation of immigrant laborers into new Americans. This mass graduation ceremony, popularly known as the "Melting Pot ceremony," was a public display of immigrants affirming their conversion to Americanism. In 1914, when the Americanization Program started at Ford, most of the workers were new immigrants. One of the first lessons they learned in the Ford program was how to say "I am a good American."[101] By 1914, Ford employed 12,880 workers, 9,109 of whom were foreign-born: Poles, Russians, Romanians, Italians, and Austro-Hungarians.[102] So popular was the Ford English "teaching plan" that it generated a national following.[103] Articles in the Ford-owned newspapers as well as those in local and national newspapers fill in some of the gaps about these ceremonies. In particular, the pageants on the Fourth of July at Ford Motor brought large crowds to witness the staged rapid transformation of the immigrant worker into an American as he emerged, wearing a suit and waving an American flag, from a large melting pot. Clinton De Witt, the director of Americanization at Ford, described the event at the national Americanization conference:

> Our program consists of a pageant in the form of a melting pot, where all the men descend from a boat scene representing the vessel on which they came over; down the gangway . . . into a pot 15 feet in diameter and 7½ feet high, which represents the Ford English School. Six teachers, three on either side, stir the pot with 10-foot ladles representing nine months of teaching in the school. Into the pot 52 nationalities with foreign clothes and baggage go and out of the pot after a vigorous stirring by the teachers comes one nationality, viz., American.[104]

The Ford Melting Pot ceremonies were held in public spaces that could accommodate thousands of viewers. The *Detroit Free Press* reported on the first public graduation ceremony in February 1916, with a graduating class of "512 husky immigrants" representing 33 nations. As the graduates emerged from the melting pot, they received their diplomas and then took their place in the audience.[105] The diplomas guaranteed that they could read, write, and speak good English, which allowed them to draw their first naturalization papers without other examinations. Over time, the Melting Pot exercises at Ford Motor became larger, more dramatic, elaborate, and intolerant. The Ford English classes, organized under the auspices of the Ford Sociological Department, were subsequently widely criticized for their "grotesquely exaggerated patriotism": "the pupils are told to 'walk to the American blackboard, take a piece of the American chalk, and explain how the American workman walks to his American home and sits down with his American family to their good American dinner."[106] Ford's Americanization program became a model for others. Its ultimate failure signaled an end to the paternalism and manipulative approach of Ford Motors to labor relations. The Melting Pot ceremonies at Ford showed the nation how the disciplined immigrant laborer could become a good American citizen (figure 6).

The Ford English School graduating class as they emerged from the "Melting Pot"

Fig. 6. Ford English School graduating class emerging from the "Melting Pot," Ford Highland Park Plant, 1916. From the Collections of Henry Ford, gift of Ford Motor Company.

Whereas the workers at Ford were subjected to the Americanization machine controlling their transformation into new Americans, other immigrants embraced citizenship as a way to escape the bondage and tyranny of European monarchs.[107] In 1891, the Chicago Polish paper *Dziennik Chicagoski* described the acquisition of American citizenship as liberatory: "Those who have lived in bondage can seek freedom here. Here they breathe freely, and rest in peace, and here, with pride, they become citizens of a free country, which is not ruled either by a czar or knout."[108] Yet, the display of immigrant bodies parading on stage under the gaze of Ford's Sociological Department reveals incongruities between citizenship as an act of consent and the elaborate citizenship ceremonies serving larger patriotic goals through repeated public performances.

The Native and new immigrant subjects who were part of the pageants of Americanization had little say in the orchestration of these public performances. Besides employing new immigrants, Ford Motor Company also employed Native men who had attended Indian boarding schools and who were perceived as embodying the lessons of Americanization taught there. Twenty-five of Ford's more than 25,000 employees in 1916 were Native men, all former students at Carlisle Indian Industrial School, representing fourteen tribes and thirteen states, three of them holding diplomas from Carlisle. To Ford officials, they were exemplary, models to be emulated by the new immigrant laborers: "These Indian students are splendid types of the Ford workman, and have proved themselves worthy representatives of their alma mater and the principles which the U.S. government has inculcated through its courses."[109] To the Native workers, Ford represented a labor opportunity, a way to make a living in a settler nation that called itself a "nation of immigrants."

The United States was never a nation of immigrants, as I argue throughout this book; it was and continues to be an occupied country, extracting resources and perpetuating the myth of a welcoming nation of immigrants. This chapter has traced the insidious ways that immigration restriction laws and federal Indian policy paved the way for organized Americanization in legislating the desirable "new American." Americanization was a central concern of the Progressive Era, an ethos and a policy imposed on new immigrants and Native Americans, yet affecting each group differently. At a time when resurgent nationalism threatened to restrict undesirable immigrants, it also sought to homogenize Indigenous people into a mass of Americanism, attempting to erase Native sovereignty and to naturalize a group displaced by colonization. The passing of the Indian Citizenship Act *after* the Immigration Act of 1924 also indicates that Americanization in an Indigenous context—also numerically smaller—followed the model of immigrant Americanization, attempting to homogenize a large and different mass of what Jodi Byrd calls "arrivants" (to distinguish from previous arrivals, the settler colonists). For Native people, Americanization and the imposition of citizenship, as extensions of settler colonialism, superimposed one civic status over another—domestic dependent, ward, and U.S. citizen. For new immigrants, Americanization meant a renunciation of political allegiance to foreign sovereigns, the acquisition of English, and civic education for citizenship.[110]

2 "You Can't Come In! The Quota for 1620 Is Full"

Americanization, Exclusion, Representation

The Indian problem is a problem because the country has taken it and nursed it as a problem; otherwise it is not a problem at all.

—Carlos Montezuma, *Wassaja*, April 1916

An aspiring writer from an immigrant background feels damned on the one side for becoming too American and damned on the other side for not being able to become American enough.

—Thomas Ferraro, *Ethnic Passages*, 1993

IN A BOOK of irreverent and politically charged cartoons, *For Indians Only* (1971), Crow Creek and Sioux artist Robert Freeman temporarily reversed the historic arc of Native misrepresentation through the lens of immigration in a cartoon titled "Papers?" (figure 7). Freeman placed a Native man at the helm of an improvised and anachronistic "immigration office," in charge of screening new settler arrivals, asking for their "papers." Freeman imagined an encounter between European settlers and Native Americans, marked not by genocide and dispossession but by diplomacy and Native agency. The Native man sits; the pilgrims stand. He speaks, they listen. One pilgrim holds a long piece of paper, marked to suggest, perhaps, his legitimacy or a long list of claims he brings to the Native man.

Drawn in the activist moment of the 1970s, the cartoon dramatized the role of papers at the heart of this book—papers as legal documents

Fig. 7. Robert Freeman, "Papers?" *For Indians Only* (1971). Ayer Collection, Newberry Library, Chicago.

legitimizing identities, papers as records and documents of presence, papers as traces of print culture left by Native and immigrant communities, as well as papers as literature, as cultural documents of distinct groups of people. Papers determine the settler state's inclusionary or exclusionary practices as well as who can or cannot be "made" American. Papers also exclude the cultural circulation of oral stories. Reversing colonial teleology, the Native man presides over an immigration office and uses his voice and posture to ask for papers. His gesture appears to question the legitimacy of the European doctrine of discovery, which granted the discovering European country title and ownership of land, turning Indigenous people into mere "tenants."[1] On one hand, historically, "papers" determined the racial composition of the country; on the other, they dispossessed Native people of millions of acres of land through war, genocide, and legislation.

In this chapter I historicize Americanization as ideology, on one hand, and federal- and state-sponsored program, on the other. I also situate the debates over national identity and citizenship in a broader racial and ethnic context. I start with the uneasy places both Indigenous and immigrant groups occupy in the American settler imaginary, in narratives of deficiency reinforced in the Americanization campaigns. Although non-Anglo-Saxon peoples were intimately implicated in Americanization, my focus on Native American and new immigrant cultural production here and in later chapters reveals the nuanced negotiations of American identity and citizenship by these two groups rarely read together. The chapter begins and ends with analyses of political cartoons, which speak to larger concerns about Americanization, exclusion, and representation.

AMERICANIZATION REDUX

When militant Americanizer Frances Kellor learned about the patriotic flag ceremonies on Native reservations in 1916 (see chapter 1), she started advocating for immigrant naturalization ceremonies: Why should not the naturalization of aliens be made a solemn and significant rite?[2] In yet another instance of settler use of Native people as a conduit for immigrant reformation, Kellor brought both groups to the American public's attention. The term "Americanization" eludes a single definition, but even in its original historical context Americanization was a highly divisive movement, with conservative connotations, which included what James R. Barrett calls "more than a hint of nativism." According to Barrett, "It was something that native [white] middle class did to immigrants, a coercive process by which elites pressed WASP values on immigrant workers, a form of social control."[3] One element missing from Barrett and the assessments of other leading historians is that the phenomenon they attribute to immigrant transformation also affected Indigenous communities.

In 1920, Peter Roberts, who had spent his career as an educator in the service of Americanization, reached a sober conclusion in *The Problem of Americanization:* "The word Americanization has become a household term—among the native-born a synonym of anxiety, dread, or duty, among the foreign-born one of misgiving, suspicion, or hope."[4] At the beginning of the twentieth century, Americanization was a new buzz word in U.S. legal, literary, and popular rhetoric. On one hand, it referred to a social, cultural, and political movement to make new immigrants and Indigenous people into Americans; on the other, it was a term used in debates over national identity and a person's fitness for citizenship.[5] The Americanization movement framed itself as inclusive, but as part of the American imperial and capitalist project, Americanization was a highly exclusive movement: a continuation of late nineteenth-century imperial consolidation tactics through westward expansion, race-based immigration policy, the genocide of Indigenous people, and the consolidation of imperial economic power through the import of new immigrant labor from southern and eastern Europe.

As a cultural and social phenomenon, Americanization originated in the nineteenth century, when questions about what it meant to be American intersected with growing nativist concerns about racial purity and fitness for citizenship. Fears about the future composition of the U.S., the efforts of the eugenics movement in lobbying for immigration restriction legislation, and racism intensified the Americanization movement. Public schools and evening classes took on "educating" immigrants, aided by settlement workers and patriotic organizations. Starting in 1907, the YMCA, led by Peter Roberts, educated new immigrants in English, civics, and Christian virtues. In addition to the hundreds of YMCA branches, the Roberts method of immigrant education was used in industrial settings. In 1914, the federal government made public schools the center of the federal Americanization program. Before World War I, instructors taught Americanization in their classes as a way "to help the immigrants cope with America." During the war, Americanization served the U.S. national interest. By 1916, the Americanization movement had been taken over by the militant nationalists, with Nativist slogans like "America first" characterizing the movement's new phase. By 1918, the work of Americanization and the war effort went hand in hand, leading to one of the movement's most nationalist phases, advocating for "100% Americanism," which dwindled after 1919.[6]

A social and political movement originating in the 1890s, the Americanization movement culminated in the immigration restriction acts of the 1920s. The Americanization movement went through several phases—the turn of the twentieth century to 1914, the years of World War I, and the immediate postwar years. Some representative organizations included patriotic groups like the Daughters of the American Revolution (DAR), the North American Civic League for Immigrants,

settlement workers, and other progressives arguing for protective legislation for the new immigrants.[7] Following a decade of war-instilled
nationalism, "the Americanization as assimilation" movement reached
its peak in the 1910s and 1920s. Americanizers called for classes in
English where appropriate, ensuring that state and federal agencies addressed the specific needs of new immigrants and promoting literacy
and knowledge of civic affairs. Schools and local governments, together
with voluntary organizations, took a lead role in this movement.

By the time the U.S. entered WWI, the network advancing the Americanization of adult immigrants included the U.S. Bureau of Education;
the U.S. Bureau of Naturalization; Americanization offices in state
governments; public school systems; Catholic, Protestant, and Jewish
organizations; the Red Cross; and women's organizations. Patriotic
groups like the Daughters of the American Revolution (DAR), the U.S.
Chamber of Commerce and its local affiliates, industrial corporations
and trade unions, public libraries, and newspapers supported the work
of Americanization.[8] As Jeffrey Mirel documented, in 1919, Chicago's
editors of foreign language newspapers joined efforts with the Chicago Association of Commerce and the Board of Education to create a
working definition of Americanization. This definition called for "the
development and possession by the individual of intelligent pride, loyalty, love, and devotion to the government, institutions, and ideals of
the US, and the practical identification of his interest with those of the
nation and its people."[9]

From the 1890s onward, patriotic societies organized in earnest in
response to the perceived threat the new immigrants posed to the nation, and public displays of patriotism and nationalism moved from the
street into the classroom and the home. Patriotism attained its highest
form of public display during Americanization Day celebrations. The
first Americanization Day in the U.S. was celebrated on July 4, 1915,
at President Wilson's recommendation. An Americanization Day Committee was formed in May 1915 to promote a "national movement to
bring American citizens, foreign-born and native alike, together on our
national Independence Day."[10] The irony of celebrating Americanization day on Independence Day was perhaps not lost on a nation ambivalent about recent arrivals from southern and eastern Europe, embracing a new brand of patriotism revived by the recent war in Europe.

But July 4 was—and still is—an opportune moment for naturalization ceremonies throughout the U.S.

The national Americanization Day Committee designed posters for the occasion, which it sent to mayors of major cities, asking them to observe July Fourth as Americanization Day. Uncle Sam took center stage, inviting (white) immigrant laborers to become citizens. One poster in particular advertised the advantages of literacy, education, and citizenship for the immigrants (figure 8).

The poster shows Uncle Sam, the Americanizer, shaking hands with a laborer in the foreground and an immigrant man receiving his "citizen's papers" in the middle ground; the Home and School complete the background with an American flag. The poster reads: "Make it a day of WELCOME to all foreign-born citizens and an INVITATION to all residents to become citizens. Make our 13,000,000 immigrants feel that they are a part of and have a share in, American institutions." The poster urges the viewer to do his part by attending the citizens' celebration on July 4, by pledging allegiance to the flag, and helping others become "Americans first." Thousands of such posters were disseminated nationally, and a prize contest for the best statement on the meaning of Americanization Day was publicized through the foreign language press. President Woodrow Wilson called the enterprise "a most successful movement." At the request of Mrs. Cornelius Vanderbilt, Tiffany designed four citizenship buttons, to be distributed at some celebrations and later used in naturalization ceremonies. The speakers on Americanization Day included foreign-born representatives of different nationalities; thousands of posters were displayed in major railroad stations.[11] Americanization Day highlighted a spectacular version of American nationalism through patriotic rituals.

In one of the first rigorous studies of the Americanization movement, which appeared in the *American Journal of Sociology* in 1919, Howard Hill noted that whereas immigrants to the U.S. between 1880 and 1885 expressed few obstacles to "successful Americanization," in 1910 only about "*one percent* of surveyed immigrants expressed the desire to become American" (my emphasis).[12] The need for a more systematic Americanization program was dictated by a combination of factors: high numbers of immigrants who spoke over one hundred languages or dialects; the large number of foreign language newspapers; millions of

Fig. 8. "Make the Fourth of July Americanization Day, 'Many Peoples—but One Nation,'" Americanization Day poster. George F. Tyler Poster Collection, Special Collections Research Center, Temple University Libraries, Philadelphia.

U.S. inhabitants unable to speak English; and the fact that only about 1 percent of adult immigrants attended school.[13] The Committee on Public Information and the National Americanization Committee sent out a survey to more than fifty thousand agencies. The information it collected revealed the number of private and voluntary organizations serving the Americanization movement: settlement houses, women's groups, home-visiting agencies, churches, and many others. Because of financial pressures on local agencies, federal aid became imperative. In 1918, Franklin Lane, the secretary of the Interior (see chapter 1), convened a conference on Americanization in Washington, D.C., attended by governors, state officials, prominent commercial and industrial leaders, educators, and publicists. The participants supported a resolution for a central body to oversee all federal Americanization work. This resolution culminated in a law passed by Congress in May 1918, authorizing the Bureau of Naturalization to issue a textbook to aid immigrants preparing for naturalization. Congressional appropriations were required to support the effective education of immigrants, "a matter vital to the national welfare."[14]

Invited to speak in Boston, Louis Brandeis, a progressive lawyer and future Supreme Court justice, gave a speech titled "True Americanism," echoing Theodore Roosevelt.[15] Unlike Roosevelt, Brandeis pointed to the idea of "true Americanism" as an intellectual pursuit, beyond the daily effort of breadwinning. Brandeis invoked a Flag Day ceremony in New York, which brought together "boys and girls representing more than twenty different nationalities warring abroad." He did not mention, however, the ongoing genocide against Native people at home. Asking the audience, "What is Americanization?" Brandeis distinguished between superficial Americanization and a more substantive one, one that allowed an opportunity to thrive. To Brandeis, it wasn't a lack of allegiance to America that hindered the immigrants; it was industrial dependence and prejudice that kept them down. Brandeis argued that every citizen must have financial independence and leisure, as well as an education beyond school.[16]

Although Americanization meant different things throughout the twentieth century, it acquired specific connotations during the Progressive Era, when federal and state programs used it in the process of *making* (new) patriotic Americans. Americanization also gave Americans the opportunity to instruct the immigrants, widening the gap between the Americanizer and the Americanized. Sociologist Michael Olneck calls Americanization a "symbolic behavior"; its ultimate goal is not a finite state but a behavior—how the immigrant *behaves* American— "an effort to secure cultural and ideological hegemony through configuration of the symbolic order."[17] Similarly, Native people adjusted to the pressures of nationalist discourse. Lucy Maddox has revealed the cultural and political constraints Native intellectuals had to negotiate as they also attempted to forge a "a public, political space for themselves, deliberately adopted, manipulated, and transformed the means already available to them for addressing white audiences."[18] Jeffrey Mirel has proposed the framework "patriotic pluralism" for understanding Americanization beyond its original grounding in patriotism and nationalism. For Mirel, Americanization is a "negotiated exchange" between immigrants and Americanizers, an exchange marked by uneven power relations. Studying several scenes of Americanization, he found that immigrants balanced "a deep commitment to the United States with an unequally strong desire to maintain crucial aspects of their cultural backgrounds and their composite American identity," retaining immigrant agency.[19] While the nativists and future restrictionists argued for the preservation of a so-called national character, Americanizers wanted to help immigrants adjust to life in the United States. Cultural and social Americanization did not depend on the immigrants' legal status as immigrants "came up with their own, often highly individualistic ideas about becoming American."[20]

THE IMMIGRANTS AND *INDIANS* OF THE AMERICAN IMAGINATION

During the Progressive Era, anxieties over new immigrants and *Indians* relegated both groups to an imagined "savagism" pitted against "civilization."[21] Once large numbers of immigrants threatened Anglo-Saxon homogeneity, this type of scapegoating targeted immigrant laborers, or "the white savages."[22] Their visibility through caricature and silent film revealed the Progressive Era outrage at their treatment and the incongruity of representation with lived conditions. Scholars such as Robert F. Berkhofer, Alan Trachtenberg, Philip Deloria, Shari Huhndorf, and David Koffman have shown how "the white man's Indian" as an imagined category negotiated social anxieties over cultural and physical differences. Huhndorf's concept of "going Native" describes a pervasive way that white people may choose to express their ambivalence about settler treatment of Native people. Drawing on encounters between Native people and Jewish immigrants, Koffman has shown that Jewish immigrants enjoyed legal and cultural benefits as white settlers in the eighteenth and nineteenth centuries. Although their whiteness was questioned, Jewish immigrants benefited from their associations with Native people "as precarious outsiders," as well as from economic and cultural alliances they forged with Native communities. The perceived enemies of mid-nineteenth-century westward expansion, *Indians* became symbols of alterity for Jewish immigrants. The rhetorical and practical uses of Indigenous tropes by Jewish immigrants ultimately served a larger cultural goal in the mid-1920s, when Jewish immigrants claimed that American Indians and Jews "be considered insiders."[23]

The crisis in national identity caused by the waves of new immigrants and their threat to "100 percent Americanism" produced an unexpected turn to the *Indian*, who donned the robe of "savagery" and became "the first American." The *Indian* as the "vanishing Indian"—a colonial invention, reinforcing the powerful illusion of what journalist John O'Sullivan called "manifest destiny" in 1845—marked the nineteenth-century representational landscape, from literature to painting to popular media. In *The Vanishing Race* (1913), Joseph K. Dixon amplified the vanishing Indian trope by documenting, in print, film, and public lectures, the putative disappearance of Indigenous peoples facing "the agents of civilization."[24] To become American, the *Indian* had to "vanish" as a Native person.

Memorializing the "vanishing Indian" took grandiose proportions in the 1910s. Wanamaker endorsed a monument to the "Vanishing Red" on Staten Island, a bronze warrior taller than the Statue of Liberty, extending his hand in welcome to the "huddled masses" of immigrants. The proposed National American Indian Memorial in New York City used the idea of the *Indian* to glorify such abstract concepts as "liberty" and "patriotism." Dixon, who was involved in promoting the memorial, spoke about it as "another World Wonder," which would "preserve and perpetuate for the inspiration of coming generations the nobility and intrepidity, the heroism and exalted qualities of Native character. This sixty-foot bronze figure would serve as a reminder to

Fig. 9. The proposed memorial to the American Indian in New York City, design by Thomas Hastings. Indiana University Museum of Archaeology and Anthropology, Mathers Ethnographic Collections. Accession Number: 1962–08–3061.

all immigrants, all the nations of the world as they come to our shore," of nothing more but a "passing race," a term popularized by eugenicist Madison Grant's *The Passing of the Great Race* (1916). If completed, the monument would speak of a defeated Indian, a warning to all: "Thus he gives, in bronze, a perpetual welcome to the nations of the world, as he gave welcome to the white man when he first came to these shores" (figure 9).[25]

The memorial's groundbreaking on February 22, 1913, drew a large crowd, including President William Howard Taft, who was in his last days in office, and an "Indian Delegation." The newspapers noted the irony of Native people attending the groundbreaking of a memorial dedicated to their own demise.[26] Despite the pomp and coverage by New York newspapers, the project ultimately failed. The memorial reinforced the vanishing Indian trope and diverted public attention from the real conditions of Native people.[27] As Frederick Hoxie notes, the National Indian Memorial "was designed to dominate the entrance to New York City." Members of the Society of American Indians were not necessarily opposed to this enterprise. In the first issue of the *Quarterly Journal*, the editor noted "the irony of building a gigantic statue to a race of men who have been so grossly injured by the evils of civilization" and concluded that the idea of the statue "is a noble one" as long as it portrayed correctly "the tribes that welcomed and nursed the feeble colonists."[28]

The memorialization of the "vanishing Indian" as the first American—and the brief moment when it had the potential to replace the Statue of Liberty and its iconography in immigrant imaginary—is worth closer scrutiny. If the Indian was the first American, why was this iconic figure also vanishing? American Studies scholars have answered this question from several perspectives. Walter Benn Michaels offered a compelling analysis of "the vanishing American" in the context of emerging nativist anxieties toward new immigrants, whose perceived difference was threatening to the old American: "If identification with the Indian could function at the turn of the twentieth century as a *refusal* of American identity, it would come to function by early 1920s as an *assertion* of American identity." Alan Trachtenberg also traced the ways that the appropriation of Native Americans as first Americans was recuperated through performance and spectacle. As Trachtenberg put it, "American identity was a process and Americanization could be learned."[29]

But what caused the shift in the American cultural (and racial) imaginary from the "vanishing Indian" to the "first American" after World War I? The affirmation of Indigenous primacy in the cultural imaginary as "the first American" (who had to "vanish" as *Indian*)—what Ojibwe historian Jean O'Brien has termed "lasting," in opposition to colonial assertions of primacy, or "firsting"[30]—coincided with the threat new immigrant groups posed to Anglo-Saxonism. This shift in the pro-Indian rhetoric also grew out of the revival of nativist fears of new immigrants. These fears eventually led to agitation for immigration restriction, fueled by "emotional nativism" and "arguments based in pseudo-scientifically supported racism."[31] Perhaps most important, the appeal to Native iconography as a paradoxical reassertion of cultural American identity also coincided with a disidentification from, nay a *refusal* in Michaels's terms, of inconvenient immigrants in the consolidation of the American empire.[32] Although their predecessors often encountered American intolerance as newcomers, the new immigrants faced different challenges. Arriving from places like the Russian empire, Austro-Hungary, Italy, or the Balkans, they came from "backward" political, social, and economic structures, with low literacy rates and little acquaintance with Protestant Christianity (most of them were Roman Catholic, Eastern Orthodox, or Jewish). Their numbers were overwhelmingly high: if, in 1875, about 10 percent of the immigrants came from eastern and southern Europe, the numbers grew to 57 percent in 1896 and to 76 percent by 1902.[33]

This reconceptualization of the *Indian* as the first American overlapped with a key moment in rethinking American exceptionalism, culminating in immigration restriction legislation, which drew "a new ethnic and racial map based on new categories and hierarchies of difference."[34] African Americans migrating from the rural South to the North often supported immigration restriction, given the increasingly competitive job market and the economic and civil privileges denied to African Americans but granted to immigrants.[35] The idea of *difference* permeated modern racial ideology, and made the list of excludable categories of immigrants longer and longer every year.[36]

THE MAKINGS OF AMERICANS: CONSIDERATIONS OF REPRESENTATION

In 1902, as millions of southern and eastern European immigrants sought refuge in North America, American writer Gertrude Stein arrived in England to visit her brother Leo. A landscape different from the poverty-stricken villages, pogroms, and small towns of eastern Europe, the English countryside offered many occasions for transatlantic meditations and many consternating questions, such as brother Leo's: "Why in the name of all that's reasonable do you think of going back to America?"[37] Expatriate writer Stein did go back to America for a short while before settling in Paris in 1903. There, at the center of the modernist avant-garde, her salon attracted many American expatriates. As if to answer her brother's question, Stein opened her thousand-page work, *The Making of Americans* (1925)—a fictionalized account of immigrant grandparents and their descendants—with a puzzling line: "It has always seemed to me a rare privilege, this, of being an American, a real American, one whose tradition it has taken scarcely sixty years to create. The old people in a new world, the new people made out of the old, that is the story that I mean to tell." From her chosen exile, away from exerting her "rare privilege" of being "a real American," Stein's attempt to tell the story of Americans and to write the great American novel resulted, instead, in failure. The great American novel she envisioned and worked on for more than a decade finally saw print in 1925 to modest critical acclaim.[38] *The Making of Americans* defied conventional novelistic form in its aesthetic experimentation and pointed to the inadequacy of (the modernist) narrative to render *the* American experience, which Stein and her contemporaries understood as the immigrant experience. Gertrude Stein failed to tell the story of "the making of Americans." Too unreadable to readers unaccustomed to high modernist linguistic experimentation, the book and its abstract poetics did not—could not—capture the drama unfolding on the American scene.

The American scene that Stein and her fellow American writers imagined also excluded traces of Indigeneity. Ralph Marvell, a character in Edith Wharton's *The Custom of the Country* (1913), described Washington Square in New York City as a "reservation" of authentic Americanism, inhabited by his mother and grandfather—the "Aborigines" of a vanishing Anglo-Saxonism threatened with "rapid extinction" by the "advance of the invading race." Wharton's narrator mused, "Ralph sometimes called his mother and grandfather the Aborigines, and likened them to those vanishing denizens of the American continent doomed to rapid extinction with the advance of the invading race."[39] Wharton's character sublimated xenophobia into a safer, imagined affiliation with the American Indian—as long as the latter was vanishing.

Wharton's fellow American writer Henry James returned to the U.S. briefly in 1904 after twenty years, to rediscover that there was "no escape from the ubiquitous alien." As he documented in *The American Scene* (1906), the Lower East Side was "a great swarming, a swarming that had begun to thicken . . . a Jewry that had burst all bounds."[40] In his travelogue, James also directed his critique at the "monstrous organism" of American capitalism, of which the immigrants were only a thin layer in the new industrial, modern landscape. James's nuanced depiction of the immigrant invasion of New York City has elicited contradictory critical responses.[41] The "American scene" that James reencountered after an imposed exile was filled with cultural, ethnic, and racial difference and tension between the "old-stock" settler citizens and the new immigrants. Fellow American realist writer, William Dean Howells, visited the Lower East Side in the 1890s and remarked on "the inmates of the dens and lairs about me," reminiscent of Jacob Riis's photojournalistic exposé, *How the Other Half Lives* (1890).[42] Howells's and James's imperial gazes, cast at the American scene, were characteristic of the reception of (new) immigrant subjectivity on American soil and in American letters, marked by aloofness, suspicion, and fear.

The turn to Americanization also indexed a view of national identity that took Anglo-Saxonism for granted, accentuated by decades of growing nativism, xenophobia, and fears of difference and materialized in the work of the ever-expanding Americanization movement and its subsequent campaigns. Americanization was imminent, indexed through many rhetorical turns. In 1897, Theodore Roosevelt called for upholding "true Americanism," which was "a question of spirit, conviction, and purpose, not of creed or birthplace." For Roosevelt, becoming American was a privilege: "To bear the name of American is to bear the most honorable of titles." True Americanism meant a renunciation of the past, a complete transformation: "Above all, the immigrant must learn to talk and think and *be* United States."[43] For Frederick Jackson Turner, "the frontier was the crucible of Americanization. In the crucible of the frontier the immigrants were Americanized, liberated, and fused into a mixed race, English in neither nationality nor characteristics."[44] As historian Desmond King has argued, "The suspicion of diversity in the decades leading up to and including the 1920s stemmed from the political dominance of one group's conception of U.S. identity," grounded in a white Anglo-American inheritance and disseminated through the Americanization movement.[45] Economics also motivated the Americanizers because it "offered a program which would solve the problem of the immigrant with the least disturbance to the economic and political life of the nation; a program which would not result in the loss of an exceedingly valuable labor supply to America."[46]

But who were the "Americans" that the immigrants met at the end of the nineteenth century? A fast-paced population growth in the U.S. at the end of the nineteenth century saw a significant shift in demographics. The population grew from almost 3.9 million people in 1790, counted by the first U.S. census, to almost 63 million Americans by 1890. By 1880, half of the labor force was in manufacturing, mining, trade, transportation, and service, no longer in agriculture. By 1920, 50 percent of the population lived in urban areas, with 72 percent of immigrants in urban areas.[47] By contrast, in 1910, the Native population counted fewer than 300,000.[48] In the U.S. exceptionalist narrative of progress and growth, the story of Native Americans is marginal; entire nations of people, who lived far away from the railroads and roads that marked "progress," were fractured by settler greed, land dispossession, and genocide. Native people had to live defending their communities from violent settler attacks, the encroachment of "civilization" programs and violence over their lands, and the continued threats to Native sovereignty. Whereas the U.S. population doubled every twenty years between 1800 and 1900, the Native population entered an alarming decline at the beginning of the twentieth century.[49] Despite these drastic changes in population and the systematic attempts at eliminating Native nations, many not only survived but entered conversations about "civilization," despite being relegated to a "savage" past. The Progressive Era witnessed a proliferation of Native popular books and magazine articles by Native authors.[50]

How did Native and new immigrant writers fit into this narrative of imminent change? In *Beyond Ethnicity,* Werner Sollors argued that works of "ethnic literature" may be read not only as representations of mediation between cultures but also as "handbooks of socialization into the codes of Americanness."[51] To a certain extent Sollors was correct, and his work of recovering forgotten works by multiethnic and Indigenous authors has shaped an entire field. Yet, Sollors's optimistic view of Americanization (historically situated), shared by David Hollinger, Lawrence H. Fuchs, and others, relied on a liberal model of a pluralistic society, where one could construct one's desired identity. Fuchs proposed the model of "voluntary pluralism," whereas Hollinger argued that a "postethnic perspective resists the grounding of knowledge and moral values in blood and history, but works within the last generation's recognition that many of the ideas and values once taken to be universal are specific to certain cultures." Yet, "blood and history" are very much part of the legacy of a violent history that cultural relativism is attempting to minimize.[52]

Sollors's and Hollinger's views are incompatible with critiques of the settler colonial state and the ongoing exploitation of immigrant labor and Indigenous land and resources, as contemporary critics of

settler colonialism like Glenn Coulthard remind us: "The reproduc-
tion of the colonial relationship between Indigenous peoples and what
would eventually become Canada depended heavily on the deployment
of state power geared around genocidal practices of forced *exclusion*
and *assimilation*."[53] In an Indigenous context, understanding exclusion
and assimilation as genocidal practices rather than glorifications of the
melting pot—diametrically opposed to the idea that one can reinvent
one's ethnicity—is a key distinction from understanding exclusion and
assimilation in immigrant contexts. If race and culture (religion, ethnicity, level of "civilization") influence our understanding of Americanization in an ethnic and immigrant context, economics (and its materialization in access to territory) is settler colonialism's main reason for
being. As Coulthard points out, following Patrick Wolfe, "Territoriality
is settler colonialism's specific, irreducible element." Like capitalism,
colonialism, as a structure of domination predicated on dispossession,
is "the sum effect of the diversity of interlocking oppressive social relations that constitute it."[54] If immigration is premised on economic
progress and accumulation, this narrative of progress comes at the cost
of continued Indigenous dispossession.

In contrast, historians like Irving Howe and Lizabeth Cohen questioned the idea of inventing one's ethnic and national identity, adding
that class and gender often impeded this process. David R. Roediger,
Michael Rogin, Matthew F. Jacobson, and others have argued that race
plays as key a role in the study of immigration. Roediger has shown
that race is a central category in studying the Americanization of immigrants. Although Sollors's work in recovering multiethnic literary
traditions has expanded the American literary canon and opened the
door for another generation of scholars, his pluralist view of American
society, where one's identity could be invented, is rather limiting. Immigrant identity formation (more broadly) and representation (more
narrowly) were also influenced by such factors as cultural hostility, isolation, economic conditions, anxieties caused by World War I, as well
as by conceptions of race.[55]

In his book *Foreigners: The Making of American Literature, 1900–
1940*, Marcus Klein asked the readers to imagine what "the loss of
America" meant in the 1910s—when, "between forty and fifty per cent
of the population was immigrant and black." Klein took the example
of Henry Adams to illustrate this perceived "loss" in the mainstream
American tradition.[56] Like Henry James's dear Washington Square,

which had been overtaken by the unkempt, "savage" immigrant motley crowd, Henry Adams's world was also gone:

> *His world was dead.* Not a Polish Jew fresh from Warsaw or Cracow—not a furtive Yacoob [*sic*] or Ysaac still reeking of the ghetto, snarling a weird Yiddish to the officers of the customs—but had a keener instinct, an intenser energy, and a freer hand than he—*American of Americans.* . . . He made no complaint and found no fault with his time; he was *not worse off than the Indians* or the buffalo who had been ejected from their heritage.[57] (my emphases)

Although distancing himself from the *Indians*, who fared much worse than he, the "American of Americans," Adams lamented the vanishing of (Anglo) Americans. For Adams and James, there was no turning back to "tradition"—i.e., settler life before immigration—and exile was the answer: "Their country had been invaded, occupied, and culturally ravaged, by barbarians."[58]

Yet, defying Anglo expectations, these "barbarians" chose to write literature. Although they spoke with accents and occasionally wrote in other languages, immigrant writers—such as Anzia Yiezierska, Abraham Cahan, Mary Antin, Marcus Ravage, and many others, including the "undistinguished Americans," popularized in Henry Holt's *The Life Stories of Undistinguished Americans* (1906)—created a body of work coeval with American realism and modernism, revealing shared aesthetic and social concerns with Anglo-American writers. If we accept Klein's tongue-in-cheek claim that "to a remarkable extent, the modernism made by Americans had a Harvard education," did immigrant and Native writers—without a Harvard education—not contribute to modernism and modernity?[59]

Mary Antin, a Jewish immigrant from Poland, who had published in magazines such as the *Atlantic Monthly*, wrote with a keen awareness of a hostile Gentile readership. At the end of her autobiography, *The Promised Land* (1912), Antin included a glossary of Yiddish terms, translating her cultural past to English-speaking readers.[60] Similarly, Antin's conational, Anzia Yiezierska, asked the question on many other immigrant writers' lips at the time: why was the immigrant writers' access to the literary market limited? Yiezierska pleaded for a chance to be heard: "We who are forced to the drudgery of the world, and who are considered ignorant because we have no time for school, could say a lot of new and different things, if only we had a chance to get a hearing."[61]

Although the immigrant ghettos were loci of literary production and consumption—literary societies, libraries, the Yiddish theater, and a vibrant publishing industry and foreign language press—until the twentieth century, John Higham argues, "Serious American literature almost totally ignored the immigrant."[62] Matthew F. Jacobson also makes a persuasive case about recovering "the inner world of the immigrants," not only to recover what immigrants experienced but also "to reconstruct the worldview through which they experienced it."[63]

Besides an increase in the number of "foreigners" of various ethnicities and national backgrounds, the Progressive Era saw an increased interest in what Henry Holt would term, the "life stories of undistinguished Americans." Initially published in the progressive newspaper *The Independent*, edited by Henry Holt, *The Life Stories of Undistinguished Americans as Told by Themselves* (1906) was a collage of new and old voices of Americans. These life stories included accounts by Syrian, Japanese, Chinese, Native American, and African American writers, along with stories by white Americans, such as a midwestern farmer's wife and a Southern Methodist minister. Whereas some of these stories were written by aspiring authors, many were "told to" stories, sometimes accompanied by editorial confessions about the literacy level of the teller, editorial intervention, the storyteller's country of origin or hidden identity, to protect the storyteller from political backlash. In one story, a Greek peddler took a direct stab at the Greek government's complicity in the Armenian genocide. Although immigrant writers had been at work for about three centuries before Holt's collection appeared, it offered a counterpoint to American exceptionalism and brought "undistinguished" Americans to the attention of a larger reading public.

The recovery of Americanization as a key episode of national formation in recent historiography and literary criticism has placed a great deal of emphasis on its emancipatory potential, on the one hand, and the limits of pluralism offered by the Crèvecoeurian myth of the melting pot, still informing views of American exceptionalism, on the other.[64] "What then is the American, this new man," Crèvecoeur asked in *Letters from an American Farmer* (1782). "*He* is an American who, leaving behind him all ancient prejudices and manners, receives new ones from the new mode of life he has embraced. . . . Here individuals of all nations are melted into a new race of men, whose labours and posterity will one day cause great changes in the world" (my emphasis).[65] Sollors and others have recovered Crèvecoeur's myth of the melting pot by emphasizing the potential of Americanization to be "emancipatory." Other scholars, like Herbert G. Gutman and Rudolph J. Vecoli, have helped reframe the Crèvecoerian myth of Americanization. More recently, Gary Gerstle has added "coercion" to the study of Americanization, contending that "any analysis of Americanization, past and present, must accord coercion a role in the making of Americans."[66]

The critique of the melting pot and the Crèvecoerian myth by historians since the 1960s points to new ways to reframe U.S. exceptionalism. These scholars have shown that immigrants traveled not only from one country to another but also from one job to another; they were not blindly lured by the nation but driven by economic interest. Second, the immigrants brought their cultures to the U.S. and fought to preserve them through education and print culture. Third, not all immigrants wanted to become Americans and protested against unfair labor practices and the imposition of Americanization as a strategy complicit with the expansion of capitalism. Others refused to naturalize or returned home.[67] This perspective adds to our conceptualization of Americanization not only in terms of nationalism and patriotism, but also in economic terms.

Questions about peoplehood informed Native and immigrant understandings of group identity, as Americanization pushed toward individualizing and assimilation. How did allegiance to one's nation affect one's adoption of or distancing from Americanization? While a question like this is exhaustive given the sheer number of Native nations and immigrant groups, common ideas about peoplehood shaped conceptions of citizenship and belonging. Although we can never know the sum of immigrant and Native voices, however distinctive they may be, the fragments available to us in writing and print, visual art, material objects, and ephemera help tell a story that challenges the myth of American exceptionalism. Focusing on individual case studies helps revisionist history in centering new immigrant and Native stories both alongside and in opposition to Americanization.

"UNCLE SAM IS A MAN OF STRONG FEATURES"

Ethnic stereotypes abounded during the Progressive Era, translating ethnic and racial anxieties originating in the early nineteenth century.

Racial and ethnic stereotypes, such as the "laziness" of *Indians*—popularized by cartoons in the popular press—were not only cultural misreadings of one (dominant) group by the other but also rhetorical acts with severe economic consequences, authorizing further dispossession of Native people.[68] By the 1870s, Irish and German stereotypes were pervasive in American popular culture. Stereotypes of Jewish, Italian, and Slavic immigrants followed after the 1890s. Immigrant stereotypes also indexed degrees of Americanization. To wit, the stronger the stereotype, the further the immigrant group from "full Americanization."[69] As Barbara Solomon argued, "In the development of a living xenophobia, outsiders were figures merely. 'They ain't folks, they're nothing but a parcel of images.'"[70] These representations indexed anxieties—such as settler anxieties of "race suicide" promoted by Theodore Roosevelt and Edward A. Ross—and marked race-based exclusions from participatory democracy based on the fiction of race. In Matthew F. Jacobson's words, "Race is not tangential to the history of European immigration to the United States but absolutely central."[71] As the cartoons I discuss below reveal, Americanization was represented as imminent; the unruly immigrants were no longer "free" to roam Uncle Sam's ark and were dragged to school; Americanization was coercive.

Along with fears of racial, linguistic, and cultural difference, racial slurs also welcomed immigrants to America.[72] Anticipating the dangers of the proliferation of such racial slurs, the first volume (1918) of the mainstream Americanization publication, the *Americanization Bulletin*, reprinted a proposed addition to the Boy Scouts' Outdoor Code that condemned the use of ethnic or racial slurs: "We pledge our service never to use, and to discourage everywhere, the use of such words as Dago, Dutchy, Froggy, Ginny, Greaser, Heiny, Horwat, Hunky, Kike, Mick, Paddy, Sheeny, Spaghetti, Wop, as applied to any foreign-born resident in the United States of America."[73] This ample repertoire of anti-immigrant slurs continued to perpetuate xenophobia while purporting to condone it. Italian poet Rosina Vieni gave these racist terms tragic proportions in a sonnet on immigration, labor, and death:

> who cares about the greenhorns, the *paesani*
> Struck dead, without the sacraments?
> What's it worth, if by misfortune or by accident
> your body falls and smashes to the floor below—
> poor Guinea, poor Dago?[74]

In 1914, sociologist Edward A. Ross surveyed the new immigrant groups in relation to the old immigrants in *The Old World in the New*, describing the new arrivals as "hirsute, low-browed, big-faced persons of obviously low mentality" and "of an inferior type," who came "straight from the hoe." To these unflattering descriptions, Ross added the "fraud" of northern and "crime" of southern Italians. He also described the "temperate Rumanians" as counterpoints to "thirsty Germans and Scotch Irish," calling the South Slavs "those Comanches of Asia." Although impressed with eastern European Jews' "humane and sensitive temper," Ross emphasized their "inborn love for money-making," their "tribal spirit," and their "wonderful adaptability" to new environments.[75]

E. A. Ross's racist lexicon had early predecessors in New England poets' lamenting the threats to Anglo-Saxonism, or what Madison Grant called "the passing of the Great Race." Thomas Bailey Aldrich, former editor of the *Atlantic Monthly*, responded to Emma Lazarus's famous poem "The New Colossus" (1883) with a poem he titled "The Unguarded Gates" (1895). Lazarus was author of the famous lines of welcome to "the huddled masses" and "the wretched refuse" in one of the most (partially) quoted poems in immigration literary history. Aldrich's poem, the product of a moment of growing nativism, rewrote Lazarus' iconic hymn: "Wide open and unguarded stand our gates,/And through them passes a wild motley throng."[76] Aldrich's image of "a wild motley throng" joined in the growing anti-immigrant rhetoric and ethnic slurs of the 1880s and 1890s. In "Democracy" (1884), James Russell Lowell reiterated that the new immigrants did not belong in America, calling them "the most ignorant and vicious of a population which has come to us from abroad, wholly unpracticed in self-government and incapable of assimilation by American habits and methods."[77] Francis A. Walker, in arguments supporting immigration restriction, wrote in the *Atlantic Monthly* in 1896 that the new immigrants were "beaten men from beaten races."[78]

Besides literary belittling of unworthy subjects, the end of the nineteenth century also witnessed a proliferation of ethnic caricature in new forms of print culture, such as the illustrated magazines *Scribner's*, *Harper's*, or *Century Magazine*. Cartoonists launched humor magazines in response to the public's growing appetite for lowbrow humor. The growing genre of ethnic caricature—legitimized by publications such as *Puck* and *Judge*—used the new genre of ethnic humor to sanction policy and to educate the reading public. Many of the exaggerated visual representations of immigrants ridiculed their exteriority, their uncanny clothes, hairstyles, or eating habits. As Henry B. Wonham has shown, "ethnic caricature typically reduces its subject to some inflexible attribute of type, fixing the margins of ethnic identity by exaggerating physiognomic and cultural indicators of origin." These exaggerated images also served, "to delineate the boundaries of legitimate citizenship for a culture unsure of its claims to authority."[79] Some cartoons of Native people in the popular press called attention to poor economic and social conditions or relegated them to savagery, drunkenness, or a distant past; others engaged pressing contemporary issues. Native publications like the *Quarterly Journal of the Society of American Indians* or Carlos Montezuma's *Wassaja* were quick to respond to misrepresentations, including cartoons commissioned especially for the journal or reproduced from the national press. The first issue of the *Quarterly Journal* reproduced the popular outcry "Lo, the Poor Indian!" with editorial commentary: "The Indian whose arm is bound by the broken shield of the government neglect may cast aside that shield when he will be asserting his independence as an individual and taking up the sword of individual action."[80] Asserting Native "individuality," the editor used Americanization rhetoric strategically, to distance Indigenous communities from their harmful representations in the popular press.

Three political cartoons of Uncle Sam from the 1880s to the early 1900s dramatize the country's changing physiognomy and the subsequent intolerance toward new immigrants and minoritized groups in the U.S. In 1880 *Puck*, the weekly magazine of graphic humor and political satire, published the cartoon "Welcome to All!," where a benevolent Uncle Sam extends his hands to welcome the newcomers to the "U.S. Ark of Refuge" (figure 10).

Uncle Sam's ark is a utopian space, reminiscent of Noah's ark yet a secular space marked by a welcoming sign at the entrance to the ark promising: "no oppressive taxes, no expensive kings, no compulsory military service, no knouts or dungeons." To Uncle Sam's right, another welcoming sign mesmerizes the newcomers with the promise of absolute freedom: "Free education, free land, free speech, free ballot, free lunch." This image established a heteronormative logic of welcoming to

Fig. 10. "Welcome to All," *Puck,* April 28, 1880. Library of Congress, LC-USZC4–954.

the U.S. Ark of Refuge, threatened by monstrous winds and creatures flying in from the east (upper right). A welcoming Uncle Sam, flanked by a large American flag and the written promises of freedom, extends his hands to those seeking shelter. Preceding the Chinese Exclusion Act of 1882 by two years, this image of Uncle Sam's affable demeanor demarcates clearly the different modes of U.S. hospitality before and after the opening of the immigration "golden door" in 1883.

The iconography of Uncle Sam underwent several subtle changes in the last two decades of the nineteenth century, from the all-embracing grandfatherly figure to the stern embodiment of a "new American" composite face in "Uncle Sam Is a Man of Strong Features" (1888), emblematic of recent changes in the country's racial and ethnic makeup (figure 11), to the disciplinarian who brings "the truant [immigrant] boy to the Little Red, White, and Blue Schoolhouse," in "American Policy" (1901; figure 12). When the Filipino and Mexican boys stray, Uncle

Sam brings them back to Miss Columbia's schoolhouse by force.[81] In the earlier cartoon, where he is "a man of strong features," Uncle Sam's face reveals the physiognomy of the (imagined) new American, and a distorted face signals the inevitability of the country's physiognomic change. The image dramatizes a stark contrast between Uncle Sam's white hair, beard, collar, and his wrinkled face, marked by the contours of immigrant features of multiple racial and ethnic backgrounds. Uncle Sam's face features old and new immigrants contorting on his chin, forehead, and ears, sustained at the center by an almost crucified Native man, who stretches out his arms to touch the new immigrants' heads. Engaging nativist fears over threats to Anglo-Saxonism and including a Native man at the center of this representation of Uncle Sam, the cartoon signaled a popular anxiety over the "visible" elements of difference brought by new immigrants and written on their bodies.

Racial scrutiny of new immigrant bodies "fit for America" would be accompanied by medical examinations at immigration stations as early as the 1890s. The often unsympathetic medical examinations, along with the growing number of "excludable diseases," which threatened the healthy body of the nation, made access to Uncle Sam's ark more difficult in the following decades.[82] Taken together, these cartoons indexed the changing lexicon of U.S. hospitality discourses, from the biblical imagery of the welcoming "ark of refuge," to the sign of imminent change written on Uncle Sam's distorted face, to the alarmist and forceful redirecting of the "truant" immigrant boy to Miss Columbia's "Liberty School." Uncle Sam violently takes a little Filipino boy by the ear to bring him to the little school, where Hawaiian, Puerto Rican, Cuban, and American Indian children—avatars of Uncle Sam's imperialism and colonialism—share in the common experience of "American education." In nineteenth-century American iconography, the rural Yankee farmer, Uncle Sam, personified the U.S. "only after a close struggle with Brother Jonathan, a tall, shrewd, impudent, rural New Englander." Miss Columbia, "a combination of Indian princess and classical goddess, stood for liberty, democracy, honesty, equality, and respect for human dignity."[83] As Meg Wesling has shown, education "as the moral imperative of American citizens" aimed at "rehabilitating racialized subjects, immigrants, African Americans, Native Americans, and Filipinos alike—within the framework of middle-class Protestant Americanism."[84] Such representations of Native people and new immi-

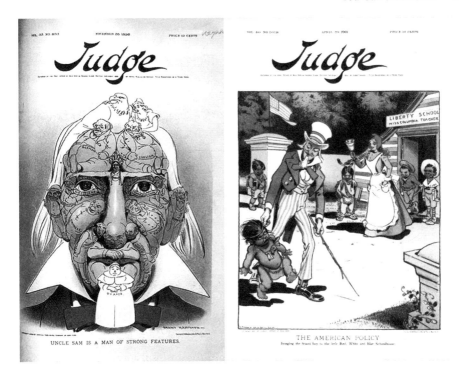

Fig. 11. (left) Grant Hamilton, "Uncle Sam Is a Man of Strong Features," *Judge*, November 26, 1888.
Fig. 12. "The American Policy," *Judge*, April 20, 1901.

grants by the dominant culture were signaling the need for change, for "civilization," reformation, and Americanization.

In this chapter I have framed the "makings of Americans"—a revered trope in American cultural history, a signifier of American exceptionalism—as a structural phenomenon of assimilating and turning difference into sameness, of solidifying settler colonial hegemony. Settler society sought the physical elimination of Native people, yet it also recuperated Indigeneity in order to assert its own difference. This periodic recuperation of Indigeneity to assert putative settler superiority found unparalleled materialization during the Progressive Era, when the conflation of the "vanishing Indian" with the "vanishing American" tropes aimed at strengthening settler colonialism's own sense of self-serving nativism. But settler hegemony did not go unchallenged: the large numbers of new immigrants who arrived in the U.S., still untrained in the norms of Americanism, challenged settler hegemony. Instead of being transformed by America, new immigrants transformed it.[85] In print and visual culture, new immigrants and Indigenous activists, writers, and artists challenged the boundaries of whiteness and the homogeneity envisioned by Americanizers. Under the guise of patriotic education, Americanization education taught normative whiteness and Anglo-Saxonism. Education as a model for rehabilitating racialized subjects reveals another insidious way that Americanization took on the attributes of a corrective narrative, as the case study of the Carlisle Indian Industrial School shows in the next chapter.

3 "That Is Why I Sent You to Carlisle"

Native Education, Print Culture, and Americanization at Carlisle Indian Industrial School, 1879–1918

When they arrived they had only the Book and we had the land; now we have the book and they have the land.

—Vine Deloria Jr., *Custer Died for Your Sins*, 1969

So keep to the English
Help Others to rise,
Leave the Indian behind you
If you wish to grow wise.

—"English Speaking," *Indian Helper*, August 13, 1886

ON JULY 19, 1923, American writer and journalist Upton Sinclair penned a letter to Richard Henry Pratt, the founder of Carlisle Indian Industrial School, lamenting "the control of the Indian schools by the big business interest of the country."[1] When Sinclair wrote to Pratt, Carlisle—the infamous off-reservation boarding school for Native students founded in army barracks in Carlisle, Pennsylvania—had been closed for five years and Pratt was approaching his demise. Sinclair's *The Goose-Step: A Study of American Education* (1923) excoriated American capitalism for its control of American education. Federal Indian policy had become complicit with what Sinclair called "the big business interest of the country" in reproducing its labor force through vocational training. Carlisle Indian Industrial School, an experiment in the forced removal of Native children to a federal Indian boarding school in the name of education and "civilization" between 1879 and 1918, made Americanization one of its central aims.

In recent decades, historians of education have shifted the conversations about boarding schools in North America toward student resilience, voice, and agency, often recovered from print documents and letters.[2] So far scholars have used the term "Americanization" to refer to the acculturation of new immigrants, relegating the forced education and transformation of Native Americans to the category of "assimilation" or using both terms interchangeably. Recognizing the nuances of Americanization in the larger context of assimilation as an extension of settler colonialism and as a tactic for solidifying empire-building is not only timely but necessary. This focus reveals subtle distinctions in the incorporation of two different groups—Native Americans and new immigrants—and the ultimate goal of both campaigns: loyalty to the nation.[3] Although we know more about the complicity of the boarding school personnel in the campaign of forced assimilation and Americanization of Native children, we still have little evidence about the students' thoughts, feelings, and understanding of their subjectivity in an oppressive environment.

In this chapter I attempt to fill this gap by turning to print as a medium for disseminating settler ideology and for communicating Indigenous thought. Scholars of early American and Native American literature have shown that Native people wrote for publication with an acute sense of their audience as early as the beginning of the nineteenth century. As Phillip Round has shown, for many Native communities, print became "a much needed weapon in their battles against relocation, allotment, and cultural erasure."[4] Examining surviving student writings, letters, and publications at Carlisle and several other federal boarding schools, I argue that Indigenous students' work in print and epistolary form offers a glimpse into a tumultuous period of forced assimilation and Americanization at Carlisle.

Print offered a platform for creative expression, built a community of readers and writers, and lay the foundations for future Native activism. Although the authorship of these writings is often difficult to ascertain, given the controlled environment of the boarding schools and the constraints of colonial archives in collecting, preserving, and curating materials produced by Native students, boarding school archives are worth studying for their contributions to what Osage literary critic

Robert Warrior calls "the American Indian intellectual tradition" and for the history of Native writing.[5] Both Warrior and Round agree that the beginnings of this educational experiment and the removal of Native children to federal Indian boarding schools, starting in 1879, coincided with the beginning of modern Indigenous intellectual history. This moment in Indigenous modernity saw an unprecedented use of print to engage larger national conversations around economic and political issues. As an anonymous student put it in the poem "My Industrial Work," published in a Carlisle periodical, life in boarding schools aligned with the rapid clock of capitalism and nationalism: "Then out in front the troops all stand, / Saluting the flag with our hats in our hand."[6] This type of engagement produced what Round calls the "first generation of intertribal activists and scholars" (see chapter 5). Here I read what Warrior calls "Native educational texts" as a necessary point of departure for understanding how students negotiated Americanization in print and for conceptualizing the Native American written tradition as part of a continuum.[7]

Although student responses to boarding school experiences are historically contingent, Native student writing during and after their time at Carlisle—in the genres of fiction, autobiography, journal articles, letters—offers a glimpse into the precarious life they lived and the rich life they envisioned. Students also used other modes of expression, such as performance and visual arts. Angel DeCora, a Ho-Chunk artist, illustrator, and teacher at Carlisle (1906–15) started the school's art department and taught the students Native art.[8] Although education was a recurrent trope during the Progressive Era, Native students in Indian boarding schools like Carlisle continued the education initiated by elders on their home reservations. Recounting his experience at Carlisle in his first memoir, Sioux student Luther Standing Bear—who arrived at Carlisle in 1879—realized that he had to learn the ways of the white man: "I thought that some day I might be able to become an interpreter for my father."[9] Native student writing is also a rich archive for exploring how the first generation of Native people educated in Euro-American schools expressed, in writing, their enthusiasm and frustrations with the daily interpellations of Americanization. Like other Native students in off-reservation boarding schools across the country, they used print to negotiate new identities in a new language. They did so often in candid ways at Carlisle, and more critically after they came of age as writers and activists in their own right. Negotiating dominant narratives, the students' rhetorically bold writings set the stage for reading the cultural work of later Native intellectuals.

Students in boarding schools read, wrote, debated, and contributed to a growing Native print culture as the federal government was imagining an American future for them, at odds with their or their communities' visions of that future. Attuned to the demands of settler time, while also removed from their ancestral places, Native children defied the logic of an imposed, domestic, and incorporated American future. Print culture enabled Native students to think, dream, and act toward a present and future beyond the confines of their industrial education.[10] Through print culture Native students positioned themselves "beyond settler time," Mark Rifkin's phrase, beyond the rigid confines of what he calls "settler modes of time"—measured by class time, years of enrollment and attendance, graduation rates, and other categories quantifying their progress toward Americanization. Writing against Indigenous temporal stasis, Rifkin asks: "In what ways is conceptualizing Native being-in-time as the inhabiting of *modernity* (or a shared present with non-natives) equivalent to a bid for inclusion within settler modes of recognition?" Were students who wrote along the directives of this institution becoming "temporally intelligible to non-Natives" in order to be perceived as less anachronistic, that is, sharing the same experience, becoming modern?[11] The body of student work in colonial archives broadens our understanding of their legacy for Native print culture. If the print culture of the early republic rendered Indigenous people anachronistic or "vanishing," were students in federal Indian boarding schools accepting or refusing such designations? Were they resisting them by becoming "intelligible" to their English-speaking, predominantly white readers, as the institution responsible for Americanizing them was training them for "industrial" work?

Although boarding school documents (including student writings, letters, and publications, as well as the school documents preserved in the National Archives) reveal competing visions for Native education and print culture, they also open a window into the students' thoughts, lives, and creative work during and after their time at the school.[12] Boarding school letters—from children to parents and from parents to children—as Brenda Child has shown, "reveal the stories of people who have for too long been anonymous and relegated to the periphery of American history."[13] Patrick Wolfe has read the abduction of Native children to mission and boarding schools as part of the larger settler colonial mission of seizing Native land; Native children and their families were in the way of colonial expansion, and eliminating such obstacles through education—and, later, enforced Americanization, under the guise of education for citizenship—was complicit with the genocidal settler colonial project.[14]

Carlisle, the first federally funded off-reservation boarding school in the U.S., provided a formal and ideological template for the Americanization of Native students. It was founded with federal support in 1879 by former army officer Richard H. Pratt, who envisioned a "civilization" program for Native students in the East, away from their Indigenous homes. The other twenty-four off-reservation boarding schools (1879–1902) were built in the West, in part because of the benefits they could bring to nearby white communities. Off-reservation schools in the West were economically sound, adding thousands of dollars to local economies through the infusion of federal funds and student labor encouraged by a curriculum grounded in vocational training.[15]

Carlisle was the first school to test the experiment of Americanization on Native students. As Richard H. Pratt put it, if immigrants could Americanize so rapidly and become self-sufficient "good Americans," why not the Indians? Underexamined school records, from pamphlets, letters, student files, the Carlisle magazines, to the carefully archived Richard Pratt Papers, reveal ambivalent, intricate relationships Native students had with an institution designed to "kill the Indian and save the man." Because Americanization attempted to erase tribal identity, which was closely connected with the idea of sovereignty and the land, Americanization also signified loss of territory.[16] The records of Carlisle Indian Industrial School provide a history of Pratt's experiment in Americanization. But an alternative archive is the students' surviving creative expression (in art, literature, and performance), albeit rooted in the colonial archive, which reveals how Indigenous students used their newly acquired literacy in English to adjust to a present of imposed Americanization as they continued to imagine a Native future. These surviving student letters and published writings reveal the ideological and affective implications of Americanization through boarding school education and patriotic training at Carlisle.

NATIVE EDUCATION

Western educational systems tend to equate education with schooling; in Indigenous communities across the world, generations of Native
children have been educated and nurtured close to ancestral lands, with
an acute sense of responsibility to fellow humans, animals, and the
earth. Before European settlers arrived in North America, Indigenous
peoples' educational systems transferred knowledge from one generation to another. Native communities included their children in many
forms of knowledge sharing through oral storytelling and direct participation (food production, tool-making, travel to gain knowledge of the
land, and so on). Native education was also a "fundamentally political
process," with active Indigenous participation.[17] Invoking Vine Deloria's call for traditional educational models, Robert Warrior argues that
education "is less about curriculum and more about probing the depths
of the philosophical terrain of what it means to be a Native learner."[18]
Although the formal education of Native children began in the early
republic, the religious and federal schools had the same goal as Americanization: to "civilize," Christianize, and assimilate Native peoples.[19]
The practice of separating Native children from parents originated in
the sixteenth century, when Roman Catholic missionaries established
missions to "civilize" and convert the "heathen" children to Christianity. In early seventeenth-century New England, Puritan missionary
John Eliot started the "praying towns"; as the missionaries converted
their parents, they also started educating Native children in the day
schools nearby. New England settlers also established the "charity
schools." Under the strict hand of Dr. Eleazar Wheelock, the missionaries and school teachers established connections with tribes, educating
the brightest Native students, among them Samson Occom (Mohegan),
who continued his studies to became a minister.[20]

The goal of colonial education was to Christianize. Like their later
federal counterparts, the mission schools were hard on the young Native students, and they ultimately failed. After Moor's Charity School
closed in 1770, boarding school education was stagnant for a while; it
was revived in 1810, when the American Board of Commissioners for
Foreign Missions established missions in China and India, as well as in
the U.S. During this time, the Choctaws, Cherokees, Creeks, Chickasaws, and Seminoles (the five "civilized tribes") also opened their own

schools, which strengthened their sense of community. Missionaries kept records in English, including Native students' writings (letters, journal entries, or religious confessions). Although problematic, these records document Native student literacy—what Hillary Wyss calls the "readerly Indians"—and a long history of Native use of literacy for creative and political purposes. Wyss describes the readerly Indian as the "docile, passive Indian figure" imagined by the missionaries, and the writerly Indian as "a speaker and actor fluent in the cultures and conventions of colonial society but also one fully committed to Native community as an ongoing political and cultural concern."[21]

As early as the colonial period, the writings of the Native students reveal the intricacies of adapting to Anglo-American education. These early models of (Christian) education also reveal the insidious ways that institutions, religious or secular, controlled students' lives and expression. Although much of this early writing was controlled and revised, there were networks of letters and document exchanges in the eighteenth century, however paternalistic the intervention of the school fathers may have been.[22] As readerly and writerly Indians, Native students in early boarding schools, like their later counterparts, were not passive vessels filled with Anglo-American knowledge.

In European and white American contexts, boarding schools were typically sites for educating the children of the elites; federal U.S. Indian boarding schools were arenas of governmental power and control over Native students' minds and bodies. Early Native education was also complicit with the theft of Native land and resources. As such, these institutions left a legacy of physical and emotional trauma, which still affects subsequent generations. In 1819, Congress passed the Indian Civilization Act to support the education of Native students. Because Native education and Christianizing went hand in hand, it also supported Christian missionaries financially. The government gave special annuities to tribes for education, and by 1824 twenty-one Indian boarding schools and day schools were in place, most of them run by Christian missionaries. Mission schools provided Native students with a rudimentary education; classes were taught in the vernacular to promote biblical teachings, although gradually mission schools added English-language instruction.[23]

Whereas the public school system undertook the "civilization" of immigrant children and adults alike in the nineteenth century—through day and evening Americanization classes—federal Indian policy and its acerbic lobbyists concocted an education policy for Indigenous people resonant with the country's federal Indian policy, which emphasized the acquisition of English, Christianity, vocational training, and the gendered-project of the nuclear family model. Formal education away from home became the main instrument of Americanizing Native children; through a combination of vocational training with reading, writing, and arithmetic, its goal was to make Native children into self-supporting Americans.

Native children, sometimes as young as five, were taken from their families, sometimes by force, for months or years, and many never made it back home. Although some students were encouraged to attend school by Native relatives, Michael Coleman estimates that one in four Native students were coerced into attending school (by government officials, tribal police, or missionaries). Compulsory education was regulated by states in the nineteenth century yet white American parents—unlike Native parents—could elect to educate their children at home.[24] Pratt's letters to recruiters of Native students for Carlisle emphasized the idea of parental consent: "All who come here must be at least one fourth Indian, in good health and of good character. . . . Consent of parents is important." After 1893, the "full consent" of the parent was necessary to send a Native child to an off-reservation boarding school.[25] In the first decades of their existence, Indian boarding schools did not account for other forms of informal education Native students had received before they left their communities, nor did they conceive of the impossibility to erase Native cultures, languages, and spirituality and replace them with Euro-American counterparts.

The idea of removing Native children from their communities and ancestral lands originated with Carlisle's mastermind, Richard Henry Pratt, who emphatically called for the complete immersion of Native students into white society: "To civilize the Indian, get him into civilization. To keep him civilized, let him stay."[26] A tangible materialization of this idea was Pratt's famous "outing" program, a form of apprenticeship, where students spent time with white families to earn wages and practice their English. Pratt believed that this form of contact with white society was "the supreme Americanizer."[27] This program, publicized nationally, elicited many congratulatory letters to Pratt. An editor from Harper and Brothers wrote: "If such conditions prevail today, it seems to me that the Indian problem is solved."[28]

The Indian problem was far from being solved; despite its promise to Americanize Native students, the outing program perpetuated the exploitation of young Native workers by their employers. Brenda Child has shown that students in boarding schools performed many forms of manual labor, working in the laundries, dairies, school gardens, and campus buildings in disrepair. At the boarding schools the classrooms were poorly ventilated and unsanitary, and the children had little time for play; the sleeping quarters were overcrowded and the clothes were scarce.[29] In a letter to his teacher A.W. Smith—founder of a school for Native children in La Push, Washington, in 1882—Native student Arthur Howeattle wrote that he would not be able to attend school during the spring because it interfered with his Native family's work season: "I want to leave school now because I've got lots of work to do."[30] Howeattle was not enrolled in a federal boarding school and could maintain ties to his community during the school year, unlike students at Carlisle or other federal boarding schools.

Indian boarding schools reproduced the logic of American capitalism through vocational training, as Alice Littlefield has also documented. In addition to reading and writing English, Native boys learned agricultural skills, carpentry, smithing, and harness-making; Native girls were trained in Euro-American domestic skills: cleaning, sewing, cooking, and preserving food.[31] K. Tsianina Lomawaima and Theresa McCarty have shown how religious organizations and the federal government envisioned boarding schools as "laboratories for a grand experiment in cultural cleansing, Christian conversion, and assimilation of laborers and domestic workers into the workforce." If the goal of federal and mission schools was to assimilate, civilize, and Americanize Native peoples, the students' domestic work, marketed as "education," served the agenda not only of Americanization but also American capitalism under the guise of vocational training and domesticity. According to Lomawaima and McCarthy, "The so-called 'civilization' of American Indians, at times simply termed 'Americanization,' mandated the transformation of nations and individuals: replace heritage languages with English; replace 'paganism' with Christianity; replace economic, political, social, legal, and aesthetic institutions."[32] Carlisle was the appropriate laboratory for Pratt to test these ideas.

CARLISLE INDIAN INDUSTRIAL SCHOOL (1879–1918)

Carlisle left a troubling legacy for the students' families and the history of Native writing in the U.S. Established in 1879 in the army barracks in Carlisle, Pennsylvania, the school advocated the total assimilation policy envisioned by reformers. As a captain and, later, general in the army, Pratt cultivated his disciplinary practices after the Civil War when he was entrusted with the "civilization" of Kiowa, Comanche, Cheyenne, and Arapaho prisoners at Fort Marion in St. Augustine, Florida. Native prisoners at Fort Marion were taught art, English, and arithmetic. The "success" of the Fort Marion program of incarceration and rehabilitation marked the beginning, in the early 1880s, of the educational campaign to Americanize a different group of prisoners: Native children. David W. Adams has called this model of boarding schools "education for extinction": Native students were expected to embrace the "civilization" program and become, through education, good Americans. This presumed transformation of Native children into Americans through a rigid educational system, on and off reservations, coincided with the nationwide attempt to turn Native people into individual landowners and participants in the new labor market created by the General Allotment Act (1887), on the path to American citizenship, the ultimate promise of a paternalistic government to its Native wards.

Carlisle promised Americanizing in record time; by preparing students for economic self-sufficiency, it made economic sense to Progressive Era bureaucrats, freeing the federal government from the treaty-mandated responsibilities of feeding and clothing Native people. In the callous estimation of secretary of the Interior Carl Schurz, it was more expensive to kill a Native person in warfare than to educate a Native child. According to David W. Adams, "it cost only $1,200 to give an Indian child eight years of schooling."[33] After the Office of Indian Affairs and Congress had approved the funds for an Indian industrial school, Pratt's experiment in training Native students for American democracy began. The first students brought to Carlisle were Sioux, recruited by Pratt himself from the Rosebud and Pine Ridge Agencies in South Dakota. Like Luther Standing Bear (Western Sioux/Teton Lakota) and his siblings, they were sons and daughters of Native chiefs and community leaders (figure 13). As the school developed, students

Fig. 13. Portrait of two visiting chiefs with a group of students, including Luther Standing Bear, standing in the middle, 1879, by John N. Choate. National Anthropological Archives, Smithsonian Institution, NAA INV 06905700; photo lot 81–12 06905700.

themselves became the recruiters.[34] During its thirty-nine years of operation, Carlisle Indian Industrial School educated thousands of Native boys and girls.

Pratt's dismissal from Carlisle in 1904 and his replacement with another army officer, William Mercer, was highly criticized in the national press by Pratt supporters, who saw it as a turn toward a more militarized life at Carlisle, which was not only ill advised and poorly timed but also detrimental to the students. School administrators at Carlisle and throughout the country had often turned a deaf ear to reports of the abuses and deaths of students. After Pratt's departure from Carlisle in 1904, Native students and school personnel reported abuses of power, especially by Pratt's replacement, Mercer.[35]

Besides physical abuse, other forms of abuse affected entire generations of student survivors of Indian boarding schools, who had been separated from family at an early age and lacked emotional support during their formative years. The students' cultural ties with their Native communities were severed as soon as they arrived at the school;

they were forbidden to speak their Native languages and were often punished for their many acts of disobedience. Their education was premised on the inferiority of tribal ways compared with "civilized" Euro-American ways. The disciplinary methods enforced in boarding schools aimed at instilling obedience. Because the schools were run by former army officers and disciplinarians, students were exposed to corporal punishment and a highly regimented life; they wore uniforms, had their hair cut short, and were prevented from speaking their Indigenous languages. As Michael Coleman put it, "Immigrant children shared far more with their American teachers than did these Indians." The Carlisle cemetery, with its 194 graves of students as of this writing, is a reminder that death was part of boarding school life.[36]

Death, a boarding school daily reality, found its way into the writings of both students and parents. A rare instance of parental response to a child's boarding school death is a poem by Clarence Three Stars, a Sioux (Kiyaksa), who entered Carlisle with its first contingent in 1879, with Luther Standing Bear, Chauncey Yellow Robe, and other Sioux students.[37] In 1908 he lost his daughter, Louisa Three Stars, to an unmentioned disease she contracted in boarding school in Pierre, South Dakota. The student paper *Oglala Light* published his poem of grief with the following note: "The above tribute written by the Father breathes forth the deep feeling of the parents and expresses, in a small manner, what a wonderful difference education and the Christian Religion have made in men like Clarence, he who did not begin school until fourteen years of age." The plea for education failed to console the grieving parent:

> You and I long for education,
> A thing that is leading on
> To where? I asked. I answer,
> Perhaps to a better land.

Clarence's unanswered question ("To where?") points to a deeper disappointment in the institutions that took children from families and failed at keeping them alive.[38]

Clarence Three Stars mourned his daughter in a poem that conflates the imagined gains of education ("You and I long for education") with possibilities of a better future ("Perhaps to a better land"). The grieving father spoke directly to his daughter, addressing her in the present tense ("You and I long for education"), and he went on to invoke the power of the Great Spirit for "courage" to "endure it all." He ends on a hopeful note, with the invocation of the Great Spirit: "we die,/and that is what we did, Louisa." The plural pronoun "we" suggests the father's painful articulation of hope. Despite the school's hopeful message for the Sioux father, Americanization in this case signified death. Besides death, Native students experienced the emotional and physical toll of coping with disease, particularly epidemics of tuberculosis, trachoma, measles, pneumonia, mumps, and influenza.

In speeches throughout his career, Pratt emphasized how the country had failed to Americanize Native people, despite its success in Americanizing "foreign immigrants."[39] Like his friend Carlos Montezuma, the Apache doctor and founding member of the Society of the American Indians, Pratt used the immigrant analogy throughout his career to make his case for Native education: "All immigrants were accepted and naturalized into our citizenship by that route and thus had a full fair chance to become assimilated with our people and our industries. Why not the Indian?"[40] Pratt's unwavering conviction that the total "absorption" of Native people could be achieved through education are landmarks of Carlisle ideology: "I believe in the total annihilation of the Indians, as Indians and tribes."[41] The violence of Pratt's language is congruent with the violence of the model of education based in white supremacist and capitalist beliefs in the Native students' total transformation in the quickest possible way into Americans. Pratt asserted that it was possible to change the putative savagery of the groups at the bottom of the evolutionary ladder through education. He was able to persuade Congress to fund his experiment by emphasizing that Native children would become *civilized* Americans: "The way to civilize an Indian is to get him into civilization. The way to keep him civilized is to let him stay." The Progressive Era was a propitious moment for this argument, as Americanization as ideology and practice garnered increased national attention.[42]

To legitimize the project of Americanization at Carlisle, school administrators used photographs and promotional materials strategically. The images the school disseminated over several decades targeted both financial assistance and broader national attention. Eric Margolis has argued that Richard H. Pratt used photography as "a propaganda-of-the-image to garner support for Carlisle and other Indian schools."[43]

The school started publicizing its famous before-and-after photographs in the 1880s, making visual transformation part of marketing the Americanization of Native students. Physical appearance was an obsession at Carlisle, and administrators controlled its image. The school had two main photographers: John N. Choate (1840–1902) and Frances B. Johnston (1864–1952), neither of whom was Native. Local photographer Choate—the photographer most widely associated with Carlisle's photographic legacy—photographed Native students as soon as they arrived. Several months later, another picture captured the student's transformation (figures 14 and 15).[44] As Hayes Peter Mauro argues, "The centrality of the visual in this process represents a uniquely American fixation: a naïve correlation between appearance and reality."[45]

The circulation of before-and-after images served to dramatize federal Indian policy. As Joanna Hearne has shown, as "evidentiary records" the photos solidified the work of the institution by compressing years and by sequencing the photographs in "before" and "after" categories to denote progress and the transition from "savagery" to "civilization." The gap between the photos further illustrates the logic of the settler colonial project, with elisions and visual erasures—especially of Native families and of life before residential schools.[46] These photographs, though not specifically about land and dispossession, encapsulate child removal, which in turn is emblematic of the "systematic removal of the Indians from their homelands," according to Jolene Rickard. In these photographs, the bodies of the children occupy most of the visual frame, and there are few details about their new environment.[47]

The photographers—Indian agents, mission staff, teachers, or visitors—frequently arranged the students in a specific way and often failed to identify the students by name, thus silencing the student point of view.[48] These photographs are deeply connected with concepts of evidence, power, and silence. Residential school photography is part of the larger category of colonial photography, where photographs enhanced colonial agendas. Particularly compelling were the juxtaposition of the before photograph with the after image against patriotic backgrounds, such as the souvenir pamphlet (1895), representing and naturalizing the imminent Americanization of the Native subject (figure 16).

The portrait on the left, showing the student in traditional clothing, is visibly enhanced by the colorized red shawl, flanked by bow and arrows, and superimposed on the image of a distant tipi. The uniformed

Fig. 14. Chiricahua Apache students arriving at Carlisle, 1885 or 1886. Library of Congress, LC-USZ62–51801.

Fig. 15. Chiricahua Apache students, after four months of training at the school, 1885 or 1886. Library of Congress, LC-USZ62–51802.

Fig. 16. Souvenir pamphlet for Carlisle Indian School, 1895. Dickinson College,
Library Archives.

portrait on the right is paired with an image of a two-story house, and
flanked by an American flag, which separates the two disparate worlds
the image has created. The pamphlet intimates—through the larger
space afforded on the left-hand side to the Indian of the past—that
transformation into an American is not only fast but also unavoidable.
The images in this pamphlet are of Sicangu Lakota student Chauncey
Yellow Robe, who was part of the first generation of students attending
Carlisle and a future activist and actor.[49] Although he was one of Pratt's
model students, like Luther Standing Bear, it took Yellow Robe twelve
years to graduate from Carlisle. He arrived at Carlisle in 1879 but did
not graduate until 1895.[50] In its first decade of existence, of the 3,800
students who attended Carlisle only 209 graduated (figure 17).[51]

The students in federal Indian boarding schools left behind an archive of writings, manuscripts, and print publications, which literary
scholars and historians have only recently started to examine as relevant archives of institutional control of student thinking and writing.

Fig. 17. Class in government, Carlisle Indian School, Carlisle, Pennsylvania, 1900. Photograph by Frances Benjamin Johnston. Library of Congress, LC-USZ62-55423.

Informed by Progressive Era optimism in the force of education, mainstream and Native boarding school publications throughout the U.S. painted a picture of "progress" through narratives of successfully Americanized Native students.

INDIAN BOARDING SCHOOL PRINT CULTURE

A fragment of a letter sent by a Pawnee father to his son, Edward Myers, a student in 1881, lends this chapter its title. "My Dear Son Edward Myers," the letter begins. "I hope you will study hard and learn all you can, mind your teachers, and be a well-behaved boy, *that is why I sent you to Carlisle for* [sic]." The letter ends with a religious invocation, a message of hope, and the promise to keep the written correspondence alive. He signs, "Your affectionate father, GEORGE (KIT-KA-HOC) LA-LU-LAY-SERH-RU-KA-SAH."[52] Education, as envisioned by the Pawnee father, was a responsibility to the Native nation, not just an act of self-making. Although the letter may have been dictated by the father at the Pawnee Agency, it shows his preoccupation with English literacy in his commitment to writing to his son, encouraging him to "write to me often." The letter also shows that Native parents were not passive and distant observers of their children's education. Although schooling created an "unwelcome distance on Indian family relationships," as Brenda Child has shown, the letters circulating between students and parents reveal that Native parents and other relatives were involved in their children's lives.[53] Although government regulations and economic factors deterred parents from visiting their children often, letters exchanged between parents and children strengthened family ties that were impossible to sustain otherwise.

Recent history of the book scholarship has explored the materiality of textual production in terms of the ideological premises of reading and writing. Scholars have shown how the words to and from Native communities may serve as correctives to previous histories where such voices were missing.[54] The print culture that federal boarding schools generated—school publications, magazines and newspapers, pamphlets, student records, and student letters—reveals Native students as more than captives to a repressive, regimented environment purporting to turn them into "good Americans." The Carlisle publications were vehicles of Americanization rather than venues for disseminating literary productions and cultural exchange, but American Indians throughout the U.S. had produced literary periodicals before Carlisle. Between 1826 and 1924, over two hundred Native newspapers and periodicals were published in the United States. The literary periodicals, however, were few because literary production required not only talent but also time, a commodity that many Native writers did not have at the time.[55]

Carlisle publications were sources of instruction and public relations, and covered relevant topics of the day (for example, allotment, Native citizenship, participation in World War I, Americanization). Partly didactic, they taught good manners, behavior, and good citizenship, capitalizing on the public's interest in the Carlisle experiment: What were the students wearing? What were they taught? What did they think of their American education? They served as reminders of the work of "educating" Native students. Reprinting letters from graduates or students who returned to their reservations or agencies and made a successful transition, they encouraged similar transitions and cautioned against the "return to the blanket." The invisible message of Carlisle publications was that they were federally funded publications endorsing a federal education policy aimed at Native dispossession—of land, language, and culture—under the guise of "education."[56]

Less than three months after Carlisle opened its doors to the first (primarily Plains) Native students, the school issued its first publication, with a bilingual title in English and Lakota: *Eadle Keatah Toh/Big Morning Star*. Printed on a small press in a converted stable, this monthly periodical underwent several name changes and was published almost continuously during the school's existence (1879–1918). *Eadle Keatah Toh* published articles on Indian "civilization," the progress of students at Carlisle, non-reservation education, Native labor, citizenship, among other topics. The staff of this publication is uncertain because no editor's name was listed. In 1900, Carlisle's two publications, *The Indian Helper* and *The Red Man*, merged into a larger, single weekly, *The Red Man and Helper*. After Pratt's dismissal as superintendent in 1904, *The Red Man and Helper* resumed its publication as *The Carlisle Arrow*, a largely commercial paper.[57] *The Indian Helper* ran parallel with *Eadle Keatah Toh* in 1884; its subtitle—"For Our Indian Boys and Girls"— reveals an imagined student readership, ranging from students still in school to students placed in the institution's famous outing program, and students returning to their reservation homes. *The Indian Helper* (later *Red Man* and *Red Man and Helper*) was "PRINTED by Indian boys, but EDITED by The-Man-on-the-Band-Stand, who is not an Indian." An image of Mr. See All, who was a precursor of the Man-on-the-Band-Stand, shows a creature of puny stature, whose binoculars suggest close scrutiny (figure 18). Mr. See All was a reminder to Native students of institutionalized surveillance and the regulatory voice of the panopticon.[58]

Among the Carlisle student publications, the *School News*, marketed as "edited and printed by Indian students," suffered the least editorial intervention. This four-page monthly bulletin was published from 1880 until 1883, when it merged with the *Morning Star*. *School News* targeted Carlisle students and prospective students, offered editorials

Fig. 18. Mr. See All, the precursor of the Man-on-the-Band-Stand at Carlisle, *The Indian Boys' and Girls' Friend*, August 1885. Beinecke Rare Book and Manuscript Library, Yale University.

praising industriousness, sobriety, the use of English, as well as student writing. The bulletin's motto emphasized the life of the mind over vocational training: "A pebble cast into the sea is felt from shore to shore. A thought from the mind set free will echo on forever more." Religion, education, civilization, and assimilation were the bulletin's main themes: "If every Indian boy and girl were in school it would not take long to civilize all the Indians."[59] Samuel Townsend, "a Pawnee Indian boy" and the paper's first editor, exhorted: "Sometime the Indians will become entirely civilized people just as good white people. If the boys and girls want to be the rulers among their people they must get the best education and learn how to work too."[60]

From the school's inception, periodicals approached the "English only" topic. The *Morning Star* ran a column titled "Only English" as early as 1882. The young Native writers' awkward use of English as a second (and sometimes third) language illustrates their struggle to master the language they were praising in their letters home. The *School News* ran the column "Talk English," which reproduced student letters. Sophie Rachel (no tribal affiliation given) wrote to her brother about speaking only English: "We must teach our own people I want to talk English every day not to talk old Sioux. Now I don't want to talk Indian anymore because I like English every day." Besides exposing Carlisle student readers to the work of their peers, these examples served institutional ideology. The poem "English Speaking" intimates that the mastery of English will ensure wisdom and communal social mobility and success:

So keep to the English,
Help Others to rise,
Leave the Indian behind you
If you wish to grow wise.

The speaker echoes Sophie Rachel's letter above; in bringing English to the reservation community, the carrier will become an agent of change: only by "leav[ing] the Indian behind" and by speaking English could one uplift oneself and one's community, the students learned.[61]

Student writings at Carlisle were complicit with the institution's ideology, popularized by Pratt, yet occasionally diverged from it. In 1913, a student responded to a teacher's prompt for a composition entitled "My Industrial Work" with a poem, printed in *Carlisle Arrow* with praise. The budding poet from "Room Eight" did not write for publication, yet his work, in modest prosodic form, offered a rhymed glimpse into the daily regimented life, painting a less flattering picture of the school than the editors perhaps realized.[62] Like much student work published in Carlisle magazines, "My Industrial Work" recorded the daily routine: napping after lunch, studying for exams, going to mass, roll call, and dinner. From rushing to brush their hair, to attending grace, to preparing for the bugle call, the students' "industrial work" is fast-paced. When the bugle calls, "the troops fall in and the roll is called," and salute the U.S. flag "with our hats in our hands." The speaker's voice recalls a moment of (imposed) patriotic allegiance, when Native children "stand in the wind" and then "march to gravy." A striking absence in this rendition of "industrial work" is the student's omission of manual labor. Whereas Indian boarding school publications boasted institutional success to the outside world, printed outbursts of innocent rendition of the harsh life behind the scenes like "My Industrial Work" offer an alternative voice recording institutional success.

The professional Native writer was a rarity in the early twentieth-century literary landscape, and American Indian intellectuals, who later pursued careers in law, medicine, or the film industry, were rarely professional writers, although some were occasional poets. Carlisle Indian student authorship is a suspicious category, given the multifarious editorial interventions by school personnel—the looming image of the Man-on-the-Band-Stand—in the student-authored texts, as well as the institutional pressures to present a positive image of Carlisle. But, over time, the institution's view of literature changed. In 1886, the *Indian Helper* revealed the centrality of vocational training to the school's mission. A poem advertising a new cooking class, addressed to girls— "Girls, Take Notice"—juxtaposed the practicality of their industrial training with the work of poetry, music, or art:

> We may live without poetry,
> Music and art;
> We may live without conscience,
> And live without heart.

Whereas "civilized man" could live without Native artists, the same "civilized man/Can't live without cooks."

Literary societies, for example, the Mercer Literary Society and the Susan Longstreth Literary Society, both for girls, were active at Carlisle.[63] Although membership in these exclusive societies was limited, literature found its way into students' daily industrial work. In 1901 *Red Man and Helper* published the poem "Books" by Sarah J. Pettinos.[64] The poem begins with an invocation to the "Living voices of the long dead Past!" and invites the readers to pour over "the bounteous streams upon the page." This ode to the "magic power" of reading had a didactic purpose: inviting students to discover the world through books: "Through you the secrets of the earth and skies/Are opened wide to our admiring eyes." The speaker's identification with the reading audience—"our admiring eyes"—naturalizes the practice of reading in a space otherwise governed by "our industrial work"; the poem's abstract images impose a western-centric approach to knowledge, disregarding Indigenous epistemologies that guided many students' lives as they navigated life at Carlisle.[65]

Students at Carlisle, along with Native writers, editors, lawyers, and politicians throughout the U.S., started a print debate over American citizenship in the publications of Carlisle Indian School as early as the school's founding in 1879. While educating for Americanization aimed at erasing tribal identity and instilling patriotism, Native students integrated Indigeneity into their writing and expressive culture. The pages of Carlisle publications included articles reprinted from the national press; Pratt's various addresses; letters between students and their parents; columns by the Man-on-the-Band-Stand, a persona embodying institutional power; news about former or current Carlisle students; editorials; letters to the editor; promotional photographs; student debates; subscription ads; wedding announcements; and news about other Indian boarding schools.

The controlling gaze of the Man-on-the-Band-Stand reminded the students at Carlisle that they were under constant surveillance.[66] Concocted as an apparition, a figure towering over the students from his space of power and privilege, the Man-on-the-Band-Stand spied, eavesdropped, and praised. He had both territorial and editorial control. Reminiscent of the panopticon, the Man-on-the-Band-Stand had the discursive power to remain engraved in the students' memory, reminding them that they were under constant scrutiny from the outside world.[67] In 1891, Marianna Burgess, a longtime Carlisle chief clerk, business manager, occasional coeditor, and superintendent of printing, published a pseudo-memoir under the pseudonym Embe. *Stiya: A Carlisle Indian Girl at Home* was serialized weekly in the *Indian Helper* and appropriated the story of a Native girl to offer a cautionary tale. *Stiya* described the eagerness of a returned Pueblo student to turn her community to the path of "civilization." Burgess's attempt at ventriloquizing Native students was filled with clichés about Native communities.[68] *Stiya* extended the invisible arm of the Man-on-the-Band-Stand's surveillance beyond the spatial and temporal confines of the school.[69] The printing office itself was a microspace of surveillance, but as writers and printers, the students found ways to indigenize the Carlisle publications, from the press emblem and logo, to mastheads, cover art, and art added to stories and poems (figures 19, 20).

The *Red Man and Helper* ran a picture of the printing office on the first page of a 1904 issue. In a large, relatively well-lit room, at least twenty young Native men are at work. The picture is taken from the back of the room, revealing the "apprentices" bent over their desks, hard at work. The apprentices received training in press work, layout, operations, and the management of the equipment, which prepared them for the printing trade. From the space of control and surveillance, the editor had continuous access to the printing process and spectatorial

A magazine issued in the interest
of the Native American
by Carlisle

Fig. 19. (left) Emblem of the Carlisle Indian Press. Beinecke Rare Book and
Manuscript Library, Yale University.
Fig. 20. The Carlisle logo. Beinecke Rare Book and Manuscript Library, Yale
University.

control over her apprentices.[70] In a 1908 article published in *Charities and Commons*, commissioner of Indian Affairs Francis E. Leupp
claimed control over "the little papers and magazines" published by
the Native students: "I am trying to arouse among the children a love
of printing the stories which their own people have told them . . . ;
*sometimes narratives of acts of prowess which would be used as epics
if the Indians had any literature;* sometimes simple descriptions of life
at home, showing what the domestic and social customs are among
the tribe to which the writer belongs."[71] Leupp gravely misinterpreted
what Native literature was, casting doubt on whether Native people
had any literature at all, and showed ignorance of the genres in which
Native students and contemporary Native intellectuals were already
prolific.

The students at Carlisle and other federal Indian boarding schools
read and wrote beyond the expectations of a rigid curriculum and despite the violence and death surrounding them. The Carlisle library
offered an alternative space, an escape from the chores of a daily industrial life. A reading room opened in 1895, and by 1918, the school's library held over 1,700 titles. Although the collection was not built with
Native input or methods of collecting, more than 40 percent of the
titles were literary. The presence of the library at Carlisle reveals that
teachers and administrators had an interest in cultivating student learn-

ing beyond the classroom, although the library offered "little if any access to new ideas in hard sciences, social sciences, and other academic topics that were seen as crucial for preparing (white) high-schoolers for the twentieth century." This scarcity of materials is indicative of the education policies of the day and the race-based theories of Native students' incapacity to study intellectually challenging subjects.[72]

The Carlisle library, aligned with progressive policies of turning Native students into good Americans, integrated a vocational curriculum imposed by the federal government. Pratt himself was proud of the library. In a speech he gave in 1901, he remarked, "The school library is of great assistance in this as in every phase of the school work."[73] Pratt created social events like Saturday evening gathering, known as "English Speaking," where students were expected to converse in English only: "In the early days the pupils were expected on that evening to report their progress in the new and difficult language," Pratt reminisced in 1901. These gatherings were occasions for interactions with students, where "the superintendent as a father . . . has come to hold a peculiarly strong place in the affections of the students."[74] The bonds affective Americanization created between young students and "the school father" influenced some students' fond memories of the institution, despite the documented physical and psychological abuse experienced by survivors and their families over generations.

After they left Carlisle, some students became professionals; others continued their education, joining the ranks of the Native American intelligentsia of the 1910s and 1920s; others returned home, struggled to make a living, and in time sent their own children to Indian boarding schools. Although the success of a handful of Native students is documentable—Pawnee student Samuel Townsend became printer for the *Chippewa Herald* at the White Earth Boarding School in Minnesota—for most Carlisle printers the future was not bright as technological changes made their training at Carlisle impracticable.

"AMERICA": BOARDING SCHOOL EDUCATION AND PATRIOTIC TRAINING

As early as January 1883, Pratt named industrial training the guiding principle of his vision for education, followed by English speaking and literary training.[75] Although the inclusion of literary training may surprise the reader, the Carlisle publications before 1900 show a wealth of literary examples—from poems by American and Native writers, to student poetry, stories, debates, and essays. After 1900, the educational policy of Indian boarding schools emphasized vocational and patriotic training. In 1901, Estelle Reel, superintendent of Indian Schools (1898–1910), outlined the new *Course of Study for the Indian Schools of the United States: Industrial and Literary,* which emphasized two categories of instruction: industrial and literary. Through daily phonic drills and dictation, the Native child was taught English and skills for self-sufficiency. To prepare the child to become "fit for life," teachers emphasized the "dignity and nobility of labor." The curriculum also encouraged music education, especially patriotic songs: "Every student should be familiar with the words as well as the music of our inspiring national songs." Reel recommended outdoor flag exercises "by the whole school, morning and evening."[76] To inspire such exercises, a picture accompanied Reel's text with the caption "Saluting the Flag" (figure 21).

A closer examination, however, reveals that it is not an image of Native students but of African American students. Taken by Frances Benjamin Johnston, who had photographed students at Carlisle, this photograph documented African American children saluting the flag at Hampton Institute in Virginia. Reel's conflation of Black and Native educational experiences was not accidental; Hampton Institute in Virginia, while occasionally accepting Native students, trained Black agricultural laborers. Samuel Chapman Armstrong, the school's superintendent, used references to Native and African American children "to represent the benefits of Americanization to each other at Hampton."[77] Reel used the image of a group of young, uniformed, students of color to help readers visualize a scene of patriotic allegiance. The landscape is desolate; a young boy holds a flag to the left, and students to the right raise their hands and gazes to the flag. Throughout the 1910s, similar flag ceremonies took place on Native reservations—for example, as part of the Wanamaker expedition of 1913 and also the ceremonies staged by Competency Commissions (see chapter 1).

Scenes of forced patriotism marked both Indian boarding school spaces and print publications. In July 1903, the *Red Man and Helper* published Kate W. Hamilton's poem "America" on its first page: "O, LAND that standest fair and free,/Serene, and safe from sea to

Fig. 21. Saluting the flag at the Whittier Primary School, 1899 or 1900. Photograph by Frances Benjamin Johnston. Library of Congress, LC-USZ62–65770.

sea./America!" It appeared on the journal's upper left-hand corner, where poems were often printed.[78] Hamilton was neither Native nor a student, but her poem amplified the ethos of the upcoming July 4 celebrations. The Native student printers who brought this Americanization poem to light arguably also indigenized it. The poem was set below an image of an eagle framed by the word "America," an aural and a visual reminder of the patriotic markers informing the mission of Carlisle, the Americanization of its students (figure 22).

The typography and page layout are reminiscent of the *Cherokee Phoenix*—the first Native newspaper, published in the U.S. as early as 1828, and first Indigenous bilingual publication—that Carlisle printers may have been familiar with. The poem appears alongside an etching of the Great Seal of the U.S., a bald eagle with its wings widely

AMERICA

AMERICA

LAND that standest fair and free,
Serene, and safe from sea to sea.
America!
Thy snow-capped mountains kiss
the sky.
Thy plains in end ess beauty lie.
O'er golden sands thy rivers shine.
Forest and rock and lake are thine:
All countries and all climes compete
To lay their treasure at thy feet,
America!

Thy starry banner gleams afar,
On many seas thy white sails are.
America!
And weary captives turn to thee
As to a hope and prophecy,
For thou, O land so strong and brave,
Thou ownest neither king nor slave.
And with thy banner fluttering free
Gots aye thy wachword. "Liberty,"
America!

A golden cup is in thy hand,
Thou holdest it at God's command,
America!
His cup of blessing, not thine own.
Thou may'st not quaff its sweets alone—
This cup of blessing sent through thee
To thirsting, sad humanity.
God keep thee to thy mission true,
O fairest land the world e'er knew,
America!

KATE W. HAMILTON.

Fig. 22. Kate W. Hamilton, "America," *Red Man*, July 3, 1903, 1.

stretched, holding arrows in its left talon, the symbol of war, and an olive branch on the right, its head turned toward peace.[79] Visually, Indigeneity and Americanism coexist in the printers' typographic presentation of the poem.

Such instances of patriotism abounded at federal boarding schools. Flags marked the students' daily existence, from their crowded dormitories to their school rooms, the library, the gymnasium, and the auditorium—just as they were pervasive in immigrant students' Americanization classes, writing, and correspondence, as the next chapter will show. Carlisle flags and American flags accompanied the Carlisle football team and band throughout the Northeast. The Carlisle parade flag was an impressive object—made of silk, with gold painted stars and fringe—displayed at the school and accompanying the band when it was asked to lend a hand in patriotic parades.[80] Patriotic markers were ubiquitous, reminders that Native students' industrial education was also an education in American patriotism. The May 1903 issue of the *Red Man* printed the program of the year's commencement exercises, which included Hamilton's "America."[81] Despite the confined spaces they inhabited and their limited agency, Carlisle students performed patriotic rituals both inside and outside the school.

In 1913, Carlisle Sioux student Rose Whipper published the poem "Pride of Our Nation" in the *Carlisle Arrow*. A call to returning Carlisle students, "Men of Carlisle," to restore Native political rights— "Give us, O give us our birthright again!"—the poem spelled out the lines of action in a direct address: "You who the wrongs of the past must efface."[82] The poem captured a sense of urgency: "Pride of our Nation, the Red Man is waiting!" Rose Whipper was at Carlisle for eight years and after leaving the school struggled to make a living as a seamstress. Little did she know when she wrote this poem that, on her own return to the Crow Creek Agency in South Dakota in 1914, she would face more hardships than the speaker in her 1913 poem could have anticipated; she found her sister, Dora, sick with tuberculosis, a disease affecting many reservations at the time.[83]

Although patriotic poetry was not central to Carlisle's publications, students were reading and writing poetry amid their "industrial work." In 1887 the *Indian Helper* reprinted the poem "A New Citizen" by Omaha student Elsie Fuller:

Now I am a citizen!
They've given us new laws,
Just as were made
By Senator Dawes.

Fuller's poem praised the Dawes Allotment Act, which granted nominal citizenship to Native allottees. In the last stanza, the speaker changed from the individual to the collective voice:

Now we are citizens,
We all give him applause—
So three cheers, my friends,
For Senator Dawes![84]

Given Fuller's young age and the poem's rhetorical shifts, from the emphasis on the individual ("Now I am a citizen!") to the collective ("Now we are citizens!") and the excessive praise of Henry Dawes, it is possible that the poem's politicized message did not escape editorial intervention. Joel Pfister makes a compelling case for reading Carlisle as an experiment in "individualizing" Native children and transforming them into productive American laborers and citizens.[85]

These poems illustrate how Native students—as readers and writers—were exposed to the grammar of patriotism at Carlisle. They demarcate chronologically a rich period in Native education and print culture, which coincided with the parallel national campaign to Americanize the new immigrants. Carlisle publications made room for such poems as Hamilton's "America" or Fuller's "A New Citizen" (1887), as similar patriotic hymns abounded in the Americanization manuals for immigrants.[86] The patriotic outbursts of Carlisle magazines contrasted sharply with students' classroom exposure to Americanization, most notably the use of English, amid daily chores and hours of labor. But the panoptic model of Americanization thrived at Carlisle, often through Pratt's paternalism and the affective bonds he forged with the students.

"DEAR SCHOOL FATHER": STUDENT LETTERS

In her 1901 course of study on Native Education, superintendent of Indian schools Estelle Reel recommended that "the smallest children should write letters to their parents or friends once a month."[87] These letters, by both students and parents, were often reprinted in Carlisle publications. Whereas the printed letters carried the weight of editorial intervention, the handwritten originals, addressed to Pratt and school personnel, reveal the affective investment of the students, often guided by the nostalgic filter of memory. The letters are on a range of topics, from birthday wishes to Pratt to accounts of their life and education after Carlisle, and they exemplify affective Americanization. Immigrant students also wrote very affectionately to their teachers, as the next chapter will show, expressing gratitude for their new cultural capital and showing their eagerness to become American, yet very few students in the immigrant archives I have consulted experienced the kind of affective bond Pratt created with the students at Carlisle. The letters sent to and from federal boarding schools by Native students and their families reveal the affective dimension of students' negotiations with their new environments, language, and modes of subjectivity inflected by Americanization. A century later, these letters, preserved in archives controlled and curated by the Pratt family and school personnel and editors who supported this experiment in Americanization, remain useful albeit limiting.

Although students internalized the all-controlling, panoptic gaze of the institution, their letters reveal that they had an ambivalent relation to Carlisle. The endearing tone and love expressed in many letters reveal as much about Pratt's legacy as they do about his students' negotiations with the legacy of an institution—harmful and damaging for many, endearing and sentimental for some. And yet, occasionally, amid the ideological morass and appreciation—which some students may have expressed genuinely—different student voices emerge. Writing letters to Pratt years after their time at Carlisle, students expressed both nostalgia for "dear Old Carlisle" and continued devotion to the "school Father." Sam Sixkiller, Cherokee, class poet in 1895 and wit extraordinaire, used one of his first epistles to update Pratt on his accomplishments, an exercise in modesty: "I have not accomplished a great deal since leaving school unless making a living honorably at whatever you could find to do be considered something." Sixkiller wrote that he hadn't discovered any "north poles," nor had he invented or flown airplanes, but that he was trying to make the best of his education: "Suffice to say that I shall endeavor at all times so to live and at that I shall be an honor to my people, a glory to Carlisle, and a fitting example of the persevering efforts of our beloved superintendent." The same energy marked a letter Sixkiller sent to Pratt almost two decades later, when he worked as a cashier and assistant manager of the *Muskogee Daily Phoenix*, which he called "the best paper in the state." Like his previous letter, his letter in 1916 expressed nostalgia for Carlisle: "My training at Carlisle was especially valuable in this position, as I could do the work in the business office at the same time having a practical working knowledge of the mechanical end." But his health was poor and he was looking for a recommendation for a job in the Indian Service. Four years later, Sixkiller wrote again to Pratt to congratulate him on his eightieth birthday, signing his letter "Your Grateful Pupil."[88] Epistolary exchanges like these were not entirely disinterested; a letter from Charles Burke, then commissioner of Indian Affairs, to Pratt in 1921 reveals that Pratt had intervened on behalf of Sam Sixkiller, his former student, to secure a promotion for him.[89] Indeed, some student letters led to favors that the "school father" was still willing to grant his former pupils many years after they had left Carlisle.

Pratt's eightieth birthday in 1920 occasioned many letters of adoration from former students. Chauncey E. Archiquette wrote from Pawhuska, Oklahoma, to congratulate Pratt. Luther Standing Bear wrote from Venice Pier, California, where he owned a business in "Indian archery."[90] Rosa La Flesche, Ojibwe, who had played an important part in the Society of American Indians in the 1910s, also wrote to congratulate Pratt and to express gratitude for his service: "It gives me great pleasure to partly express my high regard for you and gratitude for your life-time of loving thought and unselfish service for my people."[91] Pueblo student Katie Creager Day reminded Pratt that she would "never forget her days at Carlisle." A postal worker at the time of writing, she ended on a hopeful note: "I'm sure the rest of my school mates will join in hands and hearts to thank you both a thousand times."[92] Rosa Bourasa, Chippewa, wrote to Pratt in 1899 from Phoenix, Arizona, where she was employed by the Indian School Service: "What I am, I owe to Carlisle." She assured Pratt that she had secured subscribers for the *Indian Helper*, ending her letter, "your friend and school-daughter."[93]

Ralph Armstrong, who wrote about his low wages, was one of the few students who wrote to Pratt to complain. In the majority of letters preserved in the Pratt Papers, students offer updates on their lives.

John Balenti, Cheyenne, wrote in 1920 to update Pratt on his successful career as engineer in Oklahoma City. Happily married, Balenti became one of Oklahoma's assistant state highway engineers: "I can't help but think of *my dear old school days at Carlisle* and the wonderful things she has done for me."[94] Like other students, Balenti addressed Pratt as "Daddy Dear" and signed his letter "Your Loving Son." Mystica Amago, San Luiseno, continued her education in California. In 1903 she wrote to express her gratitude for Carlisle: "We all realize the good you have done to our race and we cannot help but love you for all that you have been to us all these years." Amago signed as "Your school daughter." Pratt signed his replies "Your friend and school father."[95]

Although the handwritten letters from students, along with those reprinted in the Carlisle publications, illuminate the complicated legacy of Carlisle and Pratt, their message is a continuum of adoration. Sometimes playful, sometimes plaintive, the students' letters to Pratt gesture beyond the confines of his experiment in Americanization; they point to possibilities where Native and American can coexist, when American patriotism is not at odds with Native patriotism, when "progress" is not coterminous with complete annihilation of Indigenous identities. But what of the letters expressing dissent and regret about attending Carlisle? We know that some former Carlisle teachers, like Gertrude Bonnin, expressed direct dissent in correspondence with Pratt. What of the student letters depicting death, destruction, and deferred dreams? The absence of those student letters from the archival record is as telling as it is troubling. The endearing tone and love expressed in many of these letters, some from a contemporary moment, some from a nostalgic perspective, reveal as much about Pratt's legacy as they do about the silences of his students and their negotiations with the legacy of an institution—harmful and damaging for many, endearing and sentimental for others.

Whereas print culture disseminated an Americanization ethos at Carlisle from its inception, other Indian boarding schools explored the contradictions of Americanization. The boarding school system was, ultimately, a "successful failure."[96] Although concerns over the off-reservation education of Native children emerged as early as the 1880s, after 1900 criticism increased; Native communities did not approve of their children being educated in this way, and the advantages, including opportunities for employment, for the Native students were few.[97] The Meriam Report (1928) found that the monetary provisions for Native children in boarding schools were inadequate, the children were undernourished and exhausted by physical labor. It documented "starving and overworked children debilitated by unsanitary conditions and overcrowding with resultant spread of tuberculosis and other communicable diseases." Although the report found that there were more Native students in schools funded by the state or local governments, more than twenty thousand Native children were still forced by law to attend federal boarding schools in the U.S. in 1928, subsisting on dwindling appropriations made by the Office of Indian Affairs.[98]

Carlisle Indian School's ideological ramifications left a permanent mark on Native students' encounters with disciplinary spaces, particularly in print. In his autobiographies *My People, the Sioux* (1928) and *Land of the Spotted Eagle* (1933), Sioux activist, author, and filmmaker Luther Standing Bear wrote about how he "unlearned" his Americanization once he gained enough distance from the school.[99] Native students were expected to speak, walk, and live like white Americans. Standing Bear imagined a system of education that could benefit all Americans, based in Indigenous epistemologies and conducted by Native instructors. In *Land of the Spotted Eagle*, Standing Bear proposed that "the Indian can save America" by becoming "his own historian, giving his account of the race." Advocating for "a school of Indian thought, built on the Indian pattern and conducted by Indian instructors," Standing Bear claimed that "America can be revived, rejuvenated, by recognizing a native school of thought. The Indian can save America."[100]

Despite a highly regimented and controlled life in federal Indian boarding schools, Native students were not the passive recipients of the *gift* of Americanization that the Progressive Era reformers had optimistically envisioned for them. Optimism infused the students' letters to Pratt, as well as their letters home: "Behold! I am here with my pen and brains to pour out before you and display all the information I could find, my lessons seemed harder at first and many times I felt discouraged, but I pushed my way slowly like frozen molasses, and things are getting easier day by day."[101] Native students at Carlisle and other Indian boarding schools encountered Americanization in their daily lives and in print—reading and penning poems, letters, stories— yet imagined life outside the confines of their industrial work. In spite of a regimented daily existence and a rigid curriculum of vocational training, Native students cultivated a life of the imagination informed by their traditional upbringing and the Euro-American education into which they were forced. Through literary societies, newspaper columns, letters, occasional stories, and poems published in school newspapers, Carlisle students made intellectual labor and industrial labor mutually constitutive rather than mutually exclusive. Through the print culture they generated and were exposed to, Carlisle students learned to read and write beyond the boundaries of a rigid vocational curriculum—which seldom made room for poetry or fiction—as they learned to negotiate the institution's Americanization demands with their commitments to their Native cultures.

4 "Sing, Strangers!"

Education, Print Culture, and the Americanization of New Immigrants

We shall seek the wonders of the land
And sing our last song
To the earth,
Not our earth.
We shall sing our swan song,
To the home,
Not our home.
Stranger,
Our own
Stranger.

—Ruven Ludvig, "Sing Stranger," 1924

ON JULY 5, 1924, the day after the United States celebrated another Independence Day—and shortly after it passed its most drastic immigration restriction legislation, reducing immigration to the U.S. by 85 percent—Croatian-language newspaper *Radnik* used the occasion to recount a brief history of "our powerful and great America" with two stories about the country's origin. The first story told how the American colonists took the land away from the Native Americans and introduced slavery. The second was about how modern America was built "on the blood and bones of immigrant workers"; it acknowledged land theft and the dispossession of Native Americans as part of the U.S. colonial and capitalist project. The author, a Croatian immigrant, brought Native dispossession and the exploitation of immigrants into high relief, ending with a plea to the immigrant working class to liberate itself: "We must be active participants in these struggles."[1] While a good many foreign language newspapers like *Radnik* endorsed Americanization throughout the 1910s, others—like the more progressive Polish-language *Dziennik Chicagoski*—were critical of the government's treatment of Native American people.

In this chapter I fill a gap in the current scholarship on the immigrant press and its role in the Americanization project by looking at the better-known archive of mainstream Americanization publications (for example, *Immigrants in America Review* and *Americanization Bulletin*) and the lesser-known archive of the Chicago Foreign Language Press Survey. Of particular interest in these archives is the treatment of *Indian* tropes in the foreign language press. Analogies of the "immigrant problem" with the "Indian problem" translated derogatory associations with *Indians* as markers of savagery into strategies of identification, alliance building, and occasional solidarity. Few immigrants knew Indigenous history before they came to the U.S.—and if they did, they learned a colonialist-inflected version of American history. The public schools and Americanization classes painted Native communities in the light of extinction. As the immigrant population grew and the Native one declined, the presence of Native references in the foreign language press invites further scrutiny and questions about the legibility of these groups to each other and to various reading communities. Were references to *Indians* in the foreign language press similar or different from those in the English language and mainstream publications? Were they accidental or calculated? How were the new immigrants making sense of their own place on stolen Indigenous land? Occasionally, immigrant publications acknowledged their complicity in settler history and its writing, as they negotiated pressures to Americanize while maintaining their transnational cultural ties.

As shown in the previous chapter, educating Native children in Indian boarding schools was part of the settler-colonial project of land theft and the belief in Native people's putative "racial" inferiority. In that case, the work of education performed the double task of cultural assimilation and patriotic Americanization. Similarly, the Americanization of new immigrants through education—in such venues as night schools, factories, radio stations, YMCAs, amusement parks, department or grocery stores, professional sports leagues, or movie theaters—further consolidated the U.S. empire by producing imagined compliant new citizens to supply the country's labor force. The new immigrants' predecessors, the old immigrants, from the colonial period through the nineteenth century, were not immune to the ridicule or persecution by the nativists, among them the self-declared "native Americans" of the Know-Nothing Party in the mid-nineteenth century. Likewise, the new immigrants met with an aggressive form of nativism during and shortly after World War I. In a decade marked by warnings of so-called race suicide and fears of Anglo-Saxon disappearance, Americanization was the answer to absorbing millions of new immigrants into industrial America.

In this chapter I trace some of the ways that immigrant education and print culture supported the work of Americanization. In doing so I examine a relatively new archive of immigrant student writing: letters and writing specimens produced by immigrant students in Americanization programs. Many institutions took on the mission of Americanizing the country's immigrants. Letters from former students to teachers illustrate what I call "affective Americanization," an insidious form of co-optation through the affective bonds forged across time and space by immigrant students and their American teachers, reminiscent of the previous chapter's letters Native students at the Carlisle Indian Industrial School sent to Richard H. Pratt. Reading these letters and writing specimens, I argue that the education of new immigrants was complicit with the nationalist project of Americanization as it also allowed for multiple immigrant allegiances. The short naturalization stories written by soon-to-be citizens express dual loyalties: to their country of origin and to the United States.

I also examine the role of print in the nationalist project of Americanization. An especially timely archive is that of the multilingual guides to immigrants—*Guide to the United States for the Immigrant* by John Foster Carr—as well as Silvio Floretta's notebook, which documents the role of English literacy, American civics, and patriotism in the Americanization of new immigrants. These depositories of knowledge and their circulation validated the zealous work of Americanizers. The documents from the foreign language press and its work toward Americanization, collected in the Chicago Foreign Language Press Survey, also reveal how immigrant publications occasionally acknowledged the immigrants' complicity with settler history and its writing, and how they often resorted to *Indian* tropes to affirm either ethnic nationalism or American patriotism.

AMERICANIZATION AND THE EDUCATION
OF NEW IMMIGRANTS

If the schooling of Native Americans, African Americans, and non-Anglo-Saxon immigrants in the U.S. served as a model of education standardization, it was because education and schooling were understood in similar terms. Yet, in non-Anglo-Saxon communities, education and schooling have different connotations. The economic, cultural, and social interests of the nation created and perpetuated hierarchies through education, aiming at instilling patriotism in the new immigrant or aspiring American citizen.[2] Nativism and fears of "racial difference" permeated the logic of immigration restrictionists, justifying the argument that some immigrants could not assimilate because of immutable internal (biological) differences. Italian immigrants, for instance—particularly those from the southern provinces—were at the top of the list of "unamericanizable" immigrants by the early 1900.[3] Yet, educators and social workers looked to external factors affecting assimilation to make a case for the education of immigrants. Local and national alliances, organizations, and associations contributed to the early stages of the movement toward Americanization before World War I; they included such large patriotic societies as the National Society of Colonial Dames of America, the National Society of the Sons of American Revolution, or the North American Civic League for Immigrants. These patriotic societies offered scholarships to immigrants who agreed to engage in patriotic work and published informative leaflets for the newly arrived. At the end of the nineteenth century, cities like Boston, Buffalo, Chicago, Cincinnati, Cleveland, Detroit, New York, Philadelphia, and Rochester offered education programs to new immigrants through educational alliances and immigrant societies. Founded in 1890, the Educational Alliance in New York City contributed to the Americanization of Jewish immigrants through settlement work, lectures, and classes. In 1900 the Society for Italian Immigrants opened night schools for day laborers in New York and Pennsylvania. The YMCA started its first evening schools for immigrants in New York City in 1907, spreading across 130 cities and towns in the U.S. by 1908, and reaching an estimated 55,000 immigrant men by 1912.[4]

Just as the Friends of the Indian argued for the education of Native children, at the beginning of the twentieth century there was also a growing interest in educating the new immigrants; the underlying assumption was similar to the case of Native students: that they lacked one. The education of immigrant children was supplemented by communal education and did not change upon the immigrants' arrival in the United States; what changed were the new country's expectations for what education could and should do. Whereas the majority of immigrants to the U.S. between 1820 and 1920 were peasants, many new immigrants in the 1880s came from industrial cities and were part of diverse societies, which valued education in its many forms, from the teaching of life skills or trades to literacy.[5] Because of the differences among immigrant communities, for some groups the acculturation pressures of the schools came at a cost, such as loss of language or tradition; for others, it was a smoother adaptation. Intergenerational conflicts emerged as immigrant children were socialized differently in the U.S. than they had been in their countries of birth. Italian immigrant children, for instance, who learned Italian in American high schools, could no longer communicate with their Sicilian grandparents. Similarly, Jewish children, educated in Hebrew schools had a hard time understanding their immigrant grandparents' Yiddish. For some new immigrant groups, American institutions of education were highly problematic; European Jews, Turkish Greeks, Poles, Irish, and Armenian immigrants to the U.S.—inhabiting different levels of displacement—understood schools as instruments of state persecution and set up their own schools.

If, in the nineteenth century, public schools had emphasized individual self-improvement, the beginning of the twentieth century saw a shift toward combining self-improvement with the interests of the community. This happened, in part, because of demographic changes through immigration from Russia, Italy, Hungary, and the Balkans. In 1909, the U.S. Immigration Commission reported that the parents of over 57 percent of the children in the country's thirty-seven largest cities were immigrants. It fell to public schools to educate the children of immigrants in a growing urban and industrial country. Whereas the new Slavic immigrants were the least educated by the 1950s, the Jewish new immigrants thrived.[6] From parochial schools (in Polish, German, and Irish communities) to Jewish schools of various Orthodox groups, schools for new immigrants educated in the immigrants' mother tongue and helped preserve a sense of ethnic or religious identity, often erased or muted by public schools.[7] Cultural pluralists Horace Kallen and Randolph Bourne advocated for a different version of Americanism than their predecessors, arguing for Americanization education as a process of cultural exchange rather than an imposition of the "American way." Kallen, for instance, argued that ethnic and cultural differences, those "inner" qualities representing the immigrant's descent, were essential to maintaining what he called "a multiplicity in a unity." Like Kallen, Bourne argued that the new immigrant was the product of several cultures rather than the artificial "melting" of the foreigner into the nationalist melting pot.[8] According to Peter Carravetta, Italian immigrants to the U.S. during these decades did not arrive with a strong sense of Italian identity; many immigrants also realized that they did not have to submit to the demands of "100 percent Americanism." Although in official immigration records Italians appeared alongside other "undesirable" and "unamericanizable" nationalities or "races," the restrictionists distinguished increasingly between the northern and southern Italian immigrants, finding the latter harder to Americanize.[9] As Thomas Guglielmo has shown, anti-Italian sentiment emerged from questions about the legitimacy of their claims to whiteness.[10]

Intergenerational conflicts also influenced new immigrants' levels of English-language literacy. Writing for the *New York Times* in 1907, David Blaustein decried the "effect of public schools on immigrants," arguing that it produced a "gulf between immigrants and their children." Blaustein cautioned that it further alienated immigrant children from their parents, whose Americanization was slower, and who became critical of their Americanized children and the system of education itself.[11] Second generation Italian immigrant and writer Jerre Mangione recalled his Sicilian parents' distrust of the U.S. educational system. For Mangione's father, the American school system "symbolized everything that outraged him about his adoptive country. . . . Beneath his fury was the conviction that they were encouraging immorality, disrupting family life, and undermining his position as head of the family." The Sicilian immigrant parents' distrust of the American educational system was symptomatic of larger fears of (old) cultural loss, rather than their children's (new) cultural gains.[12]

Americanization through the schools became a common theme for settlement workers and militant nationalists in the 1910s. By 1914, the federal Bureau of Naturalization and Immigration made public schools a key ally in its Americanization program. By 1921, more than thirty states had passed Americanization laws. Schools and unions organized English and civics classes for the foreign-born; private organizations, from the philanthropic to the patriotic, also launched Americanization programs. Several federal agencies joined in the movement.[13] The public schools, however, were limited in their capacity to accommodate the education of adult immigrants; teachers of the day schools, who worked with immigrant children, were unprepared to educate their adult parents and siblings effectively. Because attendance in public schools was voluntary, another problem arose: many adult immigrants worked long hours, which sometimes prevented their attending evening classes (figure 23). There was also no guarantee that adult immigrants were learning English.[14] And if they were not learning English, how could they be

Fig. 23. Class of Italian immigrants receiving instruction in English and citizenship, Newark, New Jersey, YMCA, between 1920 and 1930. Library of Congress, LC-USZ62-93091.

Fig. 24. "Without language we can't have cooperation, we can't have business, we can't have life, happiness, and prosperity. The key to citizenship is get Uncle Sam's book and *Learn English*," 1914. Library of Congress, Records of the Immigration and Naturalization Service, Education and Americanization, box 5, folder 23/2.

made into Americans? Posters juxtaposing European immigrants, such as "Mr. Foreigner," against Uncle Sam permeated the era's push for English: "The key to citizenship is [to] get Uncle Sam's book and *Learn English*" (figure 24). Uncle Sam points to the English commandment—to a presumed illiterate immigrant, "Mr. Foreigner"—as "America" looms in the distance, promisingly.

Besides teaching English, public school educators in New York City made their immigrant students proxy teachers of American domestic values in their own homes. The immigrant parents were the students, and their children became their Americanization instructors—similar to Native students' plans at Carlisle to teach their parents English once they returned to their reservations, where the school was already disseminating English-language school publications. If immigrant school children had the advantage of living in close proximity to their parents, Native students in Indian boarding schools were often separated from their families for months and, sometimes, years. Immigrant mothers were the hardest demographics for Americanizers to reach. In his speech at the Americanization Conference in 1919, S. H. Goldberger, principal of New York School 19 emphasized that public schools should reach out to immigrant mothers: "The mother has been the one most neglected. Her husband and children come in contact with American life but she remains at home. Her European training has made her shy. She has always had to work hard at home."[15]

In 1919, the *Ladies Home Journal* published a piece on the Italian immigrant author and educator Angelo Patri, principal of a public school in the Bronx. His vision of Americanization involved both the preservation of immigrant languages and the learning of English, so that disparate immigrant groups might understand the U.S. and each other. Patri's vision of Americanization brought immigrant children together, granting them agency to teach their parents. The teachers prepared blank books that the children took home to their parents and used to show their mothers how to write their names, addresses, or the names of their children. As they progressed, immigrant mothers received advanced lessons. Patri's assumption was that the children would help their mothers write and speak English, and then return the lessons to the teachers: "They are ambitious for their mothers. They do not want their mothers to appear stupid." In the school auditorium in the Bronx, Patri met with immigrant parents and children; his emphasis on empowering the children of immigrants solidified his vision of Americanization as "bringing children together."[16]

This insidious form of what I call "affective Americanization," an ideological co-optation of immigrant children through emotional appeals to make their parents into patriotic Americans, targeted immigrants through the most innocent agents of Americanization: their children. Affective Americanization as a coercive strategy of recruiting immigrant subjects into the adoptive nation originated in the militant nationalists' work and appealed to the immigrants' affection and devotion to their adoptive country. Nurses and teachers who taught immigrants in their homes also attempted to instill "American" practices and standards. In 1905, New York City schools started offering "steamer" or "vestibule" classes for immigrant children eight years and older, acquainting them with basic English language skills so that they could join regular classes with American children.[17]

Some reformers and educators were sympathetic to the role of inherited tradition in education. Educational reformer John Dewey decried the loss of immigrant traditions and the artificiality of education in the public schools, lamenting, "They even learn to despise the dress, bearing, habits, language and beliefs of their parents—many of which have more substance and worth than the superficial putting on of the newly adopted habits." In *Democracy and Education* (1916), Dewey argued for a broader conception of the common culture and a culturally pluralist curriculum.[18] In *Twenty Years at Hull House* (1910), Jane Addams recounted the refuge Chicago's immigrant community found from the crowded tenement houses at the Hull House settlement, which she had established in 1889. An experiment in Americanization, the Hull House settlement provided immigrant parents and children with hot meals and clothes, as well as kindergartens and daycare facilities, a library, music, and art classes. Hull House attempted to bridge the gap between older and younger, more Americanized immigrants.[19] New immigrants often advocated for instruction in the languages of their countries of origin. Although these efforts toward language preservation existed, their influence did not alter considerably the Americanization of immigrant children, who could function in both languages and cultures with much more ease than their parents.

Whereas some immigrant mothers learned English in their homes, many new immigrant men were Americanized in the factories where they worked. The Ford Motors Americanization Program taught industrial safety to immigrant laborers and signaled that those who did not understand English were more prone to industrial accidents. Obedience and efficiency were at the heart of industrial English programs at Ford Motors, U.S. Steel, and the YMCA Roberts program. Like other English programs in industrial settings, the YMCA program centered on punctuality, discipline, and a sense of order. A sense of regimentation marked the lessons of industrial workers: "I hear the whistle. I must hurry./I hear the five-minute whistle./It is time to go into the shop" (1911). This sequence is reminiscent of the Carlisle Indian School student's poem "My Industrial Work" (1913; see chapter 3), which captured the daily regimented life of Indigenous students, trained to become the country's future laborers: "When the whistle blows at half past five,/Once more I am up *and still alive*."[20] Inhabiting similar pressures in the new industrial landscape, both the new immigrant and the Native laborers practiced their English as they also ventriloquized the Protestant work ethic instilled in them by the factory and the industrial school, respectively, the agents of their Americanization.

"I TELL HEEM NOTHING!": IMMIGRANT LETTERS AND WRITING SPECIMENS IN THE AMERICANIZATION PROJECT

Training for citizenship and training for English literacy went hand in hand in federal Americanization programs. Amy Wan highlights three sites of citizenship production from 1910 until 1929: federal Americanization programs, union education, and university classes.[21] The first edition of the *Student's Textbook* for citizenship training in 1918 was compiled "from material submitted by the State Public Schools" and focused heavily on the work of the government, with later editions dedicated to a broader understanding of cultural citizenship. In the 1922 edition, lessons for beginners included information about institutions and mundane tasks: "I Open the Door," "I Read the Paper," "The American Flag," while intermediate lessons provided instruction on "What the Flag Stands For," "Our Schools," "City Government," and so on. By the time the immigrants arrived in naturalization classes, they had already been selected through legal and cultural mechanisms and had been implicated in the work of Americanization. Student textbooks, such as *A Standard Course for Use in the Public Schools of the United States for the Preparation of the Candidate for the Responsibilities of Citizenship* (1918), were also complicit in presenting new immigrants with an exceptionalist American history. The "discovery" narrative permeated the introduction to American history, and references to Indigenous people were in the past tense: "He has been called the true child of the forest. He knew nothing of the ways of civilization, but was a master of the secrets of the woods." Urging immigrants to become loyal American citizens, the textbook showcased examples of Native people's transformation into loyal Americans: "Indians have become American citizens. Some of them have held high offices in the

States and a few have been sent to the United States Senate or the House of Representatives."[22] The textbook implied that if Native people could become American citizens, why not the immigrants? Earlier in the twentieth century, Indigenous intellectuals like Carlos Montezuma, Gertrude Bonnin, and Charles Eastman made the opposite argument: if immigrants could be made into Americans so swiftly, why not the Indians?

In August 1924, a St. Louis naturalization officer wrote Raymond Christ, deputy commissioner of naturalization in Washington, D.C., including a copy of "A Little Naturalization Story," recounting the civics examination of an Italian man, identified only as Tony, who was "found to be in the twilight zone between satisfactory and unsatisfactory" on the topic of the election of U.S. presidents. An official asked Tony how he would explain the election of the U.S. president to a fellow immigrant from Italy, and "like a shot from a gun came his answer: *I tell heem it not hees beesness. No green horn just come to our country got any right to inquire into our beesnees. I tell heem nothing!*' The proud officer concluded his letter: 'I passed him.'" The officer passed Tony because of his declared patriotism, not his knowledge of civics or his English. Although he failed to demonstrate his qualifications, Tony was rewarded with American citizenship.[23] Americanization appealed to Tony's new sense of subjectivity, which betrayed visible animosity toward newer immigrants. This episode illustrates Americanization at work on vulnerable new immigrant subjects like Tony who, already interpellated into patriotic discourse, became the new gatekeeper of Americanism for fellow immigrants.[24]

The writing specimens forwarded by teachers in Americanization classes to government officials provide insight into an otherwise curated archive of patriotic literacy materials in service of Americanization. The students' written and graphic expression—with drawings of American flags adorning their stories and diary entries, similar to work produced by Native students in Indian boarding schools—reveal glimpses of affective Americanization. Just as Native students wrote effusive letters of adoration to Pratt after they left Carlisle, immigrant students in Americanization classes—often much older than their Native counterparts—penned their gratitude to their teachers for helping them become citizens. The letters from immigrant students to their teachers overwhelmingly praised American institutions for the opportunities they offered immigrants and their families. To showcase their students' literacy and progress, the teachers sent selected writing specimens to the Bureau of Naturalization in Washington, D.C. This progress revealed the teachers' own complicity with patriotic ideology as they distributed posters, invitations to join citizenship classes, and carefully chosen reading materials with patriotic themes to their immigrant students in several languages.

Patriotic rhetoric and imagery permeate immigrant student writing specimens. The words of the "American's Creed" and images of "Our Flag" adorned many of them. Some of the samples use perfect cursive on patriotic stationery—the American flag, embossed on the stationery—illustrating the teacher's zeal in making her students' materials even more patriotic. "The American's Creed" (1917) was reproduced in several students' writing specimens, including Gertrude Hoffman's. We might imagine that immigrant students not only copied the lines of "The American's Creed" in perfect penmanship but also recited it, with genuine hope about what citizenship might bring.[25] Hoffman's composition "Our Flag," handwritten on a piece of paper adorned with an American flag, drawn in vivid colors, exudes confidence. Hoffman, who chose to sign her composition, was an immigrant from Luxembourg, had lived in the U.S. for thirty-one years, and had been enrolled in school for seven years. She was forty-eight years old and living in Murdoch, Kansas. Although flag exercises were common public education rituals, these patriotic materials produced by immigrant adults offer a counterpoint to the Native students' work in the Indian boarding schools. If Native students had little choice in their daily patriotic routines, these collected writing specimens reveal that many immigrant students gave themselves to American patriotism willingly, or so their teachers' assembled collections of student work suggest.

In June 1924, Elizabeth O'Rourke, an instructor in Webster, Iowa, wrote a letter to the chief naturalization examiner in St. Louis to showcase the written work of her students. She asked the examiner to forward their work to Raymond Christ, commissioner of naturalization, if he found them worthy. She included writing specimens by a family of three: Mr. and Mrs. August Verhele and their son, Walter. The Verhele writing specimens convey their hopes for becoming American, compounded by fears that their level of literacy might defer the much-coveted citizenship. Mr. Verhele's penmanship is crude, and his writing filled with details about his crops. His wife's letter, in better calligraphy and English, is politically charged: "As I understand, it seems to me that an alien woman cannot have her citizen papers, in case her alien husband could not pass the examination." Although the letter doesn't directly criticize the gendered naturalization process, it reveals her declared patriotism and readiness to become American, hindered only by a bureaucratic process which precluded her working husband from attaining literacy, on which her own naturalization depended.[26]

Other writing specimens were specific about the immigrants' decision to Americanize. In his sample composition, "Why I Wish to Become a Naturalized Citizen of the United States" (1923), Sigmund A. Fridykes, a Russian immigrant, wrote: "In America, I have seen that each man, rich or poor, has an equal chance for an education. Also, his children may have the best education in the public schools." For Fridykes, becoming American meant a chance at education. Letters sent from Greely, Colorado, revealed that adult immigrant students had a harder time attending school regularly than their children. Christ Gus, a forty-one-year-old immigrant from Russia, wrote to his teacher, Miss Smith, on February 18, 1924, that he would have to miss class because he was busy with his work at home. Like Arthur Howeattle, the Native student from La Push, Washington, who wrote to his teacher about his necessary absence from school (see chapter 3), Gus wrote politely but unapologetically.

A writing specimen by Croatian immigrant Nickolas Pavich, a student in a Citizenship class in a Kansas City night school, offers generic thanks to the night school director and teacher (figure 25). In attractive penmanship, with some spelling errors, Pavich's missive bursts with patriotism: "This is a country of wonders and I am very proud to live in it. And I must give many thanks to night school Director and tiacher [sic] whom I see is [sic] taken great interest into this matter." Drawings of American flags accompanied his and his classmates' writing specimens.[27] Occasionally, calligraphy pages illustrated student penmanship. Two letters sent to Miss Florence Strevey in Massillon, Ohio, in April 1924, reveal the students' sincere affection for their teacher. The teacher transcribed the letters in full before she forwarded them to Raymond Christ. In one letter, George Papavasiliou expressed gratitude: "You helped me to lay the foundation so that I might be able to learn English." Former student Gust Marinakes also praised the teacher's

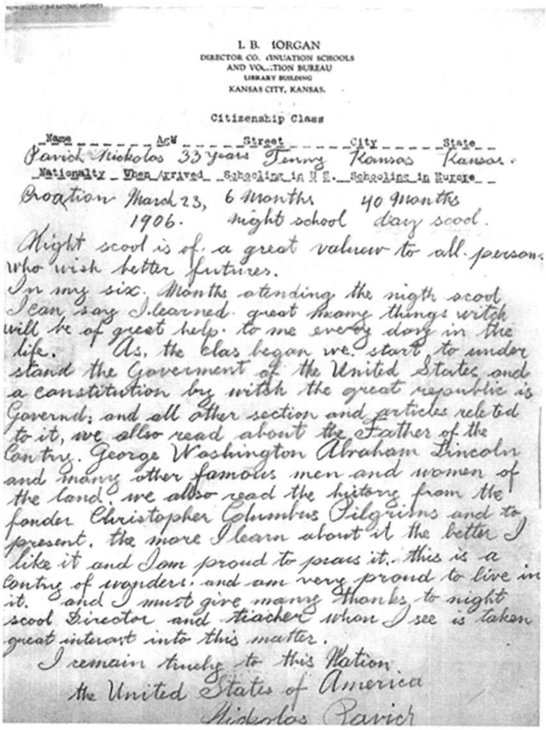
L. B. [illegible]ORGAN
DIRECTOR CO. [illegible]NUATION SCHOOLS
AND VO[illegible]TION BUREAU
LIBRARY BUILDING
KANSAS CITY, KANSAS.

Citizenship Class

Name	Age	Street	City	State
Pavich Nickolas	33 years	Tenny	Kansas	Kansas.

Nationalty	When Arrived	Schooling in U. S.	Schooling in Europe
Croatian	March 23, 1906.	6 Months night school	40 months day scool.

Night scool is of a great valuew to all persons who wish better futures.
In my six. Months atending the nigth scool I can say I learned great many things witch will be of great help. to me every day in the life. As, the clas began we start to under stand the Goverment of the United States and a constitution by witch the great republic is Governd; and all other section and articles releted to it, we allso read about the Father of the Contry. George Washington Abraham Lincoln and many other famous men and women of the land, we allso read the hitory from the fonder Christopher Columbus Pilgrims and to present. the more I learn about it the better I like it and I am proud to prais it. this is a Contry of wonders. and am very proud to live in it. and I must give many thanks to night scool Director and teacher whom I see is taken great interest into this matter.
I remain truly to this Nation
the United States of America
Nickolas Pavich

Fig. 25. Writing Specimen by a Croatian immigrant, Nicholas Pavich, sent from the Kansas City Night School to Raymond Crist, commissioner of naturalization, Washington, D.C. April 1924. National Archives, RG 85.

efforts: "Your perseverance and devotion to your work was great, and as one of America's real daughters indefatigably worked for our education to teach us the language, to write and read, and also the country's customs."[28] The affection of these students for their Americanization teachers, the agents of the state, reveals the insidious ways affective Americanization worked in immigrant training for citizenship.

Besides formal classwork and letters showcasing their progress, immigrants kept notebooks and diaries in English, recording lesson notes and homework with various degrees of formality. These repositories of knowledge acquired in English and preserved in government archives validate the zealous work of Americanizers. The notebook of Italian immigrant Silvio Floretta, 126 pages long, documents the confluence of English, American civics, and American patriotism. Born in 1896, in Cloz, Italy, he was living in Nokomis, Michigan. Like other immigrant

students, Floretta praised his adoptive country and was willing to naturalize: "I wish to be a citizen because I like the fundamental principles
of this government." Floretta's notebook contains neatly handwritten
compositions and lessons, possibly transcribed from previous drafts,
on topics ranging from the mundane to the patriotic, such as the transcribed Lesson 69, "A Good American."

With little mention of his native Italy, Floretta's notebook is a collection of "lessons" in becoming American, from observations about daily
happenings and his thoughts on becoming a good American: "My Wife
Went to the Market Last Saturday" or "The Honest Citizen." Floretta's
wife, like other immigrant wives, could not become an American citizen on her own, would have received a letter from the Bureau of Naturalization informing her that she would automatically become a citizen
when her husband did. She would have been encouraged to cooperate
with the superintendent of the schools to attend classes "where you
can learn the things which you should know to be American." Floretta
attributes physical strength and strength of character to what he calls
becoming "a good American." In Lesson 69, he writes: "Good citizenship consists in doing the small duties, private and public." Although
his collection of "lessons" perhaps targeted a small school audience,
its direct address to the reader reveals a sense of a larger audience. In
the lesson "How the Library Helps Me," about the benefits of public
libraries, the degree of detail suggests that the writer was introducing
the concept of a public library to immigrants who may not have been
exposed to it before: "Do you ever go to the library? Are you trying to
learn English? Are you trying to educate yourself in other ways? The
library will be a great help to you."[29] A rhetoric of gratitude permeates these excerpts, letters or transcriptions of letters, and notebooks,
culled from an archive curated to showcase successful Americanization
stories. These documents reveal both ideological pressures and cultural
nuances as writers negotiate their new identities in a new language.
They illustrate how affective Americanization worked in the Americanized, whose allegiances ebbed and flowed between the country of origin
and the country of naturalization.

AMERICANIZATION IN PRINT

By 1895, more than one hundred nativist publications were signaling that new immigrants were threatening America. Several of them

reached national prominence in the 1890s: the *A.P.A. Magazine*, for instance, was the nativist magazine of the decade. As the publication of the American Protective Association, an anti-Catholic secret society, during its short run (1895–97), the *A.P.A. Magazine* had as large a readership as some national magazines, such as *Harper's Weekly* or *Ladies' Home Journal*. Other nativist journals included the *United American* published in Washington, D.C. (1892–94), the *Loyal American* out of Minneapolis (1893–96), and the *American Standard* in San Francisco (1888–93). Thriving on anonymity and vitriol, these publications translated the visions of American men fond of secret societies and vigilante groups. Common concerns included "the immigrant problem" or "the American disease," using denigrating terms for immigrants: "incompetent driftwood," "foreign-born scum," "the riff-raff of Europe," or "two-legged beasts." Cheap labor, voting rights, moral character, crime, alcoholism, and national origin were other categories of scorn, but nothing riled the nativists more than the expansion of the Roman Catholic Church in the U.S., although the nativist press also paid close attention to Jewish immigrants. The targeted groups of new immigrants included the Italians, Albanians, Bulgarians, Hungarians, Poles, Russians, and Yugoslavians. Legal action and arrests, along with the growing factionalism of the nativist movement and the country's economic recovery, hastened the end of the nativist press.[30]

Although they did not share in the ethos of the nativist press, other English-language publications reveled in patriotic effusions, especially during the 1910s. The weekly *The American Legion*, the official magazine of the American Legion, a patriotic organization started by war veterans in the 1910s, published weekly pleas for "100 percent Americanism." As nativism and anti-immigrant rhetoric heightened in mainstream publications during WWI, essays on topics like "Tonic Americanism" took center stage.[31] Newspaper clippings in the John Foster Carr Papers at the New York Public Library reveal a wealth of patriotic materials disseminated by the English-language press across the U.S. A January 1920 issue of the *Evening World* expressed the gratitude of the "Americans by choice" to their new country. In November 1919, the *Evening Sun* published an anti-immigrant poem by Luella Stuart, "Aliens." After depicting the desirable immigrant in the first stanza, the speaker alerted Lady Columbia that "another brood is here," poised to "snatch your love and treasure" with their anarchism: "*Like snakes they glide in darkness, foul as ghouls that haunt the dead—/And yield no glad allegiance, save to bloody flags of red."* The poem, distributed widely, indexed an increasingly popular brand of patriotic Americanism and jingoism.[32]

The *Americanization Bulletin* and *Immigrants in America Review* reveal how Americanization enlisted the work of print in its attempt to spread Americanism across the country during one of the country's most vulnerable decades. The *Americanization Bulletin* was a weekly report on the progress of Americanization work, as reported by government agencies and private organizations. Because the federal work of Americanization was not yet centralized in 1915, Frances Kellor seized the opportunity to use print to educate readers about recent immigration and to express her belief in the necessity of Americanization. Kellor, the Americanization crusader, a lawyer turned social worker, was an authority on urban immigrants and immigration legislation and a public servant for the New York Commission on Immigration. She also set up the Division of Immigrant Education, a federal agency, which enabled the Committee for Immigrants in America to push for Americanization. Kellor also oversaw the American Association of Foreign Language Newspapers; in this role, she influenced the immigrant press with patriotic pieces and antiradical propaganda.[33]

Kellor promoted the crusade for Americanism through the short-lived publication the *Immigrants in America Review*, which exemplified nationalism at work in its one-sided approach to Americanization.[34] In 1915, *Immigrants in America Review* advanced the idea that education was "the single greatest factor in the Americanization of immigrants."[35] This paradigmatic shift held that one could become or be made into an American on the basis of education rather than race, ethnicity, or nationality. An American could be *made* in designated educational spaces (day and night schools) or through local and religious organizations (YMCA). When schooling or communal education failed or was insufficient, print culture—in English and immigrant languages—supplemented the education for Americanization. In 1918, the *Americanization Bulletin* expressed optimism that the foreign language "almanachs" published in the U.S. "will soon include Americanization propaganda in their texts."[36] According to Jeffrey Mirel, the foreign language press "promoted devotion to the U.S. and American democracy, a willingness to defend the country in time of peril, respect for law, civility in political discourse, active participation in political life, a commitment to equality, a respect for diverse points of view."[37] Federal support for Americanization, however, ended in 1919; by that time, the Bureau of Education had already closed its division of Americanization, and it published the last issue of the *Americanization Bulletin* in November 1919. State support for Americanization continued into the late 1920s.[38]

In addition to books by and about immigrants and reference works on immigration published in English, a series of pamphlets published in the 1910s taught immigrants about the U.S. *New Americans for New America: A Practical Program of Home Mission Education and Service* (1913) offered practical advice and reading recommendations, as well as references for readers interested in learning about "New Americans." A rubric of the pamphlet, the "Reference Library for Immigration," listed titles by immigrant authors like Mary Antin. Including in the pamphlet titles by "New Americans" as recommended studies of immigration suggests a more expansive consideration of immigrant authors than before. Besides Antin, the pamphlet referenced Steiner's books, *The Immigrant Tide* and *Against the Current*, as well as Jacob Riis's popular *The Making of an American*, Jane Addams's *The Spirit of Youth and the City Streets*, and Hamilton Holt's edition of *The Life Stories of Undistinguished Americans*.[39]

Immigrant guides were popular sources of knowledge on becoming American, and they often appealed to the self-taught immigrant who had neither time nor need for night school, one of the main paths toward naturalization. John Foster Carr's carefully crafted multilingual guide, *Guide to the United States* (1910–16), published in English, Italian, Yiddish, and Polish, offered advice on many topics, from societies helping new immigrants on arrival, to climate, geography, health, savings, weights and measurements, passports, learning English, the U.S. government, immigration laws, and naturalization (figure 26).

An author and lecturer, although not an immigrant himself, John Foster Carr (1869–1939) was a fervent proponent of the Americanization and education of immigrants. He was the founder and director of the Immigrant Publication Society, chartered in New York City in 1914, whose mission was "to rouse among the foreign-born an interest in America and to lead that interest on to enthusiasm for old-fashioned American ideals and for citizenship." Carr wrote his first guide at the

CAV. JOHN FOSTER CARR

G U I D A

DEGLI STATI UNITI
PER

L'IMMIGRANTE ITALIANO

PUBBLICATA A CURA
DELLA

SOCIETA' DELLE FIGLIE DELLA RIVOLUZIONE AMERICANA :

SEZIONE DI CONNECTICUT.

IMMIGRANT EDUCATION SOCIETY

241 Fifth Avenue, New York

1913.

Fig. 26. John Foster Carr, *Guide to the United States for the Immigrant.* Italian edition, 1913 [1910]. New York Public Library.

suggestion of the Royal Italian Immigration Commission and published it under the auspices of the Connecticut Daughters of the American Revolution, with the DAR emblem on the title page.[40] The English version of Carr's *Guide* included a section on "The Land of the Immigrant," which included information on different immigrant groups and their origins.[41] Carr's *Guide* began with the story of Christopher Columbus, with no mention of Native people, and ended by cautioning immigrants that interracial marriages were forbidden.[42] Indigenous people were conspicuously absent from pamphlets and guides for immigrants; if they were mentioned, it was to reinforce their "savagery" or need to be "civilized." This erasure of the country's Indigenous past amplified the settler nation's exceptionalist presentation to outsiders, sometimes through immigrant writers who internalized settler colonial discourse.

THE FOREIGN LANGUAGE PRESS
AND AMERICANIZATION

In her study of print culture in the age of nation building, Trish Loughran defines print as "American nationalism's preferred techno-mythology." The emergence of national print networks between 1820 and 1860, she argues, produced a cultural fragmentation.[43] At the end of the nineteenth century, the emergence of the immigrant press, in contrast, led to some sense of unity through shared ethnic language, although political, ideological, and religious differences persisted as immigrants built a parallel version of Americanization through the foreign language press. In 1922, sociologist Robert E. Park published *The Immigrant Press and Its Control*, a study of the foreign language press, highlighting its role in the acculturation of immigrants: "In America, as in Europe, it is language and tradition rather than political allegiance that unites the foreign populations."[44] Despite its purported sense of unity, the foreign language press also indexed fragmentation and resistance to assimilation. Whereas early studies of the immigrant press, such as Park's, focused on the question of assimilation—did the foreign language press slow down or accelerate assimilation?—recent studies have read the immigrant press as a site of ideological and identity formation. A case in point is the Hispanic immigrant press at the beginning of the twentieth century, which opposed assimilation. This resistance to Americanization characterized the newspapers of other immigrant groups, as well as other forms of expression, including literature. As Nicolas Kánellos and Kristen Silva Gruesz have shown, the underlying question of Hispanic immigrants was: why become an American citizen, when there was so much prejudice against immigrants?[45] Hispanic immigrants and their eastern European immigrant peers faced different forms of discrimination and prejudice, but they shared a common interest in dissent to Americanization in print.[46]

The foreign language press thrived in an era when newspapers educated the masses, as they also reported on social, political, economic, and cultural changes in the U.S. When the Literacy Act passed in 1917, a pivotal moment in the country's growing nativism, the U.S. had the highest number of non-English-language newspapers to date.[47] But weren't immigrants illiterate? Immigration and literacy were not entirely decoupled; as Rudolph Vecoli has shown, in the case of Italians, immigration was instrumental in the acquisition of literacy. As James Periconi has argued, "sufficiently literate in Italian in preparing to emigrate," Italian immigrants who arrived in the U.S. continued to read works in Italian and "used their modest skills in Italian to teach themselves English, at their own pace, 'without a teacher.'" The immigrants' ability to read grew, in response to the threat of a literacy test in the U.S. and as a skill to decipher information about work opportunities, immigrant manuals, or letters from home. Many immigrants in the US read and wrote. In 1900 alone, there were a thousand foreign language publications, with a circulation of over sixteen million.[48] In many ways, the foreign language press supplemented the Americanization work of the schools. But what we know less is how, like the public schools, foreign language newspapers were explicitly involved in Americanization education.

By 1920, the U.S. had 140 daily foreign language newspapers with a total circulation of almost 2 million; of these, 594 were weeklies, with over 3.6 million in circulation; 109 monthlies, with a circulation of 756,000; and 111 bilingual newspapers and periodicals.[49] Virtually every ethnic group in the U.S.—even small ones like Romanians and Lithuanians—published newspapers in their native languages. Romanian newspapers were published in the U.S. as early as 1905, with *The Romanian/Românul* (Cleveland) and *America*, the most influential Romanian American newspaper. A poem published in *The Romanian* in

1912, "D'Ale Noastre din America/Our America" by Vaida Rãceanul, captures the "tragedy of readjustment" other immigrant writers made central to their writings. In "Our America," the amateur poet pays homage to his adoptive country:

> Foaie verde ilion,
> In American sunt domn,
> Am salarul minunat,
> Ca acasã un deputat,
> Caştig douãzeci de coroane,
> Salonerul imi pune coarne,
> Ma incântã, mã descantã,
> Cu laude mã frãmântã.
> Iar eu ca sã-l mulţumesc
> Câte opt rânduri plãtesc.

Yet, the speaker also lists the immigrant's profound disappointment: "Wretched America / I used to be somebody / Till your road I took."[50] Foreign language publications like *The Romanian* allowed immigrant poets to express disappointment in America, an ethos foreign to English-language publications.

Similarly, the Yiddish modernist poets in New York, associated with such groups as *Di Yunge* (The Young) and *In Zikh* (The Introspectivists)—Mani Leib, Zisha Landau, Reuben Ayzland, Joseph Rolnick, and Moshe Leib Halpern—chose to write in Yiddish as a political act of dissimilation. Written in a language inaccessible to most American audiences, Yiddish poetry was markedly American in subject matter. It rendered the challenges of the industrial city; the streets; the diversity of people; the landscapes of California, Arizona, and New York; the trial of Sacco and Vanzetti; Central Park; and the American gangster. For these immigrants, language became their territory, the "Yiddishland" or "Yiddishkeit."[51] Although the choice of Yiddish limited their readership, the Yiddish poets used it for political and secular reasons. They invented an aesthetic tradition, placing their poetry on a par with their Euro-American modern(ist) peers.[52] Some poets of *Di Yunge* also published translations into Yiddish of Japanese, Chinese, Egyptian, and Arabic poetry, showing a range of interest in other artistic traditions, but with a keen interest in poetry. And, like many of their American contemporaries, Yiddish poets were also interested in American Indians.[53] They wrote about Native people with an acute awareness of the changing American landscape and pressures of modernity. Yiddish poets destabilized the immigrant genre par excellence—the life story—which dominated early immigrant literature in English (see chapter 6).

Immigrant identification with Indigenous suffering preceded the wave of new immigration to the United States in the 1880s. David Koffman has shown how Jewish immigrants have benefited, culturally and economically, from affiliations with Indigenous communities in the American West. Koffman reads the Jewish immigrants as "powerful agents of empire" and beneficiaries of settler colonial privileges (whiteness, citizenship, acquisition of land); as such, Jews imagined themselves between "red" and "white," resisting and participating in the colonial project aimed at eliminating the Native population and the acquisition of lands.[54] Yiddish-language poets of the Progressive Era occasionally ventriloquized Native voices to express solidarity. In Ruven Ludvig's "Indian Motifs" (1924), excerpted in the epigraph to this chapter, a Pima man takes the "palefaces" to task for seeking the desert village of a Pima tribe as a tourist attraction:

> Do not aim
> Your curiosity at *us*.
> . . . .
> Do not wake the wounds in *our* hearts.
> Do not bring the grief of mourners. (my emphasis)

Identification with the Pima man's message offers a moment of connection between immigrant displacement and Native dispossession and grief—albeit in Yiddish. The poem offers a glimpse into what I call a "convenient affiliation" between immigrant displacement and Native dispossession. Here, the Yiddish poet appropriates the voice of a Native speaker to delineate a convenient cross-ethnic and cross-racial affiliation of Jewish and Native suffering. Although, by the middle of the twentieth century, Jewish attitudes had shifted toward responsibility and advocacy for Native rights, Jewish immigrants joined other immigrant groups in using Native communities rhetorically and materially to showcase their settler superiority.

American and ethnic nationalisms coexisted in the cultural work of new immigrant groups and their publications. The publications of the *prominenti*, the Italian elite, indexed what other immigrant publications were doing at the time: dual loyalties to the country of origin and the U.S. Yet, as Rudolph Vecoli has shown, the anti-American bias of their newspapers led to frequent critiques of the U.S. as "crude, vulgar, and puritanical." Although some Italian language publications embraced Italian nationalist rhetoric—launching manifestos, campaigning on behalf of condemned Italians, or raising funds to erect statues—the journalists knew that many of their *paesani* were in America to stay. Italian-language newspapers (such as *Il Progresso Italo-Americano*, 1880–1982) condemned the abusive treatment of Italians and the lynchings of Italian immigrants in New Orleans in 1891 and condoned the behavior of Italian immigrants in the city, eager to win the respect of Americans. The *prominenti* used print culture to promote Americanization; in the process, they joined in what Vecoli calls "the invention of an Italian American ethnicity."[55] *Il Progresso Italo-Americano* was the most successful of Italian American newspapers in the U.S. Like other new immigrant groups—and like the Native American intellectuals—Italian immigrants used the Italian language press to promote a double allegiance: for *la patria* and for the United States.

Whereas the *prominenti* cultivated both forms of nationalism, the *sovversivi* or the anti-nationalists, challenged Americanization in their radical newspapers. The radicals believed in education, in the liberation of the workers' minds, and in the overthrow of capitalism. The working-class *sovversivi*, unlike the bourgeois *prominenti*, rejected Italian patriotism and American nationalism and chose not to promote the work of Americanizers. If the *prominenti* worshipped Columbus, the *sovversivi* venerated Giordano Bruno, the paragon of free thought. Instead of celebrating the Fourth of July, the radicals marked the anniversaries of the Paris Commune and the Haymarket martyrs. The Italian radical press in the U.S. was suppressed during World War I, and some of the radical newspaper editors were imprisoned or deported. After the war and during Mussolini's rise to power, the *prominenti* press was subsidized and controlled by the Fascist regime.[56] These divergent views of Americanization in the foreign language press reveal intra-ethnic group tensions and possibilities for new immigrants to fashion themselves into Americans.

In many ways, the foreign language press helped promote the work of Americanizers, yet editors of foreign language newspapers had some freedom in deciding the extent of their pro-Americanization rhetoric.

In August 1919, *La Follia* published "The Immigrant and American-ization," an article claiming that the Americanization movement was too paternalistic: "If we must Americanize our alien population, we must see to it that the process takes root from among the very people at whom it is aimed." Americanization was not a by-product of World War I, although the intensity of the movement heightened during the war: "Today all over the country the cry is Americanization. Newspapers, public and private organizations, industrial concerns, civic, religious, and political bodies, schools and universities, and all other conceivable units are making every effort to play their part."[57] In a letter sent to John Foster Carr, the author of multilingual guides for immigrants, a Lithuanian immigrant lamented: "Real Americanism doesn't consist of bigotry, the teaching of hatred and narrow-mindedness of the sort that our fathers experienced under the Czars and on account of which persecutions they have gone for the new world."[58] The foreign language press, along with the national press, had a real chance to re-frame Americanism and make its own contributions to the Americanization movement.

Case Study: The Chicago Foreign Language Press Survey

A close examination of immigrant periodicals collected in the Chicago Foreign Language Press Survey (CFLPS) reveals that the new immigrants' relation to nationalism depended on region (of emigration), religion, education and class, as well as familiarity with the English language and settler history. Some immigrant groups were articulate about what Americanization could do for their communities; others were just eager to become American. Publications printed in national languages conveyed messages in a familiar language, illegible to outsiders. Writing in Serbian, a Chicago immigrant lamented that English "was harder than stone" and noted that "Americans speak like toothless old women, like cows eating hay. . . . Your mouth must be twisted and your tongue squeezed in order to pronounce English words properly."[59] The writer's similes were basic, as was his knowledge of English, but would this writer have made the same observations in an English-language periodical at the time?

The CFLPS was a multi-institutional project to translate a selection of twenty-two Chicago foreign language newspapers, undertaken in the 1930s by the Works Progress Administration (WPA) of Illinois. Some of this work has been digitized and is now available for online searches.[60] The premise of this project was that nobody spoke all the languages of a large city like Chicago, whose foreign-born population in 1850 was higher than that of New York City. To understand Chicago was to understand the written records of its foreign language press over the previous century. In the decades leading up to the militant Americanization of the 1910s, these publications were illegible to American readers as well as to other immigrant groups. Although the CFLPS offers only a glimpse into the Chicago communities these publications represented, several common threads emerge.[61] Although the archive is incomplete and challenging, it is a key archive for studying immigrant perspectives and addressing immigrant communities directly.

Publications represented in the CFLPS shared common themes: sometimes they reiterated the patriotic messages of major national newspapers, taught their readers American history, or supported the immigrants' naturalization. As many immigrants arriving in the U.S. between 1890 and 1918 came from European empires (Russia or Austro-Hungary), and often from occupied territories, renouncing a European monarch was not a main concern: there was no (recognized) sovereign to renounce, which made American citizenship desirable. The CFLPS publications encouraged Americanization and naturalization, offering immigrants a sense of agency they could not enjoy under oppressive regimes. In 1891, the Polish *Dziennik Chicagoski* conceived of American citizenship as liberatory: "Those who have lived in bondage can seek freedom here. Here they breathe freely, and rest in peace, and here, with pride, they become citizens of a free country, which is not ruled either by a czar or knout."[62] Unlike native-born Americanizers, editors and writers of CFLPS newspapers expressed commitment to equality and respect for diverse points of view. A Polish newspaper showcased the loyalty of Polish fighters in World War I, which contrasted with a recent U.S. "imputation that we are less desirable American citizens because we have not sprung from the Nordics or Anglo-Saxons."[63] By 1923, Chicago's foreign language newspapers had taken a stance on a number of racial issues, from the racism of immigration legislation to race relations in the U.S.

Along with addressing the urgency of acquiring new information in the U.S. and responding to basic survival needs, the immigrant press offered a balance between the spoken and the written language, making information more accessible to the immigrants, who often faced literacy challenges in their native language as well as in English. In 1922, a Greek-language periodical in Chicago, *Greek Star,* praised the foreign language press for its "notable service in acquainting new arrivals with American ideals." Foreign language newspapers provided information for adapting to American life and culture. As early as the 1900s, a number of CFLPS publications denounced the lynchings of African Americans and immigrants in the South as a horrific contradiction to the American democratic ideals. The *Greek Star* described lynching as "a stain upon the brightness of American civilization."[64] Some publications were more zealous than others in conveying what Americanism was or should be. Almost two decades earlier, the same Greek-language newspaper had called for Americanizing newcomers: "It is not only beneficial to the individual to be educated in Americanism, but it is beneficial to us all, to our race, to our Mother Greece, and above all to the American commonwealth." Americanization was not only a way of surviving in the new country, but also a way of maintaining a sense of Greek identity away from "Mother Greece."[65]

Immigrant publications, nonetheless, were critical of Americanization. Lazar Churich, a Serbian immigrant in Chicago, wrote in the Serbian-language newspaper *Pamphlet* in 1907 about his "terrible mistake" of coming to America. The land was "cold" both physically and emotionally: "We must forget all that we have learned and we must, so to speak, be born again and transport ourselves into another world."[66] The Polish-language *Zgoda* also approached the issue head-on in an editorial titled "English Language vs. Polish Language" in 1897, expressing resistance to linguistic nationalism by asking fellow Polish immigrants, "In what case is the English language greater than ours?"[67] The editor reminded the readers that English was not the "original" language of the country, and that Americans themselves failed to speak "the language of the Apaches or the Sioux," whom the editor recognized as the original inhabitants of the land.[68]

A gap in the current scholarship on the immigrant press is the recurrent analogy of the "immigrant problem" with the "Indian problem." Such references and identifications translated mainstream derogatory associations with *Indians* as markers of savagery into convenient affiliations—strategies of identification, alliance building, and resistance to dominant ideologies of race and national identity. This proliferation of *Indian* tropes in "unexpected places," in Philip Deloria's term, reveals underexamined instances of cross-ethnic identification, appropriation, and occasional solidarity. As the number of immigrants grew drastically and the Native population was in a dangerous demographic decline, the presence of Native references in the foreign language press invites further scrutiny and questions. Were these references just *convenient* to immigrants? Were they exploitative and extractive? Were they similar or different from English-language and mainstream publications disseminating unflattering and ahistorical images of Native peoples? Were they accidental or timely? Native communities were certainly not vanishing from immigrant publications as the new immigrants themselves were trying to make sense of their own place on stolen Indigenous lands. Only occasionally did immigrant publications acknowledge their groups' complicity in settler history and its writing.

Different immigrant publications in the Chicago Foreign Language Press Survey resorted to different Native references for different purposes. In July 1911, the Greek *Loxias* used the analogy to shame Greek immigrants who refused to assimilate and to chastise them for clinging to the elaborate Christian Orthodox rituals, which were acceptable in Greece but not necessary in America: "We must not abuse the tolerance of our neighbors. *How should we like it if we Greeks lived near or within an Indian reservation, and while we were asleep, the Indians performed one of their queer dances, accompanied by Indian signing, as we Greeks do?*" Associating Greek religious practice with Native ceremonies as "queer dances"—to distance themselves further from proper, "American" rituals—the Greek newspaper commended the Native people who left the reservations and the "tom-tom dances" behind: "What ignorant, stubborn, selfish people we are! Indians who leave their reservations and live elsewhere have brains enough to discontinue their tom-tom dances." Referencing *Indian* savagery, the newspaper pleaded with readers to renounce antiquated religious practices and to embrace Americanization.[69] Here, references to Native people served as a rhetorical strategy for Greek immigrants, urging their peers to distance themselves from their own "savage" past as they entered an American present as potential citizens.

References to "Redskins" abounded in the publications in the CFLPS, whether as an intended slur or as the phrase du jour to refer to Indigenous people. The German-language publication *Illinois Staats Zeitung* published the piece "Indian Socialists" in 1881, arguing against what would later become the General Allotment Act of 1887, the legislation that hastened the dissolution of Native communities and caused an enormous loss of Indigenous land. Holding that Native people believed that land was the property of the community, not of individuals, the article ended by praising "the Redskins" and their resolve not to succumb to the lure of private land ownership, like their white peers, who might forget about socialism if offered free land.

Polish-language newspapers used the example of Native people as a cautionary tale for Poles: "The first citizens of this land—the Indians of various tribes—have fallen under the force of a strange culture, that they wane and die off gradually." Calling themselves the most resistant "tribe" of the "Polish race," who withstood competing imperial claims over their lands and cultures before immigrating to the U.S., the Poles have resisted assimilation: "Poles, even in foreign lands, will remain Poles; it is useless to think of assimilating them." The references to Indians here served to reaffirm Polish ethnic pride and nationalism, transplanted to the U.S.

In an 1891 editorial, the Polish *Dziennik Związkowy* reported on critiques of the U.S. government in the national English language press for its "inglorious war with the Indians" aimed at getting rid of "his red-skinned children." While maintaining a paternalistic tone, the editorial faulted the Indian agents on reservations for impoverishing many Native communities, noting that such disenfranchisement brought Native people "not only to despair, but almost to madness." Was this another instance of appropriation of Native grief and anger? Questioning the integrity of people appointed to public offices, the editorial ended by lamenting that governmental neglect and abuse may lead to the extinction of "the redskins"; it also called for order, a strategy close to the hearts of many Progressive Era thinkers: "This is the time for establishing order in the Republic of the republics." The critique of the U.S. civil service system and governmental neglect in a Polish language newspaper shows concern for fellow disenfranchised humans, a keen awareness of national journalistic reporting, and a deep political commitment to justice and the American republic.[70]

In sum, the references to Indigenous people in foreign language publications, like those in English language publications, reveal contradictory attitudes: on the one hand, reverence for a group presumed vanished or living in the past, on the other, nuanced expressions of simultaneous interethnic racism toward and solidarity with Native communities. An article in the Polish-language *Zgoda* in 1897 made anti-Indian racism unambiguous: "When Poland was fighting wars for its faith and glory, these uncivilized Indians over here were murdering themselves needlessly." The contradictory use of *Indian* tropes—as markers of savagery and as references to the "original Americans"—served to remind immigrant readers about the layered challenges to American exceptionalism posed by new immigrants and by Native peoples. In a piece advertising a Czech meeting against Prohibition in Chicago, the Bohemian newspaper *Denní Hlasatel* advertised a Native "reservation" in a Chicago park, a main attraction for a forthcoming immigrant meeting. The participants in the meeting, *Denní Hlasatel* held, would have the opportunity to witness Indian dishes cooked "Indian style" and served "by the most charming Indian maidens." In this case, the organizers sold the idea of the *Indian* as an exotic presence to attract viewers to a meeting protesting Prohibition. Bohemian immigrants in Chicago in 1922, like most urban Americans, would have recognized stereotypes of Native Americans from the Wild West shows or dime novels. Chicago had also hosted the World's Columbian Exposition in 1893, and memories of Indigenous people on display in "villages" and vitrines were not too distant for Chicagoans.[71]

In these examples of *Indian* tropes in the CFLPS, the new immigrant commitment to seek justice for fellow disenfranchised human beings is mutually constitutive rather than mutually exclusive: an immigrant group rallies against the mistreatment of American Indians, using the opportunity to critique the U.S. government and to show how the republic could be strengthened. But is this an instance of a patriotic pluralist rhetorical turn or yet another settler colonial moment serving the republic rather than the Native nations? In November 1922, the same Polish newspaper strengthened the idea of multiple immigrant allegiances in the editorial "American Patriotism." Starting from the premise that "in order to become an American patriot, one must be an Indian," the author offered this analogy as an homage to Indigenous peoples. To him, Native peoples were necessarily patriotic. He asked: "Is it possible to be a patriot of two countries simultaneously, for instance, of America and Ireland, of America and Germany, of America and Poland?"[72] And while the editorial ended by deferring a clear answer, it posed a key question at the heart of the foreign language press for the next decades. It also revealed an ongoing ignorance about a stark difference between Indigenous and immigrant ethnic groups, that the sovereignty of Native nations allows for a different political identity and relationship with the U.S. government than that of immigrant groups, old or new. This sovereign political identity is written into federal treaties signed with Native nations and rooted in mutual recognition of political identities, whereas ethnic and immigrant identities remain largely cultural and voluntary. In some cases, new immigrants decided against pursuing American citizenship, for political or cultural reasons, but continued to participate in American cultural citizenship by virtue of relocation to the U.S. The 1891 article in the Polish-language newspaper did not reveal an awareness of these issues; instead, it reproduced a settler colonial discourse of convenient affiliation and failed to understand the underpinnings of Indigenous versus immigrant (ethnic) political and cultural identity.[73] The version of Americanization that emerges from the newspapers in the CFLPS is uneven and complicated. While the editors and writers were against "100 per cent Americanism," CFLPS writers also embraced a cultural pluralism that aimed at keeping immigrant communities distinct from American society, and they often did so as proud Americans. The CFLPS writers and editors did not see a contradiction in being proud of their cultures and being patriotic Americans.

When the crusade for Americanism intensified between 1890 and 1915, Americanization education in grades K-12 and adult classes emphasized the teaching of English, history, and citizenship training. Once the U.S. entered World War I in 1917, anti-German sentiment temporarily shifted the focus of the Americanization campaign, targeting adult immigrants. By 1920, every school system serving immigrant students had incorporated Americanization into its curriculum.[74] Education also promised social mobility. But this economics of education depended on political power, most notably the combination of melting pot assimilationist views of immigration with those emerging from nativist factions, which favored Anglo-Saxonism over other national origins. After the National Origins Act passed in 1924, Americanization continued into the 1930s and 1940s. Despite occupational and educational quotas imposed on certain immigrant groups, the new generation of teachers and administrators—second- and third-generation immigrants themselves, the children of Jewish, Italian, and other new immigrant groups—were more attuned to student needs.[75] Educated in Americanism in a variety of settings, from night schools to universities, factories, and YMCAs, as well as self-taught, new immigrants joined the American reading ranks and participated, as readers and writers, in the growing American print culture.[76] Despite the stigma of the illiterate foreigner, immigrants in the U.S. read and wrote; some became famous writers in their time and in ours.

Supplementing the Americanization work of the schools, the foreign language press served the cultural needs created by displacement and provided a counterpoint to the nativist press. The immigrant press offered competing narratives of nationalism and patriotism at the heart of such American periodicals as the *Americanization Bulletin* and the *Immigrants in America Review*. It offered the new immigrants a grammar for navigating a new and unfamiliar diasporic space and also a contradictory way of preserving a sense of immigrant community while navigating—and often endorsing—the ethos of Americanization. Addressing the urgency of acquiring new information in the U.S. and responding to basic survival needs, the immigrant press made information accessible to the immigrants; it provided information about homelands and about how to adapt to American life and culture, as immigrants created their own version of Americanization. The foreign language press thrived in an era when newspapers educated the masses as they also reported on social, political, economic, and cultural changes in the U.S. These publications also indexed fragmentation, tension, and resistance to Americanization, as both American and ethnic nationalisms coexisted in the cultural work of new immigrant groups.

5 Americanization on Native Terms

The Society of American Indians,
Citizenship Debates, and Tropes
of "Racial Difference" in Native
Print Culture

I'm not the new Indian; I'm the old Indian adjusted to new conditions.

—Laura Cornelius Kellogg, at the First Conference of the Society of
American Indians, 1911

The very fact that we exist as a Society and that we publish a periodical
is an answer to the question of what the modern Indian is.

—Arthur C. Parker, *American Indian Magazine*, 1916

You have robbed, you have mistreated, and you have not bestowed
upon your red brother who gave you food, a place to lay your head and
took you as a child from the Great Spirit, the very principles that you
are fighting for.

—Carlos Montezuma, *Wassaja*, 1918

IN OCTOBER 1911 local newspapers in Columbus, Ohio, reported
on a remarkable gathering of Native Americans. The Society of American Indians (SAI) met on Columbus Day, an irony the newspapers
failed to notice.[1] The SAI was also greeted by local chapters of patriotic organizations—the Ohio Daughters of Pocahontas and the Improved Order of Red Men—which presented the attendees with small
American flags as souvenirs. The effervescence of American patriotism
reached its peak when, as the newspapers noted, SAI members sang

"America" on top of a mound, followed by "an impromptu war dance on the same elevation."[2] In the following years, the SAI would stage its own Native pageants, a growing national attraction.[3] But why would a group of professional, articulate Native men and women, wearing western clothes, intone "My Country, 'Tis of Thee," a song so antithetical to the scope of the SAI—"the revival of the natural pride of origin, the pride of the race," as penned by its first president, Reverend Sherman Coolidge?[4]

For students of Native history, it is hard, although not impossible, to imagine a few Native men doing a war dance on top of a sacred mound during the SAI's first meeting. But the Native men and women gathered on the campus of Ohio State University in 1911 had different wars to wage with white America, and their decision to sing a patriotic song before dancing a traditional dance indicated their strategic use of public spaces and performance on multiple local and national scenes. Contemporary Native critics like Robert Warrior find this image troublesome, and rightly so: "Apropos their widely shared belief in the passing by the wayside of older forms of Indianness, we could caption this photo, ironically, 'The End of History.'" Yet, not all the Native people present at this meeting of the SAI shared the belief in the passing of "older forms of Indianness." Laura Cornelius Kellogg, an Oneida from Wisconsin and SAI founding member, claimed unambiguously, "I'm not the new Indian; I'm the old Indian adjusted to new conditions," in an attempt to bridge the old with the new.[5] Yet, we may read the irony of this performance and its strategic use of Americanness in less apocalyptic terms than Warrior. Yes, the patriotic local societies welcomed the Native intellectual elite to Columbus by presenting them with American flags. But because national patriotic societies and nationalist pageants, flag exercises, and other public displays of patriotism were staples of the Progressive Era Americanization performances, we could construe this episode as a *simultaneous* reaffirmation of both American and Native nationalisms. When the SAI members performed in Columbus they expressed competing nationalisms, American and Native allegiances. On one hand, they expressed a deep commitment and allegiance to Native nations; on the other, a strategic commitment to the settler nation.[6]

The Native intellectuals of the Progressive Era—the "Red Progressives"—used a common analogy of the European immigrant to argue for citizenship and sovereignty: the immigrant could become a citizen, why not the Indian? The most politically active and savvy members of the SAI argued for political integration rather than erasure of Native identities and sovereignty through a blind replication of the imagined model of immigrant Americanization. Not only were the Indigenous Progressives more critical of Americanization than scholars have credited them, but by subverting and rewriting the mainstream discourses on "racial difference," they also authored Americanization on Native terms.

In this chapter I argue that two competing nationalisms, American and Indian—often overlapping—were at the heart of the spirited debates over American citizenship during the Progressive Era. I consider the cultural work and print culture of Native intellectuals affiliated with the Society of American Indians, the first pan-Indian national organization with an agenda for the political and intellectual future of Native communities nationally at the beginning of the twentieth century.[7] I focus here on several key SAI figures: Gertrude Bonnin, Carlos Montezuma, Arthur C. Parker, Charles Eastman, and Laura Cornelius Kellogg. I read the activist and print work of the SAI to show how Native intellectuals negotiated rhetorical practices to educate readers about Native history, culture, and resilience. In time, some Native intellectuals parted ways with the SAI for political or philosophical reasons, but they continued to argue for Native rights and American citizenship in other venues.[8] In particular, the nuanced yet central debates over citizenship in the SAI journal and in Carlos Montezuma's political newspaper, *Wassaja*, show that despite the procedural disagreements and tension in the organization—Carlos Montezuma quit the SAI, Laura Cornelius Kellogg was ousted—a constant element on the SAI print agenda was the question of what American citizenship meant for Native people. Reading these debates over citizenship in the larger national context of pro-Americanization raises further questions about the SAI members' relative pro-citizenship stance and Native communities' more critical views—and sometimes rejection—of American citizenship. The Native intellectuals discussed in this chapter were advocating for citizenship as an end to wardship as Native communities were arguing that the imposition of U.S. citizenship was a threat to tribal status and Indigenous sovereignty. Yet these two views are not necessarily diametrically opposed, as K. Tsianina Lomawaima has rightly argued; American citizenship and Native sovereignty were not mutually exclusive. Citizenship would also allow Native people to argue their cases in the U.S. courts.

In a letter to Carlos Montezuma in 1921, Jane Gordon amplified this claim: "Give citizenship to all Indians with equal rights (to go into the courts) with any other race or people here in the United States."[9]

A reexamination of the SAI publications as an archive mapping the SAI's rhetorical changes over the years affords a new opportunity to trace Indigenous arguments about "racial difference" and citizenship. In particular, this archive illuminates how Native writers and intellectuals used both the race rhetoric of the day and analogies to contemporary ethnic groups as they argued for citizenship and an end to wardship. A closer examination of how the SAI journal, the *Quarterly Journal of the Society of American Indians* (1913–16), later the *American Indian Magazine* (1916–20), and Carlos Montezuma's *Wassaja* (1916–22), reveals the rhetorical changes on the issue of citizenship among the Red Progressives over the years. These Native periodicals, although different in scope—and part of a strong Native periodical culture preceding and following the Progressive Era—offer a powerful counterpoint to the Americanization campaigns led by white progressive organizations. In 1916, the SAI journal's total circulation, for instance, included 207,300 copies of individual essays, as well as information booklets, annual platforms, conference announcements, posters, and copies of previous journal issues disseminated from 1911 to 1916. As Arthur C. Parker intimated, "This amount of literature poured into the minds and hearts of the American public cannot have helped but to effect a change in sentiment toward the Indian."[10] In contrast, as the last section of the chapter shows, Carlos Montezuma's *Wassaja* offered not just a critique of settlers' and immigrants' easier paths to assimilation and Americanization, but signaled the deficient ways that the U.S. addressed the so-called Indian problem in relation to the immigrant problem. The radical *Wassaja,* with its daring tone and appeal to Native and non-Native readers—an instance of "Indigenous editorial sovereignty" in its vision and control over the printed matter—left a strong print legacy of pro-citizenship arguments, pleas for political belonging, and Native recognition in a settler nation.

THE SAI: "AN UNFINISHED EXPERIMENT"

Initially called the American Indian Association, the SAI (1911–23) was the first pan-Indian national organization. Its platform expressed high hopes for the political and intellectual future of Native communities nationally.[11] Recent scholarship in American Indian and Indigenous studies has examined the SAI in the context of pan-Indianism, federal Indian policy, and American Indian intellectual history, from the ground-breaking work of Hazel Hertzberg to more recent work by Robert Warrior, Lucy Maddox, David Martinez, Kevin Bruyneel, Kiara M. Vigil, and K. Tsianina Lomawaima. Problematic as the SAI may appear in its optimism for progress and uplift, it differed from other Indian reform organizations in its response to the paternalism of white reformers. Whereas Indian reform organizations like the Lake Mohonk Conference framed citizenship as a *gift*, a culmination of the Americanization campaigns, the intellectuals of the SAI were interested in the effects of American citizenship on tribal citizenship and Native sovereignty. K. Tsianina Lomawaima, for instance, has shown how we can begin to understand citizenship and sovereignty as mutually constitutive rather than mutually exclusive categories: "From our twenty-first century perspective, the SAI's actions and imagination inspire possibilities of multiple, layered, mutually enriching citizenships, as well as multiple, layered partner sovereigns." For some SAI intellectuals, citizenship was the answer to questions about Native status, the promise of participatory democracy, a way out of federal paternalism, and the promise of a voice in determining Native future; for others, it was a strategic use of contemporary patriotic pluralist discourse to address and express Indigeneity.[12] From its inception in 1911, the SAI gathered an exceptional Native membership from various professions and tribal backgrounds: Marie Bottineau Baldwin (Ojibwe), Sherman Coolidge (Arapaho), Charles Eastman/Ohiyesa (Sioux), Carlos Montezuma/Wassaja (Yavapai), Charles Daganett (Peoria), Thomas L. Sloan (Omaha), Laura (Minnie) Cornelius Kellogg (Oneida), Arthur C. Parker (Seneca), Gertrude Bonnin/Zitkala-Ša (Yankton Sioux), Henry Standing Bear (Lakota Sioux), Henry Roe Cloud (Ho-Chunk), and others.[13]

The SAI journal attempted to promote Native "enlightenment," to provide a forum for addressing the welfare of Native people, "to present in a just light the true history of the race" and to preserve its records, to promote and fight for citizenship and the rights of citizen Indians, to establish a legal department to investigate Indian problems, "to exercise the right to oppose any movement that may be detrimental to the race," and to "provide a bureau of information, including publicity and statistics."[14] Concerned with disseminating accurate information about Native tribes to both American and Native readers, the SAI emphasized *the true history of the race*, in opposition to the popular representations of Native people. One main platform was citizenship: American citizenship alongside tribal citizenship, the end of wardship, and Native rights. The SAI wanted to show white America that Native values, epistemologies, and philosophies were as complex as those of people of European ancestry.[15]

When the SAI met at Ohio State University in 1911, Arthur C. Parker—SAI founding member, secretary, and longtime editor of the SAI journal—called the organization "an unfinished experiment. . . . an acid test . . . a demonstration of the qualities of the race."[16] He frequently meditated on the role of the SAI and its journal in creating the "modern Indian": "The very fact that we exist as a Society and that we publish a periodical is an answer to the question of what the modern Indian is."[17] Defining the "modern Indian" for the modern American readership was vital to enlisting support for Native political causes: citizenship and an end to wardship, autonomy, assertion of Native leadership and agency, and control over Native representation. Michelle Patterson reads the SAI members' actions as an exploitation of non-Native interest in Native culture to advance Native goals, where SAI members "carefully tread a line between pandering to a white image of 'the Indian' and advancing their own model of the acculturated Indian American."[18] Modern Americans were already exploiting *Indian* tropes in search of an "authentic" life that rapid modernization and city life could no longer offer. But perhaps a strategic use of non-Native resources and human capital characterizes better the SAI agenda than mere "pandering." Vocal SAI founding members like Montezuma and Cornelius Kellogg opposed the *Indian* of the white imagination and offered sustainable models of what Kellogg called "[old Indians] adjusted to new conditions."[19] Adjustment characterized the work of the SAI. Presenting the image of the confident "Progressive Indian American" to the world in the first issue of the *Quarterly Journal* in 1913, the SAI introduced readers to a drawing epitomizing the SAI's vision of the modern Native man (figure 27).

Drawn by non-Native artist Harold Bierce, the Progressive Indian American appeared strategically at the end of a section titled "The Indian in Caricature," which reproduced caricatures from national

The Progressive Indian American
Drawn by Harold Bierce for the *Journal.*

Fig. 27. "The Progressive Indian American" by Harold Bierce, *Quarterly Journal of the Society of American Indians* (1913). Newberry Library, Chicago.

newspapers. In contrast to the duped, poor, neglected *Indian* of the national press, the Progressive Indian American showed a confident Native man dressed in citizens' clothes, wearing the emblem of the SAI on his lapel, "the star of hope" and "the new beacon of light for the race." The Progressive Indian American "found that education, thrift, and adjustment to [new] conditions bring health and prosperity. . . . This man is not less an Indian because he has discovered the secret of success as an American in his own country."[20] Read against the caricatures of the period, this representation of the Progressive Native American was perhaps the SAI's subtle version of the imagined modern Indian, although SAI members often disagreed on what modernity was or should be for Native communities. Although the definition of the "modern Indian" changed over the years, often creating tensions between the members—

those who advocated a quick leap into "civilization," those who sought a middle ground between Indigeneity and modernity, and those with strong ties with their communities—most SAI members engaged modernity and its discontents, often in the pages of the SAI journal.

THE PRINT DEBATES OVER CITIZENSHIP AND AMERICANIZATION IN THE SAI JOURNAL

At its second national conference, in 1912, the SAI resolved to publish a journal devoted to the history of Native people and their place in American culture and history. A Native journal was certainly no aberration at the time; between 1826 and 1924, over two hundred Native newspapers and periodicals were published by nonsectarian and sectarian presses, government-supported presses, and by the American Indian and Alaska Native press.[21] The journal displayed the SAI's political and cultural commitments, with literature as a secondary—or even tertiary—interest, although some of its members were published writers. For the first time on a national scale, a Native journal was devoted to such issues as "race ethos," wardship, education, autonomy, the assertion of Native leadership, and citizenship.

If we focus our attention on the SAI's radical visions of Native modernity in the context of the push for Americanization, what do we learn about this new era in Native representation?[22] As Arthur C. Parker, the journal's first editor, explained in the first issue, published in 1913, "Never before has an attempt been made on the part of a national Indian organization to publish a periodical devoted to the interest of the entire race."[23] Although one organization could not represent the interests of all Native communities, the journal was committed to bringing "the interest of the entire race" to a national readership. The SAI motto, inscribed on the official stationery, held that "the honor of the race and the good of the country shall be paramount." Initially titled the *Quarterly Journal of the Society of American Indians* (1913–16), it changed its name to the *American Indian Magazine* (1916–20) to reflect the interest in reaching a larger readership, but it continued to include the original journal title on the title page in smaller font.

The journal presented itself as the official organ of the Society of the American Indians, with the motto: "For the Honor of the Race and the Good of the Country." Published by the American Indian Magazine

Publishing Committee of the Society of the American Indians, it was edited by three prominent SAI members—Arthur C. Parker (1913–18), Gertrude S. Bonnin (1918–19), and Thomas L. Sloan (1919–20)—and was devoted to the "immediate needs relating to the advancement of the Indian race in enlightenment." The bylaws also held that it would not publish fiction and historical accounts unless there was enough space.[24] Prominent SAI members were contributing editors, listed on the journal's first pages throughout its publication.[25] The journal's subtitle also saw a subtle change in January 1917, under Parker's editorship, from *A Journal of Race Ideals* to *A Journal of Race Progress*.[26] The transition from "race ideals" to "race progress" reveals an awareness of the journal's potential to document and enact change, from aspiration ("race ideal") to action ("race progress"). As correctives, articles by Native writers of various backgrounds offered Native views of Native cultures. Chauncey Yellow Robe's "The Menace of the Wild West Show" (1914) decried the offensive representations of Native people in a low-brow form of entertainment. Poems and short fiction gradually made their way into the journal after 1916, when it grew more eclectic in vision and politics.[27] This added feature showed readers a facet of Native writers the journal had neglected: the literary.

The SAI members wrote about Native communities and the challenges they faced. Gertrude Bonnin's work on reservations in the West also shaped her vision of the journal, which she had criticized for "concentrating too much on the abstraction of theory and policy," thus limiting its reservation audience. In 1916, writing from Fort Duchesne, Utah, to Parker, Bonnin proposed that "someone should write an *Uncle Tom's Cabin* for the Aborigine. . . . The task would be too difficult for an Indian. The perspective, entirely too close. I can hardly write a few pages of a report on conditions in one agency without being nearly consumed with indignation and holy wrath."[28] Bonnin expressed the Native writer's affective impasse in her difficulty to detach emotionally from her lived reality. Another Native activist and writer, Laura Cornelius Kellogg, professed in 1903 that "literature shall be my life work, and its aim shall be to benefit my people."[29] But after many disappointments, including the factionalism within the SAI that led her to part ways with the organization in 1913, she dedicated her life to social work, deferring her literary plans: "Later, *when my people are happier*, I hope to show that the quality of the Indian imagination has a place among the literatures of nations."[30] Although Kellogg devoted most of her life to political and activist work, she was a passionate writer and, had she not devoted much of her life to pursuing the land claims for the Six Nations, she might have rivaled Bonnin's literary accomplishments, as newspaper accounts in the 1910s intimated.[31]

In the early 1910s, few Native writers had access to the columns of mainstream newspapers and magazines. The SAI journal offered an alternative forum for voicing concerns over citizenship, racial justice, the future of American Indians, and similar issues.[32] Besides articles on these subjects and conference proceedings, the SAI journal published editorials, letters, announcements, and reprints from national and international newspapers.[33] Owned by the SAI, the journal was not a money-making scheme; it carried no advertisements, its editors and mail clerks received no salary, and it received no help from the government."[34] Appeals to subscribers were published periodically, sometimes in poem form—"I'll send the S.A.I. a dollar, I'll send one often too,/And when I can I'll make it ten, to show my colors true."[35]

The run of the SAI journal coincided with contemporaneous weekly and monthly publications of government schools, including Carlisle Indian School (Pennsylvania), Hampton Institute (Virginia), Haskell Institute (Kansas), Chilocco Indian School (Oklahoma), among others. Occasionally, the journal advertised the boarding school publications. A rubric in the June 1916 issue, "With Our Contemporaries," praised the work of contemporary publications such as the *Native American* (Phoenix Indian School), the *Indian Leader* (Haskell Institute), and the *Red Man* (Carlisle).[36] To promote other Native publications, the *American Indian Magazine* advertised Carlos Montezuma's *Wassaja*, which he started in Chicago in 1916.[37] For the first time in Native history, the SAI had a forum to voice and disseminate ideas nationally and internationally. A letter from a Danish writer to Arthur C. Parker documents the journal's popularity internationally.[38] The choice of the journal's masthead and the SAI emblem—an eagle on the left and a lighted torch to the right—changed little over the years. Ho-Chunk artist Angel DeCora chose the copper eagle to symbolize "the reawakened activity of the race and its determination through wisdom, courage, and foresight." The eagle was an object of veneration by ancestors and a symbol of wisdom and courage: "The Old Indians say that the eagle is the only bird that can fly in the face of the sun and look into its blazing countenance without closing its eyes; the *eagle can face the light, unafraid*."[39]

After six years (1912–18) Parker stepped down as the SAI journal's editor, and Gertrude Bonnin took over for a brief stint (1918–19), and during her tenure the journal's contents reflected her strong belief in the power of print to influence public opinion.[40] Under her editorship, the winter 1917 issue, a "Special Sioux Number," featured essays by the Sioux intelligentsia of the day, including Chauncey Yellow Robe, S. M. Brosius, and Charles Eastman. This strategic focus on Indigenism was balanced by a larger national focus in the following year. In the autumn 1918 issue, published also under Bonnin's editorship, Chauncey Yellow Robe wrote an impassioned plea for Americanization; a former student at Carlisle, he extolled the patriotism of Native soldiers fighting overseas, many of them not yet American citizens: "We must Americanize our glorious America under one government, one American language for all, one flag, and one God." Yellow Robe's patriotic appeal in 1918 was consistent with the journal's and the SAI's work in 1918, advocating for citizenship as an end to wardship. The same issue of the journal published the text of the proposed Indian Citizenship Bill, which would not pass for six more years, as well as excerpts from the *Congressional Record*.[41]

Thomas Sloan took over his one-year editorship in 1919 with renewed faith in the publication's appeal to a national audience. In a letter to General Hugh L. Scott in June 1920, Sloan described the journal as "a monthly publication . . . devoted entirely to the interests of the North American Indian, and which in literary and artistic quality will rank as the equal of such publications as *Harper's, Century, Scribner's, National Geographic, Asia*, and other periodicals appealing to the highest type of reader."[42] In a 1916 editorial, Parker reaffirmed the idea of the journal's appeal: "We are reaching outward as well as inward. . . . If the universities and libraries of civilization find within our pages real contributions to science, literature, history, sociology, education, and philosophy, these centers of culture will radiate a greater respect for the Red race." Throughout three different editorships, the journal maintained a vision for a national readership and its potential to instill "a greater respect for the Red race."[43] Despite Sloan's hopeful vision, the SAI journal soon published its last issue; it had a short life, like many of the period's "little magazines."[44]

What distinguished the SAI journal from publications controlled by the federal government, however, was the Native intellectuals' control of their representation as they presented themselves to the world by carefully crafting their writing, addressed to a predominantly white readership. Scott R. Lyons calls this strategy "rhetorical sovereignty" or "the inherent right and ability of peoples to determine their communicative needs and desires . . . to decide for themselves the goals, modes, styles, and languages of public discourse."[45] The SAI journal—a politically savvy and activist forum—was part of a long tradition of Native writing in English since the eighteenth century.[46] One of the SAI's aspirations was to mediate between white and red America, to "give to each an understanding of the other."[47]

The SAI journal was in high demand, and the presentation of issues nicely bound in royal morocco attests to the imagined legacy of an organization that put print culture, its preservation, and dissemination at the center of its campaign to reform its readership and change public opinion.[48] The SAI used Americanism strategically in marketing its journal. In 1915, the editor described the issues of the *Quarterly Journal* as "Books of Unquenchable Americanism" (figure 28). The bound volumes, with the title page displaying the writing plume and copper eagle as SAI emblems, reveal the Native intellectuals' idea of permanence not only in the American imaginary but also in American print culture.

If the primary goal of the SAI was to "develop and organize men and women of Indian blood as wise leaders of their race," how did Americanism fit into their plan?[49] What made it especially unquenchable? Like this statement, the meaning of Americanism itself is historically contingent, grounded in the sociopolitical moment of the 1910s, and addressing an audience sensitive to the nuances of nationalism. The putatively genuine Americanism was premised on hostility to non-Americans and foreigners: either one was an American, or one was not welcomed into the nation.[50] To position themselves in the national debates—especially over American citizenship and Native rights—the SAI intellectuals appropriated the lingo of American patriotism to suggest, perhaps, an equally "unquenchable" Indigenism.

The arguments over citizenship in the SAI journal were shaped by their political moment—before, during, and after World War I—as well as the editorial vision of each of the three journal editors (Parker,

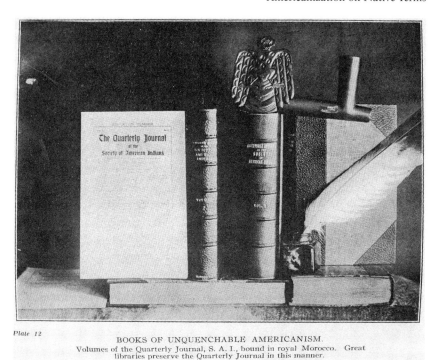

Plate 12

BOOKS OF UNQUENCHABLE AMERICANISM.
Volumes of the Quarterly Journal, S. A. I., bound in royal Morocco.   Great
libraries preserve the Quarterly Journal in this manner.

Fig. 28. "Books of Unquenchable Americanism," *Quarterly Journal of the Society of American Indians* (1915). Newberry Library, Chicago.

Bonnin, and Sloan). In 1917, as Native men joined the war effort in World War I as Americans—albeit noncitizens de jure—the Native intellectuals' attention was galvanized, as never before, around the issue of citizenship. As they positioned themselves within the debates over racial uplift alongside African Americans (the American Negro Academy, founded in 1897, of which W. E. B. Du Bois was a prominent member), the SAI intellectuals also made Native reform and citizenship their central goals.[51]

In the early years of the journal, the issues tackled ranged from religious exhortations about good citizenship to progressive arguments for "standing on a par with the best intellects of other races" (Fred E. Parker) and making way for "competent" and "efficient" citizenship (Arthur C. Parker), to the perceived incongruence of reservation life with modern citizenship (Montezuma), and legal arguments and roadmaps toward citizenship (Arthur C. Parker, Hiram Chase). Other key terms in these discussions included: "real independent citizenship" (Pratt), full citizenship, and the transformation of "potential" into "actual citizens" (Bonnin).[52] In a 1914 editorial, Arthur C. Parker argued that Native people needed preparation for U.S. citizenship; he also argued for the formation of a presidential commission that would "study existing laws," demanding Native representation at the negotiation table. The same issue reprinted a letter from President Howard Taft, expressing his support for a Native "voice" yet cautioning readers that citizenship came with responsibilities.[53]

Besides original essays and speeches by SAI members, the journal reprinted articles from national journals, newspapers, and magazines to insert the SAI conversation into the national debate over citizenship. Before the SAI meeting in Cedar Rapids, Iowa, in 1916, one local paper included an article titled "Citizenship Is the Theme of Talks by Indians."[54] When Native soldiers started fighting in World War I, the rhetoric of the SAI journal changed to patriotic appeals ("Make Them Citizens"), detailed reviews of proposed legislation—the three citizenship bills introduced in Congress—and the Indian Citizenship Campaign of 1919, a series of lectures by then SAI president Charles Eastman.[55] In a letter to SAI members, Eastman decried the overwhelming control of the Indian Bureau; with renewed faith in the mission of the SAI, he declared, "we are not a 'dying race'; we are alive and asking for our share of the liberty and democracy that we have fought for."[56] The SAI's eighth conference, held in Minneapolis in 1919, went so far as to use the slogan "American Citizenship for the Indian."[57] Even after the last issue of the journal saw print in August 1920, SAI intellectuals continued to advocate for citizenship, which was eventually granted to all Native people through the Indian Citizenship Act of 1924.

Why was citizenship one of the SAI's most powerful platforms? For one, it addressed consistently and forcefully the incongruity between the nationalist fervor toward Americanization and the incomplete citizenship model imagined for Native people. In the preface to the *Proceedings* of the SAI's first meeting, the SAI called for unified action to fight dependence, wardship, and poverty. In this Indigenous manifesto, "the thinking Indian of today" asked that, "he [sic] be treated as an *American*" to rise "to positions of the highest honor and responsibility . . . to develop normally as an American people in America."[58] The

seeming erasure of Indigeneity from the SAI plea may ring false to contemporary readers, who may read it as pro-Americanization. This is
also one of the main critiques of the SAI in our own time, as it was
in theirs. As Lucy Maddox argues, "The effort of Native Progressive
Era intellectuals to insert Indian history and local Indian issues into
a universal framework anticipated the kind of questions scholars of
American Indian histories and cultures are still asking about the American public's resistance to taking American Indian intellectualism seriously."[59] Arthur C. Parker's vision for the journal reveals a clear sense
of its audience. Sherman Coolidge's presidential address at the second
conference also called attention to Native civic responsibility by subtly changing the terms and privileging one identity over the national
category ("the Indian American") and by appealing to white America's Christian beliefs to call attention to the incompleteness of Native
citizenship.[60]

Despite occasional procedural disagreements and later factionalism
surrounding such issues as the Indian Office, peyote, and the SAI's handling of specific complaints raised by tribes, SAI members were more
or less united by the idea of citizenship. Many asked whether a uniform U.S. citizenship would allow for retention of federal protection
of Native lands and other rights. American citizenship, yet another settler colonial imposition, did not restore Native lands nor did it erase
wardship. Whereas the blanket naturalization offered by the ICA in
1924 may be read as a corrective to earlier exclusionary legislation,
citizenship for Native people proved to be an afterthought in U.S. naturalization law. Not only was there no uniform policy in place until
1924, but the ICA passed in 1924 *after* the Immigration Act, just as
Native soldiers who fought in World War I were naturalized months
after their immigrant peers who fought in the same war.[61] Considering that about two-thirds of American Indians were already citizens,
naturalized through previous treaty provisions, land allotments, and
statutory measures, the question remains: why did the SAI intellectuals
continue to advocate for citizenship?[62]

To begin to answer this question, we may consider first the lack of
Indigenous participation and agency in determining Native consent
to citizenship. The SAI sought universal citizenship for Native people
"as a way of alleviating the perennial problems caused by the reservation system."[63] As citizenship was the goal of progressive organizations

nationwide seeking to Americanize and homogenize in the context of high immigration from southern and eastern Europe, it became the main preoccupation in SAI rhetoric. The Red Progressives could not only "talk back to civilization," as Frederick Hoxie put it, but also write back to civilization, often borrowing the rhetoric of "civilization" and "racial difference" to assert Native presence and sovereignty.[64]

The uncertain legal status of Native people was one of the driving forces of the SAI citizenship debates. A pamphlet published in 1912, *The Indian and Citizenship*, by Fayette McKenzie, a sociology professor at Ohio State, called attention to Native people's lack of legal status, "perpetual inhabitant[s] with diminutive rights." This "condition of confusion in Indian affairs," McKenzie argued, was "intolerable."[65] Native people's legal status was a shared concern of SAI members. In 1912 the SAI drafted the Carter Indian Code Bill, introduced in the House of Representatives by Chickasaw congressman Charles D. Carter, spelling out the terms of citizenship. Arthur C. Parker also lobbied the Lake Mohonk Conference for support: "The Indian as neither citizen nor foreigner has occupied . . . a precarious position in our national life." Ultimately, Congressman Carter failed to gain support for the Carter Bill in 1912.[66]

The early issues of the *Quarterly Journal* argued for citizenship and for adjusting the legal status of "the Indian of the present," whose ability was "on a par with the best intellects of other races," as "the Indian citizen of to-day is an honor to his race."[67] A year later, Gabe E. Parker called for abandoning tribal relations altogether as Native people assumed the "responsibilities of American citizenship."[68] Most active SAI members remained ambivalent about the role of the reservation in advancing American citizenship. Carlos Montezuma became the reservation's most vocal enemy. In his speech to an SAI regional meeting in 1914, Montezuma referred to reservations as prisons, reiterating that just like the immigrants, Native people must learn to speak English, attend public schools, and immerse themselves in "civilization" to become American citizens.[69] In this line of argument, citizenship was desirable for Native people, yet its terms were somewhat nebulous.

From its inception, the SAI promoted the acquisition of citizenship "on a voluntary basis," yet it continued to emphasize the disparity between Native rights and the rights of the naturalized new immigrants. In his address "The Law and the American Indian" (1912), Judge

Hiram Chase argued that citizenship acquisition should be voluntary. Chase claimed that the naturalization of Native people could borrow from the immigrant model.[70] This idea was repeatedly rehearsed in the Carlisle student publications and in Pratt's correspondence with Carlos Montezuma. For the most part, the SAI publications endorsed Pratt's views and often printed his bombastic prose. In a provocative article in 1914, Pratt blamed the Indian Bureau: "Can't you see that Indian civilization and real independent citizenship means death to the Indian system? The so-called 'Indian Problem' has always been the *Indian System*, never the Indian."[71] Some SAI members agreed. Other Native activists like Eastman, Parker, and Bonnin envisioned a political future for Native nations different from Pratt's.[72] Pratt's argument for the transformation of Native people into self-supporting Americans, ready to engage with the competitive market and capital, was a favorite topic of at least two SAI members: Carlos Montezuma and Arthur C. Parker.

Although Parker's pro-citizenship stance in his editorials became more pronounced over the years, by 1915 the SAI had not made much progress toward citizenship and changing government policies. In a 1916 issue of the *American Indian Magazine*, Parker reprinted Theodore Roosevelt's piece "Indian Citizenship," where the former president called for "preparing" Native people for citizenship and cautioned that this process would take time.[73] Roosevelt's anti-Indian rhetoric and policy were consistent with his legacy as an "Indian-hater" president. His vision of Americanization—while seemingly welcoming all ethnicities into a great American melting pot—was one of "forced Americanization." For Native people, it meant forced Christianization, education, the breaking up of reservation land into individual allotments, and citizenship.[74]

In 1917, when Congressman Carl Hayden of Arizona introduced a new Indian citizenship bill in Congress (a rather controversial one, with stipulations for gradual taxation), editorials about citizenship continued to take center stage in the *American Indian Magazine*. When the U.S. entered World War I, the tenor of the journal became patriotic, as thousands of Native soldiers were drafted or volunteered to fight in the war. In their correspondence before the 1917 SAI conference, Arthur C. Parker, then president, and Gertrude Bonnin, secretary, planned a program that would include the slogan "The American

Indian in Patriotism, Production, Progress." However, after intense preparations, the SAI conference, projected to take place at the University of Oklahoma in 1917, was postponed because of the war.[75] A renewed interest in and fervor for the citizenship bill permeated later issues of the journal.

As they debated American and Native citizenship, SAI members presented arguments about "racial difference" to position Native people in the growing contemporary landscape of Indigenous, racial, and ethnic groups, using the rhetoric of racial difference of the day and analogies to American ethnic groups. A common strategy in the SAI's argument for racial difference was the comparison of Native civic and racial status with that of European immigrants. This idea did not, however, originate with the SAI members; it found its most acerbic advocate and supporter in Carlisle's mastermind Richard Henry Pratt.

In his many public addresses and private letters, including letters to Montezuma, Pratt insisted that the "Indian problem" and its solution—total assimilation—could be addressed by adopting the model of immigrant assimilation and Americanization. Pratt invoked the success of Anglicizing and citizenizing African Americans and European immigrants and called for the immediate subjection of "our Indians" to the same treatment: "Encouraging foreigners of all lands to come and settle among us has in every instance, where we have avoided the congesting of them in separate and large communities, led them to abandon their past and become thoroughly American."[76] So influential was Pratt to the SAI agenda of Americanization that some members went so far as to propose that Pratt be adopted as an Indian. Under Bonnin's editorship, Pratt's photograph was featured prominently in the SAI journal and his contributions to Americanization were praised.[77] Pro-Americanization SAI members used Pratt's arguments on different occasions, stressing the importance of the work ethic to both immigrant and Native survival. Francis La Flesche (Omaha) opined: "If the Indian were to go to work, do like the Immigrants who come here . . . he will have solved this problem that seems so difficult to us. . . . So, I say, tell the Indian to go to work."[78] Labor would thus make Native people into good Americans.

Labor and industry were virtues touted by reformers, including Robert G. Valentine, commissioner of Indian Affairs, whose prescription for Native progress relied on an ideal: "first, a solid, healthy human being, and second, a good laborer or other workman." In a 1910 article in *Sunset*, "Making Good Indians," Valentine opined that Native people did not work because they did not have to: "They are often lazy just as you or I would be lazy if we had no great worry as to where our means were coming from."[79] Fred E. Parker offered a solution for the putative Native laziness: "If the Indian were to go to work, do like the immigrants who come here—build houses, such as the German does that comes from Europe, till the soil as the native that comes from Sweden, he will have solved this problem that seems so difficult to us and to the white people. . . . So, I say, tell the Indian to go to work."[80] He attributed what he called Native people's lack of industry to a "disinclination to work" and a fondness for liquor. "Tell the Indian to go to work," he held, ventriloquizing Progressive Era rhetoric and its glorification of the Protestant work ethic. Parker's provocative statement foreshadows changes in the rhetoric around Native labor in later decades, especially during the Indian New Deal under John Collier, commissioner of Indian Affairs in the 1930s. *Indians at Work* (1933–45), a publication of the Bureau of Indian Affairs (BIA), started by Collier in 1933, served his political agenda, which included the promotion of vocational education in day schools on reservations.[81] Labor, in Collier's vision, would help Native people thrive on reservations in the Indian New Deal era.

The SAI intellectuals continued to use the immigrant analogy to signal a lack in the Native community around two pressing issues: education and health. Laura Cornelius Kellogg, founding member of the SAI and chairman of the Division of Education, was a declared enemy of the boarding school system. In her report to the SAI at its second conference, "Some Facts and Figures on Indian Education," Kellogg examined twenty-five years of federally funded Native education, tracing the contradictions of misused government funds and their consequences for Native children.[82] She pointed out the importance of Indigenous self-determination in education and saw the future of Native education as a meeting ground of tribal knowledges and epistemologies with "Caucasian" education.[83] As someone educated at white institutions, Kellogg expounded, "We want education, yes, we want to know all the educated Caucasian knows but we want our self-respect while we are getting his knowledge." She invoked the "power of abstraction in the Indian mind" and described the merits of Indigenous oratory in its "profound thought, literary merit and logic." She criticized the Office of Indian Affairs (OIA) for failing to include funds for Native students' health care, called for a transition from off-reservation schools to local public schools, and asked for appropriations for Native students pursuing higher education: "Our future is in the hands of the educational system of today. . . . Let us climb the highest mountain, without looking back till we have reached the top."[84] Kellogg ultimately criticized OIA personnel for their irresponsible handling of resources and suggested congressional appropriations to benefit Native education and health.

Whereas the link between public health and immigrants served American nativist claims for racial purity (to keep undesirable "races" out), Kellogg pointed to the ongoing extermination at home due to diseases Native students contracted at boarding schools and later spread to reservations. In both scenarios, the idea of eliminating the Native and the immigrant as threats to the healthy nation was based on fears of coexisting alongside groups that were not Anglo-Saxon Protestants and thus threatened Americanism. Although she ended her SAI speech on an optimistic note, Laura Cornelius Kellogg reminded the audience how crucial education was for Native self-determination; she also reminded them of the danger to Native students due to the lack of hygiene at the boarding schools, where they were exposed to trachoma and tuberculosis. Decrying the danger of trachoma, she deplored what she considered a criminal lack of sanitation: "Why, no immigrant can land in New York who has trachoma, but here we are exposing the youth of the race to an incurable disease. If this were done by an individual to another, it would be a penitentiary offense."[85] Kellogg sanctioned nativist fears as she advocated for Indigenous rights.

Using the immigrant analogy strategically—she was, after all, a student of Franz Boas—Kellogg referred to yet another excludable category: persons affected by contagious diseases. This new category of exclusion was added through the Immigration Act of 1907, signed by President Theodore Roosevelt, which denied admission into the U.S. to "all idiots, imbeciles, feebleminded persons, epileptics, insane persons, and persons who have been insane within five years previous; persons who have had two or more attacks of insanity at any time previously; paupers; persons likely to become a public charge; professional beggars; *persons afflicted with tuberculosis or with a loathsome or dangerous contagious disease.*"[86] Kellogg noted that, whereas immigration restriction laws responded to the exaggerated fear of alien contagion—

what Alan Kraut has called "medicalized nativism"—Indian boarding schools continued to be loci of disease dissemination without any federal acknowledgment or regulation. Only a few years before Kellogg's speech, Congress made a small appropriation to study and treat trachoma in Native communities. When she gave her speech in 1912, public health physicians still argued that the trachoma epidemic on reservations was spread by the government boarding schools.[87]

Unlike Kellogg, who raised awareness about the dire sanitation of the governmental boarding schools in the pages of the SAI journal, Arthur C. Parker expressed a more abstract concern with Native education as he also attempted to theorize rapid Americanization and Native people's place in what he called a "uniform civilization." Like Kellogg, he acknowledged that the public school was the greatest of all Americanization forces. Parker claimed that the "Indian problem" no longer emerged from what he called "racial conditions"; instead, it was a social problem. He intimated that there was no inherently biological deterrent to Native people's quick Americanization but that the Indian problem was larger, systemic. Like Carlos Montezuma, Parker directed his critique to the Office of Indian Affairs. Parker claimed that Native people should not be judged on racial terms as they entered modernity, yet he also called for the creation of a "Bureau of Race Development" to promote what he called "human efficiency" and to standardize "every racial element."[88] Why would Parker make a seemingly circular argument?

The SAI intellectuals were aware of the work of scientific racists, which targeted the "inferior" new immigrant groups (for example, the Alpine Slavs and the Jews). Immigration restrictionists invoked Darwin's theory of evolution and Mendelian genetics to support arguments about racial inferiority. In 1920, Harry H. Laughlin, a leader of the eugenics movement in the U.S., argued that the new immigrants were diluting the national racial stock and had to be stopped.[89] In a 1916 essay, Arthur C. Parker critiqued the claims to supremacy of both European and American "Aryans" popularized by contemporary race scientist Joseph P. Widney, who called Native Americans one of the "lower" and "passing" races, with little capacity to join the work of civilization." Parker maintained that "civilization" was not "the property of any race, any more than air or water or truth" and that "more men and women of Indian blood in proportion to their number are doctors, lawyers, clergymen, and teachers, than the people of any other race in America." He ended on a hopeful note: "The American Indian is in America to stay and to leave the indelible impress of his mind and blood."[90]

Like other Indigenous intellectuals, Parker expressed dissatisfaction with the OIA and its regulation of Native life, and in doing so he used yet another immigrant analogy: "If there is no Immigrant Bureau devoted to the *continual* care of foreigners seeking Americanization, there should be no special Indian Bureau." Undoubtedly, Parker was aware of the history of the Bureau of Immigration, created in 1895. At the time of his remarks in 1913, the new Bureau of Immigration and Naturalization (created in 1906) was under the jurisdiction of the Department of Labor. In his emphasis on the "*continual* care" of Indians, Parker stressed the paternalism of the OIA, which kept the Native wards under an unnecessarily prolonged panoptic gaze. In Parker's view, "a sick man, a pauper, a drunkard, an ignorant man, and a foreigner" are all at a disadvantage; however, the "human" element, not their racial background, made possible their transition from one stage of development to another: "The immigrant from Italy and the immigrant from Finland each must learn the English tongue and take on the manners of the American. . . . This means a complete entering into the social fabric of the people."[91]

In "Problems of Race Assimilation in America; With Special Reference to the American Indian," Parker compared the difficulties of assimilating Native people and new immigrants to those faced by African Americans. To address the central question—"Why has the Indian not been absorbed?"—Parker argued that the conditions of assimilation of the three groups were unequal, and that the immigrant had the easiest path toward assimilation, though he did not attribute it to the immigrants' whiteness or European descent. He held that, unlike some "foreign bloods," who encountered an even greater prejudice in the process of becoming American, the assimilated Natives posed "no grave social or racial problem" because "their aims and methods of thought are thoroughly American." Like Kellogg and Montezuma, Parker found the reservation system isolating. He intimated that, like African Americans, Native people had to prove themselves to the white world and had to overcome racial and cultural prejudice. After examining several preconditions for assimilating immigrants, among them moral energy, capital, similar values, and "good stock," Parker concluded that the European immigrant is "a white man from a civilized country" who only changes one kind of civilization for another. But his vision did not account for the agricultural and preindustrial communities in southern and eastern Europe, where many new immigrants originated. He also noted the difficulty of "the American Negro" to assimilate because of systemic racism and prejudice. Troubling race-based categories, Parker ultimately placed the argument about Native inferiority in a national context of structural barriers of prejudice against non-Anglo-Saxons.[92]

Engaging the Americanizers' theories of the melting pot—"In this great melting pot of nations, the races that are poured in will not all melt at the same degree of temperature"—Parker called attention to the disparities of inevitable assimilation:

> To the European immigrant we say, 'Come, We want you in this free country. In many respects you are like us. . . .' To the Negro we say, 'In many respects you are unlike us . . . However, we will tolerate you for after all you are a convenient laborer. . . . To the Chinaman we say, 'Stay away, we don't want you. You are vastly different from the rest of us and we dislike your looks. . . .' To the Indian we say, 'You were here first, this is true, and although we tried we could not kill you entirely. You must be segregated until you can understand us.'[93]

Parker cautioned against the incongruities of assimilation practices. His problematic ventriloquism and racist rhetoric toward Chinese immigrants—"Stay away, we don't want you. You are vastly different from the rest of us and we dislike your looks"—illustrates his contemporaries' racial prejudice, materialized in the Chinese Exclusion Act of 1882.[94] Bringing together the various degrees of discriminatory practices based on racial and ethnic group provenance—European immigrants, African Americans, Asian Americans, and Native Americans—Parker recapitulated his white contemporaries' exclusionary history as he also ventriloquized their position of privilege by reiterating the language of exclusion ("we say" and "we don't want you") to signal the absurdity of his contemporaries' theories of the melting pot.

In the racial hierarchies Parker described, only European immigrants fulfilled the requirements of assimilation. Gertrude Bonnin reacted to the absurdity of these hierarchies in the pages of the *American Indian Magazine* in 1919, disheartened that the OIA would not permit SAI members to speak on a reservation: "Though the riffraff of the people

from the four corners of the earth may enter Indian lands and home-
stead them, permitting daily contact with *the very scum of other races*,
the educated, refined, and patriotic Indian, teaching the highest ideals
of democracy is forbidden to meet with his own race, even for a day"
(my emphasis).[95] Bonnin called attention to the disparity between un-
sanctioned immigrant encroachment on Native lands and the refusal
of the OIA to let Native leaders speak on reservations, implying that
the Americanization of Native people by their Native peers on Native
terms was impossible. Parker's and Bonnin's contradictory rhetoric expressed the many paradoxes of evolutionary thinking during the Progressive Era.

The evolutionary model informing race thinking held that each race
would gradually pass through "similar structural changes of economic,
intellectual and social organization," what anthropologists described
as a progression from savagery (hunting) to barbarism (pastoralism)
and civilization (agriculture). This evolutionary model of social development influenced the design of Indian policy and immigrant programs
during the Progressive Era. The assimilation of immigrants was more
pressing, given the large numbers, at a time when Indigenous people
were believed to be vanishing.[96] Hazel Hertzberg argued that in 1919
the new direction in the SAI included a growing hostility to immigrants
and African Americans. Whereas some SAI members (Parker, Bonnin, Montezuma) occasionally bought into the nationalist xenophobic
rhetoric, they also used this rhetoric purposefully to establish an even
starker contrast between the rights granted to immigrants and African
Americans yet denied to Native people, particularly the right to citizenship. Although the evidence of hostility toward European immigrants
and African Americans that I found in SAI papers is not overwhelming,
a common strand between 1917 and 1919 was the recurring analogy
of the civic and racial status of Native people to that of the European
immigrant. As Native soldiers returned home from the war in 1919,
new arguments about Native human rights took center stage in the
SAI journal: "This is not the democracy for which our soldiers fought
and died!" Bonnin reverted to the immigrant analogy: "As they believe
in Americanizing the foreigner, so should they desire the privileges of
American citizenship for the native, the aborigine!"[97] Both nationalist
and Native visions of American citizenship—sometimes overlapping—
permeated the pages of the *American Indian Magazine*, inflecting the

arguments with competing visions and calling for the recognition of Native people as full citizens.

"AMERICA" REDUX

In 1921, after the SAI had published its last journal issue and was slowly dissolving, Gertrude Bonnin wrote the policy brochure *Americanize the First American: A Plan of Regeneration* for the General Federation of Women's Club. It included two circular charts comparing bureaucracy with democracy under two separate categories marked by two distinct circles: "What We Have" and "What We Want." Detailing the layers of bureaucracy (superintendents, supervisors, special agents), Bonnin called for an Indian citizens' association that would work directly with a reservation executive committee, an idea materialized in the National Council of American Indians (NCAI), which she helped form in 1926. In *Americanize the First American*, Bonnin pleaded with the women of America on behalf of "the Red man and his children" to advocate for citizenship and the termination of wardship: "Revoke the tyrannical powers of Government superintendents over a voiceless people and extend American opportunities to the first American—the Red Man."[98]

When *Americanize the First American* was published in 1921, its cover sheet included a picture of Bonnin framed by American flags. This presentation is not entirely accidental, given the choices she made throughout her career to serve her Native community and the white America she was navigating, as well as her strategic performance of her Native and American personas. Her visual representations in the press of the time ranged from photographs in Native regalia to the modern suit of the New Woman.[99] In her published articles and stories, Bonnin wrote under a self-given Lakota name, Zitkala-Ša, which means "Red Bird." She advocated for change and demanded freedom for Native people "to do their own thinking; to exercise their judgment; to hold open forums for the expression of their thought; and . . . to manage their own personal business."[100] Pleading for the Americanization of "the First American," Bonnin offered a biting critique of federal Indian policy, which continued to relegate Native people to the status of wards of the federal government. To Bonnin, this was not "the Red Man's America."

In 1917, Bonnin published the poem "The Red Man's America" in the *American Indian Magazine*. It offered a timely revision of "America," the song by Samuel Francis Smith, the unofficial American anthem for almost one hundred years, and the song her SAI peers had intoned and danced to only six years before in Columbus, Ohio. Variations of this immensely popular political song abound in American cultural history, from the abolitionists contesting the significance of Fourth of July celebrations for enslaved Americans, to struggles for women's rights, to rallies against capitalism. The use of Smith's "America" during times of political upheavals served to reaffirm patriotism and to voice political concerns. Rhetorical strategies for rewriting the song during times of crisis used parody and irony to call attention to key terms, such as "land of liberty" and "freedom," and their significance for the country's diverse peoples. In Robert Branham and Stephen Hartnett's reading, "patriotism, the song teaches us, is not only about supporting [the] nation's policies, but also about questioning them when . . . they need questioning."[101]

Gertrude Bonnin was not the first to rewrite this immensely popular patriotic song, but she was the first Native American to do so. African American leader and intellectual W. E. B. Du Bois also tried his hand at revising this unofficial American anthem, praising his country with the lines "My country tis of thee,/Late land of slavery" and reminding the nation that it was built on the injustices of slavery.[102] Bonnin's "The Red Man's America" lamented Native disenfranchisement and used it as a political platform to advocate for citizenship. Instead of the singular lament in Smith's poem—"Land where my fathers died,/Land of the pilgrims' pride,/From ev'ry mountainside/Let freedom ring!" Bonnin's Native speaker signaled the equally important but unrecognized part Native death played in the making of America: "Land where OUR fathers died,/Whose offsprings are denied/The franchise given wide." Bonnin's poem sanctioned American hypocrisy in its refusal to grant citizenship to "the Red Man": "My native country, thee,/Thy Red man is not free,/Knows not thy love."[103] Establishing a double audience in the poem's first two stanzas by imagining two addressees, an American and a Native one—"My country" and "My native country"—the speaker brings her "pleas" to appeal for Native enfranchisement to the first and responsibility to the second (table 1).[104]

Table 1. Left column, selections from Gertrude Bonnin's "The Red Man's America" (1917), and right column, Samuel Francis Smith, "America"/"My Country 'Tis of Thee" (1831). (Emphasis mine.)

"The Red Man's America"	"America"
My country! 'tis to thee, Sweet land of liberty, <u>My Pleas I bring.</u>	My country, 'tis of thee, Sweet land of liberty, <u>Of thee I sing;</u>
Land where <u>our</u> fathers died, <u>Whose offspring are denied</u> <u>The franchise given wide,</u> <u>Hark, while I sing.</u>	Land where <u>my fathers</u> died, <u>Land of the Pilgrims' Pride,</u> <u>From every mountain side</u> <u>Let freedom ring.</u>
My native country, thee, <u>Thy Red man is not free,</u> <u>Knows not thy love;</u> ...	My native country, thee, <u>Land of the noble, free,</u> <u>Thy name I love;</u> ...

Bonnin's rewriting of "America," with an Indigenous-centric appropriation of the song's main iconic symbols, becomes a political appeal for Native rights. When the poem was published, the U.S. had just entered World War I, and a new brand of patriotism permeated the Native and the mainstream American public spheres, as well as the pages of the SAI journal. Read in the context of Native participation in the war (many Native men enlisted or were drafted to fight as "American soldiers"), the poem "The Red Man's America" rallied the readers of the *American Indian Magazine* in the SAI's fight for citizenship. Published alongside reprints of newspaper articles about Native men and women's participation in World War I, "The Red Man's America," with its reassuring cadences, asked the "Sweet land of liberty" to recognize Native humanity and rights. This confluence of patriotism performance and Native expression speaks to the larger challenges of Native intellectuals to negotiate national and local communities, which often called for positioning themselves at the intersection of patriotic songs like "America" and traditional Native dances performed on Native-marked spaces (the "Indian mound" discussed earlier in this chapter).

Bonnin's biting critique of federal Indian policy and the perpetuation of wardship echoes the views of Carlos Montezuma.

CARLOS MONTEZUMA'S "IMMIGRANT PROBLEM," *WASSAJA*, AND NATIVE ACTIVISM

Of the intellectuals of the SAI, Yavapai Carlos Montezuma was one of the best-known Native Americans in the U.S. in the first decades of the twentieth century. His use of the immigrant trope in the context of white and Native Progressivism, expressed in his letters, speeches, as well as the pages of his newspaper, *Wassaja: Freedom's Signal for the Indian* (April 1916–November 1922), has been understudied.[105] Whereas white progressives used the analogy to immigrants to argue for a quick Americanization of Native people, Montezuma used it to keep Native and American nationalisms in tension, and to signal the government's neglect of Native people around several issues central to Native intellectuals' political and cultural work: education, health, and political identity. His radical newspaper *Wassaja*, with its daring tone and appeal to Native and non-Native readers, offers an example of what I call, following Scott R. Lyons, "Indigenous editorial sovereignty" in its vision and control over the printed matter.

Despite Montezuma's many disagreements with fellow SAI member Arthur C. Parker, they agreed on using the immigrant analogy to signal the discrepancy in each group's path to American citizenship. Montezuma borrowed the Native Progressives' argument for citizenship as an end to wardship as he developed his own analogy of the Native civic status to that of the European immigrant.[106] He offered a critique of settlers' and immigrants' easier paths to assimilation and Americanization, and signaled the deficient ways that the U.S. addressed the so-called Indian problem in relation to the immigrant problem. The adopted son of an Italian immigrant photographer and artist, Carlo Gentile, and the husband of an immigrant woman from Romania, Maria Keller, Carlos Montezuma lived and practiced medicine in Chicago, a city whose foreign-born population in 1850 exceeded that of New York City.

Throughout his career, Montezuma advocated for the Americanization of Native people—albeit a different version of Americanization than the one enforced by white reformers. Following Richard H. Pratt,

Montezuma asked: if immigrants could Americanize so rapidly and become self-sufficient "good Americans," why not the Indians? Pratt made this immigrant analogy as early as June 1881, if not sooner, according to his vast correspondence.[107] He continued to promote the analogy throughout his career. In a 1904 speech to a Baptist audience, Pratt held that the success in Americanizing Native people, had been proved by assimilating African Americans and new immigrants. Yet, he cautioned, "We shall not succeed in Americanizing the Indian unless we take him in and give him the same competitive chances."[108] Offering Native people similar opportunities and contact with other groups, Pratt argued for their total "absorption" through education. Pratt believed that contact with white society was "the supreme Americanizer."[109] The country failed to Americanize Native people for centuries, he claimed, despite the success in Americanizing "foreign immigrants."[110] Both Pratt and Montezuma resorted to the immigrant analogy to make a case for citizenship and Native education in American institutions.

Recent scholarship has positioned Montezuma's cultural and political work around the SAI, Richard H. Pratt and Carlisle Indian School, and the legacy of his work for the Fort McDowell community. Literary scholars have also started to recover his poetry, speeches, essays, by examining *Wassaja* to uncover his commitment to Native activism, radicalism, and print culture.[111] One overlooked focus of Montezuma's work is his investment in a popular topic of the Progressive Era: the analogy between Native people and recent European immigrants. Like many of his Red Progressive peers, he used it strategically to argue that Native "wards" deserved the same recognition of their political and social capital as their new immigrant peers.[112] This strategic analogy provided rhetorical ammunition in his speeches, editorials, and articles in the 1910s and early 1920s.

A founding member of the SAI in 1911, over the years Montezuma became one of its most acerbic critics. Historian Hazel Hertzberg, although generally critical of him, describes him in memorable terms: "Montezuma was by temperament and conviction a factionalist. He helped to found the Society of American Indians and then spent most of the rest of his life attacking it."[113] Sometimes borrowing Pratt's language, Montezuma argued for bringing Native people to "civilization": "We do not hesitate to take a million foreigners into our country in one year, and at once disperse and citizenize them." He emphasized: "We compelled the negro [*sic*], and invited Huns [*sic*] and Italians and the Irish and everyone else to come and live with us. Why not invite the Indians, and give them the same chance, and find out what they can do? There are only 300,000 Indians outside of Alaska."[114] If millions of immigrants were welcome to the U.S. and prepared for citizenship, Montezuma intimated, why not the Indian?

When SAI's *Quarterly Journal* became the *American Indian Magazine* in 1916, Montezuma criticized the organization's accommodationist disposition and moderate politics: "The *Journal of the American Indians* has turned into a magazine." And, like all magazines, "it cannot have any definite object but to tickle its readers at the expense of the Indians."[115] Although he would not dismiss the work of the SAI completely, especially when Wahpeton Dakota doctor Charles Eastman became its president, Montezuma remained circumspect about what the SAI could do for Native citizenship. So intense was his ire that he tried his poetic pen to express anger and disappointment, faulting SAI's inaction at the annual meeting in Lawrence, Kansas: "The sky is clear and we meet only to discuss. . . . /'Sh—! Sh—! Don't whisper about the Indian Bureau.'/We are here only to meet and discuss."[116] When his speeches, published pamphlets, and talks could no longer contain his larger-than-life vision for a Native future, Montezuma changed the status quo. He started his own weekly newspaper, *Wassaja*, with the mission, as stated in its first issue, to liberate Native people from the yoke of the Bureau of Indian Affairs, an agent of imperialism in his eyes.[117] Its polemical tone and political agenda made *Wassaja* "the most antigovernment Indian publication to that date."[118]

From the first issue in 1916 to the last issue in 1922, Montezuma's unmistakable rhetoric laid the foundations for his editorial sovereignty. Scott R. Lyons defines "rhetorical sovereignty" as "the inherent right and ability of peoples to determine their communicative needs and desires."[119] Implicit in this definition is the idea of control of meaning as well as the idea of knowledge production. As Montezuma wrote in the first issue of *Wassaja*, "The time has now arrived to present the real conditions, for the public, and for those in power, to consider and be in position to remedy the appalling slavery and handicap of the Indian race."[120] As writer, editor, fundraiser, publicist, and secretary of *Wassaja*, Montezuma was deeply implicated in recording and shaping a vision for Native people facing new economic and political challenges.

When he launched *Wassaja*—an Apache word for "beckoning" or "signaling," also the name given to him by his parents—Montezuma was aware of the power and potential of the Indigenous press. In his own "little spicy newspaper," Montezuma was hopeful for the future of Native journalism: "More Indian papers by the Indians the better. It shows the Indians are coming out to express themselves.[121] He single-handedly wrote and edited *Wassaja*, with the sole purpose of achieving "freedom for the Indians throughout the abolishment of the Indian Bureau."[122] There were other circumstances influencing his break with the SAI's stagnant politics: one of his articles was published in the SAI journal, with Montezuma's criticism of the commissioner of Indian Affairs excised.[123] This type of editorial intervention, albeit by one of his Native peers, Arthur C. Parker, did not sit well with him. Montezuma's large correspondence indicates that he had planned this activist coup in the form of a publication a decade earlier. A letter from Richard H. Pratt in 1906 lamented that Montezuma's articles did not have a wider circulation: "They are getting along to a point where they would make a pamphlet of good proportions and you must consider whether it will not be well to put them out in that form."[124] Former chief clerk at Carlisle Indian Industrial School, Marianna Burgess, echoed the sentiment in a letter to Montezuma: "You could speak the truth with a tongue of fire." Encouraging Montezuma to speak against the stereotypes of the day, Burgess voiced what many Native people reading *Wassaja* would soon learn: "the country needs you, the Indians need you."[125]

Like Pratt, who argued vociferously against the reservation, in *Wassaja* Montezuma continued to argue that "contact of people is the best of education" and called for a policy similar to that used to Americanize immigrants (learning English, attending public schools, and embracing "civilization").[126] Montezuma's argument was not, however, uncritical of his settler contemporaries. In the poem "Civilization," published in *Wassaja* in 1917, in the same month that the U.S. entered World War I, he decried the hypocrisy and artificiality of a historically abused trope: "Civilization, thou hast lost thy soul,/While carrying the cross to the heathen."[127] For him, "civilization" was not an abstract concept, but a plan for action. As early as 1903, in a piece for the *Chicago Tribune*, titled "How America has Betrayed the Indian," Montezuma conflated "civilization" with Americanization, invoking the immigrant analogy to make a case for Native belonging: "The first step towards civilization of the Indian is to place him geographically so that he can commingle with the conquering race, in the same manner and to the same extent that natives of foreign countries have become part of the people in general in our country."[128] Interaction with settlers and immigrants drove Montezuma's argument about change.

A case in point for understanding Montezuma's vision of "change" is his poem, "Changing Is Not Vanishing" (1916). By 1916, the vanishing policy was already under attack: the Red Progressives attacked it, demanding rights for Native people in national arenas; Native people on reservations fought to retain their spiritual connections with the land; scientists were challenging the myth of the "vanishing Indian." In "Changing Is Not Vanishing" Montezuma reveals his belief in a future for "the Indian race."[129] Hazel Hertzberg contends that Society of American Indians members used terms like "Indian," "our people," "the Indian people," "the Indian race" or "the race" as signs of unity: "If membership in the tribe tended to divide them, membership in the race united them."[130] The tone of the poem evolves gradually from a direct question—"Who says the Indian race is vanishing?"—to answers focused on Native survival, marked by the speaker's use of future tense three times ("the Indian will not vanish"): "The feathers, paint and moccasin will vanish, but the Indians,—never! . . . /The Indian race vanishing? No, never! The race will live on and prosper forever."[131] The "new Indian" Montezuma envisioned did not wear feathers and war paint but western, "citizen" clothing. The change is only exterior (Americanization in name), suggesting the preservation of immutable internal Native values (Indigeneity in deed). Montezuma also envisioned Native people adjusting to the demands of capitalism: "He is an industrial and commercial man, competing with the world." This line reveals Montezuma's troubled relation with capitalism, also intimated in the early issues of *Wassaja*: "In order to compete with the real world we have to meet the rascals—the sooner, the better."[132] Montezuma argued that change was not synonymous with disappearance but symptomatic of adaptation, progress, adjustment, and self-determination.

The range of materials published in *Wassaja*—from editorials to poems, reprints from the national press, and letters from Native reservations and from supporters of his cause—showed Montezuma's readers the incongruence between the assimilation of immigrants and the perpetual relegation of Native people to a complicated political status of wards of the federal government: "A foreigner that lands on the shore of America has greater rights than the Indian. . . . In a few years, the foreigner has become a citizen of the U.S., while the Indian still remains a ward." This comment is particularly poignant in its 1918 context, expressing Montezuma's exasperation with wardship at a time when Native men were fighting in World War I as Americans.[133]

Although Montezuma agreed that Native professionals could work for the Indian Service, he did not believe they *should*. Of all his SAI peers, Montezuma was perhaps the least involved in the Indian Service; his work as physician for the federal government from 1889 to 1895—as physician at the Indian School at Fort Stevenson, North Dakota, at Western Shoshone Indian Agency, Nevada, at Colville Agency, Washington, and at Carlisle, Pennsylvania—preceded his career in a private practice in Chicago. In a *Wassaja* editorial in 1917, he argued for Native self-determination: "My fellow brothers in red, do not permit the Indian Office to take care of you and your business. Take care of yourself, face prejudice, brush aside great obstacles."[134] So vast and all-consuming was Montezuma's animosity for the Office of Indian Affairs that he devoted his personal and print life to abolishing it. As David Martinez has argued, "For many Indians, Montezuma was the first Indian they knew of who dared to accuse the Indian Bureau of racism." His fight against "'bureauism' was the culmination of a life devoted to abolishing the Indian Bureau."[135] This ambition to see the Bureau abolished was the driving force behind *Wassaja*: "This monthly signal ray is to be published only so long as the Indian Bureau exists. Its sole purpose is Freedom for the Indians through the abolishment of the Indian Bureau."[136]

The opening page of *Wassaja*'s first issue carries an illustration of a Native man crushed by the weight of a log inscribed "Indian Bureau," his right hand reaching out toward *Wassaja*'s motto, "Freedom's sign for the Indian" (figure 29). Montezuma extended his crusade against the OIA through poetry. In "I Have Stood Up for You" (1919), Montezuma becomes the spokesperson for an entire Native community:

> As the Indian Bureau, like an octopus,
> Sucked your very life blood,
> I have stood up for you
>
> . . . .
> When you were judged "incompetent"
> For freedom and citizenship by the Indian Bureau—
> I have stood up for you.[137]

WASSAJA

FREEDOM'S SIGNAL FOR THE INDIANS

Vol. 1., No. 1.   April, 1916.

INTRODUCTION

The WAR WHOOP having been abandoned on account of outside pressure which was brought to bear, WASSAJA is taking its place. The name has been changed in the belief that the former name was not correctly understood.

The intent of the WAR WHOOP has been in the mind of the present editor for many years, and he believes that the time has now arrived to present the real conditions, for the public, and for those in power to consider and be in position to remedy the appalling slavery and handicap of the Indian race.

This monthly signal rays is to be published only so long as the Indian Bureau exists. Its sole purpose is Freedom for the Indians throughout the abolisment of the Indian Bureau.

It is supported by subscriptions and by private contributions from Redmen and everybody who has heart interest in the cause.

Its object is not to form a society, but to free the Indians by exposing the actual conditions of their imprisonment. If you want to help out on the expenses of printing and mailing, subscription is fifty cents a year.

We need your help if you are with us in this vital purpose.

ARROW POINTS.

Had the Indian been treated as a man, without discrimination, in the beginning of the pale-face invasion, today there would be no Indian Bureau and the word "Indian" would be only an obsolete name.

The Indian problem is a problem because the country has taken it and nursed it as a problem; otherwise it is not a problem at all.

What ye sow ye also reap. The Indian Bureau has sown, and it has brought forth nothing but pangs of sorrow and ruination to the Indian race.

It pays to make producers and wage-earners out of Indians rather than idlers and paupers. The Indian Bureau mill turns out the latter.

It does not cost much to feed and clothe the Indians, but the Indian

Fig. 29. The first issue of *Wassaja*, 1916, showing a Native man crushed by a log representing the Indian Bureau. Newberry Library, Chicago.

Besides the Indian Bureau, Montezuma criticized the American educational system, which he held responsible for limiting Native children's exposure to traditional teachings in their communities. In the pages of *Wassaja*, Montezuma was an acerbic critic of the discrepancy between the education and Americanization of new immigrants and that of Native children. Unlike Pratt, but like many educators, Montezuma argued that "educating Indian children is no different from educating children of other races. The public schools are within the reach of Indian people; why send their children to Indian schools?" Dramatizing his line of questioning to include the question "Are not the Indians real Americans?" Montezuma charged that sending Native children to Indian boarding schools, instead of American public schools, was "un-American."[138] He appealed to the educators' sense of patriotism; he held that, by separating Native children from other children, the federal government continued to erase Native presence from the American imagination, instead replacing it with the comfortable image of the vanishing Indian. In the pages of *Wassaja*, Montezuma also wrote about immigrant ignorance of Native history: "The foreigner says: 'I never saw an Indian. They are as scarce as hens' teeth. It is a good thing they were killed or restricted on reservations. It would be unsafe for them to be at large.'"[139] Montezuma also reminded his readers that adult immigrants enrolled in courses preparing them for citizenship, if they learned about Native Americans at all, learned about Native disappearance.

A more sustained interest informing Montezuma's editorials was the issue of citizenship, as well as the government's measuring of citizenship competency. In his column, "Arrow Points," he wrote:

> Born in this country and has to take out papers? You do not tell me! Is that true?
>
> Not a citizen of his own country? Who ever heard of such a thing!
>
> Was in America before Columbus and must take out papers of naturalization? Can such injustice exist?
>
> Sane Indians and over 21 years old and cannot vote? I cannot see anything but injustice in that.
>
> Indians have no voice in their affairs? Oh, that is awful.[140]

His conclusion was an unambiguous call to arms: "The Indians must become their own emancipators. There is none to carry the burden for them."[141] As he critiqued wardship, dispossession, and lack of franchise, Carlos Montezuma continued to plead for self-determination.

To advocate for citizenship for Native people, Montezuma reprinted letters from reservations recording Native people's dissent toward citizenship: "I never asked . . . for citizenship, therefore I do not know myself as a citizen," wrote Jake Culps of the Warren Springs Reservation, Oregon.[142] A reprinted story from the *New York Herald*, titled "A Japanese Naturalized," told about the admission to citizenship of Thunayoshi Takewiche, a soldier at Fort Logan. If a Japanese could naturalize despite bans on Asian naturalization (with the exception of the "reward" with citizenship of Asian immigrants fighting in World War I), why not the Indian? Montezuma's analogy reveals his exasperation at Native exclusion from the franchise: "It appears that every other nation on the face of the globe can be citizens of the United States but the Indians."[143]

In an editorial in the January 1919 issue of *Wassaja*, "Excuses to Abolish the Indian Bureau," Montezuma argued that immigrants and Black people had adapted and survived various forms of oppression and marginalization; so, too, would Native people if they were granted citizenship. Black and Native histories intersected during the Progressive Era. As historian Kyle Mays has shown, "partial citizenship affected both Black Americans and Native Americans," which had implications for the multiple forms of exclusion from the public sphere of both groups.[144] The January 1919 issue of *Wassaja* also introduced a new masthead, illustrating Montezuma's continued reliance on the immigrant analogy to plead for Native rights, a visually effective appeal (figure 30).

Designed by non-Native artist Joe Scheuerle, the *Wassaja* frontispiece shows Montezuma to the east, on the right, pointing to the Statue of Liberty and holding his famous pamphlet "Let My People Go," in which he pleads that "reservation Indians" be freed from the confines of the reservation. To the left stands a traditionally dressed Native man, holding a tomahawk in his right hand and a torch in his left. In pointing to the Statue of Liberty, Montezuma also gestures at its modern surroundings: the American city. To the left, the tipi behind the Native man suggests the restricted mobility of the reservation environment, a contrast to the possibility of movement and modernity Montezuma embodies, to the right. Both men flank *Wassaja*'s title and its message to the world: "Wassaja: Freedom's Signal for the Indian."

Edited by Wassaja (Dr. Montezuma's Indian name, meaning "Signaling") an Apache Indian.

Fig. 30. *Wassaja* masthead, January 1919. Montezuma points to the Statue of Liberty. Newberry Library, Chicago.

Although this visual representation of the traditional versus the modern Indian is reductive in its assumptions about Native modernity, in a private letter to the artist, Montezuma called the man on the left "the real Indian." He praised the artist's work: "The front page illustration is grand and dignified. The real Indian [is] giving signal for freedom to Wassaja, who stands pointing to the Statue of Liberty. The wigwam, the skyscraper, the faces all connect the Indian soldiers in the trenches and Indian soldiers standing erect by the side of the President. Can only marvel at the great meaning." Montezuma's wife also admired Scheuerle's work: "Joe is a great fellow. He ought to be an Indian." Montezuma concluded his letter to the artist: "I am an Indian and could not make such realistic illustrations."[145] Relegating Lady Liberty to the background, Scheuerle conveys in powerful visual form the message of Montezuma's popular speech, which he delivered at the SAI meeting in Lawrence, Kansas: citizenship for Native people. The iconic Statue of Liberty in the background, holding the torch of freedom, appeals to the national myth of the U.S. as a nation of immigrants, eliding Native presence and its claims to U.S. land and citizenship; its counterpoint, the torch in the foreground, held by the Native man, is a subtle reference to continued Native presence despite settler occupation.

Read in the context of immigration, the image dramatizes Montezuma's belief that Native people must be welcomed into the national body politic in the same way afforded to immigrants. As Lucy Maddox put it, Montezuma liked to say that "Indians would be much better off if they could be put on boats and then allowed to reenter the country as immigrants, with the same entitlements as new arrivals from abroad."[146] Montezuma's perhaps unexpected claim translated his despair with the lack of national regard and care for its Indigenous people as the nation embraced what Jodi Byrd calls the new "arrivants." To Montezuma, as European new immigrants, many of these arrivants enjoyed many of the same economic, racial and political benefits as their settler predecessors.[147]

In print, *Wassaja* often addressed Uncle Sam directly, appealing to readers' sense of patriotism and justice: "Indian: Say, Uncle Sam, bestow unto us your high ideals. We are not free; we are not citizens; we have no justice. We are wards, corralled on reservations, and dominated as slaves."[148] In the April 1918 issue, Montezuma took the "adopted Americans" to task, arguing that many in the U.S. "hate to classify the Indians as Americans" and accusing his white readers of hypocrisy: "You have robbed, you have mistreated and you have not bestowed upon your red brother who gave you food, a place to lay your head and took you as a child from the Great Spirit, the very principles that you are fighting for."[149] The tone of Montezuma's rhetorically charged accusation might have alienated his (white) readership had the article been published in the pages of the SAI journal. Its inclusion in *Wassaja* offered Montezuma the venue to position himself rhetorically as an inconvenient Native intellectual challenging his contemporaries. This was the responsibility and power of Montezuma's editorial sovereignty. In "his feisty monthly newsletter," Montezuma sustained an intertribal dialogue through the community of readers *Wassaja* brought together across national and reservation borders.[150] Although the SAI newspapers negotiated carefully Native concerns with larger American political and legal battles, Montezuma's radical *Wassaja*, with its daring tone and appeal to Native and American readers, offered an example of Indigenous editorial sovereignty. Montezuma spoke the truth with a tongue of fire, as Marianna Burgess had urged him; he had to speak for his people because (he believed that) they couldn't speak for themselves. Although this claim was deliberately exaggerated, it reveals Montezuma's attempt at indigenizing American publications.

Like Montezuma and Bonnin, the Native intellectuals of the SAI used their public performances of patriotism to indigenize the American public sphere, but unlike some of his SAI peers, Montezuma focused on the Native present. Montezuma wanted to change the image of the *Indian* in popular venues: "Fennimore Cooper's Indians do not exist today.[151] He invoked the colonial misnaming of Indigenous people as *Indian*, which he considered "incorrect and offensive": "What if we received Englishmen by calling them Johnny Bulls, Germans as Sauerkrauts, Irishmen as Pats and Mikes, and Italians as Dagoes?"[152] Reversing the lens of stereotyping, Montezuma assumed the voice of Native people who could not speak English: "for the past twenty-five years thousands of foreigners have been admitted into our country who at the time were ignorant [illiterate]," who "could neither read, write, nor talk our language," but who "today are classed among our best citizens."[153] Why not the Indian? Resorting to the immigrant analogy to signal discrepancies in the Americanization of his people, Montezuma continued to ask this question throughout his life.

As Native intellectuals negotiated multiple audiences and expectations, they also used print culture to spell out, to author, the Indigenous terms of Americanization, even as those terms were sometimes problematic. The SAI Native intellectuals—educated professionals of the intellectual elite, who sought to advance political and social agendas—were drawn into what we might loosely call two competing nationalisms: American and Indigenous. As they sometimes advocated for the former at the expense of the latter, they also cannily performed patriotism to enable Native persistence and cultural expression, and they firmly rejected assimilation in the name of Native nationalism. Through the print culture they shaped the national debates they engaged in, they advocated for Native citizenship as an end to wardship, critiqued the melting pot and Americanization, and asserted a continued Native present and future.

6 "This Was America!"

Americanization and Immigrant Literature at the Beginning of the Twentieth Century

The adoptive American has always been and will always remain a composite American.

—M. E. Ravage, *An American in the Making* (1917)

Where were you brought up? Among Indians?

—Abraham Cahan, *The Rise of David Levinsky* (1917)

LIKE THEIR NATIVE peers, new immigrant writers and thinkers explored Americanization as both trope and ideology. As multilingual writers and readers, they confronted the demands of the American literary market and those of Americanization. From the Yiddish poets in New York, who chose to write for a narrow audience, to better-known writers like Mary Antin, Abraham Cahan, and Marcus E. Ravage, Americanization was at the heart of immigrant writing during the Progressive Era.[1] Some early immigrant writers in the United States adopted a settler colonial stance to legitimize their claims to Americanness. In Anzia Yezierksa's novel *Bread Givers,* protagonist Sara Smolinsky identifies with Columbus and "the pilgrim fathers" when she leaves the ghetto to attend an American college: "I felt like Columbus starting out for the other end of the earth. I felt like the pilgrim fathers who had left their homeland and all their kin behind them and trailed out in search of the New World."[2] Stereotypical references to Indigenous people by early immigrant writers also populate immigrant writing.[3] The frequent association of the uncouth new immigrant with the "savage" *Indian* during the Progressive Era—the question posed to David Levinsky's greenhorn self by his American supervisor—"Where were you brought up? Among Indians?"—reiterates Anglo-Saxonism as the model of Americanization, sanctioning Indigenous and immigrant behaviors as uncivilized, unwelcome.

In this chapter I turn to Americanization in new immigrant literature, using Jewish American writers as case studies because of their prolific contributions to the literature of Americanization and its critique. Juxtaposing two Americanization stories—a fictionalized account and an autobiography, both published in 1917—I chart several strategies new immigrant writers used in their encounters with Americanization and negotiations of the pressures of the literary market. In Marcus Eli Ravage's autobiography, *An American in the Making* (1917), the pressures of the genre of immigrant memoir on the new immigrant author are symptomatic of larger, coercive demands that immigrants Americanize. In his celebrated novel, *The Rise of David Levinsky* (1917), Abraham Cahan challenged the optimistic version of Americanization.

At the beginning of the twentieth century, immigrant writers wrestled with the idea of becoming American in the genres of poetry, short fiction, life stories, and the novel. If American writers such as Henry James, Gertrude Stein, and Edith Wharton could write with some aloofness about the putative immigrant invasion, immigrant novelists like Cahan, Anzia Yiezierska, Henry Roth, and others saw the task of the immigrant novel—in English—as complementing that of the immigrant autobiography. Studies of the immigrant novel continue to invoke authors like Willa Cather or Gertrude Stein, who wrote *about* immigrant families from the vantage point of a comfortable middle-class American writer. Scholars of autobiography look more closely at stories of Americanization and their relation to the myth of the American melting pot.[4] Although Werner Sollors has made a compelling case about ethnic literature as an exercise in "group documentation and self-analysis," my analysis shares more with Thomas Ferraro's claim that immigrant literature is "compelling beyond the individual ethnic sphere."[5] As I read it, the immigrant novel by first generation immigrant writers focused on Americanization, difference, humanity, and craft.

By making both immigrant manual labor and immigrant intellectual labor coterminous rather than mutually exclusive categories, Ravage and Cahan invite us to rethink our readerly assumptions about what an immigrant story should be and what it can be. In their writings, a "composite" new American emerges as simultaneously aspiring toward and at odds with the ideal "new American" imagined by both Euro-American writers and the national Americanization campaigns. This strategic positioning of the new immigrant as a "composite" American shares similarities with Indigenous intellectuals' positioning vis-à-vis modernity, as they also negotiated new social, political, and literary spheres. Like their Native intellectual peers, new immigrant writers and activists negotiated and revised the script of Americanization as they authored new immigrant literature.

AMERICANIZATION AND THE NEW IMMIGRANT MEMOIR: MARCUS E. RAVAGE'S AN AMERICAN IN THE MAKING

Marcus Eli Ravage (né Revici, 1884–1965) arrived in New York City in 1900, following a massive wave of immigration to North America, and settled on the Lower East Side, where more than a third of recent European Jewish immigrants had settled by 1924.[6] He wrote historical and political studies, was a European correspondent for *The Nation*, and contributed fiction and nonfiction to *Harper's*, the *New Republic*, *Century Illustrated Magazine*, and *Puck*, among others. When he died in 1965, his *New York Times* obituary described him as a "Romanian-born American author" who "came to New York's Lower East Side at the age of sixteen, and worked as a peddler, bartender and in a sweat-shop as he struggled to learn English in night school. The story of his experiences as an immigrant was widely used in high schools."[7]

An American in the Making: The Life Story of an Immigrant, written at a time when the immigrant writer was competing with socio-logical accounts of "the immigrant story," tells an unexpected story of Americanization. Speaking, in part, to contemporaries' theories of Americanization and against the growing nativism of the late 1910s and 1920s, Ravage responds to previous representations of "the immi-grant" by both immigrant and American writers. He shows how a first-generation immigrant writer, public intellectual, and journalist engaged the political and cultural debates surrounding Americanization.[8] In *An American in the Making*, Ravage rewrites not only the immigrant's tragedy of readjustment but also the genre of immigrant autobiogra-phy. His "American in the making" is neither fully Americanized nor a greenhorn but a subject aware of his objectification in contemporaneous sociological studies and photojournalistic exposés. This immigrant memoir, centered on the impossibility of complete transformation and the emergence of a "composite" American, is at odds with the idea of the American imagined and presented by the national Americanization campaigns.

Written in four parts, *An American in the Making* re-creates the immigrant's journey from a shtetl in Vaslui, Eastern Romania, to New York's Lower East Side, the American Midwest, and back to New York.[9] The postscript, added to the second edition in 1935, tells of Ravage's brief return to his hometown in Romania—where he encounters "dilapidation and decay and stark ugliness"—and his eventual move to France. Like many immigrant memoirs, it fulfills readerly expectations of familiar tropes: the lure of America, deracination, a heart-breaking farewell to family, the first days in New York, and adventures of transformation.[10] Unlike most immigrant autobiographies of this era, *An American in the Making* makes internal migration—from the temporary safety of Little Romania and the Jewish ghetto in New York City to Columbia, Missouri—central to his transformation. To complete his internal migration, Ravage's autobiographical persona, Max, like Anzia Yiezierska's main character in *Bread Givers* (1925), Sarah Smolinsky, has to leave the ghetto in order to "make [himself] for a person" by attending a university in the Midwest, "the land of the true Americans." He recounts: "in the autumn of 1906, I started out on my great adventure. . . . I was going to the land of the 'real Americans.'"[11] Internalizing his contemporaries' geocultural stratifications of American regions—the East was taken over by the purported immigrant invasion—Ravage appeals to a familiar narrative of American national identity formation, one that took the American Midwest as the quintessentially American space.

Re-creating yet also challenging familiar binaries of the immigrant memoir genre (alien/citizen, Jewish/Gentile, diasporic/local, native/immigrant, and the problematic settler colonial binary Old World/New World), *An American in the Making* joined a growing canon of autobiographies in English by first-generation immigrant authors, including Danish American Jacob Riis's *The Making of an American* (1904); Bohemian American Simon Pollak's *The Autobiography and Reminiscences of Simon Pollak, M.D.* (1904); Henry Holt's edition of working-class immigrant narratives, *The Life Stories of Undistinguished Americans* (1906); Chinese American Yung Wing's *My Life in*

China and America (1909), Russian Jewish Mary Antin's *The Promised Land* (1912), and Slovakian American Edward Steiner's *From Alien to Citizen* (1914).[12] According to family legend, *An American in the Making* brought Ravage an invitation to breakfast at the White House with President Wilson.[13] Reviewers were quick to link the story to the author's lived experience: "The publishers assure us that the tale is true." Although some early reviews tended to address its appeal to a public appetite for "real" life stories—a genre popularized, for instance, by Henry Holt's 1906 collection *The Life Stories of Undistinguished Americans*—other reviewers praised its aesthetic merits: "As moving as the best of novels, this story of *actual experience* is something more than a mere personal narrative."[14]

Whereas sociologists were interested in the impact of Americanization on immigrant groups, Ravage was interested in the impact of Americanization on the individual. When sociologist Robert E. Park reviewed Ravage's memoir for the *American Journal of Sociology* in 1918, he praised it for being "a valuable source-book on the subject of the immigrant," suggestive of "a dawning racial consciousness" in an immigrant writer who does not seem as happy or as assimilated as his predecessor immigrant autobiographers.[15] Defying conventional expectations of the immigrant memoir as a social document rather than a literary text, Ravage foregrounds immigrant agency and a "dawning racial consciousness" that sociologists like Park were beginning to theorize.

The Immigrant Autobiography and the Politics of Representation

Just as Americanization, as policy or ideology, walks the fine line between liberty and coercion, consent and dissent, so does the genre of immigrant autobiography, which negotiates narrower, group identity representations with larger claims to universality.[16] Ravage's autobiography represents the first-generation Romanian Jewish middle-class immigrant male story, as it also speaks to more universal concerns about labor, authorship, and Americanization. As Sidonie Smith and Julia Watson have argued, recent scholarship has started to look more closely at "these other stories of Americanization among populations dominated and spoken for by the myth of the American melting pot";

Smith and Watson show how some autobiographers "link their auto-biographical writing to social critique."[17]

In his memoir, Ravage departs from a familiar trope, that of the self-made and assimilated immigrant, popularized by Jacob Riis's successful autobiography, *The Making of an American* (1904). The resemblance of titles suggests that Ravage may have used Riis's title strategically in his own memoir to link his work to social critique. In the last chapter of *The Making of an American,* Riis included a section on his life "twenty years later," unambiguously titled "The American Made."[18] Writing his memoir at the age of fifty, Riis gave a felicitous ending to his story of content middle-class Christian life in America, a happy family, and public recognition and admiration by Danish and American dignitaries, including the Danish king Christian and then-president Theodore Roosevelt. Riis's message was one of optimism: "Ahead there is light."[19] But there wasn't much light for Ravage and his new immigrant peers. Although Ravage, unlike Riis, saw his Americanization as a "volcanic" process, he conveyed the new immigrant's ultimate disappointment in America.[20]

Ravage placed his narrative in the larger national project of understanding not only how America sees the new immigrant but also how the immigrant sees America: "It is the free American who needs to be instructed by the benighted races. . . . Only from the humble immigrant, it appears to me, can he learn just what American stands for in the family of nations."[21] The idea of mutual discovery distinguishes Ravage's memoir from those of many of his immigrant contemporaries. Lending it a pedagogical function, Ravage sets out to tell the story not only of what an immigrant was but also what he *could* be in America, as the country itself was revising its political, scientific, and sociological definitions of what an American *should* be.

An American in the Making opens with the chapter "Life Story of an Immigrant," with Ravage living in Vaslui, Romania, then recounts the lure of "Nev York," the causes and preparations for departure, and the transatlantic journey to the United States. In part 2, Ravage narrates his arrival, shocking for the young immigrant, who experiences "a revulsion of feeling of the most distressful sort" as he is ushered in by the "rough officials" at Ellis Island.[22] Clutching his bundles, he walks to Rivington Street, "trudging through those littered streets," and comes to a bitter realization: "So this was America."[23] Whereas the Yiddish newspapers that Marcus was reading in Romania emphasized how badly immigrants were wanted in America, he soon discovered that his desirability as an immigrant depended mainly on his labor and quick assimilation. The sweatshop became his "cradle of liberty" and his "first university." Young Ravage, now "Max the Sleever"—a fitting name for his occupation in the ghetto sweatshop—discovers "the intelligentsia of the slums," who introduce him to new books, lectures, performances, and art.[24] Failing to win a coveted scholarship at City College, Ravage settles for the University of Missouri.

Like Ravage, other immigrant writers responded to the changes brought by immigration. Fellow Jewish immigrant Mary Antin claimed complete assimilation and radical change from her former self—"I am absolutely other from the person whose story I have to tell. . . . My life I have still to live; her life ended when mine began."[25] Ravage acknowledged the impossibility of returning home: "it is farewell forever" and "a person gone to America was exactly like a person dead."[26] If other immigrant groups could return home if they desired, the pogroms and persecution made immigration irreversible for Jewish immigrants.[27] Although immigration restrictionists argued that unintegrated immigrant neighborhoods, like Ravage's Rivington Street, represented the threat of balkanization, which "would compromise the integrity of the nation," they also cautioned that the absorption of all the immigrants "would make America unrecognizable to itself."[28] Ravage understood this paradox of the Americanization debates.

Whereas Ravage's immigration experience was similar to that of other conationals and Eastern European Jews—most of them farmers and laborers—what set his story apart was his desire to become a writer. If writing in English "in itself was an act of emigration" from the conservative ghetto, as Marcus Klein has argued, for Ravage writing in English was a liberatory act. Although many of his fellow Jewish authors chose to write in Yiddish for cultural or political purposes, Ravage joined the Jewish intelligentsia who claimed a symbolic space in American literature by writing in English.[29] While he built on the growing genre of immigrant memoir, Ravage resisted the totalizing impact of similar stories of Americanization, for example, Mary Antin's iconic opening of *The Promised Land*: "I was born, I have lived, and I have been made over." Instead, Ravage narrated change, mobility, and turmoil in the new immigrant's psyche: "We are not what we were when you saw us landing from the Ellis Island ferry."[30] He told a story of success and disappointment, gain and loss, transformation and stagnation, always with an eye toward the process—the story of "an American in the making."

Although he built common ground with his imagined, white middle-class readership, in the introduction to *An American in the Making* Ravage confessed that the subject of his story differed from the immigrant of the American imagination. He also addressed the native-born readers directly on several occasions: "You fortunate ones who have never had to come to America." He described the moment of the encounter between the immigrant and the native-born imagination as something "fit for a farce": "In his peculiar, transplanted life, he sells nondescript merchandise in fantastic vehicles, does violence to the American's language, and sits down on the curb *to eat fragrant cheese and unimaginable sausages. He is, for certain, a character fit for farce*" (my emphasis).[31] These exaggerations of the American public's farcical encounter with the immigrant served to amplify how different the new immigrants were from the old. In his study *The Old World in the New* (1914), sociologist E. A. Ross underscored the undesirability of new immigrants; his racist lexicon provided a vivid popular illustration of the putatively repulsive new immigrant. Ravage revised the contours of these reductive strokes: "When I hear all around me the foolish prattle about the new immigration—'the scum of Europe,' as it is called—that is invading and making itself master of this country, I cannot help saying to myself that Americans have forgotten America."[32] Ravage highlighted the paradox of the Americanization debates: that immigrants were a threat to the nation and their absorption would alter the nation irrevocably.

Ravage's autobiography gave new immigrants a voice and agency in contemporaneous debates over Americanization. The "immigrant experience" as a literary trope has been the subject of many genres of American literature. Established American writers like Willa Cather (*O, Pioneers!*, 1913, and *My Antonia*, 1918) and Upton Sinclair (*The Jungle*, 1906) incorporated in their works themes of alienation and poverty, second-language acquisition, and the costs of Americanization. Others went so far as to pass as immigrant writers: Broughton Brandenburg posed as an Italian immigrant.[33] Like Jacob Riis and Mary

Antin, or Native writer Gertrude Bonnin/Zitkala-Ša, who serialized their autobiographies in such periodicals as *The Outlook, The Churchman, Century Magazine,* or the *Atlantic Monthly,* Ravage serialized his autobiography in *Harper's Magazine.* Americanization brochures often included references to immigrant memoirs, recommending them for teaching English and civics. A growing interest in immigrant lives made immigrant memoirs appealing to the general reading public in the 1910s. Despite its critical stance on Americanization and immigration policy, Ravage's memoir was widely used in the New York public schools. Like the paradox of Americanization, such was the paradoxical reception of a story of and by "a real American."

Ravage's cultural authority stemmed largely from his negotiation of the prescriptive norms of Americanization (as ideology) and autobiography (as *the* genre of immigrant literary production). Thomas Ferraro argues that such immigrant narratives introduced the public to "the debate within ethnic homes over alternative American dreams."[34] For Ravage, the alternative to the American dream was his coming of age as a public intellectual, a secular Jew, and an American multilingual author. For immigrant writers like Ravage, literature was not only "a useful venue for the contest of political ideas," as Matthew F. Jacobson has argued, it was also "a forum for protesting present conditions . . . and for challenging the oppressors' legitimating narratives of persecution and conquest."[35] If American literature accentuated the opposition between the nation's insiders and outsiders, immigrant writers who chose to write in national languages accentuated that distance even further. However, writers like Ravage brought the eastern European immigrants closer to the American national narrative by choosing to write in English.

Americanization Redux

In the 1910s, as Ravage was on the way to becoming a respected journalist and autobiographer, the epitome of the "Americanization as assimilation" movement reached its peak. As we have seen in earlier chapters, Americanization was a highly divisive movement: on one hand, the nativists and future restrictionists argued for the preservation of a so-called national character; on the other, Americanizers wanted to help immigrants adjust to life in the U.S. Steven G. Kellman claims that

Ravage wrote his memoir "in part to assuage anxieties over a foreign invasion."[36] It is a pertinent interpretation, but Ravage was also engaging the political discourses of the time, from the urban sociologists' belief in incorporating the immigrants, to the militant nationalism at the beginning of World War I, to immigration policies aimed at keeping the undesirable immigrants out, to larger political debates over American identity.

Anglo-Americans saw the new arrivals as savage, dirty, or a threat to the Progressive Era sense of social order.[37] Ravage himself felt the intensity of the cultural gaze measuring his difference—first, only briefly in the New York ghetto, and then more consistently and painfully after his arrival in Missouri: "That first week in Missouri I found out what it was to be a stranger in a foreign land."[38] Ravage considered anti-Semitism as a logical explanation for his peers' rejection: "Why, these chaps had not the remotest idea what a Jew was like!" Aware of the "stage caricature" of the Jew, who "sold clothing and spoke broken English," Marcus concealed his Jewishness during his first three years at the university. But as his midwestern colleagues studied him, he also studied them. When they played and talked about sports, Max wanted to talk about socialism. The sheer brutishness of his colleagues shouting and pounding on tables during sports events repulsed him: "I thought I had wandered into a barbarous country."[39] To Missourians, Ravage was a bit of an oddity, yet when he was in the national spotlight, the *Daily Missourian* wrote proudly about the writer and former student. Just as Ravage claimed the Missourian chapter as key to his education and transformation, so did the Missourians, who recognized "the foreigner" in "search for the genuine American" and who could become "one of them."[40]

An American in the Making was published before the U.S. entered World War I in 1917, during a time of heightened nativist anxieties, and it dramatized emerging conceptions of American identity.[41] Before the war, Ravage could still imagine Americanization as a process, with a glimpse of immigrant agency. As a naturalized American citizen (in 1912), Ravage understood the influence his memoir could have on his readers by engaging three competing theories of American identity that informed the years preceding its publication: while critical of the theories of Anglo-conformity (100 percent Americanism) and the melting pot ("the Crèvecoeurian myth of Americanization"), Ravage dramatized the possibilities offered by cultural pluralism, as theorized by Kallen and Bourne.[42] Challenging the optimistic views of the assimilationists, Kallen and Bourne articulated a version of Americanism, grounded in the belief that immigrants could teach America as much as America could teach them. Like them, Ravage believed that the survival of immigrant cultures would enrich the adoptive country. At the end of a decade punctuated by these debates, heightened nationalism and nativism generated by World War I and the rise of scientific racism, both assimilationists and cultural pluralists deferred to the restrictionists, who claimed that new immigrants were destroying the national racial stock.

Challenging theories of Anglo-conformity and the myth of the melting pot at the heart of the Americanization movement, Ravage echoed Kallen's theory of cultural pluralism, which argued for preserving ethnic and cultural differences. For Kallen, those "inner" qualities representing the immigrant's descent were essential to maintaining what he called "a multiplicity in a unity."[43] Ravage's physical presence caused anxiety in his classmates. He lacked their manners, etiquette, language, and hygiene. In Missouri, Max was the greenhorn, all over again, and his readjustment was slow, painful, often filled with thoughts of suicide. Consenting to change so he could survive in the midwestern academic environment, Ravage also pondered the artificiality of his transformation. With wit, he concluded, "Those capitalists and oppressors were making me into a gentleman."[44] Yet he ultimately saw his difference as salutary to his identity as an "American in the making."

Just as he echoed Kallen's idea of pluralism as a challenge to Anglo-conformity and assimilation, Ravage also endorsed the idea of American pluralism as dissent to Americanization, as theorized by contemporary radical social critic Randolph Bourne. In "Trans-National America" (1916), Bourne argued that the new immigrant was the product of several cultures, a trans-national subject, rather than the artificial "melting" of the foreigner into the nationalist melting pot. Invoking the failure of the melting pot, Bourne argued that, like Europe, America was "a cosmopolitan federation of national colonies," a "world federation in miniature."[45] The idea of a federated America did not rely on a central, Anglo-Saxon culture but on multiple cultures. In a section titled "How do you like America?" Ravage spoke directly to Bourne's vision by referring to the East Side ghetto as a "miniature federation of semi-independent, allied states" of a "highly compact union."[46] Unlike Bourne, whose idealism placed the new immigrant in rather abstract spaces, Ravage humanized the miniature federation of the ghetto. His vision of Americanization in *An American in the Making* offered an alternative to "melting," a transformative blending of home country and host country traditions.

By the time the U.S. entered World War I, the network advancing the Americanization of immigrants had grown significantly, to include the Bureau of Education, the Bureau of Naturalization, newly created Americanization offices in state governments, public school systems, religious organizations, the Red Cross, and women's organizations.[47] The Americanization campaigns organized by reformers reached far and wide. About one million immigrants enrolled in formal public school Americanization classes, but fewer actually completed them.[48] Although Ravage did not anticipate the full extent of immigration restriction policy, he believed in the power of education in the immigrant's adaptation and eventual Americanization. Like many Americans, Ravage believed that education could solve social problems. Although he attended public schools, the ghetto was Ravage's most-lasting encounter with things American. With its exchange of books in Yiddish, Russian, German, and English among the intelligentsia, the evening lectures, and the East Side theater, the ghetto offered Ravage an education. He read Sholem Aleichem, the poetry of I. L. Peretz in Yiddish, studies by foreign writers (Gorky, Andreiyev, Tolstoy) and attended performances at the Progressive Dramatic Club long before he started speaking English. Not all immigrants wanted to become American, but we hardly ever read this explicitly in immigrant narratives. Ravage records the immigrant's disappointment in America: "My Americanized compatriots were not happy, by their own confession."[49] The preservation of the old country's religions, political allegiances, rituals, languages, and the cultivation of cultural institutions (churches, synagogues, schools, clubs, or newspapers) offered spaces of *alternative Americanization*, where immigrants found a home. Ultimately, the education envisioned by Americanizers was, for Ravage and millions of other new immigrants, incongruous with the reality of their lived experience.

While the nativists agitated for restriction, the new immigrants continued to build their own associations, clubs, newspapers, and a growing network of cosmopolitan communities. For the Jewish immigrants, the wide circulation of Yiddish newspapers facilitated their encounter with American topics even before they left their homelands. Young Marcus and his family read Yiddish newspapers brought from America by Couza, an estranged village relative, who returned occasionally as "the prophet from America." Yiddish connected Ravage with the imagined land of opportunity: "I conceived of New York as a brave, adventurous sort of place where life was a perilous business, but romantic for that very reason." His coming of age as a writer coincided with an unprecedented dissemination of mass circulation newspapers, including a growing foreign language press. Ravage's memoir ends with his first year at the University of Missouri, where, armed with a desire to succeed, he defeats loneliness, alienation, and discrimination. Unable to find a space of his own, Ravage came to the bitter conclusion that he did not, in fact, belong anywhere.

M. E. Ravage's Americanization and the Challenges of a (Literary) Genre

In 1915, Horace Kallen captured the crux of the celebrated immigrant autobiographies of the day: "The Riises and Steiners and Antins protest too much, they are too self-conscious and self-centered, their 'Americanization' appears too much like an achievement, a *tour de force*, too little like a growth."[50] The Ravages, as it were, soon rectified what Kallen thought to be a flawed model. Ravage's intellectual honesty offered a useful example of immigrant writing focused on growth, difference, and critical distance from Anglo-Saxonism. Although it was read as a story of a "thoroughly Americanized" immigrant by some of Ravage's contemporaries, *An American in the Making* defied the conventions of the immigrant genre by drawing attention to the process of assimilation as always incomplete, and the impossibility of return for Jewish immigrants. The new identity that Ravage forged was neither alien nor American, but "American in the making."

If new immigrants were foreign compared to their old, Anglo-Saxon immigrant peers, was their writing also exotic, different, alien? Sau-Ling Cynthia Wong reminds us that "just as immigrants are often seen as less than fully American, immigrant autobiography has been customarily assigned to the peripheries of American autobiographical scholarship."[51] For Ravage, Americanization is a multilinear process, where freedom as much as coercion play equally important roles in "the making of Americans" (along with social and historical forces, such as race, class, and gender). Becoming American "cannot be understood in 'emancipationist' terms alone, as immigrants invariably encountered structures of class, race, gender, and national power that constrained, and sometimes defeated their efforts to be free." At the same time, coercion, as much as liberty, has influenced "the process of becoming American."[52] Ravage's conformity to the genre of immigrant autobiography, imposed by the demands of the literary market and the nativism of the 1910s, was only partial. Two years after he published *An American in the Making*, Ravage continued to argue for Americanization in the pages of the *New Republic*. In "Democratic Americanization: A Critique and a Policy," he called on the country to Americanize itself: "Before the immigrant can be won over, we must Americanize America itself. We must lift American institutions. . . . We must come to look upon the immigrant as he is, a boon to us and an equal, instead of a nuisance and an uninvited invader."[53] Ravage also challenged the form and politics of immigrant autobiography, acknowledging that this intervention allows us to read immigrant autobiography as also critical of Americanization.

If immigrant autobiographies served larger political goals of appeasing nativist and xenophobic fears of racially different others, they were also a pivotal archive in the emergence of immigrant literature. Because of the role they played in the American identitary project during the Progressive Era, they served a dual purpose: they created a reading public for these narratives and they educated the public about the immigrants' purported difference. Immigrant autobiographies responded to the way the cultural and social demographics were changing as a result of massive waves of immigration. Ravage and his peers were writing about a search for immigrant cultural citizenship and autonomy. While restrictionists looked for ways to make immigrants more excludable, the immigrant writers attempted to make them more includable. In his review of Ravage's memoir, sociologist Robert E. Park commended his literary and political project. Acknowledging that the immigrant writer was well aware of immigrant representations in the mainstream press, Park argued that the immigrant had reflected on it and had started "to write back."[54] Indeed, for Ravage, writing in English was a way of writing back, of accessing the American literary market, and of becoming American on his own terms—as a writer.

AMERICANIZATION AND THE IMMIGRANT NOVEL: ABRAHAM CAHAN, *THE RISE OF DAVID LEVINSKY*

Although they read each other, it is not clear that M. E. Ravage and Abraham Cahan ever crossed paths in New York City's Lower East Side. If, for Ravage, becoming an American coincided with becoming a writer, for Cahan's fictional David Levinsky, becoming American was coterminous with becoming an entrepreneur who used capital to exploit fellow immigrant laborers. Whereas fellow immigrant writers used the literature they produced as platform to call attention to the limits of legal citizenship in the intellectual immigrant's search for cultural citizenship, in *The Rise of David Levinsky* (1917) Abraham Cahan meditated on the costs of the immigrant capitalist's Americanization in arguably one of the most popular immigrant novels ever written.[55] In this section I turn to the novel's contribution to the genre of the immigrant novel— a popular genre with a long and insufficiently examined history—and its potential recovery as a counternarrative to the Americanization ethos and policy during the decades leading to immigration restriction legislation in 1924. *The Rise of David Levinsky*, a nod to William Dean Howells's *The Rise of Silas Lapham* (1885), earned the praise of Howells, the dean of American letters, who hailed Cahan as "the new star of American realism." Howells was enthusiastic about Cahan's fiction: "We have in him a writer of foreign birth who will do honor to American letters . . . He is already thoroughly naturalized to our point of view; *he sees things with American eyes*" (my emphasis). Yet, Howells's enthusiasm was directed less at Cahan the immigrant novelist and more at Cahan as an already Americanized immigrant author, who saw "things with American eyes."[56] To be accepted in the rarified world of American letters, could the "new star of American realism" be less than Americanized? Could he be recognized for his literary virtues if he were "to see things" differently?

Whether the immigrant as an intellectual or a capitalist were the "goals of immigrant ambition" or not, as Randolph Bourne noted in his compelling review of Ravage and Cahan for the *New Republic* in

1918, they are useful categories to conceptualize immigrant representation, especially in the rare instance when the representors were themselves immigrants who published in English.[57] Like other immigrant writers of his generation, in his novel Cahan challenged the popular, optimistic version of Americanization, which entailed an unproblematic transition from greenhorn to citizen, a transformation central to many immigrant novels. Whereas, for Ravage, Americanization signified a continuous transformation, Cahan created in *David Levinsky* what Bourne called in his review "the story of the undesirable American on the make," the successful businessman whose turn from exploited into exploiter of fellow immigrant workers offered Cahan an occasion for social critique. Levinsky's Americanization also coincided with his entrance into modernity, a social and cultural scene that left a lasting mark on his immigrant persona, just as he transformed modernity as an immigrant. In this section, I examine the context preceding and surrounding the publication of the novel in 1917, and argue that *The Rise of David Levinsky* stages Cahan's response to nativism and anti-Semitism. Cahan's protagonist, David Levinsky, fashions his Americanized persona to survive and adapt in the new, urban environment. His determination to Americanize leads to a series of unfulfilled, deferred dreams, such as college education and marriage. By privileging his desired new identity and by repressing other forms of identification, Cahan's character opens up a line of critique of constructions of race and ethnicity. I end this section with a discussion of the immigrant novel as a legitimate genre in 1917 and beyond, and offer some thoughts on bringing the immigrant novel in conversation with other questions of nationality, race, and ethnicity.

Abraham Cahan was born in a small Lithuanian village, Podberezy, near Vilna, in 1860. He left for the U.S. with a false passport shortly after the assassination of Czar Alexander II in 1881 and the ensuing pogroms. He arrived in the U.S. on June 6, 1882, eighteen years before Ravage. Whereas Ravage left behind a loving family in Romania, the protagonist of Cahan's novel is an orphan, who witnessed the death of his mother at Gentiles' hands shortly before his departure from Antomir, in the anti-Jewish violence that accompanied the Russian occupation of Lithuania in the early 1880s.[58] In both Romania and Lithuania, "poverty and governmental anti-Semitism led many thousands every year to decide to go to America."[59] Max Ravage was determined to go to America "on foot." The cry "to America" also inspired David Levinsky: "It spread like wild-fire, even over those parts of the Pale of Jewish Settlement which lay outside the riot zone."[60] The anti-Semitism Ravage and Cahan witnessed at home resurfaced in New York City, as new hierarchies of difference fueled nativism and xenophobia.

Cahan's novel, along with his other fictional and journalistic work in English and Yiddish, contributed to the consolidation of the genre of the immigrant novel.[61] The Jewish immigrant novel, of course, has a much longer history in the U.S., from Nathan Mayer's novels of mid-nineteenth century to Isaac Mayer Wise's didactic and historical novels from the late nineteenth century. It wasn't until the large immigration wave of the 1880s that the Jewish American novel came to prominence and recognition in the U.S.[62] Whereas, for immigrant writers like Ravage, Americanization presupposed a continuous transformation, Cahan offered in David Levinsky a critique of "the American on the make," the capitalist who played the game of Americanization for profit. Randolph Bourne concluded his critique of the novel: "Mr. Cahan makes a subtle back-fire of criticism more deadly than the most melodramatic socialist fiction," offering "a corroding criticism of the whole field of ambitions and ideals of this pushing, primitive society, more telling than any caricature or railing."[63] Levinsky is not an eager immigrant ready to Americanize; he is a successful businessman whose turn from exploited into exploiter provides Cahan with an opportunity for social critique.

The Rise of David Levinsky was the first immigrant novel to receive national attention and, with it, a review on the first page of the *New York Times Book Review*. Despite its early favorable reception, it has received less attention than it deserves as an immigrant novel.[64] Levinsky's story of success and failure has fascinated generations of critics who have read his rise and fall as a critique of capitalism and loss of spirituality, a rags-to-riches story—a bildungsroman—Abraham Cahan's autobiographical account, "a classic of American literature."[65] Some critics have read it as a genre piece, an example of realism, ghetto realism, or naturalism; others have focused on the character's trauma and the psychological demands of Americanization on the immigrant's psyche. Understanding this novel in the context of the Americanization movement and heightened nationalism soon after its publication in 1917 helps rethink both immigrant subjectivity and the cultural work of the immigrant novel in negotiating the simultaneous pressures on the immigrant writer: Americanization (ethnic) group affiliation, access to an English readership and the American literary market, and representing the diverse experience of immigration against pressures of homogeneity.

The Immigrant Novel as Life Story: "The Autobiography of an American Jew"

Before he published *The Rise of David Levinsky*, Cahan was a cultural critic and cultural mediator, a journalist for the *Commercial Advertiser*, and an aspiring writer who contributed stories and sketches to the *New York Post* and the *New York Sun*. His early fictional work in English, which contained the germs of his future stories, included the novels *Yekl: A Tale of the New York Ghetto* (1896) and *The White Terror and the Red: A Novel of Revolutionary Russia* (1905). Cahan planned to write another novel, which he never completed.[66] At the height of his career, he described himself as "an important American novelist," "the best foreign language editor in the United States," and "a former feature writer for various English language newspapers."[67] Jules Chametzky calls Cahan "a bridge between disparate worlds of experience. . . . Among the Yankees, a Jew; among the Jews, an expert on the American scene; in capitalist America, a radical socialist; among radicals, a moderate; an intellectual and a popularizer; a Russian soul and education jostling alongside a Jewish and American one."[68] In asserting his legacy as "an important American novelist," Cahan legitimated the category of immigrant novelist as an American novelist.

Through his fictional and journalistic work, Cahan helped many Americans find the humanity of immigrants, a group that Jacob Riis in his photojournalistic *How the Other Half Lives* (1890) had reduced to mere types or specimens, waiting for a White Savior to rescue them from socioeconomic and racial marginalization. As the founding editor of the *Jewish Daily Forward* in 1897—the most influential Yiddish newspaper, with the highest circulation of all immigrant papers in the U.S.—Cahan arguably contributed to the Americanization of Jewish immigrants. He also printed Yiddish translations of the U.S. Constitution and the Declaration of Independence in the *Jewish Daily Forward/ Forverts*, a Yiddish-language newspaper he edited for forty-three years.

Cahan helped fellow Jewish immigrants *find* America long before he conjured the memorable David Levinsky; he wrote a history of the United States in Yiddish, making the history of his adopted country available to a large Jewish readership in the U.S. and abroad. Cahan's editorials in the *Forward* "criticized America's failure to live up to the country's ideals of liberty and democracy in its treatment of workers and black Americans." Close to 250,000 students used his *English Teacher* (1891) to learn English. Like his fellow immigrant writers, Cahan taught English in a night school and was certified by the New York City Board of Education.[69] Although he continued to write in Yiddish and English, Cahan cultivated a taste for Yiddish literature in the *Forverts*—as the Jewish intelligentsia disdained the Yiddish "jargon" as plebeian—by publishing the work of Sholem Aleichem, Sholem Ash, I. J. Singer, Isaac Bashevis Singer, and others. *The Rise of David Levinsky* was Cahan's last work of fiction in English or Yiddish. Writing in English was more a matter of necessity than choice for him. Unlike many of his middle-class Jewish contemporaries, Cahan realized that his Yiddish audience in America, though small, would become even smaller if the language were not preserved.[70] Ethnic enclaves tried to preserve a sense of belonging, or "the national feeling," in a familiar language. Although many immigrants shared similar political commitments, sociologist Robert E. Park argued, it was ultimately language and tradition that brought them together.[71]

Long before David Levinsky and the American Jewish question took shape in the U.S., Cahan had made a strong plea against anti-Semitism. He became an advocate for social justice through his work as a journalist and a socialist. When he raised the "Jewish question" at the International Socialist Congress in Brussels in 1891, he spoke forcefully: "The Jews are persecuted. Pogroms are made upon them. They are insulted, they are oppressed. Exceptional laws are made for them. They have been made into a separate class of people with no rights." He urged his audience to "push back anti-Semitism! Declare before the world that you condemn every form of Jewish persecution!"[72]

Cahan published the story that generated the novel *The Rise of David Levinsky* under the title "The Autobiography of an American Jew: The Rise of David Levinsky" in the sensationalist magazine *McClure's* in four installments, April to July 1913.[73] The March issue of *McClure's* included a lengthy article, "The Jewish Invasion of America," by Burton J. Hendrick, which offered an alarmist prediction of a eugenics professor that "in another hundred years the United States will be peopled chiefly by Slavs, negroes, and Jews." Announcing Cahan's forthcoming piece, Hendrick enthusiastically endorsed the story of "the Jews [who] so easily surpass or crowd out, at least in business and finance, the other great immigrating races . . . and why, in the next hundred years, the Semitic influence is likely to be almost preponderating in the United States."[74] Hendrick concluded by calling the Jews superior to other "invading races," thus setting the tone for Cahan's upcoming story.[75]

Although it is not clear whether Cahan knew about *McClure's* set-up for the story, he was well aware of the pressures of ethnic representation that the literary market was making on him as author of *Yekl* and "The Imported Bridegroom" (1898).[76] The blurb preceding the story (which ran with arguably racist illustrations by Jay Hambidge) introduced Levinsky as "an actual type" taken from "real life," fulfilling realism's new promise of extending literary representation to social groups "formerly neglected or idealized in literature."[77] *McClure's* editor added that Levinsky's story "reproduce[d] actual characters, occurrences and situations taken from *real life*."[78] The editor's distinction between a "real life" account and an "invention" called into question the fictionality of Cahan's story and reduced its aesthetic value to that of a sociological account, more consistent with investigative journalism than literary realism, denying that a Jewish writer could have imagination. But the readers of *McClure's* were in for a treat; Cahan's character negotiated subtly between his "real life" identification—*dos pintele yid,* the contested notion of the "quintessential Jew" that the public wanted to read about—and his desire to be(come) somebody else throughout the novel.[79] Cahan's decision to make an immigrant character central to an American story of transformation, told from a first-person narrative perspective, reveals his investment in the genre of the immigrant novel that his work helped solidify.

The Immigrant Novel and the Performance of Americanization

Like their American-born peers, immigrant novelists and autobiographers were invested in (re)defining ethnic identity for a predominantly WASP readership; in their endeavors, they resorted to imaginative scenarios of Americanization and struggles between the push toward cultural conformity and the pull of (ethnic) community. Cahan's David Levinsky, the unreliable narrator, contemplates his recent transformation as a "convincing personation," a performance of his many identities, including his Americanized persona: "We are all actors, more or less. The question is only what our aim is, and whether we are capable of a 'convincing personation.'"[80] Reading Americanization in Cahan's novel as performance, the immigrant character's deliberate effort to embody, to mimic, and to reframe or repress his other identities (ethnic, national, sexual) opens new possibilities for rethinking the immigrant novel as a reconceptualization of the pervasive myth of the American melting pot.

At first glance, *The Rise of David Levinsky*, written for an English-speaking, middle-class audience, is a Horatio Alger story. A Jewish immigrant becomes a successful clothes manufacturer after following a more or less predictable rags-to-riches trajectory. Born in Antomir, in Russian-occupied Lithuania, David lived with his mother and went to a traditional Jewish school in town. After his mother died in an altercation with a Gentile, trying to avenge her son (beaten in the street for his sidelocks), orphan David decided to leave for America. After his arrival in New York City, Levinsky abandoned his Orthodox clothes and religion, attended an evening school to learn English, and dreamed of becoming a scholar. One of his dreams, deferred after his cloak manufacturing business took off, was to attend City College: "Once I am to be an educated man I want to be the genuine article."[81] But he never becomes a "genuine article"; instead, he becomes complicit with American capitalism in manufacturing countless replicas of the genuine article he aspired to be. The remaining chapters of the novel revolve around his "rise" and economic success, as well as his personal failures, such as his loneliness and his failed attempts to start a family.

Throughout *The Rise of David Levinsky*, David is concerned with his appearance. He examines and imitates what he sees as "real" American gestures, demeanor, and inflections of voice. After his arrival in the U.S., he acquires new clothes and a new haircut: "I scarcely recognized myself . . . It was as though the hair-cut and the American clothes had changed my identity." Mr. Even, his benefactor, is an indirect agent of Levinsky's Americanization; he instructs the barber: "'Cut off his side-locks while you are at it. One may go without them and yet be a good Jew." Pleased with David's external transformation, his benefac-

tor exclaims: "That will make you look American. . . . One must be pre-
sentable in America."[82] The novel reveals the fashioning of Levinsky's
"American" identity and its performative possibilities. When Loeb, an
American-born Jew, starts ridiculing Russian Jews for their excessive
gesticulations, Levinsky reveals the exterior markers of his own identification as a foreigner in tension with his desire to be American. This
episode instructs David that "foreign" and "American" are embodied
identities, emerging from iterative performances following established
social codes. In a queer reading of the novel, Warren Hoffman has
argued that at the heart of the novel is Levinsky's inability to "negotiate his homoerotic feelings for other men" because such a negotiation
collided with his project of assimilation; Levinsky repressed his homo-
sexuality so that he could perform his Americanization.[83] Levinsky's
version of Americanization is a heterosexual one, despite the novel's investment in queer desire, which David ultimately represses. His performance of his sexuality and nationality reveals that his desire to become
American supersedes his desire to be recognized as a queer immigrant
during the Progressive Era.

Despite the external changes to his clothes and demeanor, Levinsky
is a constantly anxious character who tries to mask his Orthodox past
and his gesticulations, which he perceives to be "so distressingly un-
American." David internalizes his performance through self-surveillance:
"Don't be excited. . . . Speak in a calm, low voice, as these Americans
do. And for goodness' sake don't gesticulate!"[84] Yet, Levinsky does not
suppress his Jewishness; he simply acquires a new repertoire of gestures
and words that assist in his performance of Americanization. Horace
Kallen argued optimistically that Americanization did not repress but
liberated nationality.[85] Levinsky's professed Jewish secularism became
a more distinctive mark of his immigrant persona rather than a failed
attempt to "out-green" himself, to escape the mark of the new immigrant arrival, the greenhorn.

David Levinsky dramatizes his performance of becoming American,
and his studied performance invites questions about what and why
he is performing. In a study of Cahan's novel alongside James Wel-
don Johnson's The Autobiography of an Ex-Colored Man, Catherine
Rottenberg reads race and ethnicity as "performative reiteration[s]"
and argues that specific "modalities of performativity" emerge in a
subject's behavior, gestures, and speech acts when the subject attempts

to cite dominant, hegemonic categories of identification (which recognize him as subject). Thus, "subjects are interpellated into the symbolic order as gendered, classed, and raced beings"; once interpellated, they must "cite and mime the very norms that created their intelligibility . . . in the first place." This symbolic order demarcates the boundaries of the subject's identification from his "desire to be."[86]

David Levinsky's "desire to be" American mimics dominant categories of identification throughout the novel. This type of imitation calls to mind contemporary postcolonial critiques of mimicry. In Homi K. Bhabha's framework, when the colonized mimics the colonizer's institutions, behavior, language, music, appearance, and so on, he creates ambivalence in the colonizer, calling into question the colonial project through repetition and difference (the colonized sees his power and hegemony disrupted).[87] But Levinsky's position vis-à-vis the settler colonial nation is tenuous; as a Jewish immigrant, although discriminated against and inhabiting an "in-between" space in the Black-and-white racial matrix of the U.S., he enjoys the advantages of his performed whiteness. He becomes a successful capitalist who exploits other immigrants and is complicit in the settler nation's capitalist project. Levinsky's boss, Jeff Manheimer, introduces him to urban etiquette, as well as to nativism and racism: "Where were you brought up? Among Indians?"[88] He associates Levinsky's lack of manners—or his difference of manners—with racial difference, conflating cultural difference with a biological understanding of racial difference. The question translates urban and national anxieties over Native American and immigrant "savagery" and their difference from the Anglo-Saxon norm of "civilization." This norm marked nativism's widely disseminated fear of racial and ethnic difference and the threats it poses to "real Americans." Levinsky internalizes settler tropes, such as "the land of Columbus," and references to American exceptionalism as he is surveilled by America's anxieties toward "invaders." The novel also reveals Cahan's own internalized colonial discourse in Levinsky's endorsement and critique of Anglo-Saxonism.

As a white immigrant, Levinsky understands his racial advantage toward a more rapid Americanization (than African Americans or Native Americans), yet he is aware of the codes for whiteness, where "Gentile" signifies whiteness and Jewish does not. Becoming a "true American" is synonymous with becoming white, responding to the racial imperatives of Anglo-Saxonism and its codes for the American identity he seeks to perform. Discrimination against immigrant and minority groups during the Progressive Era was a lived reality. As an immigrant and a Jew, Levinsky performs whiteness and an Americanized version of his Jewishness: "I was forever watching and striving to imitate the dress and the ways of well-bred American[s]."[89] Read in the context of Progressive Era racial classifications and categories of identification, Jewish immigrants—while not enjoying the advantages of being read as "white on arrival," as Thomas Guglielmo has argued about Italian immigrants—inhabited an in-between racial status. From this vantage point of in-betweenness, Jewish immigrants engaged the hegemonic racial regime of the time, which privileged Anglo-Saxonism. Levinsky's desire to be American also signifies his desire to become white. His in-between racial status leads to what Rottenberg calls a disaggregation of Jewishness from *race* and its morphing into *identity*. This morphing of race into ethnicity "has not been possible for African Americans at all since the intelligibility of ethnicity depends on the prior construction of black-white binary opposition."[90] In morphing his whiteness unto Jewishness, Levinsky did not renounce his Jewishness but adjusted its performance to the social codes of Americanization.

One of the modes of surveillance David Levinsky encounters as he unsuccessfully tries to Americanize is the policing of his linguistic persona. Immigrant Levinsky is linguistically incompetent and anxious about his social performance. Reading *The Rise of David Levinsky* alongside Henry James's *The American*, Donald Weber has argued that Cahan's novel charts "the growth of shame, repression, self-hatred, and denial in the immigrant psyche." Weber shows that, while Christopher Newman, James's protagonist, is "at ease with his American manners," Levinsky "remains forever anxious about his social position."[91] Competing forces shape Levinsky's linguistic identity, staging an ongoing struggle between the pull of Yiddish and the desire for English. Unaccustomed to English pronunciation, David first scoffs at the idea of linguistic difference: "English impressed me as the language of a people afflicted with defective organs of speech." Levinsky hires a native speaker as a language tutor and realizes that imitation is key to his acquisition of linguistic and cultural capital: "I would hang on his lips, striving to memorize every English word I could catch and watching intently, not only his enunciation, but also his gestures, manner, and mannerisms, and accepting it all as part and parcel of the American way of speaking." Levinsky's sense of linguistic inferiority precludes what he perceives to be the ideal of Americanization. To him, "people who were born to speak English were superior beings. Even among fallen women I would seek those who were real Americans."[92] "Real Americanism," Cahan signals in the nativist and gendered undertones he implicitly critiques, will always distinguish Levinsky from his American-born peers. Levinsky's complete Americanization is, therefore, impossible.

The chasm between Levinsky's greenhorn aspirations and the reality of his Americanized life widens with age. At fifty-two, looking back on his thirty years in the U.S., he faces a classic immigrant identity crisis: David, the charity scholar of Talmud back in Lithuania, and David, the wealthy cloak manufacturer in the U.S., remain at odds: "I can never forget the days of my misery. *I cannot escape from my old self. My past and my present do not comport well*" (my emphasis).[93] His sense of displacement circularly opens and closes the novel, as he ponders the gains of accumulated capital and the loss of the greenhorn's presumed innocence. Levinsky's success and failure ultimately emerge from his negotiation with and ambivalence toward integrating and reconciling an ethnic past with an American present, at odds throughout the novel.

But David Levinsky's performance of Americanization has its limitations. He is, in Randolph Bourne's words, "an American on the make," Cahan's cautionary tale about Americanization gone wrong when capitalism gets in the way. In Bourne's astute reading, "Mr. Cahan makes a subtle back-fire of criticism more deadly than the most melodramatic socialist fiction," offering "a corroding criticism of the whole field of ambitions and ideals of this pushing, primitive society, more telling than any caricature or railing."[94] When Levinsky imitates hegemonic categories of identification that would make him legible as American, he simultaneously calls into question Americanization and its prescriptiveness. Although by the end of the novel he becomes a successful clothes manufacturer, David ultimately sees his difference as a lack: "That I was not born in America was something like a physical defect that asserted itself in many disagreeable ways—a physical defect which, alas, no surgeon in the world was capable of removing."[95] An inability to decipher American space and cues marks the greenhorn's journey. Internalizing his "un-American" behavior as a lack, Levinsky points to the impossibility of ever becoming American.

The Immigrant Novel and the Immigrant Trope

Recent attention to immigrant subjectivity has generated an interest in the immigrant novel, a genre popular in the twenty-first century but less so in the early 1900s, when sociological interest in immigrants shifted readers' attention to life stories, autobiographical accounts of immigrant journeys, and obstacles overcome.[96] Thomas Ferraro asks: "How, in fact, do immigrants become writers? . . . In what ways have recent arrivals deployed the established literary forms of the established culture? What have immigrant writers achieved for themselves and their groups by *variously* participating in national literary and rhetorical traditions?"[97] Ferraro's questions gesture at the larger immigrant literary tradition that Cahan's work has inspired, as immigrant writers continued to position themselves within the American literary and rhetorical traditions. As Matthew F. Jacobson has argued, for immigrant writers literature was not only "a useful venue for the contest of political ideas" but also "a forum for protesting present conditions . . . and for challenging the oppressors' legitimating narratives of persecution and conquest."[98] More pressingly for this study, immigrant writers went beyond the tropes of "the immigrant experience" by examining how American literature made room for immigrant tropes and how immigrant practitioners have influenced and transformed American literature.

The "immigrant experience" as a literary trope has been the subject of many genres of American literature. In their work, established American writers like Willa Cather and Upton Sinclair incorporated themes of the immigrant experience, from alienation and poverty, to second-language acquisition and the costs of Americanization. The trope of immigration attracted considerable attention from Gentile American writers, who wrote about successful or stalled Americanization experiences, often in less than flattering terms. Although literary critics are still divided on this issue, Henry James and Edith Wharton were "at least arguably anti-Semitic." Marovitz reads James's "grotesque representation of 'a Jewry that had burst all bounds'" as "ambivalent." I read James's anti-Semitism as emblematic not necessarily of his own anti-Semitism but of the "American scene" he describes through nativist and expatriate eyes.[99] Henry James's return to the American scene in 1904 proved an uneasy encounter with "the New Jerusalem" (his term for the East Side Jews), whose crowdedness and "multiplication with a vengeance" threatened the realist celebrity's bourgeois dispositions: "There is no swarming like that of Israel when once Israel has got a start. . . . The children swarmed above all—here was multiplication with a vengeance."[100] James's distaste for Jews and other immigrants, expressed in *The American Scene,* established a complicated relation between high realism and the more democratized realism proposed by William D. Howells in what he called "the aesthetic of the common" (or, between highbrow and lowbrow realism). In Cahan's novel, David Levinsky is policed and surveilled by America's anxieties toward foreign "invaders" and by realism itself as a mode of surveillance.

Although most early reviewers of Cahan's novel found ways to read it autobiographically, later studies focused on its literary appeal, its craft, and the difference between Cahan and his protagonist.[101] The craft of Cahan's novel is worth further attention, as both an immigrant novel and an American novel. Thomas Ferraro captures the crux of the immigrant writer in America: "An aspiring writer from an immigrant background feels damned on the one side for becoming too American and damned on the other side for not being able to become American enough."[102] Along with Anzia Yezierska and Mary Antin, Abraham Cahan popularized the immigrant novel in English at a time when the genre and its practitioners were under the scrutiny of modernity and one of its major social crises: immigration restriction. As a mediator between cultures and languages, emerging realist immigrant writer Cahan positioned himself in dialogue with emerging American modernity, writing about and for a group that became one of modernity's main challenges: the urban new immigrants.

Like other immigrant writers of their generation, Abraham Cahan and Marcus E. Ravage challenged the optimistic version of Americanization. Cahan's David Levinsky was not the eager immigrant ready to Americanize. Ravage's immigrant autobiography took a revisionist approach to Anglo-Saxonism.[103] Calling into question the superficiality of Americanization, Ravage not only positioned himself in relation to the American national identity narrative in *An American in the Making*, but also reframed it as he rewrote it. Rendering the immigrant character's desire and reluctance to Americanize, Cahan's *The Rise of David Levinsky* paved the way for immigrant fiction in the U.S. that would flourish throughout the twentieth century and beyond. Writing about immigrant subjectivity, old and new, requires closer attention to histories predating such forced or voluntary relocations, complicit or not in the American empire-building project, that immigrant literatures both document and imagine.

7 Spectacular Nationalism

Immigrants on the Silver Screen, Americanization, and the Picture Show

The phonograph is a marvel sure,
With a charm that's all its own;
And it's hard to overrate the lure
Of the mystic telephone.
The telegraph, with its mighty range,
Is a wonder, as we know.
But nothing yet is half as strange
As the Moving Picture Show.

—*The Moving Picture Show*, 1908

IF PRINT AS commodity was at the heart of national consciousness formation by the end of the nineteenth century, as Benedict Anderson has argued, cinema—a new medium for imagining the nation and a new commodity—also shaped the idea of national consciousness.[1] Anderson defined the nation as "an *imagined* political community"; to him, it was imagined because "the members of even the smallest nation will never know most of their fellow-members, meet them, or even hear of them." He located key forms of imagining the nation in eighteenth-century Europe print culture: the newspaper and the novel. The former, an ephemeral medium; the latter, "the first modern-style, mass-produced industrial commodity." While Anderson did not consider cinema as a medium for imagining the nation—in the sense that film theorists do when they refer to national cinema—his work opens up new lines of inquiry into the ways in which moving pictures, the next mass-produced industrial commodity after print, helped *imagine* the nation during a crucial moment of transformation of the United States, both technologically and demographically. The early twentieth century witnessed a heightened sense of nationalism and nativism precipitated by recent waves of European immigrants to the U.S. and leading to the campaign to Americanize the communities perceived as threats to American homogeneity.

As a community imagined through language, the nation inspires love and profound sacrifice; but how do the subjects coerced into or unwilling to speak the language of the settler nation—new immigrants and the American Indians—participate in it? Although Progressive Era reformers acknowledged silent film's potentially negative effects on so-called impressionable audiences—such as women, children, immigrants, and working-class Americans—they agreed on one fundamental idea: that film could educate. In recent decades, film historians have revealed the social and political roles of film across history.[2] Besides local organizations doing the work of Americanization on small or large scale, the federal government itself used the new film industry in the service of Americanization, especially at the height of the Americanization movement, during and after World War I. What I call "spectacular nationalism" in this chapter signals the visual affective connection of the (new) immigrants with their adoptive country. Spectacular nationalism emerged as a form of immigrant affect, a new line of feeling connecting immigrant subjectivity with both the country of origin and the United States. Affective Americanization, reinforced and disseminated through silent film, also indexes immigrant multiple allegiances. Like print and other cultural texts, silent film carried and elicited feelings in audiences. Although such emotions were often stifled by institutional control, especially during the more militant phase of Americanization in the 1910s, affective Americanization as a specific site of the encounter between institutions and immigrant subjects marked the immigrant viewers' encounters with both film and institutional and national ideology.[3]

In its initial context, as previous chapters have revealed, "Americanization" and "Americanism"—terms signifying the movement (to Americanize) and the (nationalist) ethos, respectively—were often used interchangeably during the 1910s and 1920s to signify the process of acculturating immigrants (through language, customs, behaviors, and so on). The Americanism Committee of the Motion Picture Industry, for instance, convened in December 1919 in Washington, D.C., to set the parameters of the Americanization campaign, which had enlisted the support of the film industry. As nativism and nationalism intensified

during and after World War I, the term "Americanization" acquired
negative connotations; if hyphenated identities thrived at the turn into
the twentieth century, the war-era nationalism shaped Americanization
into a patriotic enterprise, compounded by fears of racial and ethnic
difference and threats to Anglo-Saxonism. According to Gary Gerstle,
"coercion, as much as liberty, has been intrinsic to our history and to
the process of becoming American."[4]

Americanizers seized the opportunity to exploit the potential of
this new medium to reach wide audiences. As early motion pictures
"maintained lasting relationships with preexisting visual forms" (such
as photography), as Giorgio Bertellini has shown, these relationships
perpetuated ideologies of national and racial difference.[5] But how does
the settler nation include or exclude its aspiring citizens, through print
or silent film, when nationalism and nativism preclude the nation from
seeing the difference of its subjects? The push toward homogeneity of
the Americanization campaigns, in the name of so-called patriotism
and authorized xenophobia, reveals the possibilities and the limitations
of cinema in visualizing the settler nation.

In this chapter (and next) I ask: what cultural work did silent film
do for Americanization, the active and sometimes coercive campaign to
make new immigrants into *good* Americans? I argue that, just as Americanization did not produce compliant citizens overnight, silent film as
a powerful new medium of persuasion influenced American viewers'
transformation only in part. Of particular interest to this chapter is the
use of film in industrial and educational contexts, which sometimes
overlapped, purporting to both "educate" and Americanize the new
immigrants to the United States, particularly immigrant workers. The
films I have chosen to read as case studies—industrial, educational, and
nontheatrical films, such as *An American in the Making* (1913), *The
Making of an American* (1920), and others—illustrate the potential of
silent film as both mimesis (or representation of ideology) and as ideology. How did silent film contribute to the mission of Americanization?
Were new immigrants the innocent viewers that the American government, industrialists (like Henry Ford), and Progressive Era educators
and Americanizers were imagining for immigrant children and their
families? Were they complicit? Were they doubly exploited through the
popular images that aimed to "represent" them and in their own un-

critical reception of such films, duped by the illusion of the medium? To answer these questions, I draw on scholarship in Immigration Studies and Film Studies, as well as archival materials in the National Archives, the Library of Congress (MBRS), Northeast Historic Film, and the New York Public Library.

Although both American corporations like Ford Motor Company and the federal government used film strategically and complicitly in their efforts to Americanize the new immigrants, early American cinema was also critical of Americanization, as it negotiated new immigrant concerns about labor, literacy, gender, and representation. Miriam Hansen addresses the metaphor which understood film as a universal language that emphasized "egalitarianism, internationalism, and the progress of civilization through technology." With the rise of the nickelodeon in the United States, film offered the potential to instruct and entertain through the medium's "non-verbal mode of signification."[6] Building on Hansen's work, Giorgio Bertellini considers the larger ideological work of film on early twentieth-century audiences, noting that "to understand how films were experienced at the time of their first viewing is one thing; it is another to understand how they operated, semiotically and ideologically."[7] As industrial and educational films helped disseminate an ideal version of the desired American, silent film also helped perpetuate what Bertellini calls existing "visual patterns of national and racial differences."[8]

The images on screen—as escapist attempts from daily lives of toil or as private enjoyments away from the hustle and bustle of family and work—could also influence the immigrants' sense of ethnic or national identity and reinforce ideologies of national and racial differences. Sabine Haenni's work on the ethnicized public sphere in Midtown Manhattan reveals that European immigrants were emotionally invested "in a mediatized European immigrant scene."[9] If immigrant viewers had access to silent films, their interpellation into nationalist ideologies was not uniform. Judith Thissen finds that early silent films were complicit with the Americanization of their Jewish audiences, whereas Giorgio Bertellini argues that Italian immigrant audiences in the U.S. became, in fact, more Italian after watching films. Italians, the second largest group of new immigrants (after the Jews), watched Italian films in their U.S. neighborhoods, and rather than becoming more "American," they became more "Italian."[10] In this instance, silent film failed the Americanization project as immigrant-themed films appealed more to group allegiances in the country of origin rather than in the U.S.

NATIONALISM ON CELLULOID: SILENT FILM, EDUCATION, AND PATRIOTISM

As the Americanization campaign expanded both locally and nationally during the patriotic 1910s, silent film as a seemingly democratic (and democratizing) public sphere was a meeting ground for ideological formations vis-à-vis racial and ethnic difference. In recent decades, film scholars have started to reexamine the role of cinema at the beginning of the twentieth century, when film reached both audiences who frequented movie exhibiting places and large audiences in industrial settings.[11] Silent film could serve the education mission of the Progressive Era while also endorsing political platforms and supporting the work of the Americanization campaigns across the United States.

The moving picture show arrived in the United States at the end of the nineteenth century. Its arrival coincided with the closing of the western frontier for white settlement and the opening of the immigration door to immigrants from southern and eastern Europe in 1883. Unlike previous immigrants, the new immigrants were "white on arrival," in historian Tom Guglielmo's term, although historians still debate the degree of whiteness of these new immigrants.[12] The question of race (and whiteness, in particular), not of nationality, would come to determine the racial composition of the United States for several decades through immigration restriction legislation.[13] The new immigrants' foreignness in the Americanization campaigns was determined primarily in terms of Anglo-Saxonism; because a good many new immigrants were southern and eastern European, their transformation through Americanization programs, as well as their claims to citizenship, relied on their ability to prove their whiteness or their worthiness to become white.[14] Like the new immigrants, on its arrival cinema in America was foreign—mostly French—and threatened the stability of the emerging American cinema industry. As Richard Abel has shown, by 1905, the French company Pathé Frères supplied most of the films for the American market to the extent that French films not only came to dominate the early American market but they also determined the shape of American cinema in the next decades.[15]

At the beginning of the twentieth century, in the United States and in Europe, cinema became coterminous with modernity—as a new technology of representation and as a new cultural commodity of mass production and consumption. Major shifts in the film industry affected the Americanization efforts through film. Film as a new technology had multiple "social and cultural uses"; industrial film, in particular, through its networks of production, distribution, circulation, and exhibition offered a venue for Americanization materials. The circulation and distribution of these films—often free of charge—led to what Marina Dahlquist calls "the institutionalization of film." Moreover, cinema censorship efforts (and the move to clean up the motion picture industry) and the attempts to make the movie industry more middle class mirrored the widespread Americanization efforts more broadly, from local, state, and national programs.[16] At the same time, films were "screened and publicly debated in an America that was rife with particularly exacerbated racial, class, and political conflict in the wake of World War I."[17] Film translated Americans' desires, anxieties, and beliefs, at the same time that these anxieties helped form and nurture them.

In the United States, film emerged as a popular form of mass culture between 1900 and 1910, a decade marked by growing fears of "alienism" and a growing national(ist) panic about the new immigrants' putative difference. The French provenance of many of these early films only deepened this (white) American anxiety. As Richard Abel put it, "With an 'alien' body like Pathé at its center, how could American cinema be truly American?"[18] Film historians distinguish between two eras in silent film: the early period 1905–17 and the period 1917–29, marked by the rise of the Hollywood studio system. Early films were exhibited in a variety of spaces, from storefront theaters and nickelodeons, parks and cafés, to vaudeville theaters and opera houses, churches, schools, department stores, and YMCAs. After 1914, when the beginning of the war in Europe made it harder to bring European films to the United States, war news and American-based or patriotic films brought propaganda to American screens.[19]

As the film industry developed, immigrant filmmakers and exhibitors expanded their theatrical venues to reach an ever-growing audience.[20]

By the turn of the twentieth century, motion picture producers like Carl Laemmle and Adolph Zukor also exhibited the films they produced; immigrants became significant participants in the movie industry, not only as exhibitors and producers but also as distributors and actors.[21] At the beginning of the twentieth century, a typical moving-picture theater seated fewer than three hundred people, had poor ventilation, and was of questionable cleanliness. In a study on "commercial recreations" in New York City, published in 1911, Michael Davis documented that the films shown in these theaters were of suspicious quality. Nevertheless, the moving-picture show at the time provided the main form of recreation and was, according to Davis, "by far the dominant type of dramatic representation in New York." Davis's critiques also extended to the musically crude songs that provided sound background for the silent films, which occasionally included patriotic songs.[22] This inclusion of patriotic songs to accompany the images on screen was perhaps not accidental, especially when the audiences were predominantly working class and immigrant. Through visual and aural stimulation, the Americanization movement could find new recruits among immigrants and perform the work of affective Americanization.

Whereas critics like Davis condemned the quality of store shows and the films they exhibited, civic leaders and Americanizers found the potential of the new medium welcome. In 1910 Francis Oliver, the chief of the Bureau of Licenses in New York City, found silent film to be "a potent factor in the education of the foreign element and therefore an advantage to the city." To him, motion pictures offered the immigrants who could neither read nor write a chance at understanding their adoptive country.[23] Cultural and film critic Ernest Dench wrote in 1917 that silent films could supplement the English-language instruction. "English loses its force," whereas the moving picture, "a more powerful medium" than the page or spoken word, appeals to the eye and brings different nationalities together.[24]

As it became clear to both politicians and film industry executives that films could help in the Americanization effort, state and local efforts were mobilized, from Detroit to St. Louis to Rhode Island. Writing in 1917 about "Americanizing Foreigners by Motion Pictures," Ernest Dench advocated for the use of the motion picture—"which appeals to the eye"—to bring the many immigrant nationalities together in the U.S. He praised the work of Ford Motor Company and its Motion Picture

Department, led by Frank Cody, and applauded efforts by the St. Louis municipal authorities to educate local immigrants about the region and American industries. Although he mentioned no titles, Dench pointed out that the films shown in St. Louis were exhibited in "a Catholic church, police station, Jewish synagogue, and a public school." The effect of displaying Americanization films free of charge in such spaces was unexpected: on the first evening, he recounted, "Ten thousand children of Italian, German, Greek, Irish, and Russian parents were present, along with their guardians." The reach of the new medium was unprecedented. Dench credited the city of Pawtucket, Rhode Island—with nine-tenths of its inhabitants foreign-born—for making the best use of motion pictures in the service of Americanization. Dench also credited the Committee at the Civic Theatre in Pawtucket for hiring interpreters in several languages (Polish, Italian, or Hebrew), who would explain briefly the message of the intertitles before the screening began. In this way, film could both educate and entertain the immigrant audiences.[25]

The consumption of an emerging national cinema reveals more than its use as a source of entertainment and education; it also reveals its ideology, through articulations of nationalism and interpellations of spectators into national(ist) discourses. Despite the aura of didacticism, film provided an escape from daily life and, at the same time, was a source of acculturation to American life. Facilitating English-language literacy (immigrants could learn English by reading intertitles aloud), films also played a key role in creating the immigrant spectator. The socialization provided by the new medium (as entertainment and as education), first by the nickelodeon, later by the feature film, offered immigrant spectators an opportunity for socialization inside and outside the movie theater. In this way, film served a function similar to that of the school, the press (including the immigrant press), and the organizations supporting immigrant communities in their assumed transition to Americanness. But before silent film allowed immigrant spectators to dream, it became indispensable in the Americanization movement.

INDUSTRIAL AND EDUCATIONAL FILM: AMERICANIZATION AT FORD MOTOR AND BEYOND

The Ford Motor Company's Motion Picture Department, in collaboration with the company's Sociological Department and English program, used motion pictures to educate its immigrant workers in labor efficiency and Americanism.[26] Welfare programs Americanizing the immigrant workers at Ford were transposed on film to promote worker productivity and efficiency. Ford's experiment in welfare capitalism, known as the five-dollar day, started in 1914; it consisted of a profit-sharing model aimed at making Ford workers change their attitudes toward work to meet the rigors of mass production while also being compensated accordingly if they met specific standards of efficiency. As Stephen Meyer documents, "The preindustrial culture of immigrant workers had to be restructured to meet the requirements of new and more sophisticated industrial operations."[27] The corporate assumption about unskilled immigrant laborers was that they wanted to be "elevated" in industrial standards of efficiency and in conditions of domestic life, as the work of Ford's Sociological Department attested.

The Ford English School expanded the Ford Americanization program by taking it into the classroom. Here, adult immigrant workers received the rudiments of English-language training and an introduction to American culture. The efforts of Peter Roberts, the YMCA educator, were enlisted in the training of immigrant workers at Ford's Highland Park factory in Michigan. Ford's Americanization work before World War I served as a model for Americanization programs nationally. Although Ford Motor Company was not alone in these efforts during World War I, as manufacturers were uneasy about the immigrant workers in their factories, the Ford Americanization program became a model of transformation, showing that Americanization programs could remake and reform immigrant workers into productive Americans.[28]

In Ford's endeavor to educate its workers in Americanism and efficiency, two categories of Ford films served the work of Americanization: first, the films produced by Ford's Motion Picture Department between 1913 and 1919; second, the so-called educational films, produced between 1919 and 1925, when a postwar militant version of Americanization infused both national rhetoric and the rhetoric of Ford films. Although Ford films played regularly in traditional theatrical venues, in this section I focus on Ford films shown in nontheatrical settings. In the 1910s, more than 70 percent of Ford Motor Company employees were foreign-born. The Ford Sociological Department attempted to Americanize its immigrant employees through mandatory attendance in the company's English program. Immigrants were also introduced to middle-class domesticity by relocating to new living quarters, appropriate for the new citizen the company imagined. In addition to American history, civics, and the English language, the immigrant workers at Ford were introduced to table etiquette and American living standards.[29] Ford's interest in the educational potential of film led to the creation of the Ford Motion Picture Department at Highland Park in 1913, making Ford the first American industrial company with a motion picture department. Ford trained workers and disseminated news to wide audiences; the materials often included news about the company's products. Ford's Motion Picture Department had an annual budget of $600,000 and "produced films that were among the most widely distributed and seen in the silent era."[30] From 1914 until the 1920s, it was one of the largest film producers in the world. As David Lewis put it, by 1918 Ford was "the largest motion picture distributor on earth."[31]

The films produced by Ford's Motion Picture Department were shown in schools and factories throughout the U.S. These pedagogical endeavors included documentaries, newsreels, and travelogues, attempting to offer "a mirror" of American life. As Ford movies were presenting the viewers with an idealized vision of America, they were also self-serving in selling the Anglo-American ideal of the self-made man. Just like cars, Americans could be "made." Ford Motor Company's immigrant workers hailed from fifty-three different countries and spoke more than one hundred different languages. Henry Ford's documented anti-Semitism reveals another facet of his nativism; blaming the Jews for the degeneration of American society in private, he made it his public mission to "make" the "peasants" in his employ into good Americans.[32] The company's large distribution efforts supported these ambitions. In the early years, the films produced by Ford were grouped into the series *Ford Animated Weekly*, distributed at no charge to movie theaters and nontheatrical exhibition spaces. In 1917, Ford films were shown in three thousand theaters a week to an audience of four to five million people; in 1924, *Ford News* claimed that sixty million people worldwide had seen Ford films.[33] The postwar political economy contributed to an exacerbated rhetoric of nationalism and patriotism. Americanization was key to the Ford films, "amid anxieties about immigrant loyalty to company and nation."[34] Could immigrant workers become loyal Americans while they also maintained ties with their countries of origin? Could Ford films disseminate the American-ization ethos by appealing to immigrants' affective registers while also instructing them to become productive (and safe) workers?

Moving pictures made by Ford's Motion Picture Department in-structed audiences in mass production and capitalism, and offered the possibilities of a new visual pedagogy to transform workers into com-pliant industrial citizens.[35] Among the films produced by Ford—many now lost—is *English School*, a short 35 mm film from 1918, which includes scenes of a teacher lecturing in a classroom and adult students talking to each other.[36] One of the early films made at Ford, *English School* also shows immigrant workers who lined up at the Employers' Association Bureau but were turned away because of their inability to speak English. After the film was shown in Detroit and other industrial cities, Ford Motion Picture estimated that night school attendance in-creased more than 153 percent in a year. The *Immigrants in America Review* noted in 1915 that one of the large movie exhibitors in Detroit also displayed a slide showing the film. Posters of Uncle Sam shaking an immigrant laborer's hand on July 4, 1915, the first Americanization Day (see chapter 2), were prominently displayed in other theaters.[37]

English literacy was the theme of many of the industrial films pro-duced in the service of Americanization. Ford films included: *The Story of Old Glory* (ca. 1916), about the American flag; *Where the Spirit That Won Was Born* (ca. 1918), about Philadelphia's historic sites; *Landmarks of the American Revolution* (ca. 1920), about the Revo-lutionary War; and *Presidents of the United States* (ca. 1917). Other films showcased the beauty and modernity of American cities: *Pitts-burgh, Pennsylvania* (ca. 1917), *Washington, D.C.* (ca. 1918), *New York City* (1919). These Ford films, distributed gratis to movie the-aters and nontheatrical exhibition spaces (including factories, schools, and prisons), capitalized on the growing visual instruction movement of the 1920s. They introduced viewers to American modernity, with stories of industrial progress and a visual history of the United States. Helping audiences see themselves—on and off screen—was part of the pedagogic mission of Ford's Motion Picture Department. Films like *En-glish School* were geared to immigrant and working-class audiences, to those perceived as deficient in understanding and performing American citizenship. In addition to "visualizing citizenship" for these audiences,

Ford films contributed to the Progressive Era's mission of social and economic order.[38] At its own factories, Ford's Americanization program orchestrated large graduating exercises, with the famous "melting pot" ceremonies (discussed in chapter 1). The exacerbated sense of patriotism of these ceremonies called attention to their artificiality and to the company's use of patriotic exercises for capitalist gain, fueled by immigrant labor.

The newsreel-like series *Ford Educational Weekly* advertised the potential of film to teach "millions" and to assist in "'Americanization'— the Teacher's New Task" (figure 31). First asking, alarmingly, "Can it be done—with the children of foreign-born parents running into the millions?" the advertisement gives the answer: "Yes—it can, and it must!" *Ford Educational Weekly,* started in 1916, was distributed at low cost to cinemas.[39] Defining Americanization as "loyalty to home as well as country," the films purported to "cover history, industry, science, home life, and art." Distributed by the Goldwyn Distributing Corporation in twenty-two cities across the United States, the films appealed to the teachers' sense of citizenship and loyalty: "Every loyal school teacher

Fig. 31. "Americanization"—the Teacher's New Task. *Moving Picture Age*, January 1920.

should know what the *Ford Educational Weekly* really is. We want to tell you, and we want your helpful suggestions as to what new films we shall make." The ad included some coupon offers and the promise to connect schools with the best projector suppliers. The images used in the ad also conveyed the utility of a good projector to classroom instruction, as well as the multiplicity of spaces and times the projector helped the viewer navigate. On the screen, a middle-class family leisurely reads and converses in a sitting room, while to the left is an episode from the signing of the Declaration of Independence.

The simultaneous visualization of domesticity and history alerts the viewer to the medium's potential for Americanizing "the youth of the land." The references to domesticity and Americanization as the construction of a (primarily white) middle-class domestic and heteronormative space were consistent with the norms of domesticity imposed by Ford's Sociological Department—which would soon be terminated, along with the Americanization program, during the financial crisis caused by the 1920–21 recession. While recognizing the potential of visual instruction for educating and Americanizing the children of immigrants, *Ford Educational Weekly* also revealed the parameters of (white) American citizenship visible in the Americanization programs following World War I. According to Lee Grieveson, "The Fordist dream of a productive pedagogical cinema failed in the late 1920s and early 1930s." Ford terminated its Motion Picture Department in 1932, bringing an end to its visual pedagogy project, because of practical problems in using film in educational contexts before the 16 mm film was available and because of the increased costs after the advent of sound film.[40] Henry Ford's narrow conception of American citizenship alienated him and his corporation from Progressive Era groups. A decade later, Charles Chaplin's *Modern Times* (1936) offered an acerbic critique of the Ford assembly line and the dehumanizing effects of the Fordist project.

The Ford welfare model declined after World War I, but Ford's Americanization program soon became a model in many states. The ultimate failure of the Ford Americanization model signaled an end to the paternalism and manipulative approach of Ford Motor to labor relations. After immigration laws were in place following the Immigration Act of 1924, Americanization programs through the factory could no longer create what Stephen Meyer calls "a fully malleable workforce," its goal in the previous decade. Immigrant workers were no longer arriving in large numbers and shifts in informal worker training—where more experienced workers trained the less experienced ones—made the Ford Americanization program obsolete.[41] Other industrial conglomerates, such as U.S. Steel, produced and distributed industrial and educational films that served the gospel of Americanization and advertised the company's humane side. States also commissioned industrial films to support their Americanization work.

Some industrial films produced and distributed during the 1910s served similar aesthetic and ideological goals to those manufactured by Ford, and reveal further the potential for film to be harnessed in the work of both Progressive Era Americanizers and industrial capitalism. Among these films were *An American in the Making* (1913), sponsored by U.S. Steel, and *The Making of an American* (1920), sponsored by the Connecticut State Board of Education. The similarity of these films' titles suggests their congruent industrial and ideological mission: the "making" of an immigrant into an American at the scene of industrialization and education.

An American in the Making, an industrial film commissioned by the U.S. Steel Corporation in response to growing national concerns about industrial safety and cheap immigrant labor, purported to represent the humane side of U.S. Steel, an industrial conglomerate thriving on non-unionized, non-skilled, and low-wage workers.[42] The one-reel short industrial film (15 minutes) told the story of a Hungarian immigrant, Bela Tokaji, who was "made over" into an American in six years by becoming a good laborer, after learning the safety instructions of the U.S. Steel Corporation and marrying his English teacher (figures 32 and 33).

Shot on location at Ellis Island, in Gary, Indiana, and at two midwestern steel companies in Illinois and Ohio, the film, which starts in a rural setting in Hungary, jumps forward to an American industrial setting: city scenes, industrial scenes, and scenes of education. One key industrial scene is filmed in front of the Illinois Steel Corporation, where Bela pauses in front of a multilingual instruction board at the entrance (min. 4:10). Safety guidelines are written in English and three East European languages, suggesting the ethnic makeup of the Illinois Steel immigrant labor force.

Immigrant labor safety is at the heart of *An American in the Making*, which leaves out all other types of immigrant safety (emotional,

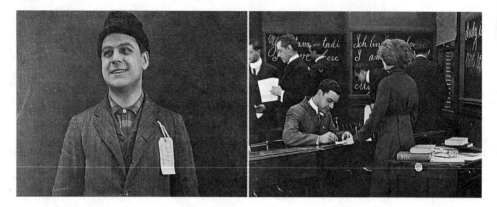

Fig. 32. (left) Film still from *An American in the Making* (1913). Bela Tokaji, optimistic as a new immigrant arrival.
Fig 33. Film still from *An American in the Making* (1913). Bela's transformation as a night school student.

physical, and so on). In 1910, a congressional investigation found that more than 40,000 U.S. Steel workers (almost half of its employees) earned less than eighteen cents an hour, and half of them worked twelve-hour shifts. President William Howard Taft had initiated an antitrust suit in 1911, which the company was still fighting when the movie was released. Therefore, U.S. Steel "had reasons to dramatize on film its safety measures and its concern for workmen."[43] If one of the goals of the early industrial films was to educate audiences about technology and to demystify the industrial process, a commissioned industrial film like *An American in the Making* did that and so much more; it conflated capitalism, Americanization, and domesticity to serve the financial interests of a corporation. By paying little attention to the subject's story or background—Bela is Hungarian but he represents the generic, malleable southern and eastern European immigrant—this industrial film sold audiences on the possibilities of Americanization and capital accumulation. Cinematic details throughout the film suggest the imperfections of Americanization and the film's own complicity in perpetuating them. When the protagonist's old parents hand him a letter and passage money from his brother in America, the letter is written in a version of Czech, although Bela is Hungarian. For a non-unionized industrial conglomerate like U.S. Steel, the laborers' racial and ethnic identities made little difference. While labor unions lobbied for restricting immigration due to a surplus of unprotected immigrant hands, corporations like U.S. Steel were ready to welcome them for minimum wage.[44] Americanization encouraged and supported cheap (immigrant) labor.

In *An American in the Making*, the film industry becomes complicit with both Americanization and capitalism. The film's emphasis on the protection of laborers reveals more about the fears of conglomerates like U.S. Steel to lose capital gains than it does about loss of immigrant lives. The viewers are interpellated into American exceptionalism as economic prosperity through narratives of safety: Bela's accumulation of economic and social capital comes from his mastery of the industrial safety equipment. Showing a film like *An American in the Making* to immigrant workers in industrial plants like U.S. Steel was part of a larger national systematic effort at Americanization.[45] *An American in the Making* was screened by the U.S. Bureau of Mines and by the National Association of Manufacturers, and it was distributed widely by the National Association of Manufacturers, often accompanied by the blurb "Every European liner that steams into New York Harbor brings in its steerage, Americans in the Making." A successful, albeit exploitative American corporation like U.S. Steel needed a film to clear its name. Bela's Americanization depends on U.S. Steel: he takes the company-sponsored English classes, learns to dress in western clothing, dates his English teacher, and settles into a comfortable middle-class home in only six years. This fractured mode of representation glosses over Bela's years of hard labor and life as an immigrant, showing instead his swift access to American domesticity. This framing of utilitarian industrial educational material with a narrative arc around immigration reveals the potential of silent film to turn the industrial safety material into "spectacle" at the same time it attempts to present it as a successful story of Americanization.

The longer and more developed silent *The Making of an American* (1920) had a clear marketing agenda: the recipe for successful Americanization. Made for the Connecticut State Board of Education by the Worcester Film Corporation, *The Making of an American* targeted industrial workers in Connecticut. It promoted the image of the well-rounded immigrant, whose success relied heavily on literacy and mastery of English. The story of Peter Bruno, an Italian immigrant with a large moustache and an uncouth appearance, revolves around his inability to speak English, his night school education, and his rise in social and leadership status.

Despite the film's polemic and predictable fictionalized plot, it serves as a useful historical document about immigration and literacy.[46] Italian immigrants formed the second largest immigrant group in the United States at the turn of the twentieth century, which may explain the choice of an Italian immigrant as a metonymy for illiterate southern and eastern European immigrants. The film shows similar "appeals to all foreigners," including safety warnings in other southern and eastern European languages. Almost killed in an elevator shaft because of his inability to read the sign "danger," Peter emerges victorious at the end of the film not only as a proficient English speaker and Americanized immigrant but also as a civic leader. In *The Making of an American*, English saves Peter's life. He becomes the head of the safety council, where he continues to fight for the well-being of his fellow immigrants. The last intertitle, in caps, reiterates the film's didacticism: "IF YOU KNOW MEN OR WOMEN WHO DON'T KNOW ENGLISH, URGE THEM TO GO TO NIGHT SCHOOL." The film promotes a lesson in literacy that includes social mobility, but it also reveals the limits to the future of the literate immigrant laborer. The Connecticut Board of Education defined Americanization as "any process which makes a man or woman a loyal, active, and intelligent citizen is Americanization," a definition the film readily endorsed.[47]

The reception of *The Making of an American* exceeded initial expectations, with over 100,000 viewers nationally during 1920 and many copies sold to other states. In one six-month period, sixty-three factories in Connecticut established Americanization classes. English was the film's metonymy for Americanness, an idea already written into immigration restriction laws by the Literacy Act passed in 1917. The bill (which passed over President Wilson's veto) marked not only the beginning of the immigration restriction policy but also an increased emphasis on English-language acquisition as the essential mark of Americanness. Produced during the militant phase of the Americanization movement following World War I, *The Making of an American* is a cautionary tale, a rethinking of the ingredients necessary for "making" an American in the next decade. Subsequent immigration restriction categories (besides literacy) and the growing nativism, coupled with an economic crisis, soon led to the drastic restriction of immigration from

countries like Peter Bruno's beloved Italy and other southern and eastern European countries through the Johnson-Reed Immigration Act of
1924.

AMERICANISM IN ACTION: MOTION PICTURES
AND AMERICANIZATION EFFORTS

Silent film was here to stay, as was its promise to educate and Americanize the immigrant industrial worker. The popularity of moving pictures with immigrant workers and children was a major argument for
the government's use of the medium strategically in Americanization
campaigns. In 1919, newspapers reported with confidence, "Movies
Will Aid Work of Making Good Americans." The goal of the Americanization campaign using celluloid was to reach over 1,900 schools
throughout the U.S., a project under the direct supervision of the Bureau of Naturalization, Department of Labor:

> Thousands of feet of celluloid are now awaiting the zero hour to go
> over the top in a drive that will carry the gospel of 100 per cent Ameri-
> canism to every corner of the land. The pictures will visualize for the
> foreigners in our midst the message that is being sent out to them
> through the bureau of naturalization. They will show them precisely
> what the government of the United States stands for and what it aims
> to do for its citizens.[48]

In promotional materials, the federal government enlisted the new medium to "aid in the work of making good Americans." The plan was to
exhibit these films in night schools that served immigrant laborers. The
films would "revel in the country's colonial history—from the landing
of Columbus to the present day"—with no acknowledgment of the
country's Native inhabitants. The settler colonial version of American
history, with its erasure of Indigenous presence, dominates overwhelmingly what immigrants were taught in public schools and night classes.
The immigrant students would not have learned about their contemporary Indigenous activists, such as the intellectuals of the Society of
American Indians, who were advocating for an end to the erasure of
their history.

A newsletter issued by the chief naturalization examiner in Chicago
on May 26, 1919, announced in all capital letters the imminent arrival

Fig. 34. Newsletter No. 5, "Americanization, Naturalization, and Citizenship," Chicago, May 26, 1919. National Archives, RG 85.

of "MOVING PICTURE FILMS AND FILM POSTERS." The films, it noted, were "for use in the instruction of the foreign-born in preparation for citizenship. They visualize the subjects covered in the Free Government Textbook furnished by this Bureau. There is to be no charge for the use of these films except the necessary express charges." A rectangular advertisement at the center of the newsletter urged the reader to "get acquainted with your country" through the "official pictures of the Bureau of Naturalization" (figure 34). The commissioner of naturalization added his hope that the films would "assist the schools to induce not only the foreign born men and women, but the native born Americans who may require further instruction of the kind furnished by the English and citizenship classes, to enroll for regular instruction."[49]

At the National Conference on Americanization Industries in Boston, Massachusetts (June 22–24, 1919), the topic of Americanization through film came up in several speeches. In his address on "Americanization in Industries," Merle R. Griffeth, publicity agent for General Electric, related an episode at a GE plant in Schenectady, New York, where the foreman decided to produce a film on Americanization to educate the immigrant workers, to show them "how the different nationalities have progressed from the time they left their homes in the old country to their present bettered condition in their American homes." At another GE plant, in Pittsfield, Massachusetts, an employee advocated for using the workers' lunch hour to show a fifteen-to-twenty-minute Americanization film.[50] Companies found these industrial films desirable because they used the employees' time efficiently and also encouraged workers to advance the work of capitalism.[51]

In an attempt to make and distribute films promoting "faith in America," representatives of the motion picture industry were summoned to Washington, D.C., in December 1919 by secretary of the Interior Franklin Lane to form the Americanism Committee of the Motion Picture Industry. The goal of the committee was to inaugurate an active screen campaign for Americanism, following a resolution by the Joint Committee on Education of the Senate and House "that the Motion Picture Industry of the U.S. be requested to do all that is within its power to upbuild and strengthen the spirit of Americanism within our people."[52] This project promoted what Secretary Lane called "concrete Americanism," enlisting the services of leading producers, artists, directors and distributing agencies.[53] Providing entertainment to immigrants and Americans alike, silent films also engaged Americanization in the service of nationalism, publicized through government venues (e.g., the Americanization conferences) and publications like *Motion Picture News* (*MPN*). Shortly after the meeting of the Americanism Committee, the January 1920 issue of *Motion Picture News* announced that the National Film Corporation of America was planning to adapt screen plays from eight stories in popular magazines (for example, *Ladies Home Journal*) in order to push Americanization.

The Americanism Committee projected that these films would be "America first products," written by American authors and using American settings. The production manager of the National Film Corporation of America, I. Bernstein, pledged to the Department of the Interior his practical support "in its scheme for Americanization through motion pictures."[54] *Motion Picture News* also announced that filmmaker Ralph Ince would make a series of Americanization pictures. The first in the series was *The Land of Opportunity* (1920), a two-reeler written by Lewis Allen Browne, about America as "land of opportunity," seen through the lens of Abraham Lincoln's life: "In commemoration the birth of the great Emancipator, *The Land of Opportunity* is released to exhibitors and it would be to the advantage of all of them to present this picture not only as a tribute to Lincoln but as an ideal subject in showing America as a wonderful land of opportunity." This film, like many similar settler projects, revealed no trace of Indigenous part in the making of "the land of opportunity." Real Art Pictures, producer and distributor of the film, used the occasion of Lincoln's birthday to promote the Americanization movement. The film was widely marketed as "the initial Americanization Production" of the Americanism Committee, chaired by Secretary Lane. The ad for the film included the names of the other committee members involved in its production: Lewis J. Selznick, the distributor, and Adolph Zukor, the producer.[55] The politicians and movie distributors agreed: film could serve—and save—the nation.

One of the first tasks of the Americanism Committee of the Motion Picture Industry was to work with film exhibitors to screen *Land of Opportunity*. The release, planned for Lincoln's birthday, was part of the national campaign to promote the Americanization movement, reaching far and wide: from Buffalo, Cleveland, Cincinnati, Detroit, and Minneapolis, to Omaha, Kansas City, St. Louis, Atlanta, Pittsburgh, and Philadelphia. The committee declared the week of February 8–14, 1920, Americanization week; it included other patriotic exercises in all the major cities of key interest to Americanizers. Exhibitors were encouraged to use musical "compositions exclusively of American authorship," including "American numbers that are valuable from a standpoint of patriotism."[56] During Americanization week, every theater on Broadway booked *The Land of Opportunity,* advertised as an antidote to post–World War I radicalism, "the most forceful blow at parlor Bolshevism ever made into a screen production."

Government officials, who viewed the film in Washington, D.C., were pleased with the film's mission to combat radicalism and unrest.[57] Secretary Lane himself—who showed similar interest in instilling patriotism on Native reservations in the 1910s (as we've seen in chapter 1)—met with film exhibitors on February 9, 1920, to remind them of the new medium's potential—nay, opportunity—to bolster public sentiment: "The whole idea of this program is that we shall try to revivify the spirit of our people." Lane's appeal was calculated: "You made the people of the country feel that the motion picture was as real as the newspaper or as the pulpit." Despite these efforts, the film drew a meager audience; it was poorly received by a public that seemed less interested in patriotic films than politicians and movie executives had anticipated. Steven J. Ross attributes the failure of this genre of Americanization films to its message of economic submission and the depreciation of the value of labor: "The anti-left, anti-labor films of the war period were paralleled by the emergence of the movie industry as a major big business and by increased militancy among its workers." Yet, in the early 1920s, film exhibitors took the opportunity to use film to sell American patriotism throughout the country.[58]

Along with private and voluntary organizations, state and municipal agencies were implicated in the work of Americanization, and federal agencies showed an interest in using film as they strove to create a more "practical Americanism campaign." A circular letter distributed to film producers in May 1920 by Secretary Lane on behalf of the American-ism Committee of the Motion Picture Industry asked the film industry "to do all that is within its power to upbuild and strengthen the spirit of Americanism within our people."[59]

On May 19, 1920, Secretary Lane wrote a letter to George Kleine, a Chicago optician and entrepreneur who made and sold film-making equipment, asking him to serve as a member of the advisory council of the Americanism Committee of the Motion Picture Industry of the U.S. One of the Americanism Committee's tasks was to develop themes for what Lane called "a practical Americanism campaign." A film distribu-tor in Chicago, Kleine was one of the first to distribute films to theaters. Throughout the 1910s, Kleine worked with the Department of War in the distribution of films for patriotic causes. One of these, in July 1917, was Edison's *Star Spangled Banner,* with the main purpose of recruiting men for the Marine Corps.[60] During World War I, Kleine dis-tributed documentaries, among them *America's Answer* (1918) about the arrival of American troops in France. When the American Motion Picture Programs, totaling thirty weekly program units, were released in January 1924, they promised to offer "eye-training for American citizenship." The programs included such titles as *Yanks, The Immi-grant, America: Enduring Power of Service*, and *America: The Garden with a Protected Soil.*

Although the Americanism Committee failed in its ambitious plan of releasing one film a week, the movies that it released received wide distribution and critical attention for a short period before the movie industry shifted its focus to a profit-driven business model.[61] The re-strictive immigration policies put in place in 1924, the consolidation of Americanism as an intransigent race-based Anglo-Saxon ideology, coupled with the consolidation of the studio system, and a host of emerging labor issues, took the spotlight off Americanization in silent film. Arising fears of Bolshevism, with fantasies of revolution, and threats of labor strikes shifted the thinking of Americanizers after the war. Yet, for a few years in the 1910s and early 1920s, the promise of silent film to advance the work of Americanization galvanized the attention of politicians, the film industry, and neighborhood exhibitors ready to make Americanism their platform.

CASE STUDIES

The silent film served the Americanization crusade through industrial and educational films, yet other feature films reveal the medium's complicity in the Americanization project beyond the classroom and the factory. Silent film engaged and challenged the nationalist project of Americanization by calling attention to such issues as citizenship and national belonging, exclusion, and the ideal American citizen— or "the good American"—that many viewers were interpellated into through the educational and industrial films. In this section I examine two nonindustrial silent films, *Making an American Citizen* (1912) and *The Immigrant* (1917), which engaged in a critique of the Americanization movement and its unrealistic and prescriptive approaches.[62] Alice Guy Blaché's *Making an American Citizen* called attention to the gender barriers limiting access to American citizenship, and showed the prescriptiveness of American behavior through a series of "lessons in Americanism" that the immigrant had to learn. Similarly, Charles Chaplin's iconic *The Immigrant* offered an acerbic parody of the "immigrant problem" and a sympathetic treatment of the immigrant subject, poking fun at the regimentation of immigrant travel and the arrival of immigrants "in the land of liberty."

Alice Guy Blaché's *Making an American Citizen* (1912)

Alice Guy Blaché's commercial feature film *Making an American Citizen* took on a task similar to industrial or educational films, yet rather than employing the didacticism of pedagogical film, it subsumed the "lessons" it attempted to teach the immigrant into a larger cautionary tale about prescriptive Americanism. A pioneer director in the U.S., Blaché was also arguably the first female director in the history of cinema.[63] She made *Making an American Citizen* for her own film company, Solax, which she and her husband, cameraman Herbert Blaché, founded in 1910, after moving to the U.S. from France in 1907. In France, Alice Blaché was a director at Gaumont, and her pioneering work earned her the Legion of Honor in 1953.[64] Solax is credited with producing films of quality, despite their didacticism, which also permeates *Making an American Citizen*. The film calls attention to the gender barriers limiting access to American citizenship and reveals the prescriptiveness of American behavior through a series of "lessons in Americanism" that the visible alien has to learn. Basing its storyline on the lessons in Americanism, the film suggests the impossibility of "making" an American citizen. Gwendolyn Foster makes the case for reading this film as an early, white feminist tract.[65] Although it uses gender as a lens for representing immigrant acclimation to the American scene, the film offers a biting critique of heteronormativity—with the family at the heart of Americanization as domestication.

The film makes the domestic sphere the primary site of the "lessons in Americanism," yet maintains a critical stance toward Americanization as an almost overnight reformation. Its plot is perhaps too straightforward: a Russian couple immigrates to the U.S., the boorish brute of a husband, Ivan Orloff (Lee Beggs), learns a series of "lessons in Americanism," and by the end of the film is "completely Americanized," cured of his crude (i.e., un-American) behaviors. The film begins on a Russian dirt road, where the soon-to-be-reformed Ivan and his unnamed wife encounter a few fellow emigrants, who invite them to share their journey to America. As did Marcus Ravage (see chapter 6), these immigrants start their journey on foot. To become an American citizen and a good husband, Ivan has to adopt middle-class propriety. The character's rendition as unrestrained, often abusive and brutish, offers the viewer a highly schematic, dichotomous understanding of two loaded concepts at the time, "civilization" and "savagery," often also used in films about Native Americans.

In making Ivan spectacularly repulsive, *The Making of an American Citizen* relegates the immigrant husband to barbarism and savagery, categories at odds with "civilized" Americanism. In an early scene, Ivan's exhausted wife draws a cart up a hill while the husband occasionally whips her. The immigrant couple's expected transformation is total; the American gentleman they first encounter after landing at Ellis

Island teaches them to perform Americanism and whiteness. Yet, Ivan continues to abuse his wife. In one poignant episode, exhausted from the voyage and the weight of the family bundle she carries, the woman falls as Ivan continues to poke her. Just as Ivan prepares to administer another series of blows, the American citizen intervenes and teaches him his first lesson in Americanism: he instructs Ivan to carry the luggage and gives the woman the stick and poking authority. The couple leaves the frame as the American man lingers in front of the camera, smiling at his accomplishment.

This memorable tableau frames the film's many poignant contradictions about what "makes" an American citizen: is it propriety, courtesy, kindness, a fair division of labor, or industriousness? Several lessons in Americanism reveal the ingredients for "making" an American citizen. One lesson takes place in the couple's tenement apartment in a Russian ghetto in New York City. As Ivan throws his wife on the floor, a neighbor intervenes. In a next scene, set in their New Jersey country home, where they move next, the wife is hard at work in the garden while Ivan sits on the porch, smoking his pipe. When she pauses to rest, Ivan tries to force her to resume her work just as another neighbor walks by. As the scene comes to an end, Ivan keeps threatening his wife, reluctantly tilling the garden and obeying his neighbor's admonition to work the garden himself. Another scene takes place in the family kitchen, where "Ivan's wife begins to live in the American Way." The final scene of Ivan's education in Americanism is the penal system, a warning that whatever cultural institutions cannot do in service of Americanization, the prison system will complete. This time the American citizens' intervention is drastic: Ivan is sentenced to six months of penal servitude for his (un-American) domestic transgressions. All's well that ends well when Ivan repents and reforms: "Ivan begins to profit from all the good advice he has received." He returns home a changed man: "completely Americanized!" the last intertitle announces. The immigrant's actions are under his neighbors' constant scrutiny, just as the immigrant subject is surveilled by the agents of Americanization—from immigration officers at Ellis Island, to neighbors or random citizens, to the legal and penal system.

As an immigrant director who relocated to the United States only five years before making this film, Alice Guy Blaché was aware that

Americanization targeted the new immigrants, attempting to make them into respectable American citizens. In choosing a violent husband and an abused wife—who becomes the agent of her husband's miraculous reformation at the hands of nosy American citizens and American law—Blaché calls into question the gendering of Americanization by pointing to the wife's voicelessness. *Making an American Citizen* reveals that American citizenship is attainable after a series of moral reformations of the heterosexual (white) couple. Choosing a nameless immigrant female character, Blaché insists that American citizenship is a male privilege in 1912, eight years before the Nineteenth Amendment granted American women the right to vote. Her choice of actor Lee Beggs to portray the violent Russian immigrant husband is also telling, as he played many Jewish characters in other Solax films. Ivan's brutishness is at odds with good citizenship in the United States. The character's fast reformation is also a critique of the Progressive Era's blind faith in the complete assimilation of even the most resistant east European immigrant, epitomized by Ivan. Ivan's slippage into the perceived un-American behavior and his repeated transgressions are likely to reoccur. Ultimately, Blaché makes the viewers question whether one can ever become "completely Americanized!" as the film's last intertitle announces.

Charles Chaplin's *The Immigrant* (1917)

Charles Chaplin's *The Immigrant* took Americanization as part of immigrants' adaptation to the new country but did not make it central to their lives. The film, among Chaplin's own favorites, captured the director's passion for humor, romance, and satire. In his unmistakable comedic style, and through a repertoire of exaggerated gestures, Chaplin revealed the confining environment of transatlantic steamers and re-created familiar scenes that appealed to the public's encounters with real or imagined immigrants. The grotesque scenes of voyage, the exaggerated physical features of the Russian immigrants, and the ruthlessness of immigration officers who treated people like cattle, challenge the viewing public's assumptions about the difference and the racial and ethnic homogeneity of immigrants. Chaplin uses familiar immigrant tropes—the crowded decks and the seasick, third-class passengers, the first sight of the Statue of Liberty, the memorable space of Ellis Island, the encounter with immigration officers—in an original cinematic representation of immigrant subjectivity.

Chaplin, the comic genius, "the man who has made more people laugh than any other man who ever lived," was himself an immigrant. Born into a British family of Jewish musical hall entertainers in London, he had a busy career before moving to the U.S. in 1913, after a successful U.S. tour.[66] Chaplin retained his British citizenship and never became an American citizen. In 1952 he was accused of communist sympathies and barred from entering the United States.[67] A voluminous FBI file, started by J. Edgar Hoover, includes investigations into Chaplin's political views and personal life. Chaplin's leftist sympathies, his political views, and the daring topics he touched on in his later films earned him Hoover's early description as one of Hollywood's "parlor Bolsheviki."[68]

Produced for Mutual, Chaplin's *The Immigrant* had a wider distribution than the silent films discussed earlier in this chapter, and it gave viewers a new take on immigrant travel and arrival: the tragic-comic. Unlike other films about immigration, *The Immigrant* was irreverent; rather than laughing *at* immigrants' idiosyncrasies, Chaplin laughed *with* them.[69] Released in 1917, *The Immigrant* entered the American scene the same year as Marcus E. Ravage's and Abraham Cahan's accomplished stories about Americanization. By the time Mutual released Chaplin's film, which he wrote and directed, he had already starred in sixty American silent films during his four-year sojourn in the U.S.[70] Starring Chaplin, Edna Purviance, Eric Campbell, Albert Austin, and Henry Bergman (all of Anglo-Saxon ancestry, all working for Chaplin's team at Mutual), the film assumed Americanization as the culmination of the immigrant's difficult journey to a new country. *The Immigrant* tells the story of an unnamed immigrant—a synecdoche for the mass of unnamed immigrants aboard the steamer. With Chaplin as his inimitable Tramp character, the film chronicles his adventures on the transatlantic trip and his predicament after arrival. Immigration affords Chaplin a productive opportunity for comic relief; laughter and tears, joy and sorrow, life and death place the other anonymous immigrants at the center of the journey, making their humanity a key component of the immigrant story.

The Immigrant opens with the still of a crowded steamer heading to America. The next image transitions to a deck where immigrants lie on the floor, coping with the seasickness and hopelessness. On the filthy third-class deck, Charlie meets his future wife (played by Edna Purviance) and later offers her his seat in the rocking dining hall.[71] A good gambler, he earns back the money Edna's mother had lost to a gambling thief. The ghostly face of Edna's mother foreshadows her imminent death. *The Immigrant* ends with Charlie and Edna stepping into an office labeled "Marriage License" in New York City, making immigrants' future and success depend on the nuclear family and the generosity of an American benefactor who employs them, and whose deus ex machina intervention provides the film's happy ending.

The film's most memorable tableau is the scene of "arrival in the land of liberty," which offers a biting critique of American hospitality (figure 35). During triage at Ellis Island, Chaplin's character furtively kicks an immigration officer's behind—a scene that caused considerable uproar, especially when Chaplin was accused of anti-American activities

Fig. 35. Film still from *The Immigrant* (1917). The scene of arrival in New York harbor.

in the 1950s—in response to the officer's similar violent act on the immigrant's body. This scene of fleeting optimism is short-lived; the immigrants are soon roped in and separated from the rest of the passengers. The Tramp is silenced, receives an entrance ticket, and leaves the scene. The physical punishment the immigrant experiences upon arrival is a metaphor for the larger forms of violence the Americanization crusade used, over and over, on and off screen. The film's final tableau captures, through the actors' facial expressions—smiles, frowns, and grimaces— the joy of arrival, the weariness of the trip, and the hope for a better future in the United States.

Despite the aura of didacticism, silent film provided an escape from daily life and was a source of acculturation. Facilitating English-language literacy among immigrants with its intertitles—which they could read aloud during screenings—film also played a key role in creating the "immigrant spectator." As film consumers in public places, immigrant spectators became aware of spectators from similar or different ethnic and racial backgrounds. Yet, in its consumption, the emerging national cinema was more than a source of entertainment and education; it also reveals its ideology, through articulations of nationalism and interpellations of the spectators into national(ist) discourses.[72]

Both theatrical and nontheatrical silent films socialized and instructed viewers, while also amplifying the exposure of immigrant and American-born audiences to xenophobia and racism, markers of their daily experiences. Stereotypes abounded in early portrayals of Italian immigrants in silent film, from *The Black Hand* (1906) and *The Organ Grinder* (1912), to the more popular *The Italian* (1915) and *Tony America* (1918). Groups such as Italians and Jews were targets of a new genre of films that emerged in the early 1900s, especially educational films promoting good American citizenship in the context of a national panic about the new immigrants' difference and unassimilability.[73] Early Hollywood resorted to Italian immigrants as ideal European (white) immigrants and models of assimilation and Americanization, such as Peter Bruno, the protagonist of *The Making of an American*. These films targeted working-class and immigrant audiences, purporting to "teach" these audiences how to be or become "good" Americans.

By the end of the 1920s, half of the U.S. population went to the movies; by the 1930s, most of the country went to the movies.[74] The images on screen could influence the immigrants' sense of ethnic or national identity and reinforce ideologies of difference. If immigrant viewers had access to silent films, their interpellation into the ideologies behind the films was not uniform. While it is difficult—if not impossible—to reconstruct the makeup of the first audiences, early immigrant viewers, while influenced by what they saw, were critical receptors rather than empty vessels waiting to be filled with "lessons" on how to become American. Spectatorship emerged "as a response to the same conditions that produced readership," as Judith Mayne has shown. Connecting the emergence of the eighteenth-century, middle-class female reader and late nineteenth-century immigrant spectator, Mayne argues that there are fundamental similarities defining the early conditions of readership and spectatorship, particularly in what she calls "the illusion of social participation" to groups otherwise relegated "to the margins of meaningful activity," such as white, middle-class female readers of novels in eighteenth-century Great Britain and immigrant audiences of silent films in America. Urban immigrant and proletariat audiences had never before thought of themselves as an "audience." Film also provided them with a way to use their limited time: to escape through the spectacle on screen and to fantasize, with an increased awareness of the private sphere and of themselves. Although the images on screen sometimes opened the eyes of immigrant spectators to fantasy as escape, they also created opportunities for fantasy as a form of resistance, what Mayne calls "an imaginary refusal of real conditions of existence." In this way, movies did not produce (mainly) compliant consumers, vessels ready to be filled with ideology, but also critical spectators, able to distinguish increasingly between the public and the private sphere, or between ethnic or national allegiances.[75]

As cinema became a new vehicle for "imagining the nation," in Benedict Anderson's terms, nations like the U.S. learned to imagine themselves and their ideal citizenry through moving images. The industrial and educational films discussed in this chapter contributed effectively to the affective work of Americanization. Motion picture theaters—like factories or night schools—became powerful arenas for educating the immigrant, not the least in American patriotism. By enlisting the motion picture industry's service to help promote Americanization, the federal government took this "education" one step further. If moving pictures promised to facilitate cross-cultural communication between people belonging to different nationalities and speaking different languages, they were also used strategically by federal and local governments in their Americanization efforts, reaching their peak during and after World War I.[76]

8 From "Vanishing Indians" to "Redskins"

American Indians on the Silver Screen

An interesting and important fact about the poor, vanishing American Indian is that he is not poor and he is not vanishing.

—*The Youth's Companion*, 1911

If the directors of the moving picture companies knew how foolish their women and girls look in the Indian pictures, with from one to three turkey feathers in the top of their heads, they would be more careful.

—John Standing Horse, Carlisle Indian School,
Motion Picture World, 1911

To act as an Indian is the easiest thing possible, for the Redskin is practically motionless.

—Ernest Dench, *Making the Movies*, 1915

FROM ITS INCEPTION, the American film industry was complicit with the insidious forms of American nationalism, manifest in the industry's move toward "American" subjects. From the nineteenth-century Wild West shows to the early westerns, representations of *Indians* on stage and on screen reproduced frontier violence and the settler idea of manifest destiny in ways that relegated Native people to either a primitive, vanishing, or exotic past, keeping Native actors and performers on the margins of representation. As Beverly Singer put it, this oversaturation of early film—or what she calls "the war-painted years"—with stereotypes "sacrificed the humanity of Native people."[1] At best, such representations were approximations, with little understanding of Native history and Native lives. Nineteenth-century dramatists had offered American audiences "the idea of the Indian," which Robert F.

Berkhofer identified as a white image or stereotype, an invention, a simplification.[2] This simplification followed white audiences' skepticism and distrust of *Indians* in the form of what Philip Deloria calls "American myths of modernity." Deloria asks: "After decades of efforts to pacify, civilize, educate, and assimilate Native people into American culture and society, did one have to take Indians seriously as Americans? How was that supposed to work? Were 'civilized' Indians really civilized or were they playing the part? Were they truly modern?"[3]

The silent film industry played no small part in this process of negotiating modernity on Native terms, even when those terms were uneven. If moving pictures helped in the work of imagining the settler nation, how did they represent one of the country's long-standing objects of fascination, the *Indian*?[4] How did these representations participate in the broader project of articulating national identity? In this chapter I examine some of the possibilities and limitations of the cultural work that silent film did in the Americanization project and the broader understanding of Indigenous representation and its relation to modernity. In silent feature, documentary, and ethnographic film, the *Indian*'s hypervisibility was a reminder of the absence of Indigenous people and their histories from the American settler colonial imaginary and a document of their continued presence despite settler violence against the Native body and image. Although many images preserved on celluloid have been destroyed or lost in the last century, some survived. Wherever they are available, silent film representations broaden our understanding of the medium's role in representations of national identity and racial difference, however problematic those representations may be.[5]

In this chapter I build on Indigenous and non-Indigenous film critics' work on the early westerns, well-known and newly discovered silent films, which performed two simultaneous tasks at the time. On one hand, they solidified American whiteness and served the work of American nationalism, patriotism, and Americanization; on the other hand, as *Indian* films became a widely recognizable genre, they paved the way for Native representation and self-representation, created opportunities for Native upward mobility, and provided occasionally a platform for the critique of federal Indian policy.[6] From early documentary footage (such as Native school scenes in New Mexico or Pennsylvania) to ethnographic film—lamenting the fate of a "vanishing race" or the "wards of the nation"—to early and later Westerns (including the "Indian drama," the western's precursor), silent films helped usher in Indigenous modernity, however uneven the process was at the time. In the first two decades of the twentieth century, and before the arrival of sound film (in 1927, with *The Jazz Singer*), American Westerns appealed to working-class immigrant audiences and aided in the work of Americanization—although the version of the imagined nation they offered was primarily white, domestic, and Christian.

Scholars of silent film and Native and Indigenous Studies have established that early films helped transpose on celluloid Americans' desires, anxieties, and beliefs, as they also helped form and nurture them. Silent films, many of them produced outside the U.S., also cultivated growing national anxieties about "foreign films." Film critic Richard Abel has shown that the Western, which he calls a "white supremacist entertainment," played no small part in solidifying, on the screen, the political and social work of the Americanization project.[7] Building on Abel's work, I turn to "reel Indians" on screen and behind the camera, and ask: what happens when the *Indian*, a construct of the settler imagination, becomes not only the object but also the subject of representation? Examining such feature films as *White Fawn's Devotion* (1910), *The Vanishing American* (1925), and *Redskin* (1929), as well as early documentary, ethnographic films, and film fragments in colonial archives, in this chapter I show that while mediating between the demands of the genre and a commitment to tribal specificity, these films began to challenge misconceptions about Native representation. A film like *White Fawn's Devotion*, for instance, directed by Native director James Young Deer/Young Johnson, offers a cinematic alternative to the trope of the vanishing Indian found in ethnographic films and Westerns. Other films, such as *The Daughter of Dawn* (1920), resorted to melodramatic conventions to depict love triangles, defied federal Indian policy and census data, and used an all-Native cast rather than white actors in red face.

Over the last four decades, Native visual media in North America has offered—in film and photography—an antidote to settler colonialist nostalgia through what film critic Joanna Hearne calls "Indigenous revisionism." Hearne has shown how Native filmmakers "navigated the power structures of Hollywood" and how they integrated the historical archive of Native (mis)representation into their contemporary work.[8]

This revisionism entails not only decolonizing Native filmmaking, or what Beverly Singer calls "wiping the war paint off the lens," but also a renewed understanding of early Hollywood representations of Native people in the twentieth-century context of settler colonialism and its push toward Americanization and assimilation. Building on Hearne's work of historical recovery, as well as that of other film scholars, I contribute to this decolonial and revisionist analysis by examining settler-produced films about Native people, including the popular Western genre, through an Indigenous Studies lens; by analyzing films by Native directors and films with a Native cast; and by identifying moments of slippage or undecidability (the Derridean aporia) in the settler colonial visual narrative, which allows for more nuanced readings of Native presence on and off screen.[9]

THE *INDIANS* OF THE SETTLER IMAGINATION: VANISHING INDIANS, WILD WEST SHOWS, WESTERNS

Moving pictures, like print culture, helped in the work of imagining the settler nation, and they also helped represent one of the country's most long-standing objects of fascination, *the Indian*, a signifier in the American imagination with little connection to its referent. At the beginning of the twentieth century, Native Americans became popular subjects (and objects) of representation in early silent films by pioneering film producers. Their popularity was not accidental. Throughout the nineteenth century, Native people had been central to American popular culture, from captivity narratives, songs and ballads, to poems and fiction, travel and sketch books, dime novels, plays, paintings, and photographs. The white American gaze, cultivated through both print and the recent medium of silent film, was fascinated by a combination of *Indian* exoticism, mystery, and putative danger. The camera picked up on this in its love of the action of Indian-white combat; stock narrative episodes from dime novels became adaptations for the screen. The fetishization of Native regalia and other markers of Native identity (feathers, moccasins, long hair, and so on) in early silent film set the tone for the industry's dissemination of stereotypes throughout the twentieth century as film became the new medium of both leisure and mass education. One of the most popular genres translating these anxieties was the Western, which grew in popularity between the 1890s and the 1920s. Drawing on the postbellum Western romances, cinematic Westerns typically depicted violent conflicts between white settlers and Native people. Westerns also validated settler colonial ideology, both a nostalgic reminder of the so-called vanishing race and a glorification of the dominant (white, capitalist, Christian) culture.[10] The idea of the "vanishing Indian" was deeply ingrained in the American psyche during the Progressive Era, the legacy of nineteenth century's legal, literary, and dramatic attempts to perpetuate in print and on stage what I call elsewhere the "last Indian syndrome."[11] This ideological formation captured mid- and late-nineteenth century audiences' fascination with an exotic image of Native people, incompatible with the categories of whiteness, citizenship, and modernity.

A young Jewish woman at an East Side nickelodeon in New York City declared herself "rapt and entranced" by an *Indian* film in 1911.[12] As immigrant spectatorship was closely connected to ideas of uplift and assimilation in the broader project of Americanization, reformers embraced the idea of *Indian* films. If the *Indians* (or Mexicans) that the audiences saw onscreen could be assimilated and act "American"— with white actors playing the lead Native roles—so could the new immigrant arrivals from eastern and southern Europe. Yet, the logic of this analogy deserves further attention: the *Indians* of the Westerns were obstacles to settlers, to be disciplined and tamed, yet their constant threats to the settler westward expansion and onscreen violence made such taming questionable. In this logic, the unassimilable Natives of the Westerns had to be eliminated through violent settler acts. The Western's high popularity as a universalizing and ideological idiom also created and solidified the category of the American spectator socialized in white supremacy.

Buffalo Bill Cody's Wild West show, which started in 1883, was one of the most popular entertainments at the end of the nineteenth century. It catered to settler American audiences and new immigrant audiences negotiating their own sense of belonging in an Anglo-Saxon settler nation. The reenactments of frontier violence in the live performances on which it thrived were later captured in film. A decade after Cody started his Wild West show, historian Frederick Jackson Turner launched his famous "frontier thesis" in an acclaimed academic paper he delivered at the American Historical Association in Chicago in 1893. Turner's frontier thesis strengthened the belief in the inevitable demise of Native people as Native people, as they acquired a new, American identity on the frontier, which Turner called "the line of most rapid and effective Americanization." For Turner, "going Native" on the frontier signified one of the crucial stages of the settlers' emerging American identity. Being like *Indians* through what I call throughout this book convenient affiliation—strategies of identification, alliance building, and resistance to dominant ideologies of race and national identity, across racial and ethnic lines, aimed at elevating settler agency and relegating Native people to the past—was desirable in the process of transforming new immigrants into Americans. Americanization presented Indigenous people as compliant, stoic, adaptable—if at all alive. The violence of settler identification as Native continued beyond the closing of the frontier. According to historian Richard White, Buffalo Bill's Wild West was more effective than Turner in advancing American exceptionalism.[13]

The formula of the Wild West shows, reenacting *Indian* attacks on cabins and wagon trains, provided a template for Indian-white conflict and was central to the history of early cinema. Native people, including leaders like Sitting Bull, and Native actors—for example Lilian St. Cyr, Ho-Chunk, and James Young Johnson, Nanticoke—joined the Wild West shows. Native employment in Wild West shows and, later, the film industry, provided mobility across the United States and Europe, as well as a source of revenue for the tribes whose food supplies were dwindling in the 1880s and 1890s. The Wild West shows circulated the images of the "vanishing Indian" at home and abroad—from world fairs in Chicago (1893), Omaha (1898), St. Louis (1904), or Portland (1905) to shows in Great Britain and other European countries (1887–1906).

A regular feature of the Miller Brothers 101 Ranch Show, an extension of Cody's Wild West show, was a segment called "Immigrant Act." Surviving photographs document a scene of Sioux men attacking settler wagons, demonizing the image of *Indians* and reinforcing the victimization of settlers, further legitimizing settler violence (figure 36).[14]

The images of *Indians* attacking settlers' cabins, ubiquitous in the early Wild West shows and etched in the settler nation's imaginary, became staples of both early and later westerns. Although Progressive Era reform groups protested repeatedly against the dehumanization of Indigenous people that resulted from these violent frontier perfor-

Fig. 36. "Immigrant Act," segment of the Miller Brothers 101 Ranch Show, featuring a Sioux attack on the settlers, Kansas City, 1930. E. M. Botsford Papers, Southwest Collection/Special Collections Library, Texas Tech University, Lubbock.

mances and "the image of the Indian," the dissemination of Wild West shows on celluloid continued after Cody's death in 1917.[15] The title of this episode —"Immigrant Act" (1930)—was perhaps misdirected; in its implication of the "immigrant" in the act of violence committed by the Sioux "warriors," we can read the scene as an attempt to build common ground with the (new) immigrant audiences watching similar performances. This episode creates a sense of complicity between the immigrant viewer and the old settlers on screen, who participate in Native dispossession by settling in the West. In the settler imaginary, the putatively violent *Indians* must be eliminated through an "immigrant act." The caption of the photograph, "Immigrant Act," makes the new immigrant viewer complicit in the histories of settler violence.

In an Attempt to make the film industry more "American," half of the Westerns produced between 1907 and 1910 were *Indian* stories or stories with a Native (or Mexican) central character. These early films offered melodramatic stories of good versus evil characters, as well as Native characters in relation to white protagonists, with "a sense of honor, justice, or self-sacrifice."[16] It their peak of popularity, between 1910 and 1912, studios released close to fifteen Westerns a month. They told stories of ruthless whites and hostile Native warriors, interracial marriage, failed Indian-white alliances, mixed-blood children and their Native sacrificing mothers, and the omnipresent white savior figure.

By 1909 the Western was the leading genre in the U.S.: "American" in subject matter, sensational, filmed in attractive, scenic landscapes. Film magazines described the Western as "a quintessentially American topic."[17] In its promotion of Americanization, the genre thrived on contradictions: it appealed to the audiences' imagined sense of American wholesomeness, yet it capitalized on the violence perpetrated on Native bodies in beautiful landscapes. The Western tapped into the familiar territory of the uncritical adoration of the picturesque American landscapes in such films as *An Indian's Gratitude* (1913) and *The Red Man and the Child* (1908). Although foreign films had dominated the nickelodeon era, the threat they posed to the sense of American identity—during the high tide of immigration in the early 1900s—led to their subsequent exclusion, through institutional structures (such as the National Board of Censorship) and print (trade press and national magazines) in an attempt to promote and disseminate preeminently American products. As film critic Richard Abel put it, the Westerns embodied the "good, clean, wholesome, national, patriotic, educational films." The magazine *Moving Picture World* insisted that American film manufacturers offer the American public materials "to assimilate anything that was alien."[18]

The extreme popularity of the Western genre during the silent era—in the United States and abroad, where many films about cowboys and Indians found a welcoming market—set the tone for the reception of a genre whose longevity would have devastating effects in misrepresenting Indigenous cultures.[19] As the film industry developed, the Western evolved, from the permissive years of the silent era to the "redskins" of the sound era.[20] Producers, exhibitors, and moviegoers used a variety of terms to describe the genre—including "cowboy and Indian pictures," "Wild West films," "frontier melodramas," and "shoot'em-ups."[21] Although the Western glorified life on the western frontier, the first ones made in the U.S. were filmed on the East Coast—in New Jersey, New York, and Connecticut—or what contemporary film critics call the "eastern Westerns." D. W. Griffith directed around thirty Indian-themed films during the industry's early years, and his films consistently portrayed Native Americans as villains—a case in point is the famous *The Battle at Elderbush Gulch* (1913)—noble savages, or vanishing *Indians*; some of these westerns featured a "noble redskin" as guide or savior to the white hero.[22]

By 1910, a fifth of the films released in the U.S. were Westerns.[23] Luther Standing Bear, the Lakota Sioux activist, actor, and Carlisle Indian School graduate, made appearances in Cody's Wild West shows and in silent films, often uncredited. He was hired as a consultant for the movie industry in 1912, and is likely to have appeared in a dozen films (uncredited), working with Douglas Fairbanks, William S. Hart, Charles Ray, and Thomas Ince, among others. In his autobiography, *My People, the Sioux* (1928), Standing Bear decried the use of what he called "white imitators" in Native roles, as Native actors were prevented from participating fully in the film industry. Luther Standing Bear recalled his own frustration with the film industry and the damage of the "Indian pictures" for Native representation:

> I have seen probably all of the pictures which are supposed to depict Indian life, and not one of them is correctly made. There is not an Indian play on the stage that is put on as it should be. I have gone personally to directors and stage managers and playwrights and explained this to them, telling them that their actors do not play the part as it should be played, and do not even know how to put on an Indian costume and get it right; but the answer is always the same, "The public don't know the difference, and we should worry!"[24]

Standing Bear also recalled his conversations with Thomas Ince, the producer and owner of the Inceville film studio: "I told him that none of the Indian pictures were made right. . . . We talked for a long time, and when I arose to leave, he said: 'Standing Bear, some day you and I are going to make some real Indian pictures.'" Ince and Standing Bear never made those "Real Indian pictures"—which would have to wait several more decades to be made—but early Hollywood cinema had more of what film critic Michelle Raheja calls "Native presences" than the following decades of the studio system.

Luther Standing Bear was not the only Native person critical of the film industry's profiting from "the image of the Indian." The Native critique of *Indian* misrepresentations became public in 1911, when tribal leaders visited Washington, D.C., and demanded that President Taft take action against the industry's continued visual attack on Native

communities. National and local newspapers, as well as Indian boarding school publications, covered the event. From Carlisle Indian Industrial School, John Standing Horse wrote: "If the directors of the
moving picture companies knew how foolish their women and girls
look in the Indian pictures, with from one to three turkey feathers
in the top of their heads, they would be more careful."[25] One film in
particular galvanized Native protest: *The Curse of the Redman* (Selig,
1911). The film told the story of Native man Zarapai, who attended an
Indian boarding school but when he returned to his tribe found that
he didn't belong anywhere; equipped with all the stereotypes, the film
made Zarapai drink, murder a fellow Native man, and ultimately com-
mit suicide. The year 1911, when Native leaders traveled to Washington and protested against the misrepresentations of Native people, also
saw the formation of the first pan-Indian national organization, the
Society of American Indians (SAI). Throughout the 1910s, the SAI (see
chapter 5) used print strategically to protest similar representations in
film and the national press and to offer a contemporary version of the
"modern Indian."

One pervasive trope in early silent film was the white settler's saving
brown women from other white men/settlers, whom the press of the
time often described as "emigrants." Other film genres were equally
problematic in representing Native Americans, especially when they
capitalized on a phenomenon we could call gratitude for the settler, an
extension of what postcolonial studies scholar Gayatri C. Spivak calls
"saving brown women from brown men." Silent film glorified the white
male savior, whose main function was to save the Native woman from
both brown and white men.[26] In such instances, white "heroes" were
in control of the visual narrative, humanizing the Native characters,
guiding or teaching them, and extracting Native gratitude. *Dove Eye's
Gratitude* (Bison, 1909), *Red Wing's Gratitude* (Vitagraph, 1909), *The
Mesquite's Gratitude* (Kalem, 1911), and *An Indian's Gratitude* (Selig,
1913) are examples of this type of storyline. White heroes protected
Native women from abuse by other white or by Native men; in the
end, the Native heroine—though "grateful"—often had to die. In *Red
Wing's Gratitude*, a white man intervenes to protect and save Red Wing
from her ignoble father (a Brule Sioux "chief"). Just as the American
citizens intervene to discipline Ivan Orloff into nonviolent domesticity
in Alice G. Blaché's *Making an American Citizen* (see chapter 7), "a

little company of emigrants" intervenes, stopping the Native father's brutality. The demonization of Native kinship structures in *Red Wing's Gratitude* results in the glorification of the Anglo-American family. The "emigrants" (settlers) prevail in the final scene, "in time to drive off the redskins and make comfortable the Native girl's last moments." Ultimately, the Native woman's gratitude to the settler results in her untimely death.[27]

In 1910, the trade journal *Moving Picture World* started a debate, well known in the American film circles, on the question "What is an American subject?" It called for "American-made pictures on American subjects" for a predominantly working-class and immigrant spectatorship. So beautiful were some of the Native landscapes in these films that spectators and reviewers delighted in its beauty and underplayed the Western's equally visible violence on Native subjects and its ideological implications and references (such as the ubiquitous American flags and other patriotic markers). In the next several years, as the film industry became complicit with the growing hyper-nationalism of the 1910s, the Western would embody—and for decades to come—the ethos of wholesomeness and patriotism promoted by the Americanization campaigns.[28]

BEYOND THE "VANISHING INDIAN" OF ETHNOGRAPHIC FILM

Like other film genres, ethnographic film articulated and contested the vanishing Indian trope. Early ethnographic cinema used Euro-American narrative techniques, simultaneously documenting and exoticizing a purportedly "pure" version of Native presence or identity. Despite their problematic documentation of Native subjects through an imperialist lens, ethnographic materials provide a visual documentary archive of the era worth recovering alongside materials where Native communities had some agency.[29] In recent decades the National Archives and the Library of Congress collections have made available a larger catalogue of Native representations on film.[30] One recently rediscovered film documents part of Joseph K. Dixon's Expedition of Citizenship to the American Indian: *The Romance of a Vanishing Race* (1916). The film offered on a celluloid version of what Edward Curtis had captured through staged photographs: an idealized and studied image of Native Americans. On three different expeditions to the American West, Dixon collected at least 11,000 photos and 50 miles of film.[31] The twenty-nine-minute film was the product of careful editing of 13,000 feet of film, and the result of an arduous journey by a team led by Dixon himself. One of the few reviews of the film in 1917—"American Indian's History Filmed"—claimed boldly that Dixon visited "all the extant tribes."[32] To promote his film and to show off the materials he had collected during his expeditions, sponsored by Philadelphia business Rodman Wanamaker, Dixon took to the lectern in Philadelphia in 1917. His lectures were accompanied by slide shows created from pictures he and his crew had taken. Ads reminded audiences that his endeavor was authorized by the U.S. federal government: "Dr. Dixon visited every Indian tribe in the country, having gone with the sanction and approval of the government."[33] The prospect of a Native future was inconceivable to Dixon and his crew, who succumbed to "despair" when facing census numbers about the dwindling numbers of the Native population in the United States. At the end of *The Romance*, Native people vanish into the sunset.

Dixon's *The Romance of a Vanishing Race* asked similar questions to those that Indigenous and non-Indigenous intellectuals were asking in print, lectures, and literature during the Progressive Era: "Is he happy, prosperous—has he the full liberty of a free born American—is he a beneficiary of the advantages of civilization?" Most pressingly, *The Romance* continued to ask what the Wanamaker Expedition of Citizenship to the American Indian had asked in 1913: "Is he a citizen of the United States enjoying all the rights and privileges we do?" The descriptions of Native peoples, objects, and landscapes in Dixon's film conformed to the lexicon of salvage anthropology, with the Navajo described as "child[ren] of the desert" and rows of plains *Indians* presented on horseback, sinking into the sunset. *The Romance* did exactly what the title promised: it relegated Native tribes to an ahistoric past, devoid of any signs of modernity—except for several rifles here and there. *The Romance* feebly attempted to engage in the critique of Indian affairs: "Because he was masterful in fighting a masterful foe—because he resented broken treaties and gross injustice—we called him a savage." Although it relegated Native tribes to the background of the story, where they became one with an idealized landscape, the film acknowledged Native warfare with admiration.

Like Dixon's *The Romance of a Vanishing Race,* other ethnographic films, such as *The Wards of a Nation* (1920), obscured the political status of Indigenous nations as debates over Native exclusion from American citizenship preoccupied Native and non-Native activists, from the Society of American Indians to the Friends of the Indian. Ford Motion Picture laboratories—which reached many immigrant viewers from the film department's start in 1914, also discussed in chapter 7—distributed *The Wards of a Nation,* a film which reinforced the pervasive idea of Native people as wards of the U.S. government and obscured the sovereign status of Native nations written into treaties with the federal government. To audiences watching in the dark, the "wards of the nation" were targets of their Christian pity. *The Wards of a Nation* dwells on the image of a pensive Native man who wears a headdress and looks out into the distance. Intertitles extol Christian virtues: "The Lord is my shepherd; therefore, I lack nothing." Scenes of tent life, outdoor feasts, and dances are interspersed throughout the film, with little reference to tribal specificity. The remaining materials on the reel offer an odd juxtaposition of religious pageantry with "Indian Rites of Old," which capture on celluloid scenes from ceremonial dances for the tribal council in Missoula, Montana, by Blackfeet, Nez Perce, and Flathead Indians.

What Dixon and other enthusiasts of Native ethnographic material failed to realize was that performances for white audiences (and the camera) were part of a long history of diplomatic protocol, where Native ceremonies to white diplomats or politicians were nothing more than studied performances.[34] Like the *Indian* melodramas of the time, *Wards of a Nation* wove in baptism and conversion to Christianity as a sign of assimilation, painting a happy face of Christianity in Native communities and showcasing Native people who smiled and embraced white domesticity: "Old warriors now kneel with their white brethren in Christian worship." Ethnographic film performed a double rhetorical move: on the one hand, it purported to capture on celluloid communities, seemingly frozen in time, "vanishing"; on the other, it allowed for Indigenous presence on camera, however distorted. At the same time, the filmed subjects in *Wards of a Nation* played the docile "wards" in front of the camera not as an acceptance of wardship but as a survival tactic.

This is not to say that Native people did not have their own performance traditions, but in an attempt to turn Native people rapidly into Americans during the Progressive Era, the Office of Indian Affairs banned tribal dances and ceremonies, seen as vestiges of "savagery" and, obstacles to a capitalist, Christian, and domestic modernity.[35] Despite all these limitations, Native Americans continued to use American patriotic holidays as opportunities to perform their ceremonies and dances.[36] Several instances of Native resistance to an absurd, fake ceremony of Americanization were immortalized in film by Joseph K. Dixon's *Romance of a Vanishing Race* (1916), issued three years after Dixon led the Wanamaker Expedition of Citizenship to the American Indian (1913).[37] In that rare footage filmed at Fort Belknap, Montana, a Native man in traditional regalia walks by the American flag and refuses to sign the fake declaration of allegiance; more pointedly, he pauses and spits near the flag. Like his Native contemporaries, whose acts of resistance were not captured on film, the Native man's refusal sanctions the long history of ceremonial and diplomatic encounters whereby Native "actors" embodied the defeat, the passing of land or goods to the settler colonists, and their silent assent to their own dispossession. This orchestrated performance of American patriotism during Dixon's Expedition of Citizenship was as artificial as the ethnographic turn in *The Wards of a Nation*, attempting to capture a fabricated idea of Native assent or "authenticity" yet ultimately making room for (performed) Native agency within the confines of a genre explicitly designed to erase it.

A counterpoint to the vanishing Indian trope of the ethnographic film is the representation of Native children in Indian boarding schools, captured in two short snippets of early documentary—*Indian School Days* (1898) and *Club Swinging at Carlisle Indian School* (1902)—preserved by the Library of Congress. They record Native children in educational settings: one in New Mexico, the other in Pennsylvania. Although they were highly repressive and regimented spaces—in their suppression of Native languages, clothes, and culture more broadly—the Indian boarding schools were also loci of Native negotiation of Americanism, citizenship, sovereignty, and modernity. *Indian School Days* was filmed by Thomas Edison from a single camera position. Among the earliest footage of Indian boarding schools, it records scenes from the Isleta Indian School in New Mexico, a name shown prominently in the first scene of the surviving footage. Native children come out of the school building, pass in front of the camera, laugh, hold hands, then turn around and reenter the school; at one point, a male Native teacher ushers them back inside the school. The laughter of the little boys and girls looks infectious, humanizing an otherwise regimented scene of Americanization; the humanity of the observed subject prevails, disorienting the imperial gaze that the ethnographic film thrived on.[38]

Club Swinging at Carlisle Indian School is an equally powerful visual document of Native education in Indian boarding schools. Filmed from a single camera position, the surviving two-minute footage shows a couple of hundred Native students at Carlisle engaged in a fitness exercise. The footage also captures the Carlisle barracks in the background. The students are dressed in dark uniforms; the boys wear white shirts and the girls, white collars. Most of the students perform the highly symmetrical and orchestrated routine of club swinging. When the footage starts, a female student misses a beat in the rhythm, and, although she tries to recover her pace, she cannot keep up with the exercise. She looks around at the synchronized movements around her, smiles at the students who continue the exercise, and improvises.

This fleeting moment of hesitation, of Derridean aporia (a moment of undecidability) captures a fissure in the Americanization enterprise and the search for order and conformity of the Progressive Era. The scene is yet another moment of Native nonconformity on celluloid, echoing the direct dissent expressed by the Native man who refused to sign the fake declaration of citizenship. Such moments of Indigenous affirmation and presence are rarely preserved on film. They do exist, but they continue to be overlooked and finding them requires careful mining of the archives. Although they do not fulfill fantasies of empire, violence, or westward expansion of what Richard Slotkin has called a "gunfighter nation"—and even though they were still produced in settler colonial contexts by agents of empire (abroad) and Americanization (at home)—ethnographic films like *Indian School Days* and *Club Swinging at Carlisle Indian School* ultimately disrupt the mythical narrative of American (settler) formation widely popularized by the Westerns.[39]

INDIAN DRAMAS AND CROSS-RACIAL ROMANCE

At its core, the Indian melodrama used the cult of domesticity to show that the Americanization of Native families was not only possible but also imminent. Although Indian melodramas, a popular subgenre of the early Westerns, were in decline by 1913, film producers resorted to them when major shifts in federal Indian policy called for it. They relied on such tropes as child-rearing, sexuality, and education.[40] As Joanna Hearne has shown, some of the Indian dramas "contrast the acquisition of land and export of gold, oil, and children from the West with the importance and value of family and even tribal obligations." In *Maya, Just an Indian* (1913), the union of a white man and a Native woman leads not to the production of children but of land or gold. A recent Carlisle graduate returns to her unnamed Native community and falls in love with a white prospector, whom she marries and helps acquire gold off her land. Her father agrees to tell her where "the gold is hidden" only if she promises "not to see the paleface again." Maya leads prospector Bill to the gold, but suspecting his unorthodox intentions, she fills his bags with sand and pebbles before he leaves for the East, where he later starts a family. Two years later, when Maya learns that Bill's white wife, now raising their small child, has "lung trouble," she rushes to their house carrying a knife, but once there she does not kill the ailing mother and child; instead, Maya leaves her knife and some gold on the table, before hurrying away toward a cliff, where she lifts her hands in despair. The open ending of *Maya, Just an Indian* offers the possibility of both survival and suicide; ultimately, the Native woman sacrifices herself so that the white nuclear family can survive.[41]

Indian melodramas naturalized the extraction of Native land and children—two of the major tactics of settler dispossession, according to anthropologist Patrick Wolfe—with devastating consequences for Native communities.[42] Several Indian dramas about the education of young Native people in the East deserve an even closer scrutiny than they have received—from *The Curse of the Redman* (1911), the film that led to Native protests in the nation's capital in 1911, to *Braveheart* (1925), *The Scarlet West* (1925), or *Redskin* (1929). In particular, *Redskin* offered a glimpse into the lives of Native students in western Indian boarding schools, showing the education offered there as the clear path to Americanization. *The Scarlet West* tells the story of the son of a generic "Indian chief" who is educated in the East; later rejected by his community, he becomes an army captain, an agent of empire. When he hears about Custer's defeat at Little Big Horn (1876), he decides to return to his people. Promotional materials advertised *The Scarlet West* as employing 4,000 Indians, 2,000 frontiersmen, 3,500 horses, and 4,000 "Real U.S. Cavalry." It also emphasized the film's sensationalism: "And then when a savage loves a general's daughter, what happens? Anything could happen." Similarly, in *Red Love* (1925), Carlisle school graduate Thunder Cloud (Sioux) falls in love with Starlight, "the half-breed daughter of Sheriff LaVerbe," whom he abducts and takes to his hideout. Believing he had killed the villain Bill Mosher in an altercation, Thunder Cloud and Starlight are on the run, followed by Little Antelope, a member of the Native police, also in love with Starlight. When Thunder Cloud recognizes Little Antelope as his younger brother, he turns himself in, stands trial, and is found not guilty of having slain Mosher (who later makes an unexpected appearance). All's well that ends well: Thunder Cloud is exonerated and Starlight agrees to marry him at the end of *Red Love*.[43]

Early silent film was invested in promoting and reinforcing the idea of fixed racial difference. If directors like Thomas Ince offered idyllic *Indian* stories, reminiscent of the works of nineteenth-century novelist James Fenimore Cooper, filmmakers like D. W. Griffith turned to Native individuals and their relations with class, culture, or race. Ince's *Indians*, either friendly or hostile—*The Indian Massacre* (1912); *Custer's Last Fight* (1912, 1925); *Blazing the Trail* (1912)—were not assimilable into America's imagined ideal citizenry. Griffith's melodramas were about lost paradises—the old South or the imagined pastoral life of Native people, who fought land-grabbers, miners, or the U.S. Army, eliciting the audience's sympathy in films like *The Red Man and the Child* (1908), *The Mended Lute* (1909), or *The Massacre* (1912). The story of the American West in this context is the story of *Indian* massacres and Native people's removal from their lands. In Griffith's *The Massacre*, a Native family is killed by the cavalry while the settler family survives; *The Battle at Elderbush Gulch* (1913) depicts violent *Indian* attacks on settlers. Griffith's films rendered the nostalgia for a white past, captured a few years later in his infamous *Birth of a Nation* (originally titled *The Clansman*, 1915), the first film to be shown at the White House, which paid homage to the Ku Klux Klan and demonized the hypersexualized Black male characters played by white actors in blackface. Just as Native leaders had protested the misrepresentation of their people by the film industry in 1911, the NAACP brought Black protesters together in New York City in 1921 for similar purposes. At a screening of the film in New York City, African American ex-servicemen distributed pamphlets illustrating the white supremacist mission of the Ku Klux Klan, while Black women marched around with placards decrying the film's racism: "We Represented America in France, Why Should *The Birth of a Nation* Misrepresent Us Here?"[44]

Similarly, the three-reeler *The Indian* (1914) dramatized contemporaneous American fantasies about assimilation and highlighted the perils awaiting the non-Americanized Native person. The film represents Indigenous people stereotypically, using white actors in red face, wearing too much makeup and wigs held by headbands, playing into white fantasies of plains *Indians*. Set in a generic *Indian* village in the West— just as the name of the film intimates a representation of a generic *Indian*—the film juxtaposes the fates of the twin sons of War Eagle, an "Indian chief," who are separated early in life, after a fight between the U.S. Cavalry and their unnamed tribe on the Great Plains. One of the boys (Red Feather) is raised by his Native father; the other (Blue Feather) grows up in the white family of an army general. The general raises Blue Feather as a playmate for his daughter Gladys, or "White Lily." When the general's daughter is kidnapped by a corrupt Indian agent, Blue Feather, the Americanized brother, saves her, while his twin brother is killed in the altercations. The final tableau shows the reconciliation between Native and white families. Blue Feather, the Americanized brother lives on, without having met his twin, the *Indian*, and the Native father has suddenly gained another son. In an exchange with Gladys, Blue Feather, the Native playmate, exclaims: "White Lily, I hate all palefaces but you." Ultimately, both Native brothers give their life to serve and save White Lily. As a larger metaphor, whiteness lives. The film also alludes to a possible interracial romance between Gladys and Blue Feather, but this subplot is not developed.[45] In the years before this film was made, the possibilities of interracial romance were at the heart of the work of Hollywood's first Native power couple—James Young Johnson and Red Wing/Lilian St. Cyr—however briefly, but after 1914 interracial romance no longer interested filmmakers. The *Indian* was both a reminder of the absence of Indigenous peoples from the American settler imaginary and a document of their presence.

CASE STUDIES

In this section I examine four instances of Native representation in silent film, and argue that the silent film industry helped negotiate modernity on Native terms, even when those terms were uneven. Because of the early film industry's openness to ideas of "authenticity" and cultural accuracy, and emphasizing Native survival, actors like James Young Deer/Young Johnson and Lilian St. Cyr intervened in the early years of the American Western and offered a more accurate, sometimes critical, stance on Native representation than did white directors and producers. Young Deer's *White Fawn's Devotion* (1910) explored the audience's uneasiness with interracial families in the silent era's most permissive years and offered a counternarrative to racial separatism and fears of racial mixing. *The Daughter of Dawn* (1920), a film with an all-Native cast, whose Native protagonists did not die, was ahead of its time. *The Vanishing American* (1925) reinforced the Americanizers' agenda as it also chastised it; although critical of federal Indian policy, it did not reach beyond the scope of a sympathetic melodrama. Similarly, *Redskin* (1929) both endorsed Americanization and critiqued the inhumanity of the Indian boarding schools. Although it challenged the fantasy of Americanization, Native control over representation was minimal. With an unfortunate title, *Redskin* foreshadowed future directions of Native representation on screen in the next decades.

"Real Indians" on Screen and behind the Camera: James Young Deer

Whether to document, critique, or invent a new tradition of Native representation, James Young Deer/James Young Johnson and Lilian St. Cyr/Red Wing mark a pivotal moment in North American Indigenous film. They created an incipient form of what Michelle Raheja calls "visual sovereignty," the creative self-representation of Native visual artists while working within the boundaries of the studio system.[46] In his productive career as director, producer, and actor in Westerns, between 1908 and 1913, Young Johnson joined other Native activists and writers of his generation to provide an alternative to the pervasive vanishing Indian trope of the settler imaginary. He used the conventions of the Western to foreground survival, Native and mixed-race family ties, and tribal sovereignty.[47] *White Fawn's Devotion* (1910) departs from the conventional Indian-themed Western to tell a story of survival, family unity, intergenerational and community relations, and the legacy of settler colonialism.

In *Making the Movies* (1915), cultural critic Ernest A. Dench addressed "The Dangers of Employing Redskins as Movie Actors." He was concerned that Native actors suffered from an excess of "realism," an unrelenting behavior in front of the camera, which could jeopardize the white cast's well-being: "Once a white player was seriously wounded when the Indians indulged in a bit too much realism with their clubs and tomahawks." To Dench, Native actors and extras "naturally object[ed] to acting in pictures where they are defeated," and they sometimes smuggled real bullets into the action, which enhanced their realist performance yet made them more threatening to the crew. Many white directors of later Westerns shared Dench's view, as the Western as a national and international genre was co-opted into the work of the Americanization project as a form of what Richard Abel calls "white supremacist entertainment."[48]

Nanticoke actor and director James Young Deer/James Young Johnson may not have shared Dench's views. He had an unremarkable career in the Wild West shows, performing occasionally with his wife, Lilian St. Cyr (aka Princess Red Wing) in New York and Philadelphia. He was employed by such U.S. film companies as Kalem, Lubin, Vitagraph, and Bison. He played a small part in D. W. Griffith's *The Mended Lute* (1909), a film with an overwhelmingly white cast portraying Native people.[49] When the French company Pathé Frères started producing films in the U.S., Young Deer was appointed general manager of the Pathé West Coast Studio. Most of the films he directed and wrote are now lost, but his Westerns were credited in movie magazines as "often highly successful." Among them were *The Cheyenne Brave, The Yaqui Girl, Lieutenant Scott's Narrow Escape, Red Deer's Devotion.*[50] To understand his work, we rely primarily on reviews in specialized film magazines and brief glimpses into some of his few surviving films, among them *White Fawn's Devotion* (1910), a rare silent film with a Native director. He directed and acted in around one hundred and fifty films, a prolific pace for such a short-lived career, with his most productive three years at Pathé's West Coast Studio.[51]

Young Deer and St. Cyr capitalized on white American fantasies about *Indians* and on the white fascination with Indian princesses.[52] Young Deer and St. Cyr, a Ho-Chunk Carlisle graduate, acted in over sixty films from 1909 to 1925.[53] For a (lost) one-reeler from 1911, *Old Indian Days*, Young Deer received high praise from one of the film industry's most respected venues at the time, the trade journal *Moving Picture World:* "The showing of Indian customs, the Indian manner of living, cooking, feasting, traveling, wooing etc. is very prettily done."[54] Native subjects were not of as much interest to the audience as were their surroundings and external realities. Native history and material conditions were interesting only insofar as they served as background to ethnographic stories and landscapes, marked "authentic" by the very presence of Native people, however peripheral to the footage. Such a daring enterprise was ahead of its time, but Young Deer quickly disappeared from the public eye after a scandal in Los Angeles. Although he was exonerated, his career was over after that incident.[55] For all his personal failings, Young Deer helped revise the cinematic representation of Native people, and even though his efforts were short-lived, his work illuminates the possibilities and limitations of the early Westerns and provides a wider framework for understanding contemporary Native critiques of representations of Native people in silent film.[56]

During the early 1910s, films started offering a sharp critique of the treatment of Native people in the U.S. So popular were the *Indian* Westerns in Europe that Pathé Frères, one of the world's most powerful production companies at the time, opened its own studios in the U.S. and hired Young Deer as director and manager of its California branch.[57] After Young Deer moved to Pathé's California studios in 1909, he wrote and directed a film where he "reversed the sexes of the interracial couple," which upset his reviewers. The (now lost) *Red Deer's Devotion* (1911) received the following criticism in *Moving Picture World:* "Another feature of this film will not please a good many. It represents a white girl and an Indian falling in love with each other. While such a thing is possible, and undoubtedly has been done many times, there is still a feeling of disgust which cannot be overcome when this sort of film is depicted as plainly as it is here."[58] How ready were American audiences for interracial romance on screen and what possibilities for imagining Americanism could a film like this open?[59] Although many silent Westerns depicted violent encounters between settlers and Natives on the western frontier, often resulting in the removal, suicide, or murder of the Native characters, *White Fawn's Devotion* centered on Native survival. The early 1910s were favorable to Indian-themed films in Europe and in the U.S. In some of these early westerns, Native women were heroines.

Filmed in Pathé Frères studios on the East Coast, before the move to Los Angeles, *White Fawn's Devotion: A Play Acted by a Tribe of Red Indians in America* told the story of a settler and a Native woman living on the Pine Ridge Reservation in South Dakota. Settler Combs receives "an unexpected legacy" and has to sail to London immediately to claim it. When his wife, White Fawn, learns about his plans to leave for England—and take the couple's daughter along—the mother attempts suicide. Just as the mother succumbs to a melodramatic fall, the girl appears and finds her father holding a bloody knife. The intertitle explains: "Deceived by appearance and believing her mother to be dead, the child accuses her father of murder." Terrified, the child runs to her mother's family, whose men start chasing the settler. After a dangerous chase, where Combs shoots down a few Native men, he is apprehended and awaits punishment. The daughter is brought on scene to punish her father: "Justice by his child." All's well that ends well: the mother, who had only wounded herself, returns and saves the settler from her people's wrath: "White Fawn arrives in time to save him." The film ends with a family tableau (figure 37), which illustrates the endurance of the interracial family. Although the surviving film copy is missing the last few seconds of the original film, promotional material reveals its resolution: "The Combs take their departure and return to their home, for he feels he will be happier with his family on the plains than if he goes east and claims his legacy."[60]

White Fawn's Devotion moves away from predictable *Indian* deaths of other contemporary Westerns, the chases are realistic, and the suspense of tribal justice at the end save Young Deer's film from many of the clichés of early Westerns. Although indebted to the Western genre, the film deemphasizes the blind revenge in films such as D. W. Griffith's *The Redman and the Child* (1908), where Griffith made the Native character a murderer. Pleading with her tribe to save Combs's life, White Fawn strengthens the future of her interracial family. Her melodramatic appearance in the film's climactic scene and her emergence from self-inflicted pain suggest her endurance. The film's title also emphasizes White Fawn's agency: her "devotion" is ultimately to survival, to life. Although Combs dominates the action—he leaves, returns, is chased and eventually exonerated—White Fawn is the film's central consciousness. The film's subtitle, *A Play Acted by a Tribe of Red Indians in America*, gives agency to the Native actors, the "Red Indians."

Fig. 37. Film still, *White Fawn's Devotion* (1910). Last tableau.

Instead of "Red Indians," however, "Redskins" would dominate Hollywood Western feature films in the next decades, despite occasional attempts at seemingly benevolent representations of Native films in the "reform dramas" of the 1920s.[61] The cultural work of *White Fawn's Devotion* lies in its intervention in the dominant cinematic narratives of the 1910s; a Native director offers a vision of Native America different from that imagined by Americanizers, which gestures toward the cultural pluralism of the next decades.

A Different Kind of "Indian Drama": *The Daughter of Dawn* (1920)

Unlike the many "Indian dramas" of the 1920s that were invested in plot lines of interracial love and assimilation, *The Daughter of Dawn* (1920), a recently rediscovered six-reel melodrama, expanded and challenged viewers' expectations of the genre.[62] One of the first feature films with a cast of nonprofessional Kiowa and Comanche actors—including White Parker, the son of famous Comanche chief Quanah Parker—the film was directed by non-Native Norbert A. Myles, a

Shakespearean actor and vaudevillian.[63] When it restored the film in 2012, the Oklahoma Historical Society commissioned David Yeagley, a Comanche musician, to write a film score.[64] An early intertitle names the film's main conflict, which may be based on a Comanche or Apache story of a love triangle: "From time immemorial, the eternal triangle."[65] Comanche White Eagle (White Parker) wants to marry Dawn (Esther LeBarre), daughter of the chief Hunting Horse, former U.S. Army scout, but the chief wants Dawn to marry Black Wolf (Jack Sankadota). A fourth character turns "the eternal triangle" into a quadrangle, or what the score's composer David Yeagley called a quartet: Red Wing (Wanada Parker), who is in love with Black Wolf, suffers in silence.[66] The film points to rivalry between the Comanches and the Kiowas, and it uses action scenes—a buffalo hunt, capturing and rescuing Dawn, a contest between Dawn's two suitors—for dramatic effects. White Eagle's and Black Wolf's bravery is tested when the chief asks them to jump off a cliff for the reward of his daughter's hand in marriage. In the end, White Eagle kills Black Wolf and saves the Daughter of Dawn (who had been taken prisoner by the Comanches during a raid on the Kiowa camp). On finding Black Wolf's body, Red Wing takes her own life. In the final scenes, White Eagle and Dawn row away in a canoe, fading out into the sunset.[67]

Like most Westerns of the day, *The Daughter of Dawn* addressed audiences with varying degrees of knowledge about Native communities. The film attempted to portray faithfully the Comanche and Kiowa communities, yet as Russ Tall Chief, Osage, put it, "Tinseltown audiences watch an all Native American cast from Oklahoma perform Hollywood's interpretation of an Indian 'love triangle.'"[68] Kiowa and Comanche families around Lawton, Oklahoma, where it was filmed, passed down stories of the film, but other than photo stills preserved at the Museum of the Western Prairie in Altus, Oklahoma, historians feared the film was lost. It was never released beyond a 1920 pre-release screening in Los Angeles.

Why was *The Daughter of Dawn* erased from public memory? And how would a film like this captivate Americans? The expectation was for Westerns to depict frontier violence and the survival of white damsels in distress, often through the sacrifice of Native women. Although its plot was melodramatic and allowed for some playful intertribal exchanges, a film with an all-Native cast, where not all Native protagonists die, was ahead of its time. As its director, Norbert Myles, later documented, the Native actors he hired were good negotiators who stood by their demands.[69] At a time when Native dances, along with Native languages and cultural practices, were prohibited on reservations, this film insisted on the normalcy of tribal dances, regalia, and location. The buffalo hunt may have been a nod to the Wichita Mountains Wildlife Refuge in Oklahoma—where the film was shot—and which had acquired a buffalo herd in 1907, but it was also a reference to what I read as the U.S. government's systematic killing of the buffalo, which led to the starvation of tribes on the Plains. The film references famine from the very beginning: Dawn's father asks White Eagle whether he has seen "the game we have long been waiting for. Our women and children can go hungry no longer." Dawn's other suitor has considerable wealth, but his decision is not economic: "If one of you or both fail in this—you shall no longer be worthy of the name Kiowa and shall be driven from the tribe to live among the coyotes" (min. 49). The lead actors are Comanche but they play Kiowa characters—a subtlety contemporary white audiences would not have picked up on—a role reversal that allowed for a playful exchange and signification decodable decades later.

The rediscovery of the film and its screening after restoration has occasioned conversations between Kiowa and Comanche tribal members. Tribal members recognized and could authenticate some of the material objects and characters in the film. One elderly Kiowa audience member, Sammy 'Tone-kei' White, seeing his young mother, Em-koy-e-tie, in the film had an intense emotional response. Sammy's family had kept the story of his mother's performance alive after her passing in 1946. Describing the experience of watching his mother in *The Daughter of Dawn,* Sammy 'Tone-kei' White recalled: "My mother was walking right at me; she was so beautiful. I'm glad the room we were watching it in was dark, because it was emotional seeing her so young."[70] Joanna Hearne calls this moment of contemporary reconnecting with this long-lost film "intergenerational recognition," as the film circulates back to its original community. Through performance, setting, and mise-en-scène, the film "renews the visual record of generational continuity and aesthetic representations" of Kiowa and Comanche history.[71] The actors in the film were living on their allotments and trying to adjust to the new era of assimilation ushered in by the

Allotment Act of 1887. The rediscovery of films like *The Daughter of Dawn* reveals possibilities for Indigenous representation at odds with census data and federal Indian policy, which aimed at vanishing Native communities.

The Vanishing American (1925) and the Limits of "Sympathetic" Representation

If films participate in "a political struggle for supremacy," as Jacqueline Kilpatrick has argued, *The Vanishing American* staged the irreconcilable distance between colonial fantasy and white guilt, emblematic of the decade's struggle to restore an Indigenous place in modernity.[72] Yet, the film's ending reveals that there is no place for the Navajo hero in this modernity. The main character, Nophaie, dies at the end of the film—accidentally killed by another Native character—and the film eschews the possibility of an interracial couple. *The Vanishing American* uses a predictable sentimental plot, appeals to Christian values in its work toward Americanization, and participates in the political struggle for white supremacy. Drawing the viewer's attention to the story's illusory medium, *The Vanishing American* (1925) ends by reminding the audiences about the medium's artificiality, deemphasizing the promising political implications of the critiques the film ultimately fails to make.

In September 1925, Paramount Studio completed filming *The Vanishing American*, adapted from a Zane Grey novel.[73] The film, forgotten for many decades, was rediscovered by the American Film Institute in 1970 and has since received scholarly attention as "one of the most important films ever made about the Native American."[74] For the twenty-first century viewer, the film's recovery points to its misdirected political potential, its artistic and technical accomplishments, and its emphasis on death, loss, and disappearance. Contemporaneous silent films gave little attention to harsh reservation life, the demands—and often promises—of Americanization, and the corruption of the Office of Indian Affairs employees. Yet, a film like *The Vanishing American* appealed to viewers for its "sympathetic" look at reservation life. Although critical of federal Indian policy, its portrayal of Navajo people (represented by the fictional Nopah tribe) makes the film a good contender for a "sympathetic melodrama." Like other adaptations of

Indian-themed novels, *The Vanishing American* resorts to a sentimental plot—a white woman (Marion) and a Native man (Nophaie) fall in love; he dies and she lives—and advocates for Americanization.

Like his progressive contemporaries, poet, writer, and film critic Carl Sandburg lamented Zane Grey's fictional attempt and George Seitz's cinematic effort to impress the audience with a "passionate sentiment for the red man." In his review, Sandburg called *The Vanishing American* "a bizarre attempt at setting down on gelatin the story of the American red man in broad strokes."[75] The film was partisan to the Native causes, which contemporaneous social reformers and the Friends of the Indian championed. It criticized federal programs calling for the disintegration of reservations, and praised the efforts of the Navajo soldiers who fought in World War I and were rewarded with American citizenship. As the Native soldiers returned home, they found their reservations in a precarious state, their women abused, and their land taken under Indian Agent Booker's regime of terror.

To complete *The Vanishing American,* Paramount amassed an impressive cast and crew, including serial director George B. Seitz, and headed for the Arizona desert in beautiful Navajo country.[76] After two years of planning and shooting, the result was, according to a reviewer, "an inspiring production."[77] Although the film diverged from Grey's equally exploitative book, the contract Grey signed with Paramount required that the films based on his books be "made on the exact locations of the author's stories." The production of the film intruded on Navajo land in Monument Valley, as Paramount crewmembers "opened up a road and constructed usable cliff dwellings for the spectacular attack sequence."[78] The favorable reviews raved about the film's technical achievement, the visibility of the Arizona desert and canyons, and the "amazing" white actor Richard Dix. The reviewers downplayed the film's central concern—the Indigenous subject.[79] Critics called it an "extraordinary picture," and compared it to (the notoriously racist) *Birth of a Nation* (1915). One *Los Angeles Times* reviewer called it "one of the most ambitious motion picture undertakings in the history of the screen."[80]

Although early silent film companies like Bison or Vitagraph employed Native actors, most studios continued to employ white actors in red face. The Navajo actors cast in *The Vanishing American* served as background to a story told and performed by white actors, who occasionally wore too much makeup. In his *New York Times* column, Mordaunt Hall praised Richard Dix's performance (in red face) but criticized the makeup, which "does not always strike one as being a redskin."[81] A reviewer for the *Wall Street Journal* commented on "a lovely heroine with her exaggerated eye-work."[82] Another reviewer noticed the heroine's melodramatic acting in her blinking too much, "a sort of Morse code," and her high heels, which contrasted with the setting, "such a wild place."[83] The Paramount team took the liberty of teaching the Native actors how to act.[84] While the reviewers were quick to observe the white characters' exaggerated or anachronistic features, few noticed the invisibility of Native characters.

The Vanishing American was publicized as tribute to the "vanishing Indian." In an interview with the *Los Angeles Times*, protagonist Richard Dix shared his sympathy for the "copper colored lads" who "aren't bad fellows at all, once you get to know them." But Dix was frustrated with shooting on location in Arizona, "a million miles away from nowhere," a small price to "play Indian" in an "epic of [the] red man."[85] Dix's leading lady, Lois Wilson, was equally uncomfortable: "We have had rainstorms, sandstorms, heat that sent the mercury up to one hundred thirty degrees."[86] The making of the film was challenging for the production crew, as well. Although Paramount built camps across the Navajo reservation for the crew, the producers were too excited about the film's technical and cinematic potential to worry about how the Navajos might feel about the desecration of their lands.

The classroom and preparations for war are the film's main scenes of Americanization. In the classroom, the agent of Americanization is feminized: white teacher Marion Warner teaches the Native children, including Nophaie, "the smartest buck on the reservation." A typical class day at the boarding school imagined in *The Vanishing American* begins with the Pledge of Allegiance: one Navajo student presents the U.S. flag to the classroom while the others utter the words of the pledge. The children who act in this scene look scared and disoriented; their imagined American future includes acquiring fluency in English, loyalty to the country as good citizens, and Christianity. The film does not dwell as much on Christianity as it does on patriotism. The same classroom where young students pledge their allegiance to the U.S. flag is also a battleground for racial and masculine supremacy. When the Indian agent (Booker) sexually harasses Miss Warner, Nophaie comes to her rescue, confronting Booker and his bullies. The mise-en-scène suggests that the fight desecrates the symbolic power radiated by the presidential portraits on the wall. During the fight scene, the flag appears besides Nophaie, who is constantly interpellated by Americanization symbols as he fights a U.S. government agent.

Distressed to hear that Uncle Sam needs him to fight in the war— "The government comes to me—a haunted man—for help?"—Nophaie listens to Marion, Uncle Sam's fair spokeswoman: "You're as much an American as any of us," she tells him. The scene ends with Nophaie contemplating, in disbelief, the distance between the "haunted man" he is and the desired American he could become if he shared his tribe's horses with the U.S. troops: "American! Me!" This abrupt conversion presents Nophaie as a changed man, joining the war effort in hopes that he will be rewarded and the reservation will escape the tyranny of Indian agents: "Since we are Americans, we go fight. Maybe if we fight . . . maybe if we die . . . our country will deal fairly with our people." The scene ends with Native soldiers, led by Nophaie, leaving to fight in World War I, flanked by U.S. flags flying in the wind.[87] After Nophaie leaves the scene, Marion muses: "Pitiful. . . . Riding away to fight for the white man . . ."

But wartime service did not work to the advantage of the Native volunteers. *The Vanishing American* dramatizes the losses experienced by the fictional Nopah community as the returned soldiers find their lands stolen by the Indian agent's "experimental farm." As a shell-shocked soldier returns home, his double vision facilitates the superimposition of the two realities, before and after the war. As the unnamed soldier faces the distorted reality around him, he sees shadows of Native people walking around, a glimpse of the prewar reservation land, now forcibly taken away. The eerie scene reveals a ghostly present, marked by a single mud house and an old Native man refusing to leave his land; the world as he knew it is gone. Nophaie is angry at "this God of the white man [who] looked from those cold heights beyond the stars and let his people perish!" When he is accidentally mortally wounded by one of his own men—after he had survived the war—he asks Marion to read to him from the New Testament she had gifted him, and dies an American (i.e., a Christian). Representing the American Indian as a "vanishing American" raises questions about the film's politics of representation: does it condemn the trope of the vanishing Indian by turning its attention to genocide and cultural annihilation, filled with government neglect and impoverished communities? As Nophaie dies— "vanishes"—taking with him the hope for the future of the Nophas, the last intertitle of the film brings the audiences back to their present and the artificiality of the medium they have just witnessed: "For races of men come—and go but the stage remains." The self-referentiality of the last scene returns the viewer to the fictionality of the story, its illusory medium, and the triumph of art. The film mourns the "vanishing" Indian as the first American as it celebrates his transformation into an American. Privileging the *Indian* as the "vanishing American," the film calls attention to its own representational politics for the urban audiences of the 1920s, many of them new immigrant spectators.[88]

"I'm Going Back to My People Where I Belong": *Redskin* (1929) and Americanization

Redskin, a silent with a provocatively racist title, stages Americanization debates in unexpected ways; the sentimental plots and subplots and the non-Native director's artistic choices obscure the film's larger ideological and political potential. *Redskin* endorses Americanization as it critiques the inhumanity of the Indian boarding school system. Although purporting to tell the story of a conflicted Navajo character, its stab at cultural pluralism only reinscribes older misrepresentations of Native people on the silver screen—but this time in Technicolor. In 2007, the National Film Preservation Foundation issued a four-volume collection of rare silent films in the series "Social Issues in American Film, 1900–1934." The unfortunately titled *Redskin* is part of volume 4, "Americans in the Making." Critics have praised it for its artistic merits, and its recovery is timely in the context of decolonized readings of *Indian* films and the emergence of a strong body of Native scholarship of film and media.[89] One of Paramount's last silent films, *Redskin* was released in 1929, at the end of a decade of intense criticism of federal Indian policy, after the exacerbated nativism preceding World War I and the restrictive immigration legislation, and a year after the publication of the Meriam Report (1928), which provided data essential for reforming Indian policy through the Indian Reorganization Act (1934).

In his introduction to the film notes accompanying the series, Scott Simmon optimistically calls *Redskin* "the most authentic Hollywood fiction film about Native Americans," commending it for taking a sympathetic look at Native life.[90] Compared with its contemporaneous portrayals of Native people in film and on stage, *Redskin* was clearly ahead of its time. Although it exploded the fantasy of Americanization, Native control over representation was minimal, with an all-white cast, director, writer, and producers. *Redskin* was produced by Paramount, directed by a studio house name, Victor Schertzinger, and written by Navajo enthusiast Elizabeth Pickett (whose 1929 novel, initially titled *Navajo,* was published after the film's premiere).[91] As the title suggests, the film follows in the tradition of other Hollywood racist films—*Justice of the Redskin* (1908), *Romantic Redskins* (1910), and *The Trapper and the Redskins* (1910). *Redskin* was filmed in black and white and two-color Technicolor, a process introduced in 1917, combining black-and-white scenes in the white man's world with two-color scenes filmed on the tribal lands of the Navajo and Acoma Pueblo tribes. The film's Anglo cast included a dashing Richard Dix, who after his stint in *The Vanishing American* returned to play the Navajo Wing Foot, and Gladys Belmont as Pueblo Corn Blossom. Hundreds of Native people were employed as extras, representing the rival Navajos and Acoma Pueblos tribes. The early reviews of *Redskin* unanimously noted that it was handsome Richard Dix who sold the film.

The main plot line of *Redskin* follows Wing Foot from his peaceful childhood on the Navajo reservation as Chief Notani's son, to boarding school, college, and his return to the reservation. The name of the fictional Thorpe University he attends is a nod to Carlisle's star athlete Jim Thorpe (Sac and Fox); there, Wing Foot is a star athlete and studies medicine. The black-and-white boarding school scenes were filmed at the Chinle Indian Boarding School in Arizona and at the Sherman Indian Institute, in Riverside, California.[92] The plot is uncomplicated. Navajo Wing Foot meets Acoma Pueblo Corn Blossom and they fall in love; she is called back home, they are apart, he is banished from his tribe for defying his elders and refusing the honor of becoming the new medicine man. All's well that ends well: Wing Foot discovers oil on his land claim, shares half of it with the Acoma people, ending the long conflict between the tribes, and weds Corn Blossom in a brief traditional ceremony. As the caption reads, this reconciliation brings forth "the greatest gift of heaven, tolerance."

Redskin was a big studio film (with a budget of $400,000), shot on location in Arizona and New Mexico. Paramount carved a road of about three hundred feet to carry the heavy Technicolor equipment up the mesa, a road still functional today. The commissioner of Indian Affairs at the time, Charles H. Burke, gave permission to Paramount to make this film—as long as it provided "wholesome and instructive entertainment to the public, especially in regard to the attitude of the Government toward Indians."[93] The initial screenings were accompanied by music playing a popular radio tune, "Redskin." The song captured the writer's and the country's fascination with the *Indian*.[94] The theme song set the tone for a potential interracial romance between Wing Foot and a white flapper. As she glanced at his athletic body on the track field, the flapper demanded that her obliging white boyfriend "invite that Redskin to the dance tonight. He ought to be a new thrill—in the Ballroom!" Later, after Wing Foot has won the race and everyone is awaiting his triumphant appearance in the ballroom, the flapper, looking for him, asks, "Where's my Redskin?" "Say! What's the idea—getting all steamed up over an Indian?" asks her white boyfriend. A minor character, he provokes Wing Foot to a fistfight. Wing Foot is surrounded by white students dancing and whooping around him—"Well, if you can't dance my way, I'll dance yours!" After Wing Foot is humiliated, told he is tolerated only because he is needed on the track team, he decides to return home: "After what I saw tonight, I'm proud to be a Redskin. My mistake was in thinking I ever had a chance among you whites!"

Although sympathetic in its representation of Indigeneity on the silver screen, *Redskin* belongs to an era when the "Indian docudrama" was one of Hollywood's favorite genres, combining dramatic stories with documentary footage that romanticized "a lost tradition."[95] Cases in point are Thomas Edison's *The Vanishing Race* (1917), reviving the noble but doomed Blackfeet, who disappear into a majestic background; Robert J. Flaherty's *Nanook of the North* (1922), documenting Inuit life with a loose story line and a central character; and Edward Curtis's *In the Land of the Head-Hunters* (1914), a story about Kwakiutl on Vancouver Island, with an all-Native cast. But *Redskin* shares more thematic elements with two other films from 1925: Alan

Hale's *Braveheart*, a pro-assimilation movie, and George B. Seitz's *The Vanishing American*, which represented the failure of the federal Indian policy and the brutality of Indian agents and overemphasized such markers of Americanization as education, Christianity, modernization, and disease.[96]

Paramount's president Herbert T. Kalmus took pride in producing this film in an "age of miracles": "The Indians will tell you so! They came from far and wide to see themselves projected on a screen in the heart of the desert; they whooped and went wild at the sight."[97] While it was an age of miracles for Paramount, it was not an age of miracles for Native people. The Meriam Report of 1928 urged a move away from the failed assimilationist policy and recommended a policy of cultural pluralism. The report was also critical of the Indian boarding schools, finding them "grossly inadequate," and exposed the public for the first time to major abuses Native children suffered in boarding schools. The Meriam Report affirmed the complaints that many Native families had been making for years, for example, the federal government's failure to provide Native students with basic necessities like food and medicine.[98] Early in *Redskin*, in one of the black-and-white scenes at the boarding school, Wing Foot receives new clothes, a new haircut, a new and derogatory name (Do-Atin, "The Whipped One/The Tamed One/The Broken One"), and a new lesson in American discipline through corporal punishment—which the film, sensibly, does not show. In his refusal to salute the U.S. flag, asserting the chief's son's choice to resist patriotic interpellations, we see a fleeting moment of rebellion that other boarding school runaway students attempted as they risked punishment and sometimes death.

At Albuquerque Indian College, which Wing Foot attends, agents of Americanization come from outside Native communities, but Pueblo Corn Blossom—described as "the little Indian flapper"—teaches Navajo Wing Foot one of his first lessons in Americanization. She urges him, "'You must salute the flag.' With a startled glance at her, Wing Foot watched as Corn Blossom saluted respectfully. The little Pueblo girl, his only friend, then took his hand and with earnest explanations, guided it awkwardly to his forehead." In Picket's novel *Redskin*, Corn Blossom shows Wing Foot how to salute the U.S. flag: "'That's it!' she says, nodding toward the flag as it fluttered out on the strong desert wind. 'That stands for our Uncle Sam, who loves his Indian children!'

Fig. 38. (left) Film still, *Redskin* (1929). Corn Blossom teaches Wing Foot to salute the American flag.
Fig. 39. Film still, *Redskin* (1929). Student Wing Foot salutes the flag at Thorpe University.

she whispered softly." In the film adaptation, the intertitle reads: "That's Uncle Sam. He is going to take care of you and me" (figure 38). Years later, when he attends Thorpe University, Wing Foot voluntarily salutes the flag (figures 39).

At the end of *Redskin,* Wing Foot decides to return home: "My mistake was in thinking I ever had a chance among you whites! I'm going back to my own people—where I belong!" Read in the context of the Meriam Report, the film offers the return to the reservation and Native nation as a tangible possibility for belonging in America, in a sense the antidote of Americanization efforts. The film places Native belonging as distinct from the cosmopolitan scenes of Americanization. Wing Foot navigates several identities, names, landscapes, and languages. Taken to boarding school by force at age nine, he rebelled against the coercive rituals of Americanization, which included saluting the U.S. flag. His refusal cost him a major whipping and a failure of his first Americanization lesson; it also led to a shameful name given him by his Native fellow students: "Do-Atin," or "the Whipped One," a phrase the Navajos used to refer to a broken mustang. Wing Foot's father, Chief Notani, also called him "Do-Atin" after he refused to become the tribe's medicine man. As a student of medicine in the white man's world, Wing Foot disdained traditional medicine: "Your witchcraft killed my mother [who died in childbirth]—it is killing my grand-mother [who is going blind]—and now you want me to preach such nonsense!" As he meditated on the effects of American education on his life, Wing Foot concluded bitterly: "I am neither Indian nor White Man. Just . . . Redskin." Wing Foot's return home marks the beginning of another journey that will not gain visibility on the silver screen for several more decades.[99]

From the beginning of the silent film era, moving pictures helped in the work of imagining the settler nation; but how did they repre-sent one of the country's most long-standing objects of fascination, the *Indian*? From Wild West shows to Westerns, *Indians* on screen and on stage reproduced the logic of frontier violence and attempted to erase Native presence from modernity. Such representations dwelt on a primitive, vanishing, or exotic past, and they kept Native actors and performers on the margins of representation. If the Western thrived as a white supremacist entertainment and a source of racist ideology, other silent film genres were invested in Native presence.[100]

American Westerns appealed to the settler imaginary through an imagined nation that was white, domestic, and Christian. An influen-tial medium, documenting and informing modernity, silent film enabled white directors and producers to bring representations of Native peo-ple to white audiences and to reinforce white supremacist ideology. Although many images preserved on celluloid were destroyed or lost in the last century, surviving footage broadens our understanding of the medium's role in representing race and Indigeneity. Although a few Native performers were employed by major studios, white actors con-tinued to "play Indian" on stage and in front of the camera for decades. In *Redskin,* the character Wing Foot refuses to salute the American flag in the boarding school he was forced to attend; his defiant gesture, dis-ciplined by the agents of the state, continued the arc of Native dissent expressed in earlier films. Read alongside the episode filmed by Dixon in *The Romance of a Vanishing Race* (1916)—when the Native man at Fort Belknap, Montana, pauses to spit near the American flag, then refuses to sign the fake declaration of allegiance to the United States—this scene suggests the continuity of Indigenous resistance and the pres-ervation of allegiance to Indigenous, rather than American, communi-ties, and the possibility of strategic mutual allegiances.

Conclusion

A CENTRAL GOAL of this book has been to uncover how Americanization, as a specific early twentieth-century phenomenon of homogenization, was part and parcel of an American mythical story of national formation, rooted in nineteenth-century narratives of imperial expansion and aimed at creating compliant and patriotic citizens. As a broader nationalist and capitalist project, Americanization has occupied a part of the American imagination associated with progress, overcoming obstacles, renewal, and manifest destiny. As historian John Higham has shown, from the end of the nineteenth century to its pinnacle during World War I, "the crusade for Americanization . . . brought new methods for dealing with the immigrants," and revealed "the growing urgency" of nationalism.[1] This pervasive narrative of Americanization, especially in its militant years during World War I, obscured the painful, often traumatic side of the story of U.S. national origin, marked by genocide, relocation, trauma, and loss in both Native and new immigrant communities. Understanding Americanization through a settler colonial lens reveals the race-based assumptions that non-western communities, in their assumed "backwardness," had to be reformed. Just as colonial missionaries attempted to "bring Indians to the book," the evangelists of Americanization—from social workers to movie executives and public school teachers—preached the doctrine of patriotism and loyalty to the nation. Purporting to include, Americanization ultimately excluded. Yet, throughout this enterprise, Native and new immigrant subjects proved to be not silent receptacles but active participants in Americanization, often authoring it on their terms.

A focus on Indigenous and immigrant writing and representation during the Progressive Era reveals a consistent effort to question American exceptionalism and reject the exclusion of Native American and immigrant cultures. Thinking about these two dimensions of U.S. cultural history together, despite their historical treatment in isolation from each other, expands our understanding of the intersections of Indigenous and immigrant concerns as well as the exclusionary force of Americanization. Reframing conversations in American Studies—particularly American Indian and Indigenous Studies, Immigration Studies, and Film Studies—in this book I have revealed connections between immigration and Indigeneity, categories that are at the heart of contemporary narratives of national formation.

When I started researching this book, I was struck by the pervasive use of the phrase "making Americans" in archival documents and titles dating to the first decades of the twentieth century. The Progressive Era thrived on the rhetoric of "making Americans": the belief that, although one was not born an American, one could be "made" into one. In its original context, "making Americans" signified endless possibilities for immigrants dreaming of economic and political futures. In a way, this logic of efficiency—popularized by Ford Motor Company and its Americanization program—could solve the era's dilemma about two emerging "problems": the immigrant problem and the *Indian* problem. In the decades studied in this book, 1879–1924, the "making of Americans" took on several distinct meanings, which coincided with the ebbs and flows of the Americanization movement, from the country's more hopeful years at the end of the nineteenth century to the militancy, patriotism, and nationalism of the post–World War I years.

This book has not offered an exhaustive analysis of immigrant and Native literatures, but, rather, it is an attempt to show through case studies and relevant references the extent of immigrant and Native cultural participation in the Americanization movement. Due to the large archives of pertinent materials—considering the multitude of tribal nations and southern and eastern European immigrant cultures—this book does not aim to be a comprehensive study. Rather, it offers case studies in print and visual culture, identifying recurring themes, and suggesting methods to approach these archives in future research.

Access to archives allowed me to spend time with several key settler colonial archives. My research for this project started at the University of Illinois at Urbana-Champaign and the Newberry Library, and continued at the Beinecke Library and the Historical Society of Pennsylvania. As my work progressed, additional questions and hunches took me to the National Archives, the Library of Congress, the New York Public Library, and the Cumberland County Historical Society in Pennsylvania. Although some of the materials I read—such as the Carlisle newspapers, Carlos Montezuma's *Wassaja*, or Charles Chaplin's *The Immigrant*—are highly recognizable in their respective fields, others, such as the immigrant writing specimens in the National Archives, were part of the serendipity of archival research. A similar serendipitous encounter led me to the special collections at the New York Public Library, where the John Foster Carr Papers and other collections of immigrant writing brought me to the immigrant guides and other print materials used in Americanization campaigns.

Although Native Americans have had a vexed relationship with colonial archives—the repositories of much Native writing since the early republic—this body of work is still insufficiently examined by literary scholars. As Jacques Derrida put it in *Archive Fever*, "There is no political power without control of the archive, if not of memory."[2] For Elizabeth Povinelli, archival power also "authorizes specific forms of the future by continually concealing the history of the manipulation and management of the documents within existing archives."[3] Where are the student letters of dissent in the Carlisle and Pratt Papers archives? Or the letters sent by Native parents criticizing their children's Americanization and removal from reservations, or lamenting their deaths? In 1978, Standing Rock Sioux scholar Vine Deloria Jr. advocated for Native people's "right to know." Historian William T. Hagan positioned Native people as "archival captives": "To be an Indian is to have non-Indians control your documents from which other non-Indians write their versions of your history." Deloria and Hagan recognized how critical information and knowledge are to the sovereignty of Native people.[4] Although some of the research for this book involved tribal archives, because of the nature of the topic and the case studies I decided to use, I relied mainly on colonial archives. The voices recorded there are sometimes uneven, complicated, or unexpected. The letters that Native students sent to Richard Henry Pratt, the Carlisle superintendent, or the letters immigrant students in Americanization classes sent to their teachers reveal unexpected moments of candor, compliance, and occasional dissent. As a literary scholar, I continue to return to the print and film text for evidence, interdisciplinary connections across the groups I'm studying, and voice—however mediated by its respective medium and power structures behind its production, however lost in the myriad nuances of the Americanization scenes I examine.

This book brings Native and new immigrant writing and representation to the fore, from better-known writers like Abraham Cahan to lesser-known Yiddish poets, from public figures such as Gertrude Bonnin (Yankton Sioux) and Carlos Montezuma (Yavapai) to a lesser-known archive of Native writing in boarding schools and Native periodicals. Some figures may be entirely unknown to readers today—for example, Marcus E. Ravage, whose popular memoir *An American in the Making* (1917) was widely taught in New York City high schools in the 1920s, or Laura Cornelius Kellogg, whose book *Our Democracy and the American Indian* (1920), reprinted recently, led to her inclusion in a suffragette statue unveiled in Seneca Falls, New York, in 2021.[5] Two of my favorite archives are the immigrant writing specimens in the National Archives and the Carlisle students' letters in the Pratt Papers at the Beinecke Library, which share more similarities than I initially hoped. The silent film footage on Americanization at the Library of Congress, although limited, confirmed the role silent film played in spreading the gospel of Americanization. Archival research is laborious and unexpected; I hope my work does justice, respectfully, to the faces behind the screen and the voices behind the pen.

One unexpected turn of the project has been toward silent film and the simultaneity of this new technology with mass immigration and the Americanization efforts. The emerging film industry was key in supporting and disseminating visual materials in local and national Americanization campaigns in the early 1910s. An influential medium, documenting and informing modernity, film enabled white directors and producers to bring representations of Native people to white audiences, which reinforced white supremacist ideology and perpetuated myths of savagery. The (ideological) violence of the image continued the physical violence of the so-called savage war between settlers and Native Americans during the nineteenth century. The new medium could take the end of the nineteenth-century physical violence on the

American frontier, transpose it onto celluloid, and disseminate it to larger audiences than print could reach.

Watching patriotic parades and messages on film, a new absorbing medium, elicited emotions about complicated, sometimes multiple, patriotic allegiances. In the early twentieth-century affective economy, how immigrant subjects decoded and negotiated forms of belonging— and the imposition of more or less militant practices aiming at effective Americanization—affected both the person and the community. I offered the term "affective Americanization" to describe the structure of feeling emerging at the intersection of official discourse (federal and state governments spelling out the parameters of Americanization and acculturation), popular responses to the official discourses (such as silent film), and its larger cultural negotiations. Historian of education Jeffrey Mirel calls the new immigrants' competing allegiances "patriotic pluralism," which he describes as a new commitment to the adoptive country and a strong allegiance to the country of origin, a desire to maintain cultural ties with one's birth place despite new affective and political allegiances. Mirel's patriotic pluralism paradigm also captures the affective investment of immigrants in the United States through their vision of American democracy, at the same time that they maintained strong cultural and spiritual bonds with their cultural backgrounds.[6] Over the years, local (civic), state, and national organizations serving political and economic interests would exploit such affective allegiances for political gains, especially during the peak years of the Americanization movement (during and after World War I). Silent film helped elicit and nurture immigrant audiences' patriotic pluralist allegiances, while also entertaining them.

Silent film responded to white America's obsession with race. Early Hollywood perpetuated racial stereotypes in thousands of shorts and feature films; D. W. Griffith was a case in point, particularly in his films about Native Americans and African Americans. If other films simply glossed over the topic of race, The Making of an American (1920) conceived of Americanization as a process of "whitening."[7] In the 1910s, the popularity of films like Birth of a Nation (1915) or The Italian (1915) revealed the country's fascination with race. The typecasting of Italians revealed larger, ingrained racist and nationalist rhetoric, such as the belief that certain immigrant groups were unsuitable for citizenship. As Kevin Brownlow has shown, Irish actor George Beban, who played the lead role in *The Italian*, had a fundamental role in changing the film's initial title from *The Dago* to *The Italian*.[8] New immigrant groups, for example, Italians and Jews, were targets of a new genre of films emerging in the early 1900s, especially educational films aimed at promoting good American citizenship in the context of a national panic about the new immigrants' difference and unassimilability.[9]

Silent film, as a new medium of both entertainment and persuasion, facilitated the work of Americanization in several ways: on the one hand, it purported to educate; on the other, it served local and national Americanization projects. As Mark Glancy argues, film "gained credibility during the First World War, when it was used as a medium of persuasion by all of the major powers."[10] Reformers, industrial moguls, youth organizations, and the federal government used film to educate. The YMCA, for instance, "distributed industrial pictures and proposed that the films would provide an opportunity 'for developing the platform of mutuality between the managerial and working force in industry.'"[11] Early industrial films educated audiences about technology and tried to demystify the industrial process for the immigrant laborers. If we think of moving pictures during the 1910s as a form of "visual Esperanto" (Miriam Hansen's term) or the medium that filmmakers and inventors predicted would take over written language and replace books in schools and libraries (Thomas Edison or D. W. Griffith), silent film was a welcome educational tool and the immigrant audiences were the ideal students. Viewers of silent films, however, were not just compliant consumers and vessels ready to be filled with ideology; they were also critical spectators, able to distinguish increasingly between the public and the private sphere, or between ethnic or national allegiances.[12]

Similarly, Native people were not only engaged in modernity at a time when the settler imaginary still relegated them to the "primitive" margins of modernity, but they also shaped that modernity by challenging the expectations and anxieties about who could become an American and by participating in national debates on Americanism and American citizenship.[13] Although a few Native performers were employed by major studios, white actors continued to "play Indian" on stage and in front of the camera, often in red face, for many decades.[14] Native actors and directors were sometimes employed by large studios and, occasionally, films had an all-Native cast. Yet, the stories that Native directors like Nanticoke Young Deer/Young Johnson could tell conformed to white audiences' expectations and the industry's representational politics. Although contemporary Native filmmakers have turned the camera against the long history of Indigenous misrepresentations in print and visual culture, still pervasive in the Euro-American imagination of settler colonial countries, much damage has been done. Yet, a small group of Native actors playing *Indian* roles in early film—from Young Deer and Princess Red Wing/Lilian St. Cyr to Edwin Carewe, Minnie Ha Ha (Minnie Devereux), Molly Spotted Elk, and Luther Standing Bear—used these roles to serve their communities.

The glorification of the idea of the *Indian* found the new medium of silent film a welcome venue for large popular appeal, first in ethnographic film and later in short and feature-length studio films. In his study of "classic American literature" (1923), D. H. Lawrence diagnosed a longstanding ambivalence toward Indigenous people throughout American history: "The desire to extirpate the Indian. And the contradictory desire to glorify him." Joanna Hearne has shown persuasively how Native filmmakers have "navigated the power structures of Hollywood" and how they have integrated the historical archive of Native (mis)representation into their contemporary work.[15] Ella Shohat and Robert Stam revisited Lawrence's idea and argued that "the elimination of the Indian allows for elegiac nostalgia as a way to treat Indians only in the past tense and dismiss their claims in the present, while posthumously expressing thanatological tenderness for their memory." Shohat and Stam echoed Renato Rosaldo's concept of "imperialist nostalgia," which he coined in response to his "anger at recent films that portray imperialism with nostalgia." According to Rosaldo, imperialist nostalgia revolves around "mourning what one has destroyed."[16]

Silent film, in its simultaneous emergence with the Americanization campaigns, helped negotiate modernity on Native and new immigrant terms, even when those terms were uneven. Although the silent film era did not alter dominant representations of *Indians,* it created possibilities for alternative representations, influenced by the work of Native activists, writers, actors, and filmmakers and racial theories of the day. Silent films performed two simultaneous tasks. On the one hand, they solidified American whiteness and served in the work of American nationalism, patriotism, and Americanization; on the other, as *Indian* films became a widely recognizable genre, they paved the way for Native representation and self-representation and provided opportunities for upward mobility and a platform for Native activists and artists to engage federal Indian policy. From early documentary footage to ethnographic film and Westerns, silent film helped usher in Indigenous celluloid modernity, however uneven the process was at the beginning of the twentieth century.

As a cultural history, *The Makings and Unmakings of Americans* tells a story of Americanization that scholars have only recently started to reexamine as it brings to the fore the overlapping Americanization campaigns at the turn of the twentieth century that attempted to turn Native Americans and new immigrants into "good Americans." Drawing on Indigenous and new immigrant writing and activism in the U.S. during the Progressive Era, it addresses a gap in field-specific and interdisciplinary scholarship by thinking of Americanization as both a national and local movement to assimilate and as a mutually constitutive group strategy to withstand various forms of exclusion. At the same time, it addresses a gap that scholars of immigrant (and multiethnic) literatures can help narrow by rethinking the terms of immigrant writing and by reframing the paradigmatic model of U.S. exceptionalism and its overused designation as a "nation of immigrants," so ingrained in the U.S. racial imaginary. [17] Of particular significance to rethinking this paradigm is an examination of literary and cultural encounters between immigrants and Indigenous people, "the first Americans" glorified by Progressive Era nationalist discourse yet relegated to the margins of American history through colonial tactics ranging from genocide to removal and dispossession.

If at the beginning of the twentieth century Indigenous activists appropriated anti-immigrant and nativist rhetoric to argue against the inequities burdening Native communities—particularly the lack of recognition of Native people as legitimate citizens of the United States, at a time when immigrants were granted an easier path to citizenship than Native Americans—one hundred years later Native activists came together to express solidarity with immigrants and refugees. In 2017, Indigenous activists joined protests against another race-based U.S. immigration ban: an executive order targeting refugees and travelers from Muslim-majority countries, barring Syrian immigrants indefinitely and all refugees from these countries for at least four months. Native historians and activists Nick Estes and Melanie Yazzie, who participated in these protests against the Muslim bans—later popularized by the hashtag #NoBanOnStolenLand—reasserted Native solidarity with immigrants and refugees, reframing the chorus of the popular song "This Land Is Your Land" to "No bans on stolen lands." This reframing indigenizes a beloved patriotic refrain in an attempt to (re)educate Americans, many of them offspring of immigrants, about their complicity in the settler colonial project. It is also a reminder, in Melanie Yazzie's words, that "we were here first." This ongoing Indigenous solidarity with refugee and immigrant communities is part of a global phenomenon against settler colonial domination, extraction capitalism, and dispossession and exploitation of black, brown, and red peoples. As we witness Indigenous sovereignty movements throughout the world—contesting and reclaiming not only *recognition* by settler states but also territories—counter-sovereignty movements, largely driven by late capitalist modes of extraction, continue to erode possible alliances among Indigenous, immigrant, and refugee groups.[18] As we understand the questions at the heart of this book in a contemporary context of continued colonial occupation (a framework that the field of settler colonial studies has helped articulate more clearly), the focus on the Americanization movement—with its emphasis on patriotic education, conformity, a heightened nativism and nationalism, xenophobia and the glorification of white supremacy—contributes to a new understanding of our contemporary moment one hundred years later, as renewed fears of alienism, combined with capitalist extraction and ongoing dispossession of marginalized populations, continue to define American political economy.

Notes

Introduction

Epigraph: Paul Chaat Smith, "The Most American Thing Ever Is in Fact American Indians," *Walker*, September 20, 2017.

1. "Aborigine and Immigrant," *New York Times* (December 21, 1923): 16.

2. I italicize the word *Indian* to call attention to its constructedness in what Gerald Vizenor calls "the literature of dominance." See Vizenor, *Fugitive Poses: Native American Indian Scenes of Absence and Presence* (University of Nebraska Press, 1998), 35.

3. Amy Kaplan, *The Anarchy of Empire in the Making of U.S. Culture* (Harvard University Press, 2005), 3.

4. George Lipsitz, "The Possessive Investment in Whiteness: Racialized Social Democracy and the 'White' Problem in American Studies," *American Quarterly* 47, no. 3 (1885): 369; Carlos Montezuma, "Introduction," *Wassaja* 1, no.1 (1916): 1.

5. Desmond King, *Making Americans: Immigration, Race, and the Origins of the Diverse Democracy* (Harvard University Press, 2000), 120.

6. Thomas Guglielmo, *White on Arrival: Italians, Race, Color, and Power in Chicago, 1890–1945* (Oxford University Press, 2003). Guglielmo shows that anti-Italian sentiment emerged from questions about the legitimacy of Italian immigrants' claims to whiteness (5–6).

7. Patrick Wolfe, "Settler Colonialism and the Elimination of the Native," *Journal of Genocide Research* 8, no. 4 (2006): 387–409, 388.

8. John Bodnar, *The Transplanted: A History of Immigrants in Urban America* (Indiana University Press, 1985).

9. Ali Behdad, *A Forgetful Nation: On Immigration and Cultural Identity in the United States* (Duke University Press, 2005), esp. 14–21.

10. Edward G. Hartman, *The Movement to Americanize the Immigrant* (Columbia University Press, 1948).

11. John Higham, *Send These to Me: Immigrants in Urban America* (Johns Hopkins University Press, 1984 [1975]), 21.

12. King, *Making Americans*, 207.

13. Roger Daniels, *Not Like Us: Immigrants and Minorities in America, 1890–1924* (Ivan R. Dee, 1997), viii; Russel L. Barsh, "Progressive-Era Bureaucrats and the Unity of Twentieth-Century Indian Policy," *American Indian Quarterly* 15, no. 1 (1991): 1–17.

14. Ruth Spack invokes a similar example in postcolonial critic Ngugi wa Thiong'o's work, where he recalls that if students in Kenya were caught speaking Gikuyu, they were beaten or forced to wear a metal plate around their necks, "I AM STUPID" or "I AM A DONKEY." Spack, *America's Second Tongue: American Indian Education and the Ownership of English, 1860–1900* (University of Nebraska Press, 2002).

15. Raymond Williams defines the concept "structure of feeling" in *Marxism and Literature* (Oxford University Press, 1977), 136–41. On affect theory, see Sara Ahmed, *The Cultural Politics of Emotion*, 2nd ed. (Edinburgh University Press, 2014 [2004]); Lauren Berlant, *The Queen of America Goes to Washington City: Essays on Sex and Citizenship* (Duke University Press, 1997); Eve Kosofsky Sedgwick, *Touching Feeling: Affect, Pedagogy, Performativity* (Duke University Press, 2003); *The Affect Theory Reader*, ed. Melissa Gregg and Gregory J. Seigworth (Duke University Press, 2010); Brian Massumi, "The Autonomy of Affect," *Cultural Critique* 31 (1995): 83–109.

16. Robert H. Wiebe, *The Search for Order, 1877–1920* (Hill and Wang, 1967).

17. Michelle Raheja, *Reservation Reelism: Redfacing, Visual Sovereignty, and Representations of Native Americans in Film* (University of Nebraska Press, 2010).

18. Jill Norgren, *The Cherokee Cases: Two Landmark Federal Decisions in the Fight for Sovereignty* (University of Oklahoma Press, 2004), 28.

19. This section title is an homage to Roxanne Dunbar-Ortiz's book, *Not "A Nation of Immigrants": Settler Colonialism, White Supremacy, and a History of Erasure and Exclusion* (Beacon Press, 2021).

20. For a corrective, see Ned Blackhawk, *The Rediscovery of America: American Indians and the Unmaking of U.S. History* (Yale University Press, forthcoming). See also Susan Sleeper-Smith, Julianna Barr, Jean O'Brien, Nancy Shoemaker, and Scott M. Stevens, eds., *Why You Can't Teach United States History without American Indians* (University of North Carolina Press, 2015).

21. On the methodological implications of the framework of settler colonial studies on Indigenous Studies, see Frederick Hoxie, "Retrieving the Red Continent: Settler Colonialism and the History of American Indians in the US," *Ethnic and Racial Studies* 31, no. 6 (2008): 1153–67; Lorenzo Veracini, "Understanding Colonialism and Settler Colonialism as Distinct Formations," *Interventions* 16, no. 5 (2014): 615–33; Patrick Wolfe, "Settler Colonialism and the Elimination of the Native," *Journal of Genocide Research* 8.4 (2006): 387-409; Patrick Wolfe, "The

Settler Complex: An Introduction," *American Indian Culture and Research Journal* 37, no. 2 (2013): 1–22.

22. Daniel Heath Justice, *Why Indigenous Literatures Matter* (Wilfred Laurier University Press, 2018), 12. See also Eve Tuck and K. Wayne Young, "Decolonization Is Not a Metaphor," *Decolonization: Indigeneity, Education, and Society.* 1, no. 1 (2012).

23. Mahmood Mamdani, *Neither Settler nor Native: The Making of Permanent Minorities* (Harvard University Press, 2020), 20.

24. Lorenzo Veracini, *The Settler Colonial Present* (Palgrave McMillan, 2015), 9, 32, 40–41; Corey Snelgrove, Rita Kaur Dhamoon, and Jeff Corntassel, "Unsettling Settler Colonialism: The Discourse and Politics of Settlers, and Solidarity with Indigenous Nations," *Decolonization: Indigeneity, Education, and Society* 3, no. 2 (2014): 1–32.

25. Eve Tuck and K. Wayne Yang, "Decolonization Is Not a Metaphor," *Decolonization: Indigeneity, Education, and Society.* 1, no. 1 (2012): 6–7. I also rely on the work of the following scholars to make a case for distinctions between settlers and (new) immigrants: Kevin Bruyneel, *The Third Space of Sovereignty: The Postcolonial Politics of U.S.-Indigenous Relations* (University of Minnesota Press, 2007); Jodi A. Byrd, *The Transit of Empire: Indigenous Critiques of Colonialism* (University of Minnesota Press, 2011); Audra Simpson, *Mohawk Interruptus: Political Life across the Borders of Settler States* (Duke University Press, 2014); Glenn Coulthard, *Red Skin, White Masks: Rejecting the Colonial Politics of Recognition* (University of Minnesota Press, 2011).

26. Alan Trachtenberg, *Shades of Hiawatha: Staging Indians, Making Americans, 1880–1930* (Hill and Wang, 2004); Joel Pfister, *Individuality Incorporated: Indians and the Multicultural Modern* (Duke University Press, 2004): 52–53.

27. Jean M. O'Brien, *Firsting and Lasting: Writing Indians out of Existence in New England* (University of Minnesota Press, 2010); Lisa Brooks, *The Common Pot: The Recovery of Native Space in the Northeast* (University of Minnesota Press, 2008).

28. On the SAI newspapers and Americanization, see Stanciu, "Americanization on Native Terms: The Society of American Indians, Citizenship Debates, and Tropes of 'Racial Difference,'" *NAIS: Native American and Indigenous Studies* 6, no. 1 (2019): 111–48. On the "Friends of the Indian," see Francis Paul Prucha, ed., *Americanizing the American Indian: Writings by the "Friends of the Indian," 1880–1900* (Harvard University Press, 1973).

29. Anzia Yiezierska, "America and I," *Children of Loneliness: Stories of Immigrant Life in America* (Funk and Wagnalls, 1923), 151–71, quote on 154. "Mostly about Myself," *Children of Loneliness*, 1–28, quote on 11.

30. Beth H. Piatote, *Domestic Subjects: Gender, Citizenship, and Law in American Literature* (Yale University Press, 2013), 176.

31. Byrd, *Transit of Empire*, xxxviii.

32. Ned Blackhawk, *Violence over the Land: Indians and Empires in the Early American West* (Harvard University Press, 2006); Sleeper-Smith, Barr, O'Brien, Shoemaker, and Stevens, eds., *Why You Can't Teach United States History without American Indians*. Mark Rifkin has prompted me to think about the disciplinary

implications of the question about literariness. Rifkin, "'But Is It Literary?': Generalist Racisms, Disciplinary Insularity, and the Limits of Too-Big-to-Fail Thinking," *J19*, 4, no. 1 (2016): 130–35.

33. Roxanne Dunbar-Ortiz, *An Indigenous People's History of the United States* (Beacon Press, 2014); Manu Karuka, *Empire's Tracks: Indigenous Nations, Chinese Workers, and the Transcontinental Railroad* (University of California Press, 2019).

34. Thomas Ferraro, *Ethnic Passages: Literary Immigrants in Twentieth-Century America* (University of Chicago Press, 1993), 9.

35. David Cowart, *Trailing Clouds: Immigrant Fiction in Contemporary America* (Cornell University Press, 2006), 209.

36. Brooks, *Common Pot*, xxxv.

37. Melanie Benson Taylor, *Reconstructing the Native South: American Indian Literature and the Lost Cause* (University of Georgia Press, 2011), 16. On the dangers and the possibilities of bringing multicultural methodologies to bear on Indigenous contexts, see Monika Siebert's *Indians Playing Indian: Multiculturalism and Contemporary Indigenous Art in North America* (University of Alabama Press, 2015).

Chapter 1. Native Acts, Immigrant Acts

1. Oscar Handlin, *The Uprooted: The Epic Story of the Great Migrations that Made the American People* (University of Pennsylvania Press, 2002 [1951]), 3.

2. President Barack Obama also used this phrase in a naturalization ceremony in 2012: "For just as we remain a nation of laws, we have to remain a nation of immigrants." Remarks by the President at Naturalization Ceremony, The White House Office of the Press Secretary, July 4, 2012, https://obamawhitehouse.archives.gov/the-press-office/2012/07/04/remarks-president-naturalization-ceremony, accessed April 28, 2020. Dunbar-Ortiz, *Not "A Nation of Immigrants."* See also Mamdani, *Neither Settler nor Native* and Stanciu, "Native Acts, Immigrant Acts: Citizenship, Naturalization, and the Performance of Civic Identity during the Progressive Era," *JGAPE: Journal of the Gilded Age and Progressive Era* 20 (April 2021): 252–76.

3. On the power of settler memory in the continued disavowal of Indigeneity, see Kevin Bruyneel, *Settler Memory: The Disavowal of Indigeneity and the Politics of Race in the United States* (University of North Carolina Press, 2021).

4. Dunbar-Ortiz, *Indigenous People's History of the United States*, 10.

5. Veracini, *Settler Colonial Present*, 9.

6. This myth is alive and well: John F. Kennedy, *A Nation of Immigrants* (Harper and Row, 1964); a recent book by Susan F. Martin, *A Nation of Immigrants* (2010), also uncritically perpetuates the myth of the U.S. as a nation of immigrants, omitting Indigenous histories from the story of national formation.

7. Emma Lazarus, "The New Colossus" (1883); *Johnson v. McIntosh*, 21 U.S. 543 (1823).

8. According to historian Roxanne Dunbar-Ortiz, "Politicians, journalists, teachers, and even professional historians chant like a mantra that the United States is a 'nation of immigrants'" (*Indigenous People's History of the United States*, 50).

Immigration Act of 1924 (or the Johnson-Reed Act), H. R. 7995, 68th Congress, Sess. I, Ch. 190 (May 26, 1924), Sec. 11 (a), 159. In *Impossible Subjects: Illegal Aliens and the Making of Modern America,* Mae Ngai calls the 1924 Immigration Act "the first comprehensive restriction law" (3). See also David R. Roediger, *Working toward Whiteness: How America's Immigrants Became White* (Basic, 2005), 147.

9. Jill Doerfler has revealed the settler attempts to conflate "biological" constructions of race with the political status of Native nations in dealings with Indigenous people. *Those Who Belong: Identity, Family, Blood, and Citizenship among the White Earth Anishinaabeg* (Michigan State University Press, 2015), xxxiii–xxxiv.

10. Lisa Lowe, *Immigrant Acts: On Asian American Cultural Politics* (Duke University Press, 1996); Joanne Barker, *Native Acts: Law, Recognition, and Cultural Authenticity* (Duke University Press, 2011).

11. Carroll Smith-Rosenberg, "Inventing the Modern Citizen in the Age of Atlantic Revolution," Seminar on Gender and History, Newberry Library, Chicago, April 5, 2014.

12. Hendrick Willem Van Loon, "You Can't Come in. The Quota for 1620 Is Full." *The Survey* 51, no. 12 (1924): 666 and "Only Nordics Need Apply," *The Survey* 52, no. 2 (1924): 330.

13. "Taking the Queue Out of Quota," *The Survey* 51, no. 12 (1924): 667.

14. This was the commissioner of immigration. Ibid., 667–70. The translations of immigrant opinions by the Foreign Language Information Service are grouped under the rubric "The Neighbors Discuss the Immigration Bill," 670.

15. See Robert F. Zeidel, *Immigrants, Progressives, and Exclusion Politics: The Dillingham Commission, 1900–1927* (Northern Illinois University Press, 2004).

16. Francis Jennings, *The Invasion of America: Indians, Colonialism, and the Cant of Conquest* (University of North Carolina Press, 2010), 15.

17. David E. Wilkins and K. Tsianina Lomawaima, *Uneven Ground: American Indian Sovereignty and Federal Law* (University of Oklahoma Press, 2001), 19–97.

18. Dunbar-Ortiz, *Indigenous People's History of the United States,* 200.

19. Mae Ngai, *Impossible Subjects: Illegal Aliens and the Making of Modern America* (Princeton University Press, 2004), 37–54. On the Calvinist idea of the covenant and its use to justify Indigenous dispossession and genocide, see Dunbar-Ortiz, *Indigenous People's History of the United States,* esp. 32–55.

20. Felix S. Cohen, *Cohen's Handbook of Federal Indian Law* (Michie, 1982), 151–53. "National citizenship" is a term used by R. Alton Lee in "Indian Citizenship and the Fourteenth Amendment," *South Dakota History* 4, no. 2 (1974): 207.

21. "Indian Citizenship," *Office of Indian Affairs Bulletin* 20 (1926, reprint), Edward E. Ayer Collection, Newberry Library. "The Indian Citizenship Act," H.R. 6355, 68th Congress, Sess. I, Ch. 233 (June 2, 1924).

22. Naturalization Act of 1790, 1st Congress, Sess. II, Ch. 3 (March 26, 1790).

23. The Page Act of 1875 was the first federal legislation that enumerated specific types of people who were excluded from entering the U.S. (immigrants under contract for "lewd or immoral purposes" or "prostitution"; or persons guilty of felony); Page Act, 43rd Congress, Sess. II, Ch. 141 (March 3, 1875); the Naturalization Act

of 1870 naturalized persons of African nativity or descent; Naturalization Act of 1870, 41st Congress, Sess. II, Ch. 254 (July 14, 1879); Citizens of Hawaii became U.S. citizens in 1900; Hawaiian Organic Act, 56th Congress, Sess. I, Ch. 339 (April 30, 1900). In 1882, Congress passed a law excluding convicts, lunatics, idiots, and paupers, making disability (physical and mental) a category or exclusion on a par with crime and poverty; Immigration Act of 1882, 47th Congress, Sess. I, Ch. 376 (August 3, 1882). In 1885, the Alien Contract Labor Law passed as a response to lobbyists of organized labor, prohibiting employers from recruiting labor in Europe and from paying laborers' passage across the Atlantic; Alien Contract Labor Law, 48th Congress, Sess. II, Ch. 164 (February 26, 1885).

24. The children of naturalized persons, under the age of twenty-one and residing in the U.S. at the time of naturalization, "shall also be considered citizens of the United States." Naturalization Act of 1790.

25. The Immigration and Nationality Act (also known as the McCarran-Walter Act) passed in 1952, doing away with the racial requirement for naturalization; Immigration and Nationality Act of 1952, H.R. 5678, 82nd Congress, Sess. II, Ch. 477 (June 27, 1952). See also Ian Haney López, *White by Law: The Legal Construction of Race* (New York University Press, 1996).

26. Naturalization Act, 5th Congress, Sess. II, Ch. 54 (June 18, 1798); Aliens Act, 5th Congress, Sess. II, Ch. 58 (June 25, 1798); Alien Enemy Act, 5th Congress, Sess. II, Ch. 66 (July 6, 1798). See also E. P. Hutchinson, *Legislative History of American Immigration Policy, 1798–1965* (University of Pennsylvania Press, 1981), 45–46.

27. The Chinese Exclusion Act (1882) mandated that "no state or court of the United States shall admit Chinese to citizenship." It was not repealed until 1943. Chinese Exclusion Act, 47th Congress, Sess. I, Ch. 126, Sec. 14 (May 6, 1882).

28. The "patent" refers to the title deed given by the federal government to a person to transfer land. "In fee" refers to the ownership of land "in fee simple." The term "patent-in-fee" refers to the title document the federal government issues to terminate the trust previously created by a trust patent issued to an allottee. *Indian Land Tenure Foundation*, https://www.iltf.org/glossary, accessed February 9, 2021.

29. The Burke Act of 1906 amended the provisions of the General Allotment Act of 1887 (Dawes Act), stipulating that Native people who had received allotments under the Dawes Act would not become citizens until they became competent to manage their affairs. Forced Fee Patenting Act, H.R. 11946, 59th Congress, Sess. I, Ch. 2348 (May 8, 1906). The scholarship and historiography on the Allotment Era is vast. See especially Janet A. McDonnel, *The Dispossession of the American Indian, 1887–1934* (Indiana University Press, 1991), 89–102; Frederick E. Hoxie, *A Final Promise: The Campaign to Assimilate the Indians, 1880–1920* (University of Nebraska Press, 1994); C. Joseph Genetin-Pilawa, *Crooked Paths to Allotment: The Fight over Federal Indian Policy after the Civil War* (University of North Carolina Press, 2012).

30. John J. Newman, *American Naturalization Processes and Procedures, 1790–1985* (Indiana Historical Society, 1985).

31. Immigration Restriction Act of 1891, 51st Congress, Sess. II, Ch. 551 (March 3, 1891); John Higham, *Strangers in the Land: Patterns of American Nativism, 1860–1925* (Atheneum, 1972), 68–105.

32. The Immigration Restriction League (IRL) gathered a distinguished membership, including Massachusetts senator Henry Cabot Lodge and eugenicist Madison Grant, author of *The Passing of the Great Race: Or, The Racial Basis of European History* (Scribner, 1916)—a plea for "Nordic superiority" and an infamous example of scientific racism.

33. U.S. Immigration Commission, vol. 1, 1910. Quoted in Desmond King, *Making Americans*, 314 n. 47; Robert F. Zeidel, *Immigrants, Progressives,* 86–100.

34. The report is from 1876, reprinted on the title page in Henry S. Pancoast, *The Indian before the Law* (Indian Rights Association, 1884).

35. Dorothee Schneider, *Crossing Borders: Migration and Citizenship in the Twentieth-Century United States* (Harvard University Press, 2011): 153, 205–6, quote on 207; 209–41.

36. Naturalization Act of 1906, H.R. 15442, 59th Congress, Sess. I, Ch. 3592 (June 29, 1906); Newman, *American Naturalization Processes and Procedures,* 5–6. Schneider, *Crossing Borders,* 195.

37. King, *Making Americans,* 59.

38. The European report of the Dillingham Commission was one of the forty-one volumes produced between 1907 and 1911. Zeidel, *Immigrants, Progressives, and Exclusion Politics,* 68.

39. Zeidel, *Immigrants, Progressives, and Exclusion Politics,* 86–100.

40. Special provisions for aliens of foreign birth to acquire U.S. citizenship were made through the Act of July 19, 1919 (H. J. Res, 120, 66th Congress, Sess. I, Ch. 25); Native men who enlisted to fight in the war (and were not U.S. citizens) were naturalized four months later, through the Act of November 6, 1919 (H.R. 5007, 66th Congress, Sess. I, Ch. 95); see Cohen, *Cohen's Handbook of Federal Indian Law,* 154.

41. On the critique of citizenship as a gift to Native Americans, see Bruyneel, *The Third Space of Sovereignty,* 97–121.

42. Quoted in Amy Wan, *Producing Good Citizens: Literacy Training in Anxious Times* (University of Pittsburgh Press, 2014), 74.

43. Prucha, ed., *Americanizing the American Indian* 3.

44. Kenneth W. Johnson. "Sovereignty, Citizenship, and the Indian," *Arizona Law Review* 15 (1973): 973.

45. Wilkins and Lomawaima, *Uneven Ground,* 20, 41, 51; 19–63.

46. Johnson, "Sovereignty, Citizenship, and the Indian," 984–85.

47. Quoted in Cohen, *Cohen's Handbook of Federal Indian Law,* 207.

48. Wilkins and Lomawaima, *Uneven Ground,* 103. Felix Cohen also calls attention to the Treaty Clause as a source of federal authority over Indian affairs, 207–8.

49. Johnson, 985–86; Vine Deloria and David Wilkins, *Tribes, Treaties, and Constitutional Tribulations* (University of Texas Press, 1999), 25–26.

50. Deloria and Wilkins, *Tribes, Treaties, and Constitutional Tribulations,* 28; Cohen, *Cohen's Handbook of Federal Indian Law,* 208; Bruyneel, *Third Space of Sovereignty,* 92.

51. "Indian Removal Act," 21st Congress, Sess. I, Ch. 148 (May 28, 1830); *Cherokee Nation v. Georgia,* 30 U.S. 1 (1831). See also Francis Paul Prucha, ed., *Documents of United States Indian Policy* (University of Nebraska Press, 1990), 52–53.

52. *Cherokee Nation v. Georgia.* Prucha, *Documents of United States Indian Policy,* 58–60, quote on 59; K. Tsianina Lomawaima, "The Mutuality of Citizenship and Sovereignty: The Society of American Indians and the Battle to Inherit America," *American Indian Quarterly* 37, no. 3 (2013): 331–51; Patrick Wolfe, "Against Intentional Fallacy: Logocentrism and Continuity in the Rhetoric of Indian Dispossession," *American Indian Culture and Research Journal* 36, no. 1 (2012): 3–45, quote on 7.

53. *Cohen's Handbook of Federal Indian Law,* 641–42.

54. *Ex parte Crow Dog,* 190 U.S. 556 (1883). Prucha, *Documents,* 162–63, quote on 163 and 167–68.

55. Major Crimes Act, 23 U.S. 385 (1885); Indian Crimes Act, 90 U.S. 585–86 (1976). Prucha, *Documents,* 166, 278–79.

56. *Elk v. Wilkins,* 112 U.S. 94 (1884). Prucha, *Documents,* 166–67.

57. Deloria and Wilkins, *Tribes, Treaties, and Constitutional Tribulations,* 145–46; Hoxie, *A Final Promise,* 75; *Cohen's Handbook of Federal Indian Law,* 86, 283–84, and 642–43.

58. *Elk v. Wilkins,* 112 U.S. 94. 110 (1884) (dissent).

59. *Cohen's Handbook of Federal Indian* Law, 283. Deloria and Wilkins, *Tribes, Treaties, and Constitutional Tribulations,* 146.

60. *United States v. Wong Kim Ark,* 169 U.S. 649 (1898). Bethany R. Berger, "Birthright Citizenship on Trial: *Elk v. Wilkins* and *United States v. Wong Kim Ark,*" *Cardozo Law Review* 37 (2016): 1185–1258.

61. Prucha, *Americanizing the American Indian,* 6.

62. Hoxie, *Final Promise,* 73–74. General Allotment Act of 1887 (Dawes Act), 49th Congress, Sess. II, Ch. 119 (February 8, 1887), sec. 6, 390.

63. The Curtis Act of 1898 accomplished through legislation what the Dawes Commission could not through negotiation—it destroyed tribal governments in Indian Territory by abolishing the tribal courts. Curtis Act, 55th Congress, Sess. III, Ch. 517 (June 28, 1898); Prucha, *Documents,* 197–98.

64. By 1906, 166,000 Native people had already become citizens through the allotment process and as members of the Five Nations. Tom Holm, *Great Confusion in Indian Affairs,* 164–66.

65. Surveys taken in 1908 showed that more than 60 percent of the Native people who received fee patents quickly lost their land. McDonnell, *Dispossession of the American Indian,* 89, 93.

66. Brian Dippie, *The Vanishing American: White Attitudes and U.S. Indian Policy* (University of Kansas Press, 1982), 193; Cohen, *Cohen's Handbook of Federal Indian Law,* 153–56.

67. The authority of Congress to naturalize Native Americans has been constantly sustained by the courts. Cohen, *Cohen's Handbook of Federal Indian Law,* 643, and 643 nn. 33–39.

68. The Indian Citizenship Act also passed in order to prevent the Interior Department from extending its authority over Indian affairs even further. Robert B. Porter, "The Demise of the *Ongwehowehn* and the Rise of Native Americans: Redressing the Genocidal Act of Forcing American Citizenship upon Indigenous Peoples," *Harvard BlackLetter Law Journal* 15 (1999): 124.

69. McDonnell, *Dispossession of the American Indian,* 102; quoted in Cohen, *Cohen's Handbook of Federal Indian Law,* 155. See also Deloria and Wilkins, *Tribes, Treaties, and Constitutional Tribulations,* 148, and 186–87 n33. On Native women's involvement in the suffrage movement, see Cathleen D. Cahill, *Recasting the Vote: How Women of Color Transformed the Suffrage Movement* (University of North Carolina Press, 2020).

70. Cohen, *Cohen's Handbook of Federal Indian Law,* 154.

71. Bethany Berger's study of these two federal landmark cases is the first of its kind to examine the stakes of citizenship and naturalization in Native American and immigrant contexts. The article persuasively shows the unconstitutionality of the efforts to limit birthright citizenship. Berger, "Birthright Citizenship on Trial," 1248.

72. Jake Culps to Carlos Montezuma, "This Indian Filed a Unique Claim for Exemption from the Draft," *Wassaja,* 3, no. 3 (June 1918): 3.

73. Luther Standing Bear, *Land of the Spotted Eagle* (University of Nebraska Press, 1978 [1933]), 229.

74. Kevin Bruyneel documents that Jane Zane Gordon "set out a legal, historical, and political argument against citizenship based on the premise that 'the diplomatic status of the Indian is established' as a citizen of his or her indigenous nation." Bruyneel, *The Third Space of Sovereignty,* 109–10.

75. Clinton Rickard, *Fighting Tuscarora: The Autobiography of Chief Clinton Rickard* (Syracuse University Press, 1984), 53.

76. Ibid., 52.

77. Quoted in Bruyneel, *Third Space of Sovereignty,* 112.

78. Bruyneel, *Third Space of Sovereignty,* 115, 119.

79. John Troutman, *Indian Blues: American Indians and the Politics of Music, 1879–1934* (University of Oklahoma Press, 2009), 20–21.

80. On the political and cultural work of Native American dances, see Clyde Ellis, *A Dancing People: Powwow Culture on the Southern Plains* (University of Kansas Press, 2003); Adriana Greci Green, "Performances and Celebrations: Displaying Lakota Identity, 1880–1915" (Ph.D. diss., Rutgers University, 2001).

81. Troutman, *Indian Blues* 5, 52.

82. Ellis, *Dancing People,* 15, 13; Ellis, "We Don't Want Your Rations," *Western Historical Quarterly* 30, no. 2 (1992): 153–54.

83. Ibid., 15.

84. Ellis, "The Sound of the Drum Will Revive Them," in *Powwow,* ed. Clyde Ellis, Luke Eric Lassiter, and Gary H. Dunham (University of Nebraska Press, 2005), 11–18. On how tribes modified their dances to adjust to agents, see Ellis, "We Don't Want Your Rations," 144.

85. *The Rodman Wanamaker Expedition of Citizenship to the North American Indian,* min. 10:30. On the genealogy and work toward the failed memorial to the North American Indian, see Lucy Maddox, *Citizen Indians: Native American Intellectuals, Race and Reform* (Cornell University Press, 2005), 34–49.

86. *The Romance of a Vanishing Race: The Rodman Wanamaker Expedition of Citizenship to the American Indian,* 1913. Running time: 26 minutes. Chip Richie, Rich Heape Films, 2009.

87. Russel L. Barsh, "An American Heart of Darkness: The 1913 Expedition for American Indian Citizenship," *Great Plains Quarterly* 13, no. 2 (Spring 1993): 91–115.

88. McDonnell, *Dispossession of the American Indian, 92.*

89. See Alexandra Witkin, "To Silence a Drum: The Imposition of United States Citizenship on Native Peoples," *Historical Reflections/Reflections Historique* 21, no. 2 (1995): 353–83.

90. Dippie, *Vanishing American,* 192–94. See also the *Wanamaker Primer on the North American Indian* (Philadelphia, 1909).

91. Quoted in Vine Deloria Jr., ed., *Of Utmost Good Faith: The Case of the American Indian against the Federal Government of the United States* (Bantam,1972), 141–43.

92. The competency commissions were established by the Indian Office to test the "competence" of Native allottees for citizenship. McDonnell, *Dispossession of the American Indian,* 93–95.

93. Ibid., 95.

94. Hoxie, *Final Promise,* 180.

95. "Citizenship for Indians," *Immigrants in America Review* 2, no. 2 (July 1916): 4.

96. "Naturalization in the United States, 1910–Present," Migration Policy Institute, Washington, DC, http://www.migrationpolicy.org/programs/data-hub/charts/number-immigrants-who-became-us-citizens, accessed February 9, 2021.

97. James R. Heintze, *The Fourth of July Encyclopedia* (McFarland, 2007), 201.

98. "World's 4th Today," *Washington Post* (July 4, 1919): 1–2, quote on 2.

99. The Naturalization Oath is codified in Section 337 (a) of the Immigration and Nationality Act (INA, 1965).

100. Frederick E. Crane, "A Welcome to New Citizens," *New York Times* (May 12, 1922): 98. See also "Citizenship Fete Planned," *New York Times* (May 19, 1918): 6, and "Becoming Citizens," *New York Times* (February 1, 1924): 16.

101. Higham, *Strangers in the Land,* 247–48.

102. Stephen Meyer, "Adapting the Immigrant to the Line: Americanization in the Ford Factory, 1914–1921," *Journal of Social History* 14, no. 1 (1980): 69.

103. "To Spread Ford Teaching Plan," *Christian Science Monitor* (December 23, 1915): 7.

104. Clinton C. De Witt, "Industrial Teachers," U.S. Bureau of Education, *Proceedings, Americanization Conference, 1919* (Washington, DC: Government Printing Office, 1919), 119.

105. "512 Ford School Pupils Graduate," *Detroit Free Press* (February 28, 1916): 6. See also Werner Sollors, *Beyond Ethnicity: Consent and Descent in American Culture* (Oxford University Press, 1986), 91.

106. Other schools for immigrants employed the Roberts method of English teaching, which asked the students to act out the meaning of the words they used. Gregory Mason, "'Americans First': How the People of Detroit Are Making Americans of Their Foreigners in Their City," *The Outlook* 14 (1916): 193.

107. On the Ford Motors Americanization program, see "150 Ford Workers Receive Diplomas," *Detroit Free Press* (October 2, 1916): 2; "512 Ford School Pupils Graduate: 33 Nations Represented in English Class in Big Auto Plant," *Detroit Free Press* (February 28, 1916): 5; Sollors, *Beyond Ethnicity,* esp. 89–91; Higham, *Strangers in the Land,* 247–48.

108. *Dziennik Chicagoski,* 1891, Chicago Foreign Language Press Survey (CFLPS).

109. "Original Americans," Report from *Ford Times, Red Lake Nation News,* April 1916, 3.

110. Byrd, *Transit of Empire,* xxxiv; The Marshall Court's wording of *Johnson v. McIntosh* (1823) supports the idea of the inevitability of settler acquisition and later governance of an otherwise "inhabited country."

CHAPTER 2. "YOU CAN'T COME IN!

1. The Crown retained title to all lands occupied by Indian tribes, a limited sovereignty over the tribes, and an exclusive right to end the tribal right of occupancy. Johnson, "Sovereignty, Citizenship, and the Indian," 973–74, 980.

2. "Citizenship for Indians," *Immigrants in America Review* 2, no. 2 (July 1916): 4.

3. James R. Barrett, "Americanization from the Bottom Up: Immigration and the Remaking of the Working Class in the United States, 1880–1930," *Journal of American History* 79, no. 3 (1992): 997.

4. Peter Roberts, *The Problem of Americanization* (Macmillan, 1920), v.

5. Early studies of Americanization include Isaak B. Bergson, *Theories of Americanization: A Critical Study: With Special Reference to the Jewish Group* (Columbia University Press, 1920); Howard Hill, "The Americanization Movement," *American Journal of Sociology* 24, no. 6 (May 1919): 609–42; Edward G. Hartman, *The Movement to Americanize the Immigrant* (Columbia University Press, 1948). More recent studies include: Schneider, *Crossing Borders: Migration and Citizenship in the Twentieth-Century United States;* Philip Gleason, "American Identity and Americanization," *Harvard Encyclopedia of American Ethnic Groups.* ed. Stephan Thernstrom (Harvard University Press, 1980), 31–58; Gerd Korman, "Americanization at the Factory Gate," *Industrial and Labor Relations Review* 18 (1965): 396–419; John F. McClymer, "The Americanization Movement and the Education of the Foreign-Born," *American Education and the European Immigrant: 1840–1940,* ed. Bernard J. Weiss (University of Illinois Press, 1982), 96–116; Michael Olneck, "Americanization and the Education of Immigrants, 1900–1925: An Analysis of Symbolic Action," *American Journal of Education* 97, no. 4 (August 1989): 398–423; Christina Ziegler-McPherson, *Americanization in the States: Immigrant Social Welfare Policy, Citizenship, and National Identity in the United States, 1908–1929* (University Press of Florida, 2010); Jeffrey Mirel, *Patriotic Pluralism: Americanization Education and European Immigrants* (Harvard University Press, 2010). An early autobiography of Americanization by a "Nordic" immigrant (which does not fall under the purview of this study) is Edward Bok's

The Americanization of Edward Bok: The Autobiography of a Dutch Boy Fifty Years After (Scribner's, 1920).

6. Korman, "Americanization at the Factory Gates," 398–417, quote on 404.

7. Gleason, "American Identity and Americanization," 38–40.

8. Gary Gerstle, "Liberty, Coercion, and the Making of Americans," 525; King, *Making Americans* 2, 87; Mirel, *Patrotic Pluralism*, 25–26.

9. Mirel, *Patriotic Pluralism*, 103.

10. National Americanization Committee, *A Call to National Service* (New York, 1916), 2.

11. Kellor, "National Americanization Day," *Immigrants in America Review* 1.3 (September 1915): 18–29, 21.

12. Hill, "Americanization Movement," 610–11.

13. Ibid., 610–12, quote on 612.

14. Ibid., 623–26, quote on 627.

15. Theodore Roosevelt, "True Americanism," *American Ideals, and Other Essays, Social, and Political* (Putnam's, 1897).

16. Louis D. Brandeis, "True Americanism," *Brandeis on Zionism: A Collection of Addresses and Statements by Louis D. Brandeis* (Hyperion Press, 1942) 4–5.

17. Olneck, "Americanization and the Education of Immigrants, 1900–1925: An Analysis of Symbolic Action," *American Journal of Education* 97, no. 4 (August 1989): 409.

18. Maddox, *Citizen Indians*, 16.

19. Mirel, *Patriotic Pluralism*, 11.

20. Schneider, *Crossing Borders*, 151.

21. Anglo writers have painstakingly tried to explain the idea of the "savage" to "civilized" men, from Richard Johnson's *Nova Brittania* to Lewis Henry Morgan's *League of the Iroquois*. Roy Harvey Pearce, *Savagism and Civilization* (University of California Press, 1988 [1953]), xvii.

22. Richard Slotkin, *Gunfighter Nation: The Myth of the Frontier in Twentieth Century America* (Atheneum, 1992), 20. In a 2018 article in *The Conversation*, Jérôme Viala-Gaudefroy claimed that "in Trump's America, immigrants are modern-day 'savage Indians,'" https://theconversation.com/in-trumps-america-immigrants-are-modern-day-savage-indians-99809, accessed January 31, 2021.

23. Koffman, *Jews' Indian*, 4–5; Trachtenberg, *Shades of Hiawatha*.

24. Dixon, *Vanishing Race*, 4.

25. Quoted in Barsh, "American Heart of Darkness," 96–97.

26. Ibid., 99.

27. "The Vanishing Red" was also a poem published by Robert Frost in 1916, under different titles, including "The Vanishing American." For a critique of the poem's imperialism, see Tyler Hoffman, "Robert Frost's 'The Vanishing Red' and the Myth of Demise," *Robert Frost Review* 13 (2003): 101–4.

28. Frederick E. Hoxie, *Talking Back to Civilization: Indian Voices of the Progressive Era* (Bedford/St. Martin's, 2001), 110.

29. Walter Benn Michaels, "Anti-Imperial Americanism," *Cultures of United States Imperialism*, ed. Amy Kaplan and Donald E. Pease (Duke University Press,

1993), 372. Alan Trachtenberg makes a similar claim in *Shades of Hiawatha*, esp. 33–35.

30. Jean O'Brien, *Firsting and Lasting: Writing Indians out of Existence in New England* (University of Minnesota Press, 2010), xii, xv.

31. On the perils to Anglo-Saxonism, see Trachtenberg, *Shades of Hiawatha*, 212; on emotional nativism, see Robert A. Divine, *American Immigration Policy, 1924–1952* (Yale University Press, 1957), 3.

32. Walter Benn Michaels, "The Vanishing American," *American Literary History* 2, no. 2 (1990): 220–41, esp. 224 and 227. In *Indians Playing Indian*, Monika Siebert makes a compelling argument that, in the U.S., the appeal to the idea of "first Americans" helped strengthen the nation's historical genealogy, and helped "rewrite the colonial narrative of conquest into the nationalist narrative of progressive historical evolution" (12).

33. Statistical data collected by the U.S. Immigration Commission shows that, from 1873 to 1919, 979,370 immigrants from southern and eastern Europe came to the U.S. See Hartmann, *Movement to Americanize the Immigrant*, 15, and *Abstracts of Reports of the Immigrant Commission, I and II* (Washington, DC, 1911), 61–63, https://archive.org/details/reportsofimmigra19unitrich.

34. Ngai, *Impossible Subjects* 7–8.

35. Charles Jaret, "Troubled by Newcomers: Anti-Immigrant Attitudes and Action during Two Eras of Mass Immigration to the United States," *Journal of American Ethnic History* 18, no. 3 (Spring 1999): 14.

36. Ngai, *Impossible Subjects*, 3, 18, 121; see also Zeidel, *Immigrants, Progressives, and Exclusion Politics*.

37. Stein went back to the United States. In 1903 she started writing what would become *The Making of Americans*, which she finished in 1911 and published in 1925 in a limited edition in England.

38. Stein, *Making of Americans* (Dalkey Archive Press, 1995 [1934]), 3.

39. Edith Wharton, *The Custom of the Country* (Oxford University Press, 1995 [1913]), 47.

40. Henry James, *The American Scene* (Indiana University Press, 1968 [1907]), 87, 131.

41. See Ross Posnock, *The Trial of Curiosity: Henry James, William James, and the Challenge of Modernity* (Oxford University Press, 1991).

42. William Dean Howells, *Impressions and Experiences* (Harper and Brothers, 1896), 138–39.

43. Theodore Roosevelt, "True Americanism," *American Ideals*, 1897.

44. Frederick Jackson Turner, "The Significance of the Frontier in American History," paper presented at American Historical Association, World's Columbian Exposition, Chicago, July 12, 1893.

45. King, *Making Americans*, 14.

46. Hartman, *Movement to Americanize the Immigrant*, 8.

47. Margo Anderson, *The American Census: A Social History* (Yale University Press, 1988), 1–4, 84, 132.

48. Barsh, "Progressive-Era Bureaucrats," 4.

49. The 1900 census reported that only 250,000 Native people lived in the U.S. Hoxie, *Talking Back to Civilization*, 6.

50. Charles Eastman, one of the most popular Native authors at the time, addressed white audiences' misconceptions about Native people in his autobiographies: *Indian Boyhood* (1902), *The Soul of an Indian* (1911), *From the Deep Woods to Civilization* (1916). Other contemporaneous popular Native authors included Simon Pokagon, Gertrude Bonnin, Francis LaFlesche, Carlos Montezuma, and Luther Standing Bear. Although not all these writers addressed the issue of Americanization directly, they all engaged settler colonialism and its effects on their communities.

51. Sollors, *Beyond Ethnicity*, 7. See also David Hollinger, *Postethnic America: Beyond Multiculturalism* (Basic, 1995), 1–2.

52. For encounters between immigrants and other groups in the U.S., see Leonard Dinnerstein et al, *Natives and Strangers: Blacks, Indians, and Immigrants in America* (Oxford University Press, 1990).

53. Coulthard, *Red Skin, White Masks*, 4.

54. Ibid., 7, 15.

55. Michael Omi and Howard Winant, *Racial Formations in the United States: From the 1960s to the 1980s*, 3rd ed. (Routledge, 2014).

56. Marcus Klein, *Foreigners: The Making of American Literature, 1900–1940* (University of Chicago Press, 1981), 12.

57. Henry Adams, *The Education of Henry Adams* (Modern Library, 1931 [1907]), 238.

58. Klein, *Foreigners*, 12.

59. Ibid., 8.

60. "Glossary," in Mary Antin, *The Promised Land* (Houghton Mifflin, 1912), 289–94.

61. Yiezierska, "An Immigrant among the Editors," *Children of Loneliness: Stories of Immigrant Life in America*, quote on 134.

62. Higham, *Send These to Me*, 87.

63. Matthew Frye Jacobson, *Special Sorrows: The Diasporic Imagination of Irish, Polish, and Jewish Immigrants in the United States* (Harvard University Press, 1995), 6.

64. Gary Gerstle, "Liberty, Coercion, and the Making of Americans," *Journal of American History* 84, no. 2 (September 1997): 527.

65. Hector St. John de Crèvecoeur, *Letters from an American Farmer* (Fox, Duffield, 1904 [1782]), 43.

66. Quoted in Gerstle, "Liberty, Coercion, and the Making of Americans," 527.

67. Ibid., 536–38.

68. On race, class, and their influence on the political history of whiteness, see Matthew F. Jacobson, *Whiteness of a Different Color: European Immigrants and the Alchemy of Race* (Harvard University Press, 1998), 20–21.

69. Karel D. Bicha, "Hunkies: Stereotyping the Slavic Immigrants, 1890–1920," *Journal of American Ethnic History* 2, no. 1 (1982): 16–38; Higham, *Strangers in the Land*, 99–101, 117–19.

70. Barbara Solomon, *Ancestors and Immigrants* (Harvard University Press, 1956), 152, 175.

71. Jacobson, *Whiteness of a Different Color,* 42.

72. David R. Roediger, *Working toward Whiteness: How America's Immigrants Became White* (Basic, 2005), 35–54.

73. "Proposed Addition to *Boy Scouts' Code,*" *Americanization Bulletin* 1, no. 2 (October 15, 1918): 1.

74. Qtd. in Michael La Sorte, *LaMerica: Images of Italian Greenhorn Experience* (Temple University Press, 1985), 95.

75. Edward A. Ross, *The Old World in the New: The Significance of Past and Present Immigration to the American People* (Century, 1914), 286.

76. Thomas Bailey Aldrich, "Unguarded Gates" (1895), in *Inventing America: Readings in Identity and Culture,* ed. Gabriella Ibietta and Miles Orvell (St. Martin's, 1996), 27.

77. Quoted in Jacobson, *Whiteness of a Different Color,* 72.

78. Francis A. Walker, "Restriction of Immigration," *Atlantic* Monthly 77, no. 464 (June 1896): 822–29, quote on 828.

79. Henry B. Wonham, *Playing the Races: Ethnic Caricature and American Literary Realism* (Oxford University Press, 2004), 141–42, 31, 33, and 34–35.

80. Qtd. in Hoxie, *Talking Back to Civilization,* 111. The first issue of the *Quarterly Journal* published the article "The Indian in Caricature," *Quarterly Journal* 1, no. 1 (January–April 1913): 84–87, alongside three cartoons. "Lo, the Poor Indian! Whose untutored mind / Sees grafters on both sides, before and behind," by Bartholomew, reprinted from *Minneapolis Journal,*" 84; a satirical response to the proposed statue at Fort Wadsworth in New York Harbor, was reprinted from the *New York Press*; another version of "Lo, the Poor Indian!" by Coulyaus, was reprinted from the *New York Herald.*

81. Divine, *American Immigration Policy,* 5–6.

82. Alan Kraut makes a persuasive case for the relation between immigration restriction and public health concerns in *Silent Travelers: Germs, Genes, and the "Immigrant Menace"* (Basic, 1994).

83. John J. Appel and Selma Appel, "The Little Red Schoolhouse," in *American Education and the European Immigrant: 1840–1940,* ed. Bernard Weiss (University of Illinois Press, 1982), 17–30, quote on 19.

84. Meg Wesling, *Empire's Proxy: American Literature and U.S. Imperialism in the Philippines* (New York University Press, 2011), 3–4.

85. Higham, *Send These to Me,* 181 and 175–97.

Chapter 3. "That Is Why I Sent You to Carlisle"

1. Letter to Pratt from Upton Sinclair, July 19, 1923. Richard Henry Pratt Papers, Beinecke Library (hereafter Pratt Papers), box 8, folder 282.

2. David Wallace Adams, *Education for Extinction: American Indians and the Boarding School Experience, 1875–1928* (University of Kansas Press, 1995); Brenda Child, *Boarding School Seasons: American Indian Families, 1900–1940* (University of Nebraska Press, 1998); Michael Coleman, *American Indian Children at School, 1850–1930* (University of Mississippi Press, 1993); K. Tsianina Lomawaima, *They Called It Prairie Light: The Story of Chilocco Indian School*

(University of Nebraska Press, 1994); Clyde Ellis, *To Change Them Forever: Indian Education at the Rainy Mountain Boarding School, 1893–1920* (University of Oklahoma Press, 1996).

3. Ziegler-McPherson, *Americanization in the States*, 2–3. See also K. Tsianina Lomawaima and Theresa L. McCarthy, *To Remain an Indian: Lessons in Democracy from a Century of Native American Education* (Teachers College Press, 2006).

4. Phillip Round, *Removable Type: Histories of the Book in Indian Country* (University of North Carolina Press, 2010), quote on 5.

5. I explore this issue further in Stanciu, "'That Is Why I Sent You to Carlisle': Indian Poetry and the Demands of Americanization Poetics and Politics," *American Indian Quarterly* 37, no. 2 (Spring 2013): 34–76.

6. Anonymous, "My Industrial Work," rpt. in Robert Dale Parker, "Boarding School Poetry," *Changing Is Not Vanishing: A Collection of American Indian Poetry to 1930* (University of Pennsylvania Press, 2011), 235–36.

7. Round, *Removable Type*, 6; Robert Warrior, *The People and the Word: Reading Native Nonfiction* (University of Minnesota Press, 2005), 98.

8. Linda Waggoner, *Fire Light: The Life of Angel DeCora, Winnebago Artist* (University of Oklahoma Press, 2008). On Native and Norwegian experiences on the frontier, see Elizabeth Sutton, *Angel De Cora, Karen Thronson, and the Art of Place: How Two Midwestern Women Used Art to Negotiate Migration and Dispossession* (University of Iowa Press, 2020).

9. Luther Standing Bear, *My People, the Sioux*, 147.

10. On Native literacy and alphabetic literacy as a colonial project, see Laura E. Donaldson, "Writing the Talking Stick: Alphabetic Literacy as Colonial Technology and Postcolonial Appropriation," *American Indian Quarterly* 22, no. 1/2 (1998), 46–62.

11. Warrior, *The People and the Word*, 100–101; Mark Rifkin, *Beyond Settler Time: Temporal Sovereignty and Indigenous Self-Determination* (Duke University Press, 2017), 5–6, quote on 6.

12. See the Carlisle Indian School Digital Resource Center: http://carlisleindian.dickinson.edu/, accessed February 10, 2021. On the Canadian residential schools, see John S. Milloy, *A National Crime: The Canadian Government and the Residential School System, 1879–1986* (University of Manitoba Press, 1999).

13. Child, *Boarding School Seasons*, 7.

14. Wolfe, "Settler Colonialism and the Elimination of the Native," 388.

15. In 1890, adding a boarding school in Phoenix would add $50,000 to the local economy. Adams, *Education for Extinction*, 55–59.

16. Spack, *America's Second Tongue*, 37.

17. Child and Klopotek, "Introduction: Comparing Histories of Education for Indigenous People" in *Indian Subjects: Hemispheric Perspectives on the History of Indigenous Education*, ed. Brenda Child and Brian Klopotek (School for Advanced Research, 2014), 1–15, quote on 4.

18. Warrior, *People and the Word*, 101.

19. Lomawaima and McCarty, *To Remain an Indian*, xxi.

20. Clifford E. Trafzer, Jean A. Keller, and Lorene Sisquoc, eds., *Boarding School Blues: Revisiting American Indian Educational Experiences* (University of Nebraska Press, 2006).

21. Hilary E. Wyss, *English Letters and Indian Literacies: Reading, Writing, and New England Missionary Schools, 1750–1830* (University of Pennsylvania Press, 2012), 1–14, quote on 6; Trafzer et al., *Boarding School Blues*, 6–7.

22. Wyss, *English Letters and Indian Literacies*, 5, 36, 72–73, quote on 72.

23. Trafzer et al., *Boarding School Blues*, 9–10. On English-language instruction at Carlisle, see Spack, *America's Second Tongue*, 4.

24. Coleman, *American Indian Children*, 60.

25. Adams, *Education for Extinction*, 65. Pratt to Howard E. Gansworth, asst. disciplinarian, September 4, 1902, Pratt Papers, box 10, folder 342.

26. Richard Henry Pratt, *Battlefield and Classroom: Four Decades with the American Indian* (University of Oklahoma Press, 2003 [1964]), 283.

27. Quoted in Trennert, "From Carlisle to Phoenix," 267.

28. Henry Mills Alden to Pratt, March 13, 1900, Pratt Papers, box 1, folder 6.

29. Brenda Child, *Boarding School Seasons*, 32–40.

30. Letter dated February 3, 1893, from Arthur Howeattle, La Push, WA, A. W. Smith Papers, Beinecke Library, folder 1, Student Papers, Correspondence to A. W. Smith (from La Push, WA).

31. Alice Littlefield, "Native American Labor and Public Policy in the United States," *Marxist Approaches in Economic Anthropology*, ed. Alice Littlefield and Hill Gates (University Press of America, 1991), 221–22.

32. Lomawaima and McCarty, *To Remain an Indian*, 4.

33. Adams, *Education for Extinction*, 20.

34. Pratt to the U.S. Indian Service, January 23, 1883, Pratt Papers, box 10, folder 342.

35. Letters from school personnel (Lucretia T. Ross, Anne S. Ely) document Mercer's abuses, hinting at the molestation of employees. Eventually, as Ross records, "he agreed to leave Carlisle and the Indian Service. *He also promised not to molest any employee* at Carlisle" (my emphasis). Miss Anne S. Ely also writes in support of the "removal of his brutal majesty." Ely writes: "He should be court martialed and lose his place in the army, not be allowed to remain and be in line for promotion. . . . If you liked the work at Carlisle I wish you could have stayed for a time after the filth was cleaned out." Letter from Lucretia T. Ross, Lawrence, KS, February 1, 1908; letter from Miss Anne S. Ely to Miss Ross, sent from Mound City, KS, January 12, 1908, Pratt Papers, box 8, folder 266.

36. Coleman, *American Indians at School*, 80. Although different sources list different numbers, I use this figure (194) based on correspondence with longtime CHIIS historian, Barbara Landis. Letter to the author, October 6, 2017. Recently, the bodies of some students have been repatriated to their nations. May 25, 2021: https://www.witf.org/2021/05/25/the-u-s-army-preparing-to-exhume-the-remains-of-10-indian-school-students-from-carlisle-barracks-cemetery/.

37. His file in the National Archives indicates that, although he attended Carlisle on and off from 1879 until 1884, he later continued his education and became the state's attorney for Bennett County, South Dakota, by 1913.

38. The paragraph following the poem reads: "Louisa Three Stars, the oldest child of Clarence Three Stars, died March 5th, and was buried in the Episcopal cemetery at the Agency. About a year ago Louisa came home from Pierre school on account of sickness." "Items from the Day Schools," *Oglala Light* 9.1 (March

1908): 25, Beinecke Library, Western Americana. The editors introduced the poem with these words: "A poem written by a father (Clarence T. Stars) whose child (Louisa Three Stars) had died a year after she returned from boarding school." For the full poem, see Stanciu, "Looking for the Native Students' Voices in the Western Americana," *Beinecke Illuminated* 2, no. 1 (Summer 2015): 12–13.

39. Pratt to the Friends of Indian Education, June 1881, Pratt Papers, box 10, folder 342.

40. Pratt, *Battlefield and the Classroom*, 214.

41. Pratt Papers, box 19, folder 649, 4.

42. *Carlisle Arrow*, October 16, 1914, 1.

43. Eric Margolis, "Looking at Discipline, Looking at Labour: Photographic Representations of Indian Boarding Schools," *Visual Studies* 19, no. 1 (2004): 72.

44. Dippie, *Vanishing American*, 116.

45. Mauro, *Art of Americanization at Carlisle*, 5.

46. Joanna Hearne, *Native Recognition: Indigenous Cinema and the Western* (State University of New York Press, 2013), 20–30.

47. Jolene Rickard, "Occupation," 60, qtd. in Hearne, *Native Recognition*, 29.

48. Krista McCracken, "Archival Photographs in Perspective: Indian Residential School Images of Health," *British Journal of Canadian Studies*, 30, no, 2 (2071): 163–82.

49. Yellow Robe wrote the prologue to the film *The Silent Enemy* (1930), set in a precontact Anashinaabe community in Canada and recounting the community's struggle with starvation. He also recited the film's prologue in Lakota, although his audience believed he was speaking Ojibwe/Anashinaabe. Michelle Raheja, *Reservation Reelism*, 87.

50. Marjorie Winberg, *The Real Rosebud: The Triumph of a Lakota Woman* (University of Nebraska Press, 2004), 20–22.

51. Adams, *Education for Extinction*, 63.

52. "Letter to One of the Boys by His Father," Pawnee Agency, Indian Territory, October 21, 1881, *Eadle Keatah Toh/Big Morning Star* 2, no. 4 (November 1881): 3.

53. Child, *Boarding School Seasons*, 27.

54. Wyss, *English Letters and Indian Literacies*, 9, 11.

55. Daniel F. Littlefield and James Parins, *American Indian and Alaska Native Newspapers and Periodicals, 1826–1924* (Greenwood Press, 1984), 11.

56. On the Indian school press, see also ibid., xxviii–xxix.

57. Ibid., 317–21.

58. I develop this analysis further in "That's Why I Sent You to Carlisle: Carlisle Poetry and the Demands of Americanization Poetics and Politics," *American Indian Quarterly* 37, no. 2 (Spring 2013): 34–76.

59. Editorial, *School News* 1, no. 2 (June 1880): 3.

60. Editorial, *School News* 1, no. 8 (January 1881): 2.

61. "English Speaking," *Indian Helper* 2.1 (August 13, 1886): 1.

62. Anonymous, "My Industrial Work," rpt. in Parker, *Changing Is Not Vanishing*, 235–36.

63. "The Invincibles" was a literary society for boys at Carlisle. Members of the Susan Longstreth Literary Society (girls) are pictured in *Red Man and Helper* 18.32

(March 6, 1903): 3. The Susans were still active in 1918 when Carlisle closed. A letter from Pratt, with a donation to the society, was reprinted in *Carlisle Arrow* and *Red Man* (March 22, 1918), 30.

64. Sarah Pettinos was a Carlisle resident who sometimes contributed to the *Indian Helper.*

65. Sarah J. Pettinos, "Books," *Red Man and Helper,* May 17, 1901, 1.

66. Wolfe, "Settler Colonialism and the Elimination of the Native," 388; Amelia V. Katanski, *Learning to Write "Indian": The Boarding School Experience and American Indian Literature* (University of Oklahoma Press, 2005), 56, 84; Jacqueline Fear Segal, *White Man's Club: Schools, Race, and the Struggle of Indian Acculturation* (University of Nebraska Press, 2007).

67. For another great interpretation of the "Man-on-the-Band-Stand" and a reading of the *Indian Helper* as a rhetorical panopticon, see Katanski, *Learning to Write "Indian,"* 45–94.

68. Marianna Burgess left Carlisle in 1904, after Pratt's dismissal from his position as superintendent. *Stiya: A Carlisle Indian Girl at Home* (Riverside Press, 1891).

69. For an analysis of *Stiya,* see Katanski, *Learning to Write "Indian,"* 45–94.

70. I develop this discussion, with an analysis of the photograph in the article "That's Why I Sent You to Carlisle," *American Indian Quarterly* 37, no. 2 (Spring 2013): 34–76.

71. "Back to Nature for the Indian: An Interview with Francis E. Leupp, Commissioner of Indian Affairs, Washington," *Charities and Commons* (June 6, 1908): 336–40, quote on 339.

72. Bernadette A. Lear's extensive study of the Carlisle library is based on the school's 1918 inventory. See Lear, "Libraries and Reading Culture at the Carlisle Indian Industrial School, 1879–1918," *Book History* 8 (2015): 166–96, esp. 171–75; quote on 166.

73. "The Carlisle Industrial School for Indians" (1901), Pratt Papers, Special Files, box 30, folder 816.

74. Ibid.

75. R. H. Pratt to the U.S. Indian Service, January 23, 1883, Pratt Papers, General Correspondence and Official Papers, box 10, folder 342.

76. Estelle Reel, *Course of Study for the Indian Schools of the United States: Industrial and Literary* (Government Printing Office, 1901), 224, 5–6, 109–19.

77. Tova Cooper, "The Scenes of Seeing: Frances Benjamin Johnston and Visualizations of the 'Indian' in Black, White, and Native Educational Contexts," *American Literature* 83.3 (2011): 509–45, 544 n. 49.

78. I expand on the concept of "Carlisle poetry" in "That Is Why I Sent you to Carlisle," *American Indian Quarterly* 37, no. 2 (Spring 2013): 34–76.

79. Kate W. Hamilton, "America," *Red Man and Helper* 3, no. 45 (July 3, 1903): 1.

80. "Participation of Carlisle Indian School Band in Patriotic Parade." Correspondence, Cato Sells, commissioner of Indian Affairs, E. B. Meritt, Frederic A. Godcharles, and John Francis Jr., April 17–18, 1917, National Archives and Records Administration (hereafter NARA), RG 75, Carlisle Indian School Digital

Resource Center, Dickinson College, http://carlisleindian.dickinson.edu/docu ments/participation-carlisle-indian-school-band-patriotic-parade, accessed February 10, 2021.

81. *Red Man* 5, no. 9 (May 1913): 434–35. The graduating class of 1903 included only fifteen students, one awardee of a certificate of proficiency in stenography and typewriting, and fifty-six recipients of industrial certificates.

82. Rose Whipper (Sioux), "Pride of Our Nation," *Carlisle Arrow* 10, no. 37 (May 22, 1913): 1.

83. Ibid. See Rose Whipper's Carlisle file, held at the National Archives, digitized by the Carlisle Indian School Digital Resource Center at Dickinson College: http://carlisleindian.dickinson.edu/student_files/rose-whipper-student-file, accessed February 10, 2021.

84. Elsie Fuller, "A New Citizen," *Indian Helper* 2, no. 39 (May 6, 1887): 1.

85. See Pfister, *Individuality Incorporated,* esp. chaps. 1 and 2.

86. See *Federal Textbook on Citizenship Training* (Government Printing Office, 1936), esp. "Our Nation," which included sixty-eight lessons in American citizenship and a copy of the U.S. Constitution.

87. Reel, *Course of Study for the Indian Schools of the United States,* 224.

88. There are three letters from Sam Sixkiller to Pratt in the Pratt Papers: the first is dated February 26, 1899; the second, January 27, 1916; the third, December 6, 1920, Pratt Papers, box 8, folder 282. Sixkiller was a Carlisle prankster, remembered fondly in Pratt's documents, including stories penned by Pratt's daughter. Pratt Papers, box 30, folder 823.

89. Charles Burke to Pratt, April 30, 1921, Pratt Papers, box 2, folder 43. "My dear General Pratt, I have your letter of April 16, enclosing a communication from Sam Sixkiller, who graduated from Carlisle Indian School, now employed as a clerk at the Muskogee Indian Office, who desires a promotion. In answer, you are advised that I shall be glad to bear in mind your interest in Mr. Sixkiller."

90. Chauncey E. Archiquette to Pratt from Pawhuska, Oklahoma, September 2, 1920, Pratt Papers, box 1, folder 2. Letter to Pratt from Luther Standing Bear, from Venice Pier, California, 1920 [n.d.], Pratt Papers, box 8, folder 290.

91. Rosa La Flesche to Pratt, December 5, 1920, from San Francisco, Pratt Papers, box 4, folder 154.

92. Katie Creager Day, Laguna, NM, to R. H. Pratt, December 2, 1920, Pratt Papers, box 2, folder 66.

93. Rosa Bourassa to Pratt, November 10, 1899, Pratt Papers, box 2, folder 36.

94. Balenti to Pratt, December 1, 1920, Pratt Papers, box 1, folder 20.

95. Mystica Amago to Richard Henry Pratt, February 25, 1903, Pratt Papers, box 1, folder 2.

96. Trafzer, Keller, and Sisquoc. "Introduction," *Boarding School Blues,* 1.

97. Trennert, "Educating Indian Girls at Nonreservation Boarding Schools, 1878–1920," 288.

98. "Brief Extract from the Meriam Report, Bulletin 16, Prepared by the Eastern Association on Indian Affairs," John Collier Papers, Sterling Library, Yale University, box 19, folder 48. According to Michael Coleman, by 1900, the U.S. govern-

ment also funded eighty-one on-reservation boarding schools. Coleman, *American Indian Children*, 44.

99. Other Native writers published autobiographies about various forms of education in white institutions, from Francis La Flesche's *The Middle Five* (1900), to Charles Eastman's *Indian Boyhood* (1902) and *From the Deep Woods to Civilization* (1916), and Gertrude Bonnin's *American Indian Stories* (1921). Although nineteenth-century Native-authored autobiographies by George Copway, Black Hawk, or Sarah Winnemucca-Hopkins may have served as inspiring examples for Native students in boarding schools, these examples were not part of the Carlisle curriculum.

100. Luther Standing Bear, *Land of the Spotted Eagle*, 254–55.

101. "Extracts from Home Letters," *Morning Star*, 1886. Qtd. in Jennifer Bess, "Casting a Spell: Acts of Cultural Continuity in Carlisle Indian Industrial School's the *Red Man and Helper*," *Wicazo Sa Review* 26, no. 2 (Fall 2011): 13.

CHAPTER 4. "SING, STRANGERS!"

1. "1776–1924," *Radnick*, July 5, 1924.

2. Lomawaima and McCarthy, *To Remain an Indian,* 5, 20.

3. Peter Carravetta, "The Silence of the Atlantis," in *The Routledge History of Italian Americans*, ed. William J. Connell and Stanislao G. Pugliese (Routledge, 2018), 141.

4. Hartman, *Movement to Americanize the Immigrant*, 13–24. Data on YMCA numbers in 1912 on page 28.

5. See Wan, *Producing Good Citizens*.

6. Bernard J. Weiss, "Introduction," *American Education and the European Immigrant: 1840–1940* (University of Illinois Press, 1982), xii–xiv.

7. Leonard Dinnerstein, "Education and the Advancement of American Jews," in Weiss, ed., *American Education and the European Immigrant*, 44; John Bodnar, "Schooling and the Slavic-American Family, 1900–1940," in Weiss, ed., *American Education and the European Immigrant*, 78–95, 78.

8. Horace Kallen, "Democracy versus the Melting Pot," *The Nation* 100, no. 2590–2591 (February 18–25, 1915): 190–94, 217–20; Randoph Bourne, "Trans-National America," *Atlantic Monthly* 118 (July 1916): 86–97.

9. Caravetta, "Silence of the Atlantis," in *The Routledge History of Italian Americans*, ed. William J. Connell and Stanislao G. Pugliese (Routledge, 2018), 132–51, 134–35.

10. Guglielmo, *White on Arrival*, 5–6.

11. David Blaustein, "The Effect of Public Schools on Immigrants: How American Public School Education Often Creates Gulf between Immigrants and Their Children," *New York Times* (August 18, 1907): SM8.

12. Jerre Mangione, *An Ethnic at Large: A Memoir of America in the Thirties and Forties* (Putnam's, 1978), 18. Matteo Pretelli, "Italian Americans, Education, and Italian Language: 1880–1921," *Quaderni D'Italienistica* 38, no. 1 (2017): 61–84.

13. John F. McClymer, "The Americanization Movement and the Education of the Foreign-Born," in Weiss, ed., *American Education and the Immigrant*, 110.

14. Korman, "Americanization at the Factory Gate," 397–99.

15. S. H. Goldberger, "Using the Schoolhouses in Americanization," Americanization Conference, Washington, DC, May 12–15, 1919. NARA, RG 85, entry 26, folders 27671/7344.

16. Mary Graham Bonner, "A Real Piece of Americanization: Why Mr. Angelo Patri's School Has a Running Start in a National Task," *Ladies Home Journal* (November 1919): 83. John Foster Carr Papers, Manuscripts and Archives Division, New York Public Library (hereafter Carr Papers, NYPL), box 4, folder "Americanization, Clippings."

17. Wiebe, *Search for Order*. John Foster Carr Papers, NYPL, box 4, folder "Americanization, Clippings"; "Practical Americanization: Making Public Education Fit the Public," *Immigrants in America Review* 1 (September 1915): 87; Olneck, "Americanization and the Education of Immigrants." New York's "steamer classes" or "vestibule classes" were available to recently arrived immigrant children, eight years and older. They lasted between six and twelve months; isolating immigrant students from native speaker students, these classes used punitive measures if immigrant students spoke their native language. See Ester De Jong, "Steamer Classes," in "Immigrant Era: Focus on Assimilation," https://www.colorincolorado.org/article/immigrant-era-focus-assimilation, accessed November 2, 2021.

18. John Dewey, quoted in Handlin, "Education and the European Immigrant, 1820–1920," in Weiss, ed., *American Education and the European Immigrant,* 10; Mirel, *Patriotic Pluralism*, 31.

19. Jane Addams lamented the gap between immigrant generations, such as Italian women losing hold of their Americanized children, *Twenty Years at Hull House*, ed. Victoria Bissell Brown (Bedford/St. Martin's, 1999 [1910]), 136–47.

20. "My Industrial Work," rpt. in Parker, *Changing Is Not Vanishing*, 235–36. On the Roberts method, see Paul McBride, "Peter Roberts and the YMCA Americanization Program," *Pennsylvania History* 44, no. 2 (1977): 145–62 and George E. Pozzetta, *Americanization, Social Control, and Philanthropy* (Garland, 1991).

21. Manuals such as *Teaching Our Language to Beginners* and the *Federal Citizenship Textbook on Citizenship Training* were issued by the Bureau of Naturalization in cooperation with the Department of Education. Wan, *Producing Good Citizens*, 13.

22. *A Standard Course for Use in the Public Schools of the United States for the Preparation of the Candidate for the Responsibilities of Citizenship*, 24.

23. NARA, RG 85, box 6.

24. "A Little Naturalization Story," Library of Congress, RG 85, entry 30, box 18, folder 5.

25. William Tyler Page, "The Americans' Creed," 1917, https://www.ushistory.org/documents/creed.htm, accessed February 10, 2021.

26. Writing specimens from Webster, Iowa (1924) from the Verhele family, NARA, RG 85, Records of the Immigration and Naturalization Service.

27. Ibid.

28. Gust Marinakes to Florence Strevey, April 17, 1924; George Papavasiliou to Florence Strevey, April 12, 1924. Library of Congress, RG 85, Records of the Immigration and Naturalization Service, Education and Americanization, box 5, folder 23/2, "Exhibits—School Work."

29. Notebook of Silvio Floretta, Library of Congress, RG 85, Records of the Immigration and Naturalization Service, Education and Americanization, box 5, folder 23/2, "Specimens of Work of Pupils."

30. Rodger Steitmatter, "The Nativist Press: Demonizing the American Immigrant," *Journalism and Mass Communication* 76, no. 4 (Winter 1999): 673–83, quotes on 676.

31. For a timeline since its inception in 1919 to the present, see the official website of the American Legion, https://www.legion.org/history, accessed December 11, 2020.

32. John Foster Carr Papers, NYPL, box 4, folder "Americanization, Clippings."

33. Hartman, *Movement to Americanize the Immigrant*, 222–23; Korman, "Americanization at the Factory Gate," 405–19.

34. Korman, "Americanization at the Factory Gate," 408. One of the invited members of the editorial board of *Immigrants in America Review* was immigrant writer Mary Antin, author of the successful pro-Americanization memoir *The Promised Land* (1912).

35. "Americanizing the Alien," editorial. *Immigrants in American Review* 1, no. 2 (June 1915): 5.

36. "Foreign Language Almanachs," *Americanization Bulletin* 1, no. 2 (October 15, 1918): 1.

37. Mirel, *Patriotic Pluralism,* 102–5, quote on 105.

38. On the "Schooling of the Immigrant: Americanization and Adult Education, 1919–1929," see Ziegler-McPherson, *Americanization in the States,* 122–43. By 1923, only eight states in the country (New York, California, and Massachusetts among them) supported Americanization programs. By 1929, adult education programs replaced immigrant education programs.

39. "New Americans for New America Pamphlet," John Foster Carr Papers, NYPL, box 3, folder 1.

40. John Foster Carr Papers, NYPL, box 1, folder 1.

41. *Guide to the United States for the Jewish Immigrant: A Nearly Literal Translation of the Second Yiddish Edition,* by John Foster Carr, 2nd ed. (Connecticut Daughters of the American Revolution, 1913), Carr Papers, NYPL, box 1, folder 1.

42. Carr, however, refers to museum Indians when he describes the NYC Museum of Natural History, with "collections of Indian work, models of Indian life, relics of our ancient American civilization." *Guide to the United States for the Jewish Immigrant. A Nearly Literal Translation of the Second Yiddish Edition,* 2nd ed. (Connecticut Daughters of the American Revolution, 1913), 24.

43. Trish Loughran, *The Republic in Print: Print Culture in the Age of U.S. Nation Building, 1770–1870* (Columbia University Press, 2009), 3.

44. Robert E. Park, *The Immigrant Press and Its Control* (Harper and Brothers, 1922), 5.

45. Nicolas Kánellos, "Recovering and Re-constructing Early Twentieth Century Hispanic Immigrant Print Culture in the US," *American Literary History* 19, no. 2 (2007): 439.

46. Kristen Silva Gruesz recovered Spanish-language nineteenth-century periodicals and is a scholarly model for understanding the role of the immigrant press in challenging American exceptionalism written in U.S. national tradition. *Ambassadors of Culture: The Transamerican Origins of Latino Writing* (Princeton University Press, 2002).

47. Sally M. Miller, ed., *The Ethnic Press in the United States: A Historical Analysis and Handbook* (Greenwood Press, 1987), xiii.

48. Rudolph J. Vecoli, "The Italian Immigrant Press and the Construction of Social Reality, 1850–1920," in *Print Culture in a Diverse America*, ed. James P. Danky and Wayne A. Wiegand (University of Illinois Press, 1998), 17–18.

49. Quoted in Mirel, *Patriotic Pluralism*, 102.

50. Vaida Raceanul, "D'Ale Noastre Din America"/"Our America," *Romanian Cleveland Almanach,* 1912, Historical Society of Philadelphia Archives.

51. Benjamin Harshav attributes this idea to Chaim Zhitlovsky, a famous Yiddish author and theoretician of Jewish nationalism. See Harshav, ed. *Sing, Stranger! A Century of American Yiddish Poetry: A Historical Anthology* (Stanford University Press, 2000), xxiv.

52. "Introspectivism" (Manifesto of 1919), Benjamin Harshav and Barbara Harshav, *American Yiddish Poetry: A Bilingual Anthology* (University of California Press, 1986), 774–84.

53. Howe, *World of Our Fathers,* 442. According to Irving Howe, in the 1920s Yiddish poets also translated into Yiddish some American Indian "chants," a problematic concept dismissing the possibility that Indigenous people had an oral culture on par with literate Western literature.

54. David Koffman, *The Jews' Indian: Colonialism, Pluralism and Belonging in America* (Rutgers University Press, 2019), 7.

55. *Il Progresso Italo-Americano* was founded in New York City in 1880 as a weekly and soon became the first Italian daily, published until 1982. Carlo Barsotti, a padrone banker with little education, founded it and hired others to write and edit it. See Vecoli, "Italian Immigrant Press and the Construction of Social Reality," in *Print Culture in a Diverse America*, ed. Danky and Wiegand, 17–33, 21–23.

56. Ibid.

57. *La Follia,* August 10, 1919. John Foster Carr Papers, NYPL, box 4, folder "Americanization, Clippings."

58. Letter to John Foster Carr from the Foreign Language Information Service, December 17, 1925. Carr Papers, NYPL, box 1, folder 2.

59. Lazar Churich, "Underground in America," *Pamphlet,* 1907. Chicago Foreign Language Press Survey (CFLPS), Newberry Library, Chicago.

60. *The Chicago Foreign Language Press Survey: A General Description of Its Contents* (Chicago Public Library Omnibus Project, Work Projects Administration, Chicago, 1942). On federal oversight of the foreign language publications, see Sally M. Miller, ed., *The Ethnic Press in the United States: A Historical Analysis and Handbook* (Greenwood 1987), xvii.

61. "The Foreigners among Chicago's Population," *Illinois Staats Zeitung*, January 25, 1892.

62. *Dziennik Chicagoski,* 1891.

63. Ibid.

64. "Polish American Veterans: The Proof of Loyalty," *Dziennik Chicagoski,* (September 3, 1927), CFLPS; "Jews and Negroes," *Svenska Nyheter* (June 30, 1903), CFLPS, IIIH.

65. *Greek Star*, August 1904; *Greek Star*, 1922, CFLPS.

66. See also Bernard J. Weiss, "Introduction," *American Education and the European Immigrant,* xi–xxviii.

67. [Serbian] Lazar Churich, "Underground in America," *Pamphlet*, 1907, CFLPS.

68. "English Language vs. Polish Language," *Zgoda*, October 21, 1897, CFLPS.

69. *Loxias*, July 1, 1911. http://flps.newberry.org/article/5422062_5_0951, accessed December 11, 2020.

70. "Indian Socialists," *Illinois Staats Zeitung*, April 18, 1881. CFLPS, Newberry Library; "Let Us Be Poles" (editorial), *Dziennik Związkowy*, December 6, 1910, http://flps.newberry.org/article/5423968_8_0557, accessed December 11, 2020.

71. "Czechoslovaks Protest against Prohibition," *Denní Hlasatel*, October 6, 1922, CFLPS. http://flps.newberry.org/article/5418478_1_0509, accessed December 11, 2020.

72. On multiple allegiances of the Society of American Indians, see my article "Americanization on Native Terms."

73. "The Press Criticizes the United States Government for Mistreatment of the American Indians" (editorial), *Dziennik Chicagoski*, January 6, 1891.

74. Mirel, *Patriotic Pluralism* 20.

75. On the expansion of Americanization work into the 1930s and 1940s, especially through the YMCA, see McBride, "Peter Roberts and the YMCA Americanization Program."

76. James Periconi, "Italian American Book Publishing and Bookselling," in *The Routledge History of Italian Americans*, ed. Connell and Pugliese (Routledge, 2018), 264.

Chapter 5. Americanization on Native Terms

1. "Indian Congress Opens Two Meetings to Local Public," *Columbus Citizen*, October 11, 1911, reel 10, Papers of the Society of American Indians (hereafter SAI Papers), ten microfilm reels, ed. John W. Larner Jr., Newberry Library, Chicago.

2. "Columbus Red Men Entertain Indians," *Ohio State Journal*, October 17, 1911, reel 10, SAI Papers.

3. At the Minneapolis meeting in 1919, some SAI members performed "The Conspiracy of Pontiac," written for the occasion by Charles Eastman, with performers also including Carlos Montezuma and Gertrude Bonnin. Maddox, *Citizen Indians,* 51.

4. Sherman Coolidge, "The Function of the Society of American Indians," *Quarterly Journal* 2, no. 3 (July–September 1914): 186–90, quote on 186.

5. Robert A. Warrior, "The SAI and the End(s) of History," *American Indian Quarterly* 37.3 (Summer 2013): 224. Unless otherwise noted, all quotations from Laura Cornelius Kellogg's work come from Kristina Ackley and Cristina Stanciu, eds., *Laura Cornelius Kellogg: Our Democracy and the American Indian and Other Works* (Syracuse University Press, 2015), quote on 8.

6. On the pageantry craze at the beginning of the twentieth century, see David Glassberg, *American Historical Pageantry: The Uses of Tradition in the Early Twentieth Century* (University of North Carolina Press, 1990).

7. The joint issue of *American Indian Quarterly* and *Studies in American Indian Literatures* from the summer of 2013, edited by Chadwick Allen and Beth Piatote, is a step forward in combining historians' and literary historians' work toward recovering the legacy of the SAI one hundred years later.

8. On the work of the SAI toward citizenship and Progressive Era Native activism, see also Frederick E. Hoxie, *This Indian Country: American Indian Activists and the Place They Made* (Penguin, 2012), esp. "The Good Citizenship Gun: Thomas Sloan, Omaha," 225–76.

9. Jane Gordon to Carlos Montezuma, April 26, 1921, Edward E. Ayer Collection, Carlos Montezuma Papers, box 1, folder 65, Newberry Library.

10. "Our correspondence is heavy. Nearly 30,000 letters have been written, dictated, and signed by the Secretary while he has been in Office, not including 49,000 circular letters and about 20,000 announcements." Volume 3 of the *Quarterly Journal* had the highest distribution at six thousand copies. "Our Office Work," *American Indian Magazine* 4, no. 2 (June 1916): 167–68.

11. The SAI limited membership to people with at least one-sixteenth "Indian blood," a problematic use of the blood quantum concept but a necessary measure in the organization's view at the time, in an attempt to preserve an all-Indian membership. The SAI was not the first attempt at a national Native political organization; preceding it by a few years was the National Indian Republican Association, organized by Carlisle graduate Luzena Choteau in 1904. See David Antony T. Clark, "Representing Indians: Indigenous Fugitives and the Society of American Indians in the Making of Common Culture" (Ph.D. diss., University of Kansas, 2004), 14–15.

12. Lomawaima, "Mutuality of Citizenship and Sovereignty," 338, 335.

13. On Henry Roe Cloud, see Renya K. Ramirez, *Standing Up to Colonial Power: The Lives of Henry Roe Cloud and Elizabeth Bender Cloud* (University of Nebraska Press, 2018). Other prominent members of the General Committee of the SAI included Hiram Chase, William Holmes, Marie Baldwin, Frank Wright, Howard E. Gansworth, Dennison Wheelock, J. E. Shields, Emma J. Goulette, Rosa B. LaFlesche.

14. *Report of the Executive Council on the Proceedings of the First Annual Conference of the Society of American Indians* (Washington, DC, 1912.), 2. "Proceedings of the Second Annual Conference, Held at Columbus, Ohio, October 2–7, 1912, at Ohio State University," *Quarterly Journal* 1, no. 2 (April—June 1913): 115–255.

15. Tom Holm, *The Great Confusion in Indian Affairs: Native Americans and Whites in the Progressive Era* (Austin: University Texas Press, 2005), 53–56. Hazel

Hertzberg's study of the SAI remains the most comprehensive to date: *The Search for an American Indian Identity: Modern Pan-Indian Movements* (Syracuse University Press, 1971), esp. 59–193.

16. "Editorial Comment," *American Indian Magazine* 4, no. 2 (April–June 1916): 107.

17. Ibid., 110.

18. Michelle W. Patterson, "Real Indian Songs: The Society of American Indians and the Use of Native American Culture as a Means of Reform," *American Indian Quarterly* 26, no. 1 (Winter, 2002): 45.

19. Ackley and Stanciu, *Laura Cornelius Kellogg*, 8.

20. "The Indian in Caricature," *Quarterly Journal* 1, no.1 (January–April 1913): 84–87.

21. Littlefield and Parins, *American Indian and Alaska Native Newspapers and Periodicals*, ix.

22. "Editorial Comment," *Quarterly Journal* 1, no. 1 (1913): 1. On the political work of Native intellectuals in the nineteenth century, see Maureen Konkle, *Writing Indian Nations: Native Intellectuals and the Politics of Historiography, 1827–1863* (University of North Carolina Press, 2004).

23. "Editorial Comment: The New Quarterly Journal," *Quarterly Journal* 1, no. 1 (April 15, 1913): 2.

24. *Constitution and By-Laws of the Society of American Indians* (Washington, DC: The Society, 1916), 17, Ayer Collection, Newberry Library.

25. In 1916 (vol. 4, no. 2), the journal changed its title from the *Quarterly Journal* to the *American Indian Magazine*.

26. The subtitle change of the *American Indian Magazine* was introduced in vol. 5, no. 1 (January–March 1917).

27. The SAI journal started publishing poems in its fourth year, after it underwent a change of vision and name in 1916. On the poems published in the journal, see Stanciu, "Americanization on Native Terms."

28. Gertrude Bonnin to Arthur C. Parker, December 19, 1916, reel 1, SAI Papers.

29. "One Indian Maiden: Her Literary Plans for the Uplifting of Her Race," *New York Tribune*, February 15, 1903.

30. "The North American Indians: A Redskin Princess," qtd. in Ackley and Stanciu, *Laura Cornelius Kellogg*, 18, emphasis added.

31. On Kellogg's activist and literary work, see the introduction to the volume recovering her work for the first time. Cristina Stanciu and Kristina Ackley, "Laura Cornelius Kellogg: Haudenosaunee Thinker, Native Activist, American Writer," in *Laura Cornelius Kellogg*, 1–64.

32. Gertrude Bonnin published stories and essays in the *Atlantic Monthly* ("Why I Am a Pagan," 1901) and *Harper's Magazine* ("The Soft-Hearted Sioux," 1901). Her two published volumes are *Old Indian Legends* (1901) and *American Indian Stories* (1921). A cogent biography of Bonnin is Tadeusz Lewandowski's *Red Bird, Red Power: The Life and Legacy of Zitkala-Ša* (University of Oklahoma Press, 2016). For a comprehensive list of Native American writers before 1924, see Daniel F. Littlefield Jr. and James W. Parins, *A Bibliography of Native American Writers, 1772–1924* (Scarecrow Press, 1981).

33. Over the years, the journal garnered national praise. In the late 1910s, the *American Indian Magazine* started including international news, in rubrics such as "What the Papers Say about Indians" and "Under the Sun: Clippings on World News," *American Indian Magazine* 7, no. 1 (Spring 1919): 43, 48–50.

34. "A Plain Statement about the Quarterly Journal." *Quarterly Journal* 1, no. 4 (October–December 1913), 341–42.

35. "Send That Dollar Now," *American Indian Magazine* 4, no. 2 (June 1916): 167.

36. "With Our Contemporaries," *American Indian Magazine* 4, no. 2 (June 1916): 186.

37. "Dr. Montezuma's Wassaja," *American Indian Magazine* 4, no. 2 (June 1916): 168.

38. Reel 8, SAI Papers.

39. *Quarterly Journal* 1, no. 3 (July–September 1913): 304, emphasis added.

40. According to Maddox, Bonnin had suggested to Parker in 1916 that the SAI journal also publish a leaflet especially for reservation Indians. Parker took Bonnin's advice on some matters, publishing stories set on reservations, poetry, biographical sketches of less prominent members of the SAI, and notes from reservations. Maddox, *Citizen Indians*, 102, 107.

41. Chauncey Yellow Robe, "Indian Patriotism," *American Indian Magazine* 6, no. 3 (1918): 129–30.

42. Thomas Sloan to General Hugh L. Scott, June 25, 1920, reel 9, SAI Papers.

43. Arthur C. Parker, "Editorial Comment: A World Opportunity for the Society," *American Indian Magazine* 4, no. 2 (April–June 1916): 116.

44. *Blast*, one year; *The Crisis*, twelve years; *The Egoist*, five years.

45. Scott R. Lyons, "Rhetorical Sovereignty: What Do American Indians Want from Writing?," *College Composition and Communication* 51, no. 3 (February 2000): 447–68, esp. 450–51.

46. For a comprehensive bibliography of Native American writers of this period, see Daniel F. Littlefield Jr. and James W. Parins, *A Bibliography of Native American Writers, 1772–1924* (Scarecrow Press, 1981) and *A Bibliography of Native American Writers, 1772–1924: A Supplement* (Scarecrow Press, 1985).

47. "Making a White Man out of an Indian Not a Good Plan," *Quarterly Journal* 5, no. 2 (April–June 1917): 85. Kathleen Washburn rightly notes that this declaration was published on the inside cover of the inaugural issue. Washburn, "New Indians and Indigenous Archives," *PMLA*, 127, no. 2 (2012): 380–84, 381.

48. An editorial note urged the readers: "Keep your copies of the *QJ*, they are valuable." *Quarterly Journal* 3, no. 3 (September 1915): 229.

49. *Quarterly Journal* 1, no.1 (April 15, 1913): 69.

50. King, *Making Americans*, esp. 14–24.

51. Lucy Maddox writes about the SAI in the context of the ideology of uplift during the Progressive Era, illuminating differences between the "Indian question" and the "Negro question." See Maddox, *Citizen Indians*, esp. 10–16, 54–88.

52. Editorial, "The Path to Citizenship," *Quarterly Journal* 3, no. 1 (1915): 74; Gertrude Bonnin, "A Bill Conferring Citizenship," *Quarterly Journal* 5, no. 3 (1917): 138.

53. Arthur C. Parker, "The Road to Competent Citizenship," *Quarterly Journal* 2, no.1 (January–March 1914): 178, 182, quote on 196.

54. *Coe College Cosmos*, October 3, 1916, reel 10, SAI Papers.

55. "Make Them Citizens," reprinted from *Native American* in *The American Indian Magazine* 5, no. 3 (1917): 206; "A Declaration of Citizenship" and "Citizen Indians," *American Indian Magazine* 6, no. 1 (1918): 93; "Indian Citizenship Bill," *American Indian Magazine* 6, no. 2 (1918): 131; "The American Indian as an Equal Citizen," reprinted from the *Christian Science Monitor* in the *American Indian Magazine* 7, no. 1 (1919): 46–47.

56. Charles A. Eastman to SAI Members, January 11, 1919, reel 4, Papers of Carlos Montezuma, MD, including the Papers of Maria Keller Montezuma Moore and the Papers of Joseph W. Latimer, 9 microfilm reels, Ayers Collection, Newberry Library.

57. Hertzberg, *Search for an American Indian Identity*, 184.

58. Preface to *Report of the Executive Council on the Proceedings of the First Annual Conference of the Society of American Indians* (Washington, DC, 1912), 3–5. The first SAI conference met in Columbus, Ohio, in October 1911.

59. Maddox, *Citizen Indians*, 14.

60. Sherman Coolidge, "The Indian American: His Duty to His Race and to His Country, the United States of America," Presidential Address. *Quarterly Journal* 1, no. 1 (April 1913): 20.

61. Special provisions for aliens of foreign birth to acquire U.S. citizenship were made through the Act of July 19, 1919; Native men who enlisted to fight in the war were naturalized four months later through the Act of November 6, 1919. *Cohen's Handbook of Federal Indian Law*, 154.

62. The General Allotment Act of 1887 held that Indian allottees would become citizens of the United States and of the state where they resided if they adopted "the habits of civilized life," for which they received "certificates of citizenship."

63. David Martinez, *Dakota Philosopher: Charles Eastman and American Indian Thought* (Minnesota Historical Society Press, 2009), 106.

64. I refer here to the title of Frederick Hoxie's edited collection, *Talking Back to Civilization: Indian Voices of the Progressive Era*.

65. McKenzie, *Indian and Citizenship*, 4, 10.

66. The Carter Indian Code Bill, H.R. 18334, 62nd Congress, Sess. II. Fayette McKenzie, quoted in Maddox, *Citizen Indians*, 110.

67. Fred E. Parker, "The Indian as a Citizen," *Quarterly Journal* 1, no. 2 (1913): 133.

68. Gabe E. Parker, "The Great End: American Citizenship for the Indian," *Quarterly Journal* 2, no. 1 (1914): 60.

69. Carlos Montezuma, "The Reservation—Fatal to the Development of Citizenship," *Quarterly Journal* 2, no. 1 (1914): 69–73.

70. Hertzberg, *Search for an American Indian Identity*, 184.

71. Pratt, "Why Most of Our Indians Are Dependent and Non-Citizens," *Quarterly Journal* 2, no. 3 (1914): 223, emphasis in the original.

72. Charles Eastman published the article "The Indian as Citizen" in *Lippincott's* in 1915, where he engaged with an earlier scheme of citizenship proposed

by Fayette McKenzie: tribal ward, allotted ward, citizen ward, and full citizen. Instead, Eastman argued for citizenship and its privileges for Native people without the erasure of Native cultures.

73. *American Indian Magazine* 4, no. 4 (1916): 326.

74. Lawrence Hauptman, "Governor Theodore Roosevelt and the Indians of New York State," *Proceedings of the American Philosophical Society* 119, no. 1 (1975): 1–7, 1.

75. Arthur C. Parker to Gertrude Bonnin, July 5, 1917, reel 1, SAI Papers.

76. Pratt, "The Indian? No Problem," paper read at the Women's New Century Club, Philadelphia, January 10, 1896, The Library Company, Philadelphia.

77. *American Indian Magazine* 6, no. 4 (Winter 1919): 160.

78. Reverend Coolidge made the motion to adopt Pratt at the SAI second meeting; the motion was seconded by Thomas Sloan. Arthur C. Parker interjected, "We do not need to adopt Gen. Pratt as an Indian, he is already one—none better," and then moved on to the business agenda. See *Quarterly Journal* 1, no. 2 (1913): 136, 137.

79. Qtd. in Russel Lawrence Barsh, "Progressive-Era Bureaucrats," 6; Robert G. Valentine, "Making Good Indians," 611.

80. Fred E. Parker, "The Indian as a Citizen" in *Proceedings of the Second Annual Conference of the Society of American Indians*, 138.

81. In the 1930s, commissioner of Indian Affairs John Collier formed the division of the Civilian Conservation Corps (CCC), which created jobs for Native men. John J. Laukaitis, "*Indians at Work* and John Collier's Campaign for Progressive Educational Reform, 1933–1945," *American Educational History Journal* 33, no. 2 (2006): 97–105.

82. Ackley and Stanciu, *Laura Cornelius Kellogg,* 159.

83. Most SAI members used the term "the Indian" most frequently, but they often referred to "the Indian race" or the "race," as Hertzberg observes. SAI members and Indian public intellectuals also used the phrases "our people" and "the Indian people," with the words "people" and "tribe" being synonymous occasionally. Hertzberg, *Search for an American Indian Identity,* 71.

84. Laura Cornelius [Kellogg], "Some Facts and Figures on Indian Education," in Ackley and Stanciu, *Laura Cornelius Kellogg,* 154–66.

85. Ibid., 163.

86. Immigration Act of 1907, section 2.

87. Priscilla Wald, "Communicable Americanism: Contagion, Geographic Fictions, and the Sociological Legacy of Robert E. Park," *American Literary History* 14, no. 4 (Winter 2002): 653–85, 654. See also Kraut, *Silent Travelers*, 4; Child, *Boarding School Seasons*, 55–58. Adams, *Education for Extinction*, 133–34.

88. Arthur C. Parker, "The Editor's Viewpoint: What Makes the Indian a Problem?" *Quarterly Journal* 1, no.2 (1913): 105.

89. Mirel, *Patriotic Pluralism*, 37–44.

90. Arthur C. Parker, "The White Aryan and the Red American," *American Indian Magazine* 4, no. 2 (April–June 1916): 121–26, quotes on 124, 126. Joseph P. Widney, *Race Life of the Aryan Peoples* (Funk and Wagnalls, 1907).

91. Arthur C. Parker, "The Editor's Viewpoint: What Makes the Indian a Problem?" *Quarterly Journal* 1, no. 2 (1913): 104–7, quotes on 106, 105, and 104.

92. Arthur C. Parker, "Problems of Race Assimilation: With Special Reference to the American Indian," *American Indian Magazine* 4, no. 2 (1916): 285–304, quotes on 285, 299, and 290.

93. Ibid., quotes on 303.

94. On the legal construction of race in the United States, see Ian Lopez, *White by Law.*

95. Gertrude Bonnin, "Editorial Comment," *American Indian Magazine* 7, no. 2 (Summer 1919): 63, emphasis added.

96. Parker, "What Makes the Indian a Problem?," 105; Barsh, "Progressive-Era Bureaucrats," 2–3.

97. Gertrude Bonnin, "Editorial Comment," *American Indian Magazine* 7, no. 2 (1919): 63.

98. Gertrude Bonnin, "Americanize the First American." The cover sheet of the pamphlet included a picture of Bonnin framed by a number of American flags. Papers of Mary Walden, Special Collections, Newberry Library, Chicago.

99. See Cathleen D. Cahill, *Recasting the Vote: How Women of Color Transformed the Suffrage Movement* (University of North Carolina Press, 2020).

100. P. Jane Hafen, introduction to *Dreams of Thunder: Stories, Poems, and the Sun Dance Opera by Zitkala-Ša* (University of Nebraska Press, 2001), xxi, xvii.

101. Congress selected the "Star-Spangled Banner" as the national anthem in 1931. On the cultural history of the song, see Robert J. Branham and Stephen J. Hartnett, *Sweet Freedom's Song: 'My Country 'Tis of Thee' and Democracy in America* (Oxford University Press, 2002), 14–34.

102. W. E. B. DuBois, "My Country 'Tis of Thee," Poetry Foundation, https://www.poetryfoundation.org/poems/43026/my-country-tis-of-thee.

103. Samuel Francis Smith, "America"/"My Country 'Tis of Thee," first performed on July 4, 1831, in Boston. See https://www.loc.gov/item/ihas.200000012/.

104. Gertrude Bonnin, "The Red Man's America," *American Indian Magazine* 5, no. 1 (January–March 1917): 64.

105. Here I draw on the Montezuma Papers at the Newberry Library and his editorials and letters from Native communities, reprinted in *Wassaja.*

106. Pratt to Carlos Montezuma, August 27, 1902, box 3, folder 153, Carlos Montezuma Papers, Newberry Library.

107. Pratt Papers, box 10—General Correspondence and Official Papers, folder 342.

108. Pratt, "Speech Given before the Baptists, 1904," Pratt Papers, box 19, folder 653.

109. Quoted in Robert A. Trennert, "From Carlisle to Phoenix: The Rise and Fall of the Indian Outing System, 1878–1930," *Pacific Historical Review,* 52, no. 3 (1983): 267.

110. Pratt to the Friends of Indian Education, June 1881, Pratt Papers, box 10, folder 342.

111. Kiara Vigil, *Indigenous Intellectuals: Sovereignty, Citizenship, and the American Imagination, 1880–1930* (Cambridge University Press, 2015), 101–64. Other recent relevant studies of Montezuma's work include: Rochelle R. Zuck, "'Yours in the Cause': Readers, Correspondents, and the Editorial Politics of Carlos Montezuma's *Wassaja*," *American Periodicals* 22, no. 1 (2012): 72–93; Julianne Newmark, "A Prescription for Freedom: Carlos Montezuma, *Wassaja*, and the Society of American Indians," *Studies in American Literature* 25, no. 2/*American Indian Quarterly* 37, no. 3 (Summer 2013): 139–58; David Martinez, "Carlos Montezuma's Fight against 'Bureauism': An Unexpected Pima Hero," *Studies in American Literature* 25, no. 2/*American Indian Quarterly* 37, no. 3 (Summer 2013): 311–30.

112. Montezuma died the year before Native people were granted blanket citizenship by the Indian Citizenship Act of 1924.

113. Hertzberg, *Search for an American Indian Identity*, 44.

114. Montezuma, "Reservation Is Fatal," 71.

115. "Arrow Points," *Wassaja* 1, no. 2 (1916): 3.

116. "Clear Cut Attitude of Procedure of the Society of American Indians at the Lawrence Conference as Seen by Wassaja," *Wassaja* 1, no. 2 (1916): 4.

117. Critics have called *Wassaja* a newspaper, a newsletter, a pamphlet, and a journal. I use newspaper, which is a more capacious term signaling the Native print culture tradition on which it builds.

118. Littlefield and Parins, *American Indian and Alaska Newspapers and Periodicals*, 385.

119. Lyons, "Rhetorical Sovereignty," 450–51.

120. "Introduction," *Wassaja* 1, no. 1 (1916): 1.

121. *Wassaja* 3, no. 2 (May 1918): 1.

122. Montezuma advertised *Wassaja* as "a little spicy newspaper," quoted in Maddox, *Citizen Indians*, 113.

123. Peter Iverson, *Carlos Montezuma and the Changing World of American Indians* (University of New Mexico Press, 1982), 101.

124. Pratt to Carlos Montezuma, November 22, 1906, box 3, folder 153, Carlos Montezuma Papers, Newberry Library.

125. Marianna Burgess to Carlos Montezuma, n.d., box 1, folder 25, Carlos Montezuma Papers, Newberry Library. Burgess was chief clerk, business manager, occasional co-editor, and superintendent of printing at Carlisle from the 1880s until 1904.

126. Montezuma, "The Reservation Is Fatal to the Development of Good Citizenship," *Quarterly Journal* 2, no. 1 (1914): 69–74, 71.

127. Montezuma, "Civilization," *Wassaja* 2, no. 1 (1917): 2–3.

128. Quoted in Iverson, *Carlos Montezuma and the Changing World of American Indians*, 38.

129. Montezuma used the language of his day referring to "the Indian race."

130. Ibid.

131. "Changing Is Not Vanishing," *Wassaja* 1, no. 4 (1916): 4.

132. "Arrow Points," *Wassaja* 1, no. 3 (1916): 4.

133. By 1918, more than ten thousand Native Americans had enrolled in the U.S. Army, 85 percent as volunteers, but Native soldiers were not granted Ameri-

can citizenship, by special act of Congress, until July 1919, months after their peer immigrant soldiers. See Montezuma, "The Indian Is Right," *Wassaja* 3, no. 7 (1918): 1; Holm, *Great Confusion in Indian Affairs,* 178; *Cohen's Handbook of Federal Indian Law,* 154.

134. Quoted in Cathleen D. Cahill, *Federal Fathers and Mothers: A Social History of the United States Indian Service, 1869–1933* (University of North Carolina Press, 2011), 231.

135. David Martinez, "Carlos Montezuma's Fight against 'Bureauism: An Unexpected Pima Hero," *Studies in American Indian Literatures* 25, no. 2/*American Indian Quarterly* 37, no. 3 (Summer 2013): 321, 311.

136. *Wassaja,* 1, no. 11 (1917): 1; *Wassaja* 1, no. 1 (1916): 1.

137. "I Have Stood Up for You" was not Montezuma's first stab at poetry. He published other poems in *Wassaja*: "Changing Is Not Vanishing," "Civilization," "Steady, Indians, Steady," "Indian Office," and "Indians Playing the Game." All these poems are collected and introduced in Robert Dale Parker, *Changing Is Not Vanishing,* 286–94.

138. Montezuma, "The Educators and the Indian Schools," *Wassaja* 1, no. 5 (1916): 2.

139. Ibid.

140. "Arrow Points," *Wassaja* 1, no. 6 (1916): 4.

141. "Arrow Points," *Wassaja* 1, no. 7 (1916): 4.

142. "This Indian Filed a Unique Claim for Exemption from the Draft," *Wassaja* 3, no. 3 (June 1918): 3.

143. "A Japanese Is Naturalized," *Wassaja* 3, no. 9 (December 1918): 2.

144. Kyle Mays, "Transnational Progressivism: African Americans, Native Americans, and the Universal Races Congress of 1911," *Studies in American Literature* 25, no. 2/*American Indian Quarterly* 37, no. 3 (2013): 244.

145. Carlos Montezuma to Joe Scheuerle, December 14, 1918, reel 4, Carlos Montezuma Papers, Newberry Library.

146. Maddox, *Citizen Indians,* 75.

147. See also Iverson, *Carlos Montezuma and the Changing World of American Indians,* 147–48.

148. *Wassaja* 2, no. 9 (1917): 4.

149. "Who Are the First Americans?" *Wassaja* 3, no. 1 (1918): 3.

150. John Larner, the editor of The Papers of Carlos Montezuma, calls *Wassaja* "his feisty monthly newsletter," Papers of Carlos Montezuma, reel 1. On Montezuma's legacy as a misunderstood editor, see Zuck, "'Yours in the Cause,'" 72–93.

151. *Wassaja* 1, no. 6 (1916): 1.

152. "Indian This and Indian That," *Wassaja* 1, no. 11 (1917): 3.

153. *Wassaja* 1, no. 12 (1917): 1.

CHAPTER 6. "THIS WAS AMERICA!"

1. The tone of Cahan's advice column in the *Forverts/The Forward,* "Bintel Brief," changed post–World War I, away from praising Americanization and toward cultural pluralism. Mihãilescu, *Eastern European Jewish American Narratives, 1880–1930* (Lexington Books, 2018), 28.

2. Anzia Yiezierska, *Bread Givers* (Persea, 1999 [1925]), chap. 16.

3. In *The Promised Land*, Antin recounts an encounter with a wooden Indian in front of a cigar store in Boston and the storekeeper's warning: "look out for wild Indians!" (chap. 17).

4. Sidonie Smith and Julia Watson, *Reading Autobiography: A Guide for Interpreting Life Narratives*, 2nd ed. (University of Minnesota Press, 2010), 123–24.

5. Sollors, qtd. in Thomas Ferraro, *Ethnic Passages: Literary Immigrants in Twentieth-Century America* (University of Chicago Press, 1993), 6.

6. In the 1910s Ravage attended the graduate program in English at the flagship university in Illinois—a university whose corridors this writer also walked a century after Ravage. The annual reports of the commissioner general of immigration record that immigration from Romania began in 1881, with eleven immigrants; the first Jewish immigrants from Romania were recorded in 1872. Sherban Drutzu and Andrei Popovici, *Românii in America [The Romanians in America]* (Cartea Românească, 1926), 234–35.

7. Obituary, *New York Times* (October 12, 1965): 47.

8. The second, expanded edition appeared in 1935; the third edition, with a preface by Louise Ravage Tresfort, the writer's daughter, in 1971; a fourth edition, edited by Steven Kellman, in June 2009.

9. The "Postscript—Twenty Years Later" was added to all subsequent editions.

10. *An American in the Making*, 204.

11. Ibid., 130–31.

12. A host of later memoirs gave the genre wider representation and legitimacy in the literary market: Edward Bok, *The Americanization of Edward Bok* (1920), Constantine Panunzio, *The Soul of an Immigrant* (Macmillan, 1921); Michael Pupin, *From Immigrant to Inventor* (Scribner's, 1923); Abraham Cahan, *The Education of Abraham Cahan* (Jewish Publication Society of America, 1969 [1925]); Bok's and Pupin's memoirs received the Pulitzer Prize (in 1921 and 1924, respectively).

13. Suzanne Clausen Ravage, *Growing Up Rootless* (Fithian Press, 1995), 11.

14. Albert Shaw, "Review of An American in the Making," *American Review of Reviews: An International Magazine* 56 (1917): 664.

15. Park, "Review of *An American in the Making*," 839.

16. I develop this argument further in "Marcus E. Ravage's *An American in the Making*, Americanization, and New Immigrant Representation," *MELUS: Multi-Ethnic Literatures of the United States* 40, no. 2 (2015): 7.

17. Smith and Watson, *Reading Autobiography*, 123–24.

18. Riis, *Making of an American*, 421.

19. Ibid., 437.

20. Ravage, *American in the Making*, 135.

21. Ibid., 7.

22. Ibid., 47–48.

23. Ibid., 51.

24. Ibid., 100.

25. Antin, *Promised Land*, xi.

26. Ravage, *American in the Making*, 8 and 17.

27. For a detailed account of the new immigrants' return to Europe, see Wyman, *Round-Trip to America: The Immigrants Return to Europe, 1880–1930* (Cornell University Press, 1996) and Zeidel, *Immigrants, Progressives, and Exclusion Politics*, esp. 51–67. Zeidel refers to returning immigrants as "birds of passage" (51).

28. Wald, "Communicable Americanism," 665.

29. Klein, *Foreigners*, 20. As Matthew F. Jacobson has shown, the Yiddish community in the U.S. "developed its own, distinctly American themes and styles" from the Yiddish theater to literary production (Abraham Cahan, Morris Rosenfeld, or Leon Korbin). Jacobson, *Special Sorrows*, 95–96.

30. Antin, *Promised Land*, xi; Ravage, *American in the Making*, 9.

31. Ravage, *American in the Making*, 8, quote on 7.

32. Ibid., 7.

33. Broughton Brandenburg posed as an Italian immigrant, a story recounted in *Imported Americans: The Story of The Experiences of a Disguised American and His Wife Studying the Immigration Question* (Stokes, 1904).

34. Ferraro, "Ethnicity and the Marketplace," *Columbia History of the American Novel*, ed. Emory Elliot (Columbia University Press, 1991), 382.

35. Jacobson, *Special Sorrows*, 96–97.

36. Steven G. Kellman, introduction to M. E. Ravage, *An American in the Making: The Life Story of an Immigrant* (Rutgers University Press, 2009), xiv.

37. Wald, "Communicable Americanism," 654.

38. Ravage, *American in the Making*, 139.

39. Ibid., 142, 144.

40. "An American in the Making," *Evening Missourian* (November 16, 1917): 4.

41. Maria Lauret, "When Is an Immigrant's Autobiography Not an Immigrant Autobiography? *The Americanization of Edward Bok*," *MELUS* 38, no. 3 (2013): 7.

42. Leslie J. Vaughn, "Cosmopolitanism, Ethnicity, and American Identity: Randolph Bourne's 'Trans-National America,'" *Journal of American Studies* 25, no. 3 (1991): 443–59.

43. Kallen, "Democracy versus the Melting-Pot," 220. See also Daniel Greene, *The Jewish Origins of Cultural Pluralism: The Menorah Association and American Diversity* (Indiana University Press, 2011).

44. Ravage, *American in the Making*, 140, 141, quote on 167.

45. Bourne, "Trans-National America," 89, 93.

46. Ravage, *American in the Making*, 63.

47. Mirel, *Patriotic Pluralism*, 5.

48. Aneta Pavlenko documents the low attendance of Americanization classes and the coercion of non-English-speaking immigrants to attend public schools: "More than thirty states passed Americanization laws which obligated aliens unable to speak or read English to attend public evening schools. . . . Thirty-four states also passed official English-language policies which declared English the only language of instruction and effectively closed most bilingual and native language programs." "'Ask Each Pupil about Her Methods of Cleaning': Ideologies of Language

and Gender in Americanisation Instruction (1900–1924)," *International Journal of Bilingual Education and Bilingualism* 8, no. 4 (2005): 275–97, 279, 289.

49. Ravage, *American in the Making*, 61.

50. Kallen, "Democracy versus the Melting-Pot," 193.

51. Sau-Ling Cynthia Wong, "Immigrant Autobiography: Some Questions of Definition and Approach," *American Autobiography: Retrospect and Prospect* (University of Wisconsin Press, 1991), 142. See also Richard Tuerk, "At Home in the Land of Columbus: Americanization in European-American Immigrant Autobiography," *Multicultural Autobiography: American Lives*, ed. James Robert Payne (University of Tennessee Press, 1992), 136.

52. Gerstle, "Liberty, Coercion, and the Making of Americans," 558.

53. Qtd. in Mihăilescu, *Eastern European Jewish American Narratives*, 117.

54. Park, "Review of *An American in the Making*," *American Journal of Sociology* 23, no. 6 (May 1918): 838.

55. David M. Fine calls *The Rise of David Levinsky* "the most important novel written by a Jewish immigrant" and H. L. Mencken refers to it as "one of the best American novels ever written." Qtd. in Lipsky, "Introduction," *The Rise of David Levinsky* (Modern Library, 2001 [1917]), xi–xix, xviii. See also David M. Fine, "In the Beginning: American Jewish Fiction, 1880–1930," *Handbook of American Jewish Literature: An Analytical Guide to Topics, Themes, and Sources*, ed. Lewis Fried (Greenwood Press, 1988), 16.

56. Howells's enthusiasm for *The Rise of David Levinsky* was less intense than his praise of Cahan's previous work. Qtd. in Chametzky, *From the Ghetto: The Fiction of Abraham Cahan* (University of Massachusetts Press, 1977), 68–69.

57. Randolph Bourne, "Americans in the Making," *New Republic* 14, no. 170 (1918): 30. On the costs of the immigrant capitalist's Americanization, see Eli Lederhendler's *Jewish Immigrants and American Capitalism, 1880–1920: From Caste to Class* (Cambridge University Press), 2009.

58. From October 1905 to the end of 1906, "pogroms had devastated 661 towns, killed 985 people, widowed 387 women, and orphaned 177 children." Zeidel, *Immigrants, Progressives, and Exclusion Politics*, 61.

59. Glazer, *American Judaism* (University of Chicago Press, 1957), 61.

60. Cahan, *Rise of David Levinsky*, 60.

61. On the genealogy of the Jewish American novel, see Derek Parker Royal, "Plotting a Way Home: The Jewish American Novel," *A Companion to the American Novel*, 1st ed., ed. Alfred Bendixen (Wiley and Sons, 2012), 241–58.

62. Ibid., 244.

63. Ravage, *American in the Making* 31; Bourne, "Americans in the Making," 30.

64. Sanford E. Marovitz, "*The Rise of David Levinsky*," *Abraham Cahan* (Twayne, 1996), 162.

65. Chametzky, *From the Ghetto*, viii.

66. The title of Cahan's new novel would have been *The Chasm*. Jules Chametzky speculates that Cahan never completed *The Chasm* because he found it difficult to reconcile his old and new experiences in literary form: "The chasm was wider than Cahan had sometimes thought and to bridge it more difficult than he expected" (75).

67. Moses Rishkin, ed. *Grandma Never Lived in America: The New Journalism of Abraham Cahan* (Indiana University Press, 1985), xvii.

68. Chametzky, *From the Ghetto,* 115.

69. Steven Diner, *A Very Different Age: Americans of the Progressive Era* (Hill and Wang, 1998), 99.

70. Chametzky, *From the Ghetto,* 54.

71. Park, *The Immigrant Press and Its Control,* 55, 5.

72. Qtd. in Jacobson, *Special Sorrows,* 50.

73. *McClure's* initially announced this forthcoming story as "The Confessions of an American Jew," a title Abraham Cahan changed later to "The Autobiography of an American Jew." Cahan, "The Autobiography of an American Jew," *McClure's* (April 1917): 92–106, 92–93.

74. Burton J. Hendrick, "The Jewish Invasion of America," *McClure's* 40 (March 1913): 165.

75. Ibid., 125.

76. Marovitz, "*Rise of David Levinsky,*" 136.

77. Kaplan, *Social Construction of American Realism,* 21–22.

78. Cahan, "Autobiography of an American Jew," 92–93.

79. Jacobson, *Special Sorrows,* 96.

80. Cahan, *Rise of David Levinsky,* 194.

81. Ibid., 164.

82. Ibid., 101.

83. Warren Hoffman, "The Rise and Fall of David Levinsky: Performing Jewish American Heterosexuality," *Modern Fiction Studies* 51, no. 2 (Summer 2005): 393–415, 394–97, quote on 394.

84. Cahan, *Rise of David Levinsky,* 318, 329.

85. Kallen, "Democracy versus Melting Pot," 220.

86. Catherine Rottenberg, "Race and and Ethnicity in *The Autobiography of an Ex-Colored Man* and *The Rise of David Levinsky:* The Performative Difference," *MELUS: Multi-Ethnic Literatures of the United States* 29, nos. 3/4 (2004): 312; Cahan, *Rise of David Levinsky,* 312–13.

87. Homi K. Bhabha, *The Location of Culture* (Routledge, 1994), 86–89.

88. Cahan, *Rise of David Levinsky,* 182.

89. Ibid., 260.

90. Rottenberg, "Race and and Ethnicity," 317–18.

91. Donald Weber, "Outsiders and Greenhorns: Christopher Newman in the Old World, David Levinsky in the New," *American Literature* 67, no. 4 (1995): 734.

92. Cahan, *Rise of David Levinsky,* 126, 135, 171.

93. Ibid., 518.

94. Bourne, "Americans in the Making," 30.

95. Cahan, *Rise of David Levinsky,* 284.

96. A case in point is Henry Holt, *Life Stories by Undistinguished Americans* (1906).

97. Ferraro, *Ethnic Passages,* 7.

98. Jacobson, *Special Sorrows,* 96–97.

99. Marovitz, "*Rise of David Levinsky,*" 108

100. James, *American Scene*, 131.

101. Lipsky, "Introduction," *Rise of David Levinsky*, xii–xiii.

102. Ferraro, *Ethnic Passages*, 10.

103. Pavlenko, "Making of an American," 49.

Chapter 7. Spectacular Nationalism

Epigraph: Rpt. in Richard Abel, *The Red Rooster Scare: Making Cinema American, 1900–1910* (University of California Press, 1999), 20.

1. Richard Abel, Giorgio Bertellini, and Rob King, "Introduction," *Early Cinema and the "National"* (John Libbey, 2008), 1–2; Bertellini, *Italy in Early American Cinema: Race, Landscape, and the Picturesque* (Indiana University Press, 2010), 1–18.

2. On the institutionalization of educational cinema in the 1910s and 1920s, see Marina Dahlquist and Joel Frykholm, "Introduction," *The Institutionalization of Educational Cinema: North America and Europe in the 1910s and 1920s*, ed. Marina Dahlquist (Indiana University Press, 2020). Dahlquist and Joel Frykholm reveal "the social and political roles cinema has played historically" (1–2).

3. Ahmed, *Cultural Politics of Emotion*, 2nd ed., 8–9.

4. Gary Gerstle, "Liberty, Coercion, and the Making of Americans," *Journal of American History* 84, no. 2 (September 1997): 524–58, quote on 558.

5. Bertellini, *Italy in Early American Cinema*, 280.

6. Miriam Hansen, *Babel and Babylon: Spectatorship in American Silent Film* (Harvard University Press, 1991), 76.

7. Giorgio Bertellini, "National and Racial Landscapes and the Photographic Form," in *Early Cinema and the "National,"* 27–41, 30–32.

8. Bertellini, *Italy in Early American Cinema*, 27, 10.

9. Sabine Haenni, *The Immigrant Scene: Ethnic Amusements in New York, 1880–1920* (University of Minnesota Press, 2008), 194.

10. Bertellini, "National and Racial Landscapes and the Photographic Form," 29–45.

11. I develop this argument in "Making Americans: Spectacular Nationalism, Americanization, and Silent Film," *Journal of American Studies* 56, no. 2 (May 2022). Dahlquist and Frykholm, "Introduction," 1. Katy Peplin, "Ford Films and Ford Viewers: Examining 'Nontheatrical' Films in the Theatres and Beyond," in *The Institutionalization of Educational Cinema: North America and Europe in the 1910s and 1920s*, ed. Marina Dahlquist (Indiana University Press, 2020), 201–19, 202–3; Gregory A. Waller, "Institutionalizing Educational Cinema in the United States during the Early 1920s," 220–47, 220; Bertellini, *Italy in Early American Cinema*, 280.

12. See especially Guglielmo, *White on Arrival*; Roediger, *Working toward Whiteness*; Jacobson, *Whiteness of a Different Color*; James R. Barrett, "Americanization from the Bottom Up: Immigration and the Remaking of the Working Class in the United States, 1880–1930," *Journal of American History* 79, no. 3 (1992): 996–1020; and James R. Barrett, *History from the Bottom Up and the Inside Out: Ethnicity, Race, and Identity in Working-Class History* (Durham: Duke University Press, 2017).

13. Guglielmo, *White on Arrival*, 5–6.

14. Film historian Kevin Brownlow makes a similar argument in *Behind the Mask of Innocence: Sex, Violence, Prejudice, and Crime: Films of Social Conscience in the Silent Era* (Knopf, 1990), 308.

15. Richard Abel, *Red Rooster Scare*, xi.

16. Charney and Schwartz, "Introduction," *Cinema and the Invention of Modern Life*, ed. Leo Charney and Vanessa R. Schwartz (University of California Press, 1995), 1–14; Dahlquist and Frykholm, "Introduction," 1.

17. Waller, "Institutionalizing Educational Cinema in the United States during the Early 1920s," 220.

18. Abel, *Red Rooster Scare*, 11–14, quote on 14.

19. Steven J. Ross, "American Workers, American Movies: Historiography and Methodology," *International Labor and Working-Class History* 59 (Spring 2001): 81–105, 86.

20. On the nickelodeon boom in Manhattan and the ethnic composition of its audience in the early 1900s, see Ben Singer, "Manhattan Nickelodeons: New Data on Audiences and Exhibitors," *Cinema Journal* 34, no. 3 (Spring 1995): 5–35; on film, urban progressivism, and modern leisure, see Lary May, *Screening Out the Past: The Birth of Mass Culture and the Motion Picture Industry* (University of Chicago Press, 1980). On exhibition venues and spectatorship, see also Richard Allen, *Projecting Illusion: Film Spectatorship and the Impression of Reality* (Cambridge University Press, 1997); Charles Musser, *The Emergence of Cinema: The American Screen to 1907* (University of California Press, 1990); Patrick Mullins, "Ethnic Cinema in the Nickelodeon Era in New York City: Commerce, Assimilation, and Cultural Identity," *Film History* 12, no. 1 (2000): 115–24; and Richard Butsch, *The Citizen Audience: Crowds, Publics, and Individuals* (Routledge, 2009).

21. Hansen, *Babel and Babylon*, 255; Sharon S. Kleinman and Daniel G. McDonald, "Silent Film and the Socialization of America: Lessons from an Old New Medium," *Journal of American and Comparative Cultures* 23, no. 3 (Fall 2000): 79–87, 81.

22. Michael M. Davis Jr., *The Exploitation of Pleasure: A Study of Commercial Recreations in New York City* (Russell Sage Foundation, 1911), 22–24.

23. Editorial, "Favorable Comment on Moving Pictures by Civic Authorities," *Moving Picture World* 7 (July 2, 1910): 13.

24. Ernest Dench, "Americanizing Foreigners by Motion Pictures," *Motion Picture Education* (Cincinnati: Standard Publishing, 1917), 195–97, 196.

25. Ibid., 196–99.

26. Mayfield Bray, *Guide to the Ford Film Collection in the National Archives* (1970). Also available here: https://ia800504.us.archive.org/24/items/guidetoford filmcoobrayrich/guidetofordfilmcoobrayrich.pdf. The film *English School* (1918) is referenced on p. 65. Accessed July 11, 2021.

27. Stephen Meyer, "Adapting the Immigrant to the Line: Americanization in the Ford Factory, 1914–1921," *Journal of Social History* 14, no. 1 (1980): 69.

28. Ibid., 77.

29. Loizides, "'Making Men' at Ford," 116.

30. Lee Grieveson, "The Work of Film in the Age of Fordist Mechanization," *Cinema Journal* 51, no. 3 (Spring 2012): 25–51, 26.

31. David L. Lewis, *The Public Image of Henry Ford: An American Folk Hero and His Company* (Wayne State University Press, 1973), 115. Grieveson, "Visualizing Industrial Citizenship," *Learning with the Lights Off: Educational Film in the United States*, ed. Devin Orgeron, Marsha Orgeron, and Dan Streible (Oxford University Press, 2012), 107–23, esp. 112–13.

32. *Henry Ford,* PBS, "American Experience," 2013, documents Ford's antisemitism, which also included antisemitic pieces in one of his newspapers, the *Dearborn Independent.*

33. Qtd. in Grieveson, "Work of Film in the Age of Fordist Mechanization," 29.

34. Lee Grieveson has shown that there were two trends in the production of pedagogic films at Ford: the Ford ideal in manufacturing and the social and industrial welfare. Ibid., 27, 30

35. Ibid., 26, 29.

36. Bray, *Guide to the Ford Film Collection in the National Archives,* Publication No. 70–6 (National Archives, 1970), 70.

37. Esther Everett Lape, "The 'English First' Movement in Detroit," *Immigrants in America Review* 1, no. 3 (September 1915): 47. Hartman, *Movement to Americanize the Immigrant,* 128.

38. Grieveson, "Work of Film in the Age of Fordist Mechanization," 28.

39. Ibid., 27.

40. Ibid., 46–47, quote on 46.

41. Meyer, "Adapting the Immigrant to the Line," 79.

42. *An American in the Making,* filmed by Carl L. Gregory of the Thanhouser Film Corporation.

43. Scott Simmon, "Program Notes," *Treasures III: Social Issues in American Film, 1900–1934* (National Film Preservation Foundation, 2007), 122.

44. The number of Hungarian immigrants who came to the U.S. between the 1890s and 1914 is estimated to be around 450,000, https://www.filmpreservation.org/sponsored-films/screening-room/an-american-in-the-making-1913, accessed February 12, 2021.

45. Hill, "Americanization Movement," 612–16.

46. In December 2005, *The Making of an American* was added to the National Film Registry, https://www.loc.gov/item/mbrs00016771/, accessed February 12, 2021.

47. Archivist Mark H. Jones, whose research was used in Northeast Historic Film's preparation of this film edition, found these documents in the Connecticut state archives. Author's correspondence with Northeast Historic Film Archivists, September 2009.

48. "Movies Will Aid Work of Making Good Americans" [1919?], newspaper clipping, NARA RG 85, Records of the Immigration and Naturalization Service, Education and Americanization Files, 1914–1936, box 20.

49. Newsletter No. 5, "Americanization, Naturalization, and Citizenship," Chicago, May 26, 1919, NARA, RG 85, box 1596, folder 27671/7216.

50. "Americanization in Industries," *Proceedings of the National Conference on Americanization Industries.* Boston, June 22–24, 1919, 33–37, 88.

51. Grieveson, "Work of Film," 25.

52. George Kleine to Kendal Banning, director of Division of Pictures, Washington, DC, July 4, 1917. George Kleine Papers, Library of Congress, box 65.

53. "The Immigrant and the 'Movies': A New Kind of Education," *Touchstone and the American Art Student Magazine* 7, no. 1 (1920): 327–28.

54. "National Film States Plans: Will Picture Eight Popular Magazine Tales Which Will Push Americanization," *Motion Picture News* (1920): 650.

55. "Land of Opportunity," *Motion Picture News* (1920): 1279.

56. "Realart Pushes Americanization," *Motion Picture News* (1920): 1681.

57. "Broadway Houses Book Selznick Picture," *Motion Picture News* 19 (1920):1873.

58. "News from Correspondents," *Motion Picture News* 19 (February 21, 1920): 1878. Steven J. Ross, *Working-Class Hollywood: Silent Film and the Shaping of Class in America* (Princeton University Press, 1998), quotes on 130–31.

59. George Kleine Papers, Library of Congress, box 1, folder "The Americanism Committee of the Motion Picture Industry of the United States," 1920.

60. George Kleine to Kendal Banning, director of Division of Pictures, Washington, DC, July 4, 1917. George Kleine Papers, Library of Congress, box 65.

61. Ross, *Working Class Hollywood*, 129.

62. Richard Abel, "The Cinema of Attractions in France, 1896–1904," in *The Silent Cinema Reader*, ed. Lee Grieveson and Peter Krämer (Routledge, 2004), 70.

63. Alison McMahan, *Alice Guy Blaché: Lost Visionary of Cinema* (Continuum, 2002).

64. Blaché made all of Gaumont's films in Paris between 1896–1906 before becoming the head of Solax in New Jersey. Richard Abel, *Americanizing the Movies and "Movie Mad" Audiences, 1910–1914* (University of California Press, 2006), 246.

65. Gwendolyn A. Foster, *Performing Whiteness: Postmodern Re/Constructions in the Cinema* (SUNY Press, 2003), 54–57.

66. From 1916–1917, Chaplin was hired by Mutual, where he made *The Immigrant*, along with eleven other two-reel films. Theodore Huff, *The Early Work of Charles Chaplin*, 2nd ed. (BFI, 1961).

67. Chaplin returned to the U.S. only once, in 1972, when he received his Academy Award for Outstanding Career Achievement.

68. A brief version of Chaplin's FBI file is now available at http://www.paperless archives.com/chaplin.html, accessed February 12, 2021.

69. On immigrant spectatorship, see Judith Mayne, "Immigrants and Spectators," *Wide Angle* 5, no. 2 (1982): 32–40; Abel, *Americanizing the Movies and "Movie Mad" Audiences*; Melvyn Stokes and Richard Maltby, *American Movie Audiences: From the Turn of the Twentieth Century to the Early Sound Era* (BFI, 1999).

70. In 1998, *The Immigrant* was selected for preservation in the U.S. National Film Registry by the Library of Congress as "culturally, historically, or aesthetically significant." http://www.filmsite.org/filmreg.html.

71. Edna Purviance starred as Chaplin's leading lady in thirty-five films he made between 1915 and 1923.

72. See Andrew Higson, "The Concept of National Cinema," *Screen* 30, no. 4 (Autumn 1989): 36–47.

73. Kleinman and McDonald, "Silent Film and the Socialization of America," 83–84; Marina Dahlquist, "Teaching Citizenship via Celluloid," in *Early Cinema and the "National,"* ed. Richard Abel, Giorgio Bertellini, and Rob King (John Libbey, 2008), 118.

74. Ross, *Working-Class Hollywood,* xiii.

75. Mayne, "Immigrants and Spectators," 38–40, quote on 39.

76. Bertellini, *Italy in Early American Cinema* 27, 10. See also Charles R. Acland and Haidee Wasson, "Introduction: Utility and Cinema," *Useful Cinema* (Duke University Press, 2011), 1–14.

CHAPTER 8. FROM "VANISHING INDIANS" TO "REDSKINS"

1. Beverly Singer, *Wiping the War Paint Off the Lens: Native American Film and Video* (University of Minnesota Press, 2001), 14.

2. Robert F. Berkhofer, *The White Man's Indian: Images of the American Indian from Columbus to the Present* (Vintage, 1979), 3.

3. Philip Deloria, *Indians in Unexpected Places* (University of Kansas Press, 2004), 54.

4. I use this italicized version to suggest the removal of the signifier *Indian* from the real conditions and lives of Indigenous peoples. See Gerald Vizenor, *Fugitive Poses: Native American Indian Scenes of Absence and Presence* (University of Nebraska Press, 1998), 35.

5. Film scholars estimate that close to 75 percent of silent films were lost due to the flammability of the nitrate film. Anthony Slide, *Nitrate Won't Wait: A History of Film Preservation in the United States* (McFarland, 2000), 5–6.

6. For Young Deer's genealogy, see Joseph A. Romeo's "The Moors of Delaware," http://www.moors-delaware.com/gendat/moors.aspx?Mode=Member&MemberID=J525J1876. See also Waggoner, *Starring Red Wing!: The Incredible Career of Lilian M. St. Cyr, the First Native American Film Star* (University of Nebraska Press, 2019).

7. Abel, *Red Rooster Scare,* 151–75.

8. Hearne, *Native Recognition,* 6–8.

9. Robert Stam and Ella Shohat, *Unthinking Eurocentrism: Multiculturalism and the Media* (Routledge, 1994), 118, Hearne, *Native Recognition,* 30, 40.

10. Buffalo Bill Cody's and white filmmakers' masculinist approaches to American identity were also part of late-nineteenth century discourse on *Indians*. See Gregory S. Jay, "'White Man's Book No Good': D. W. Griffith and the American Indian," *Cinema Journal* 39, no. 4 (2000): 7–9; Hearne, *Native Recognition,* 182.

11. Cristina Stanciu, "'The Last Indian' Syndrome Revisited: *Metamora*, Take Two," *Intertexts* 10.1 (2006): 26–27.

12. Journalist Mary Heaton Vorse documented this episode, quoted in Abel, *Red Rooster Scare,* 170 and 282 n. 141. See also Lewis E. Palmer, "The World in Motion," *Survey* 22 (1909): 355–65.

13. Quoted in Deloria, *Indians in Unexpected Places*, 62.

14. "Photographs: Entertainers and Native American Performers, 1923–1952 and undated," folder 4, E. M. Botsford Papers, Southwest Collection, Texas Tech University Lubbock. Botsford was a cowboy who performed in the Buffalo Bill Show, Pawnee Bill Show, and Miller Brothers 101 Ranch Show until the 1930s.

15. On the history of the Wild West shows, see L. G. Moses, *Wild West Shows and the Images of American Indians, 1883–1933* (University of New Mexico Press, 1996). Philip Deloria speculates that, on the Pine Ridge Reservation, "the most significant regular flow of money onto the reservation between 1883 and 1913 may have come from Lakota performers traveling nationally and internationally." *Indians in Unexpected Places*, 69.

16. Abel, *Red Rooster Scare*, 164–65.

17. Quoted in Abel, "Our Country/Whose Country?" 68.

18. Abel, *Red Rooster Scare*, 78–84, quote on 84.

19. For a relatively recent study of the misrepresentation of Native people in Hollywood films, see Peter C. Rollins and John E. O'Connor, eds., *Hollywood's Indian: The Portrayal of the Native American in Film* (University of Kentucky Press, 1998). For the popularity of the Westerns in Europe, see Abel, *Americanizing the Movies and "Movie-Mad" Audiences, 1910–1914*.

20. Richard Abel writes persuasively about the Western as "white supremacist entertainment" in "'Our Country/Whose Country?' The Americanization Project of the Early Westerns," in *Back in the Saddle: Again: New Essays on the Western*, ed. Edward Buscombe and Roberta Pearson (BFI, 1998), 77-95, esp. 81–83. For studies of the genre's revival, see Slotkin, *Gunfighter Nation and Jane Tompkins, West of Everything: The Inner Lives of Westerns* (Oxford University Press, 1992).

21. Andrew Brodie Smith, *Shooting Cowboys and Indians: Silent Western Films, American Culture, and the Birth of Hollywood* (University Press of Colorado, 2003), 6, 9, 37.

22. Ibid., 4.

23. Scott Simmon, *The Invention of the Western Film: A Cultural History of the Genre's First Half-Century* (Cambridge University Press, 2003); Abel, *Red Rooster Scare*, 152; Jay, "White Man's Book No Good," 2.

24. Luther Standing Bear, *My People, the Sioux*, 285.

25. *Motion Picture World*, 1911, qtd. in Raheja, *Reservation Reelism*, 41.

26. Gayatri C. Spivak, "Can the Subaltern Speak?" in Robert Dale Parker, *Critical Theory Reader*, 675–93.

27. Deloria, *Indians in Unexpected Places*, 80–94. According to Linda Waggoner, *Dove Eye's Gratitude* and *Red Wing's Gratitude* are no longer extant. The plot of *Red Wing's Gratitude* is from *The Film Index*, October 16, 1909. My gratitude to Linda Waggoner for her contributions to this paragraph. Correspondence with the author, August 2019.

28. Hansen, *Babel and Babylon*, 79–80.

29. Joanna Hearne, "Telling and Retelling in the 'Ink of Light': Documentary Cinema, Oral Narratives, and Indigenous Identities," *Screen* 47, no. 3 (2006): 307–8.

30. Although several films in the collection have been digitized, many of the films referenced or discussed in this chapter are still widely unavailable to audiences outside the Library of Congress.

31. Dippie, *Vanishing American,* 212.

32. "American Indian's History is Filmed," *Valdez Daily Prospector* (February 1917): 2.

33. "To Show Indian Pictures; Dr. Dixon to Lecture on *Romance of a Vanishing Race,*" *Evening Star* (May 24, 1917): 9.

34. On early Native performance and diplomacy, see Stephanie Fitzgerald, "'I Wunnatuckquannum, This Is My Hand," in *Native Acts: Indian Performance, 1603–1832,* ed. David Bellin and Laura L. Mielk (University of Nebraska Press, 2011), 145–68.

35. Dances such as the Scalp Dance, Sun Dance, and War Dance became criminal offenses according to the OIA "Rules Governing the Court of Indian Offenses," 1882. On the dance bans, see Gabriella Treglia, "Using Citizenship to Retain Identity: The Native American Dance Bans of the Later Assimilation Era, 1900–1933," *Journal of American Studies* 47, no. 3 (2013): 777–800.

36. Ellis, "We Don't Want Your Rations"; Rayna Green and John Troutman, "By the Waters of the Minnehaha: Music and Dance, Pageants and Princesses," *Away from Home: American Indian Boarding School Experiences, 1879–2000,* ed. Margaret L. Archuleta, Brenda J. Child, and K. Tsianina Lomawaima (Heard Museum, 2000), 60–83; Troutman, *Indian Blues,* 8.

37. *The Rodman Wanamaker Expedition of Citizenship to the American Indian,* 1913, running time: 26 minutes (Rich Heape Films, 2009).

38. *Indian School Day* (1898), Thomas A. Edison, Inc., restored by the Library of Congress in 1999, length: 49 seconds, https://www.loc.gov/item/00564534/, accessed February 12, 2021.

39. *Club Swinging at Carlisle Indian School* (Mutoscope, 1902), 1:59 minutes; cameraman: Arthur W. Marvin; copyright: American Mutoscope and Biograph Co., held at the Library of Congress.

40. Hearne, *Native Recognition,* 9–19.

41. *Iola's Promise* (Biograph, 1912); *Maya, Just an Indian* (Frontier, 1913).

42. Wolfe, "Settler Colonialism and the Elimination of the Native"; Joanna Hearne, "The Cross-Heart People: Race and Inheritance in the Silent Western," *Journal of Popular Film and Television* 30 (Winter 2003): 181–96, 182–83; Aleiss, *Making the White Man's Indian,* 13.

43. *The Scarlet West* (First National, 1925) has not survived in full, but the Library of Congress has the trailer available for viewing. Director John G. Adolfi; cast: Robert Frazer, Clara Bow. *Red Love* (Lowell Film Productions, 1925). Director: Edgar Lewis; story: L Case Russell.

44. Melvyn Stokes, *D. W. Griffith's The Birth of a Nation* (Oxford University Press, 2008), 236.

45. *The Indian* (1914) by Klaw and Erlanger, New York City. Cast: Linda Arvidson, Charles Perley, Alfred Paget, Bert Williams, Lewis Wells, Violet Reid.

46. Raheja, *Reservation Reelism,* 200.

47. Hearne, *Native Recognition,* 192–93. I am grateful to Linda Waggoner for pointing me to the larger arc of Young Deer's career, beyond his work in cross-racial romances. See Waggoner, *Starring Red Wing!*

48. Ernest Alfred Dench, "The Dangers of Employing Redskins as Movie Actors," *Making the Movies* (Macmillan, 1919), 92–95. Abel, "Our Country/Whose Country?" 81.

49. Waggoner, correspondence with the author.

50. Kevin Brownlow, *The War, the West, and the Wilderness* (Knopf, 1979), 331–34.

51. Although we cannot confirm all of Young Deer's production and directorial credits, *Moving Picture World* mentioned in 1912 that Young Deer completed his 100th film for Pathé. *Moving Picture World* (June 29, 1912): 1218. According to Angela Aleiss, approximatively 150 movies are attributed to Young Deer for Pathé's West Coast Studio. Aleiss, "Who Was the Real James Young Deer? The Mysterious Identity of the Pathé Producer Finally Comes to Light," *Bright Lights Film Journal* 80 (May 2013): 1-10, 8.

52. Aleiss, "Who Was the Real Young Deer?" 2–4.

53. On Lilian St. Cyr's artistic career and activism, see Linda Waggoner's biography, *Starring Red Wing!*

54. *Motion Picture World* (July 1, 1911): 1508.

55. On Young Deer's tortuous career, see Simmon, *Invention of the Western Film*, 30 and 303 n. 36; Aleiss, *Making the White Man's Indian,* 16; Aleiss, "Who Was the Real Young Deer?"; and Waggoner, *Starring Red Wing!*

56. Native directors, such as Victor Masayesva (*Imagining Indians*, 1991) and Chris Eyre (*Smoke Signals*, 1998), continue to critique the Western in their works. Hearne, "Cross-Heart People,"193.

57. Aleiss, *Making the White Man's Indian*, 1–2.

58. Simmon, "Program Notes," 70.

59. Although she was not the protagonist of *White Fawn's Devotion*, Princess Red Wing/Lilian St. Cyr was the protagonist of other films made by Pathé and Young Deer, for example, *The Red Girl and the Child* (1910).

60. Qtd. in Simmon, "Program Notes," 70.

61. The first feature-length Western is Cecil B. DeMille's *The Squaw Man* (1914), starring Lilian Margaret St. Cyr, uncredited, based on a melodrama of the same title from 1905.

62. According to Karen Shade, the film was found "completely intact in 2004 in North Carolina." The film (80-plus minutes) was acquired by the Oklahoma Historical Society and restored in 2012. "All Native Silent Film Restored, Screened," *Native American Times* 9 (November 2012): 1, 8.

63. *The Daughter of Dawn* was written by Myles and Richard Banks of the Texas Film Company and produced by Banks. It had a preview showing in Los Angeles after its completion in 1920 but was never released. The Library of Congress selected it to the National Film Registry in 2013.

64. David Yeagley (1951–2014), Comanche musician, wrote the film score, which was performed by students from Oklahoma City University.

65. Linda Sue Warner and John Wooley suggest that the love story originates in "an Old Comanche Legend" but the details of the original story are not available in these sources; Linda Sue Warner, "The Daughter of Dawn," in *Race in American*

Film: Voices and Visions That Shaped a Nation, ed. Daniel Bernardi and Michael Green (Greenwood Press, 2017), 213; John Wooley, *Shot in Oklahoma: A Century of Sooner State Cinema* (University of Oklahoma Press, 2011), 69.

66. Comanche composer David Yeagley opined: "There are the tribal struggles of a group. . . . An intertitle in the film refers to the archetypal love triangle, but that's a mistake. It's a quartet." Quoted in Wooley, *Shot in Oklahoma,* 71–72.

67. According to the original script, now at the Library of Congress, the film had 303 scenes. Leo Kelly, "*The Daughter of Dawn*: An Original Silent Film with an Oklahoma Indian Cast," *Chronicles of Oklahoma* (Fall 1999): 292; Hearne, *Native Recognition,* 112–14.

68. Quoted in Hearne, *Native Recognition,* 113.

69. Quoted in Kelly, "*Daughter of Dawn,*" 290, 292.

70. Kerry McQueeney, "Extraordinary 1920 Silent Film with All-Indian Cast Re-released after a Painstaking Restoration Project." *Daily Mail,* July 16, 2012, http://www.dailymail.co.uk/news/article-2174260/The-Daughter-Of-Dawn-Foot age-restored-1920-silent-film-Indian-cast.html, accessed February 12, 2021.

71. Hearne, *Native Recognition,* 114.

72. Kilpatrick, *Celluloid Indians,* xvi.

73. Harper and Brothers planned the publication of the book so that it would coincide with the release of the film but altered the book considerably after pressures from religious and social groups. Aleiss, *Making the White Man's Indian,* 35.

74. Ralph E. Friar and Natasha Friar, *The Only Good Indian . . . The Hollywood Gospel* (Drama Book Specialists, 1972).

75. Carl Sandburg, "Review of *Vanishing American,*" in *The Movies Are: Carl Sandburg's Film Reviews and Essays, 1920–1928,* ed. Arnie Bernstein (Lake Claremont, 2000), 301–2.

76. The cast also included Richard Dix (as Nophaie, the Navajo "warrior"), Lois Wilson (as the white teacher, or "White Desert Rose"), Noah Beery (the villain, i.e., the Indian agent), Malcolm McGregor, Shannon Day, Charley Crockett, Bert Woodruff, John Dillion, Dick Howard, and Bruce Gordon, as well as a large number of Navajos as extras.

77. Mordaunt Hall, "The American Indian," *New York Times* (October 16, 1926): 18.

78. Brownlow, *War, the West, and the Wilderness,* 344–45.

79. A Paramount publicity release also centered on Dix: "There is no greater story than the passing of the Indian. . . . The whisper of the winds of history was on it—Dix was amazing." Qtd. in Brownlow, *War, the West, and the Wilderness,* 344.

80. The review presented in great detail the lengthy process of production and noted that the filming of *The Vanishing American* "kept 500 whites on the Navajo Indian reservation, from 160 to 200 miles from a railroad, for four months, and brought 10,000 red men before cameras for the first time in their lives. "New Zane Grey Film Finished by Paramount," *Los Angeles Times,* 1925, A11.

81. Mordaunt Hall, "The Screen," *New York Times* (October 16, 1925): 18; Sandburg, "Review of *Vanishing American,*" 301.

82. Metcalfe, "Lo, the Poor Indian," 3.

83. Hall, "American Indian," 18.

84. The film featured Native Americans from the Soboba Reservation in San Jacinto, California. Linda Waggoner, correspondence with the author.

85. Grace Kingsley, "Richard Writes: Dix Tells of Adventures in the Desert," *Los Angeles Times* (July 18, 1925): 7.

86. Quoted in Brownlow, *War, the West, and the Wilderness*, 345.

87. In the restored version from 2000, the audience members clapped as the Native soldiers left the scene. This identification with the bravery of Native soldiers exemplifies, perhaps accurately, an instance of their desire to "play Indian." See *The Vanishing American*, color-tinted black and white, 108 minutes, not rated, Film Preservation Associates, distributed by Image Entertainment, 2000 [1925].

88. A longer version of this section appears as "Indigeneity on the Silver Screen: *The Vanishing American* (1925) and the Limits of 'Sympathetic' Representation" in a special issue on Indigeneity in *Acta Iassyensia Comparationis*, Fall 2021, 59–70.

89. On the role of television in shaping contemporary Native representations, and considering Native people actors, producers, and viewers of sitcoms as well as subjects of comedy, see Dustin Tahmakera, *Tribal Television: Viewing Native People in Sitcoms* (University of North Carolina Press, 2014).

90. Simmon, "Program Notes," 132–34.

91. This was Elizabeth Pickett's last screenplay for Hollywood, following a series of documentaries about the Pueblos she made in 1925. Elizabeth Pickett, *Redskin* (Grosset and Dunlap, 1929).

92. Chinle was established in 1910, close to Canyon de Chelly, where *Redskin* was filmed.

93. Quoted in Simmon, "Program Notes," 133.

94. The theme song of the film was also titled "Redskin," https://digitalcollections-baylor.quartexcollections.com/Documents/Detail/redskin-theme-song-of-the-paramount-picture-redskin/1128017?item=1223648, accessed November 12, 2021.

95. Aleiss, *Making the White Man's Indian*, 30.

96. Quoted in ibid., 180, n. 17.

97. Interview with Philip Sheuer, *Los Angeles Times*, February 17, 1929.

98. Child, *Boarding School Seasons*, 32.

99. Liza Black's *Picturing Indians: Native Americans in Film, 1941–1960* (University of Nebraska Press, 2020) recovers the work of the next generation of Native actors on and off screen in midcentury Hollywood Westerns.

100. Film critic Richard Abel calls the Western a "white supremacist entertainment" ("Our Country, Whose Country?" 81–83). The genre, although temporarily relegated to low-brow status by academics, has received new critical attention since the 1990s, with a renewed interest in the genre's ideological potential and its representation of gender norms.

CONCLUSION

1. John Higham, *Strangers in the Land: Patterns of American Nativism, 1860–1925* (Atheneum, 1972), 234.

2. Jacques Derrida, *Archive Fever: A Freudian Impression*. Trans. Eric Prenowitz (University of Chicago Press, 1995), 4.

3. Elizabeth Povinelli, "The Woman on the Other Side of the Wall: Archiving the Otherwise in Postcolonial Digital Archives," *Differences* 22, no. 1 (2011): 151.

4. Jennifer O'Neal, "'The Right to Know': Decolonizing Native American Archives," *Journal of Western Archives* 6, no. 1 (2015): 1–17, quote on 6. William T. Hagan, "Archival Captive: The American Indian," *American Archivist* 41, no. 2 (1978): 135–42.

5. The statue, "Ripples of Change," will include Laura Cornelius Kellogg, Harriet Tubman, Martha Coffin Wright, and Sojourner Truth. "Town of Seneca Falls Gifted New Suffragette Statue." November 18, 2020, https://www.prnewswire.com/news-releases/town-of-seneca-falls-gifted-new-suffrage-statue-301176354.html.

6. Mirel, *Patriotic Pluralism,* 10, 105.

7. Roediger, *Working toward Whiteness,* 9–10. Roediger writes about the centrality of race to the new immigrant experience. Although "race" and "ethnicity" were terms used interchangeably in the early decades of the twentieth century (he refers to Isaak Baer Berkson's *Theories of Americanization,* 1920, as "theories of ethnic adjustment"), Roediger shows how the new immigrants did not become "the white ethnics" until the 1970s, when *The Oxford English Dictionary* first used the term (18–27).

8. Brownlow, *Behind the Mask of Innocence,* 319.

9. Kleinman and McDonald, "Silent Film and the Socialization of America," 83–84; Dahlquist, "Teaching Citizenship via Celluloid," 118.

10. Mark Glancy, "Temporary American Citizens? British Audiences, Hollywood Films, and the Threat of Americanization in the 1920s," *Historical Journal of Film, Radio and Television* 26, no. 4 (October 2006): 461–84, quote on 465.

11. Lee Grieveson, "The Work of Film in the Age of Fordist Mechanization." *Cinema Journal* 51, no. 3 (Spring 2012): 25–51, 40.

12. Judith Mayne, "Immigrants and Spectators," *Wide Angle* 5, no. 2 (1982): 32–40, quote on 39.

13. Philip Deloria, *Indians in Unexpected Places* (University of Kansas Press, 2004), 54–55.

14. Close to thirty Native performers were credited in early twentieth-century films: Big Bear, Blue Eagle, Edward Little, Chief Many Treaties (William Hazlett), Nipo Strongheart, Molly Spotted Elk, Chief Thunder Cloud, Dove Eye Dark Cloud, White Eagle (Jack Miller), Chief Phillippi, Two Feathers, Little Thunder, Bog Moon, Daniel Yowlatchie, Luther Standing Bear, Jim Thorpe, Will Rogers, and others. Deloria, *Indians in Unexpected Places,* 78.

15. D. H. Lawrence, *Studies in Classic American Literature* (Viking, 1923), 36; Hearne, *Native Recognition,* 6–8.

16. Renato Rosaldo, "Imperialist Nostalgia," *Representations* 26 (1989): 107–22.

17. See Stanciu, "Native Acts, Immigrant Acts."

18. On counter-sovereignty as a mode of political authority, see Manu Karuka, *Empire's Tracks*; Lenard Monkman, "'No ban on stolen land,' say Indigenous activists in U.S," *CBC News,* February 2, 2017, https://www.cbc.ca/news/indigenous/indigenous-activists-immigration-ban-1.3960814, accessed July 19, 2021; this article also quotes Native historians and activists Nick Estes and Melanie Yazzie.

Acknowledgments

I OWE A large debt of intellectual and personal gratitude to a wonderful network of supporters—archivists, mentors, colleagues, friends, and family—incurred during the long process of researching and writing this book and I am happy to offer some words of gratitude here.

From its inception as a dissertation at the University of Illinois at Urbana-Champaign to its completion, this project benefited from the following generous fellowships: the Balch Institute for Ethnic Studies Fellowship, Historical Society of Pennsylvania; the Center for Democracy in a Multiracial Society Fellowship, University of Illinois; the Emerging Scholars Professional Development Fellowship, Association for the Study of American Indian Literatures; the Lauter-McDougal Dissertation Fellowship, University of Illinois; the Yiddish Summer Institute Award, Program in Jewish Culture and Society, University of Illinois; the Committee on Institutional Cooperation (CIC) Graduate Student Research Fellowship, Newberry Library; a Pre-Doctoral Fellowship in American Indian Studies, Michigan State University; the Monticello College Foundation Fellowship for Women, Newberry Library; the Reese Fellowship in American Bibliography and the History of the Book in the Americas, Beinecke Rare Book and Manuscript Library, Yale University; the American Association of University Women (AAUW) Postdoctoral Fellowship; a National Endowment for the Humanities (NEH) Summer Stipend Award; an Obama Fellowship, Johannes Gutenberg University, Mainz, Germany; and a Fulbright Scholar Award. Additionally, a seed award from the College of Humanities and Sciences at VCU and several research grants from the Humanities Research Center at VCU made archival trips to the National Archives, the Library of Congress, and New York Public Library possible. Three NEH summer institutes I attended also made access to archival materials possible, in addition to superb intellectual company and new friendships: "From Metacom to Tecumseh" (Newberry), "Bridging National Borderlands in North America" (Newberry), and "On Native Grounds" (Library of Congress); I would like to acknowledge all the fellow participants, teachers, and institute leaders Scott M. Stevens, Benjamin H. Johnson, Laraine Fletcher, and George Scheper.

Many thanks to the staff members at the Newberry Library (especially John Aubrey, Danny Greene, Patricia M. Norby, and Liesl Olson), the Beinecke Rare Book and Manuscript Library (especially George Miles), the Historical Society of Philadelphia, the Library Company, the University of Illinois Archives, the Barnard College Archives, the Henry Ford Archives, the Indiana University Museum of Archeology and Anthropology, the Temple University Libraries Special Collections, the New York Public Library Special Collections, and the Motion Picture, Broadcasting, and Recorded Sound Division (MBRS) at the Library of Congress.

At the University of Illinois, a number of wonderful mentors and colleagues in the Departments of English and History and the American Indian Studies Program provided a supportive environment and rigorous training. My dissertation committee has been generous beyond the call of duty: J. B. Capino, Gordon Hutner, William J. Maxwell, and my tireless dissertation director Robert Dale Parker—who still reads (a lot of) what I write and continues to send letters of recommendation for all fellowships imaginable. Bob Parker is the reason I am the scholar and writer I am today and I am grateful for his generous support over almost two decades. Additionally, a wonderful assembly of mentors inspired and supported me at Illinois: Kristina Ackley, Dale Bauer, Nina Baym, Jodi A. Byrd, Stephanie Foote, Fred Hoxie, LeAnne Howe, John and Kara McKinn, Bruce Michelson, Debbie Reese, David Roediger, Michael Rothberg, Siobhan Somerville, Julia A. Walker, and Robert Warrior. Michigan State University awarded me a full-year pre-doctoral fellowship in the American Indian Studies Program; the late Susan Applegate-Krouse was a wonderful mentor and friend during my stay in East Lansing, and Janis Fairbanks, Gordon Henry, Mindy Morgan, and Bill Penn were also gracious local hosts and interlocutors.

Valued colleagues at other institutions offered advice and read many chapter drafts. Ned Blackhawk has encouraged this work from its inception, through the CIC graduate student conferences held at the Newberry Library and across the Big Ten universities. The network that faculty in Native American and Indigenous Studies created for graduate students in the early 2000s has been truly generative of collaborations over the following decade(s). Fred Hoxie read drafts of this project and offered continued encouragement and feedback at all stages, from book proposal to final draft. I'm especially grateful to him for a class in Indigenous history, which I audited in graduate school at Illinois, and for all the professional advice over the years. Jackie Rand continues to be the mentor and friend I am grateful to have, who shows up at panels, reads drafts, and facilitates professional connections. Other scholars in Native American and Indigenous Studies I deeply admire have shaped my thinking and writing over the years: Chadwick Allen, Ned Blackhawk, A. LaVonne Brown-Ruoff, Kevin Bruyneel, Brenda Child, Jill Doerfler, Roxanne Dunbar-Ortiz, Joe Genetin-Pilawa, Mishuana Goeman, Joanna Hearne, Brian Hosmer, LeAnne Howe, Miranda Johnson, Manu Karuka, K. Tsianina Lomawaima, Drew Lopenzina, Mary Anne Lyons, Jean O'Brien, Beth Piatote, Mark Rifkin, Phillip H. Round, Oliver Scheiding, Siobhan Senier, Audra Simpson, Scott M. Stevens, David Stirrup, Robert Warrior, Kelly Wisecup, Hertha D. Sweet Wong, as well as the CIC consortium and later NAISA (Native American and Indigenous Studies Association) fellow graduate students, faculty, and (later) colleagues who supported and cheered me on at various stages of the project.

For their insightful feedback, I would also like to acknowledge the anonymous readers for Yale University Press. It has been a pleasure to work with a fantastic team at Yale University Press. I thank Adina Popescu-Berk and Sarah Miller, wonderful acquisitions editors, as well as Margaret Otzel and Ash Lago, for their guidance and their hard work on this book. Eliza Childs has been the best copy editor an author could hope for, and I thank her for her patience and guidance. I am immensely grateful to Ned Blackhawk, the series editor of the Henry Roe

Cloud Series on American Indians and Modernity at Yale University Press, for believing in this project from the start and for his continued support.

Other readers, interlocutors, and audiences deserve special thanks: Joel Pfister, who was a superb interlocutor and lunch companion during a month I spent doing research in New Haven; the late Alan Trachtenberg, whose belief in this project and phone calls meant the world to me; the late Jeffrey Mirel, who talked to me on the phone when I embarked on revising my dissertation into book form and offered great advice and encouragement; Barb Landis, archivist extraordinaire, for welcoming me to Carlisle, Pennsylvania, and for being a generous reader and supporting friend; Linda Waggoner and Clyde Ellis, whom I met at Carlisle Journeys, a conference Barb Landis organized in October 2014 at Carlisle, and who have been trusted readers and cheerleaders; Joanna Hearne, who generously read the film chapters during her Fulbright fellowship in Canada—such an act of generosity makes me hopeful for the future of academia; Phillip H. Round, who always reads very carefully and asks many insightful questions; the cohort of fellows at the Newberry— Mary Blaine Campbell, Tobias Higbie, Margaret Meserve, Phillip H. Round, Michael Schreffler—who commented on earlier drafts; J. B. Capino, who offered expert advice on the film chapters and treated me to yummy meals in Chicago and Champaign; and Bob Parker, who read everything many times over and continued to encourage me when things got bleak during the pandemic.

I would also like to acknowledge the generosity of many audiences I was fortunate to share parts of this work with over the years at Sogang University, South Korea (Kyung-Sook Boo); University of Amsterdam (Kristine Johanson); the Latvian Academy of Culture (Iveta Ķešāne); Roma Tre University (Sabrina Vellucci), University of Macerata (Valerio Massimo De Angelis), and Sapienza University (Giorgio Mariani) in Rome; Université Paris Nanterre (Nicoleta Alexoae-Zagni); several universities I visited in Romania during a Fulbright Scholar Award (Iasi, Bucharest, Cluj, and Sibiu); several universities whose invitations I was unable to honor due to the Covid-19 pandemic in spring 2020, when my Fulbright year was cut short; the Obama Institute in Transnational American Studies at Johannes Gutenberg University in Germany for hosting me for a series of lectures and workshops, and for offering wonderful feedback on chapters 3 and 5—my gratitude to Oliver Scheiding, Alfred Hornung, René Dietrich, and Frank Newton. I also thank Michael Coleman for his questions and feedback during a virtual lecture I gave in April 2021 at the University of Warsaw.

MELUS has been one of the most welcoming intellectual homes, which I found at the beginning of my career and which continues to welcome and nourish me. For their collegiality, generosity, friendship, and intellectual company, I would like to acknowledge the following: Lori Askeland, Mary Jo Bona, Kyung-Sook Boo, J. J. Butts, Keely Byars-Nichols, Matthew Calihman, Martha Cutter, Mayuri Decka, Melissa Dennihy, Mauricio Espinoza, Tracy Floreani, Fred Gardaphe, Christopher Gonzales, Amy Gore, Letitia Guran, Sherry Johnson, Joe Kraus, Lesley Larkin, Anastasia and Neal Lin, Kim Martin Long, John Lowe, Leah Milne, J. Stephen Pearson, Stella Setka, Werner Sollors, Amirjit Singh, Gary Totten, Agnieszka Tuszynska, Isabel Quintana Wulf, and the late Jo Anne Ruvoli and Doug Stewart.

My colleagues in the English department at Virginia Commonwealth University, especially the last three chairs (Katherine C. Bassard, David Latané, and Catherine E. Ingrassia) have offered support, resources, and time away from teaching to honor national fellowships and archival trips. Sachi Shimomura, our tireless associate chair, made sure that my teaching schedule was manageable and the classes I was assigned to teach stayed exciting. The office support staff at VCU also deserves a shout out: Virginia Schmitz, Margaret D. Schluer, Kelsey Capiello, and Gregory Patterson. Several research assistants also deserve thanks, especially (now Dr.) Santos Ramos and (now Dr.) Michael Means. Other colleagues at VCU have offered encouragement, feedback, and insightful questions, and camaraderie: Winnie Chan, Marcel Cornis-Pope, Joshua Eckhardt, Antonio Espinoza, Richard Fine, Nick Frankel, David Golumbia, Les Harrison, Catherine E. Ingrassia, Mary Caton Lingold, Bryant Mangum, Katherine S. Nash, Terry Oggel, Jenny Rhee, Paul Robertson, Sachi Shimomura, Ryan Smith, and Rivka Swenson. I thank my first mentor at VCU, Marcel Cornis-Pope, for welcoming me to Virginia and for being an all-around wonderful human being. Katherine C. Bassard and Catherine E. Ingrassia have been tireless mentors and cheerleaders over the years, and I'm immensely grateful for their friendship. As I was finishing the revisions to this book, I took on the demanding job of director of the Humanities Research Center (HRC) at VCU; I am very grateful to the HRC advisory board for a smooth transition and all their support.

Over the years I have been fortunate to be part of several writing groups, and I would like to thank every single group member: the HRC First Book Writing Group at VCU (Myrl Beam, Chris Cynn, Jesse Goldstein, and Brandi Summers), the "Write That Thing" virtual group (Cathleen D. Cahill, Adriana Greci Green, Karen Lynn Marerro, Claire M. Bourne, and Lyndsey Passenger Weick), the "Writing Mavens" (Lissette Piedra, Chi-Fang Wu, and Patrisia Macias), and the NCFDD coaches writing group (Lorena Garcia and Kari Zimmerman). Michelle Boyd and Joycelyn Moody have provided much-needed expert advice and support during our writing retreats in Georgia. My University of Richmond colleagues and friends, especially Monika Siebert, Kevin Pelletier, and Elizabeth Outka, offered much-needed cheer and writing company over the years; Monika read many drafts, entertained our children, provided expert culinary guidance in Richmond and London, and assured me that the end was in sight. To Monika and her daughter Maria, I am deeply grateful for their friendship.

Friends and family provided love, support, food, child care, wine, and many welcome distractions over the long process of revision. Rashid Robinson deserves special thanks for keeping me company in the early hours of the morning during a pandemic summer of virtual writing, revisions, and sheer panic about the world (2020), and for checking in periodically. Erin Castro and her exercise group offered much-needed camaraderie during the pandemic through Zoom yoga and strength exercises. Melissa Girard read countless drafts of chapters and articles. Other close friends in Richmond, Virginia; Champaign-Urbana, Illinois; Columbus, Ohio; and Romania have kept me going: Margaret Altonen, Matt Connors and Sarah Beauchamp, Codrin and Laura Cuțitaru, Karo and Jeff Engstrom, Oana Falasca, Gary and Kim Holcomb, Lisa Oliverio and Alan Thorn, Luminița and Ionel Oniciuc, Daniel and Ioana Carmen Păstinaru, Isabel Quintana-Wulf and Rashid Robinson, Veronica and Radu Popescu, Frank Ridgeway and Susan Gregson, Kerstin Rudolph and Will Morris, John Cole Scott and Katherine Herrera, Galina Slavova-Hernandez and Jerry Hernandez, Joe and Karen Sokohol, Cristi and Oana Vlas, Mihaela Gainusă-Wood and Greg Wood, Violeta and Sorin Tanase, and Marcela Ursu (Mandru).

For their hospitality during my many research trips to Chicago, thanks to Florin Ion, Elena Leonte, and Matei Stroilã.

Most importantly, my family helped maintain my sanity during the last couple of decades as I straddled two continents, several homes, research, writing, and life. My husband Bogdan's parents, Romeo and Alexandrina Stanciu, did not live to see this book in print but supported my choice of an academic career and family across the ocean. My parents, Maria and Vasile Buruianã, have been constant sources of unconditional love, immense patience, child care and entertainment, great food and stories, and so much support during our American adventure of 20-plus years. Our children, Maya Margot (K, 14) and Matilda Marie (Tilly, 7), continue to remind me of the joys of life, laughter, and the importance of *not* writing. Above all, I thank Bogdan Stanciu, my very patient and brilliant partner, chef, stand-up comedian, fellow traveler, chauffeur, occasional motivational speaker, and film buff extraordinaire. To him and to our family this book is lovingly dedicated.

A section of chapter 1 was first published as "Native Acts, Immigrant Acts: Citizenship, Naturalization, and the Performance of Civic Identity during the Progressive Era," *JGAPE: Journal of the Gilded Age and Progressive Era* 20 (April 2021): 252–76. Cambridge University Press.

A section of chapter 3 was first published as "'That Is Why I Sent You to Carlisle': Indian Poetry and the Demands of Americanization Poetics and Politics," *American Indian Quarterly* 37.2 (Spring 2013): 34–76. University of Nebraska Press.

A section of chapter 4 was first published as "'I Tell Heem It Not Hees Beesness. I Tell Heem Nothing!': Americanization, Immigrant Education, and Ethnic Identity at the Turn into the Twentieth Century," *Italian American Review* 11.1 (2021): 27–50. University of Illinois Press.

A section of chapter 5 was first published as "'Americanism for Indians': Carlos Montezuma's 'Immigrant Problem:' *Wassaja*, and the Limits of Native Activism," *Studies in American Indian Literatures* 33.1–2 (Spring–Summer 2021): 125–57. University of Nebraska Press.

Another section of chapter 5 was first published as "Americanization on Native Terms: The Society of American Indians, Citizenship Debates, and Tropes of 'Racial Difference,'" *NAIS: Native American and Indigenous Studies* 6.1 (2019): 111–48. University of Minnesota Press.

A section of chapter 6 was first published as "Marcus E. Ravage's *An American in the Making*, Americanization, and New Immigrant Representation," *MELUS: Multi-Ethnic Literatures of the United States* 40.2 (Summer 2015): 5–29. Oxford University Press.

A section of chapter 7 was first published as "Making Americans: Spectacular Nationalism, Americanization, and Silent Film," *JAS: Journal of American Studies* 56.1 (February 2022): 1–37. Cambridge University Press.

Index

References to figures and tables are indicated by "*f*" and "*t*" following the page numbers.